W9-CFL-260

Sisters

Sisters

Raina Telgemeier

with color by Braden Lamb

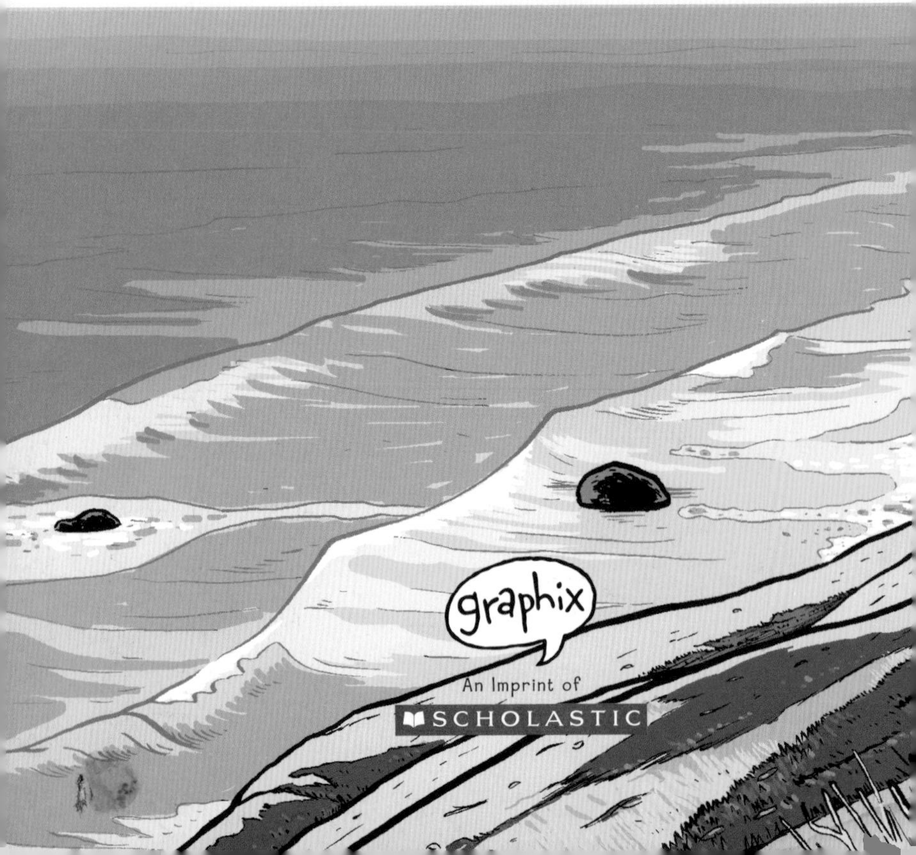

graphix

An Imprint of

SCHOLASTIC

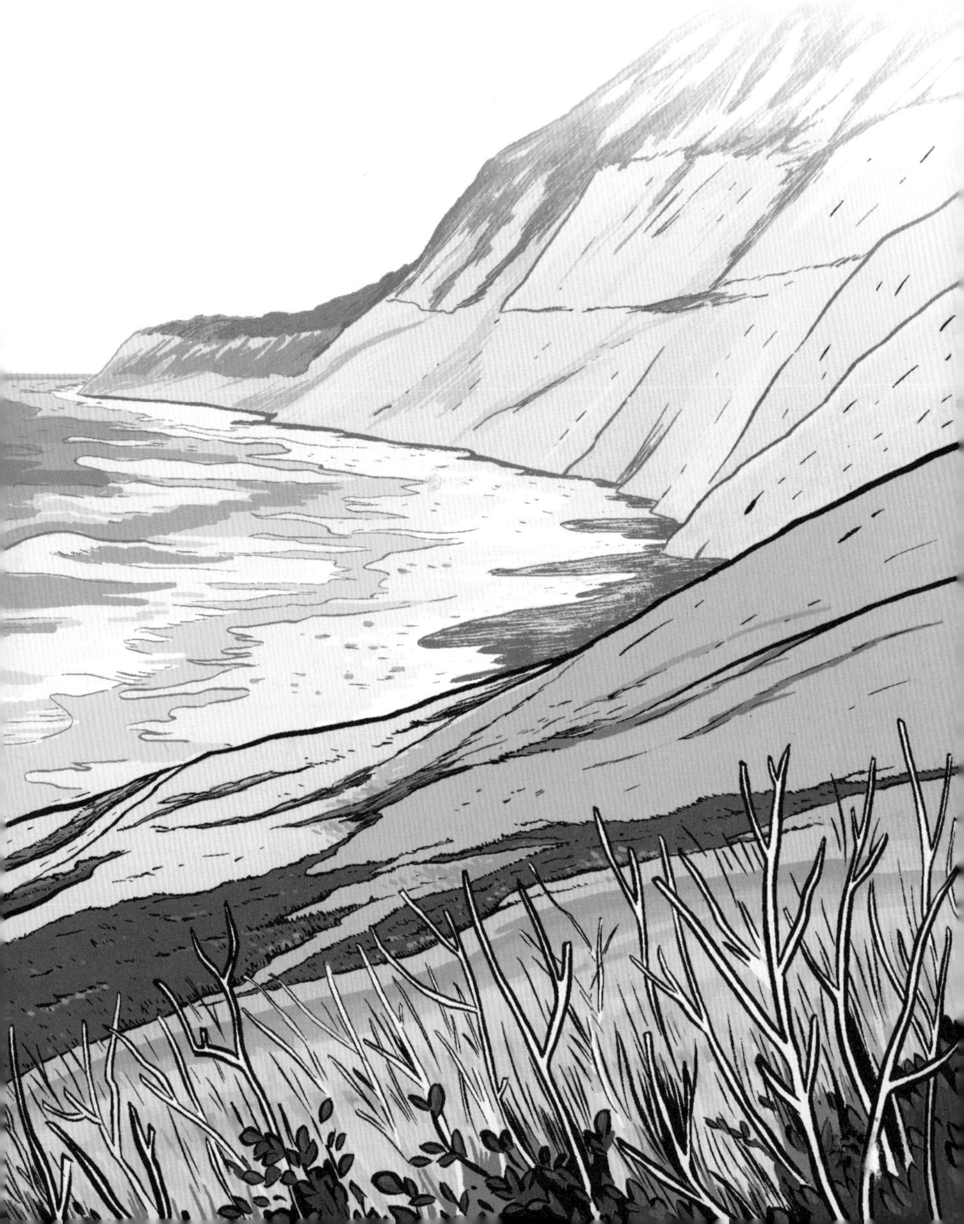

For Amara, obviously

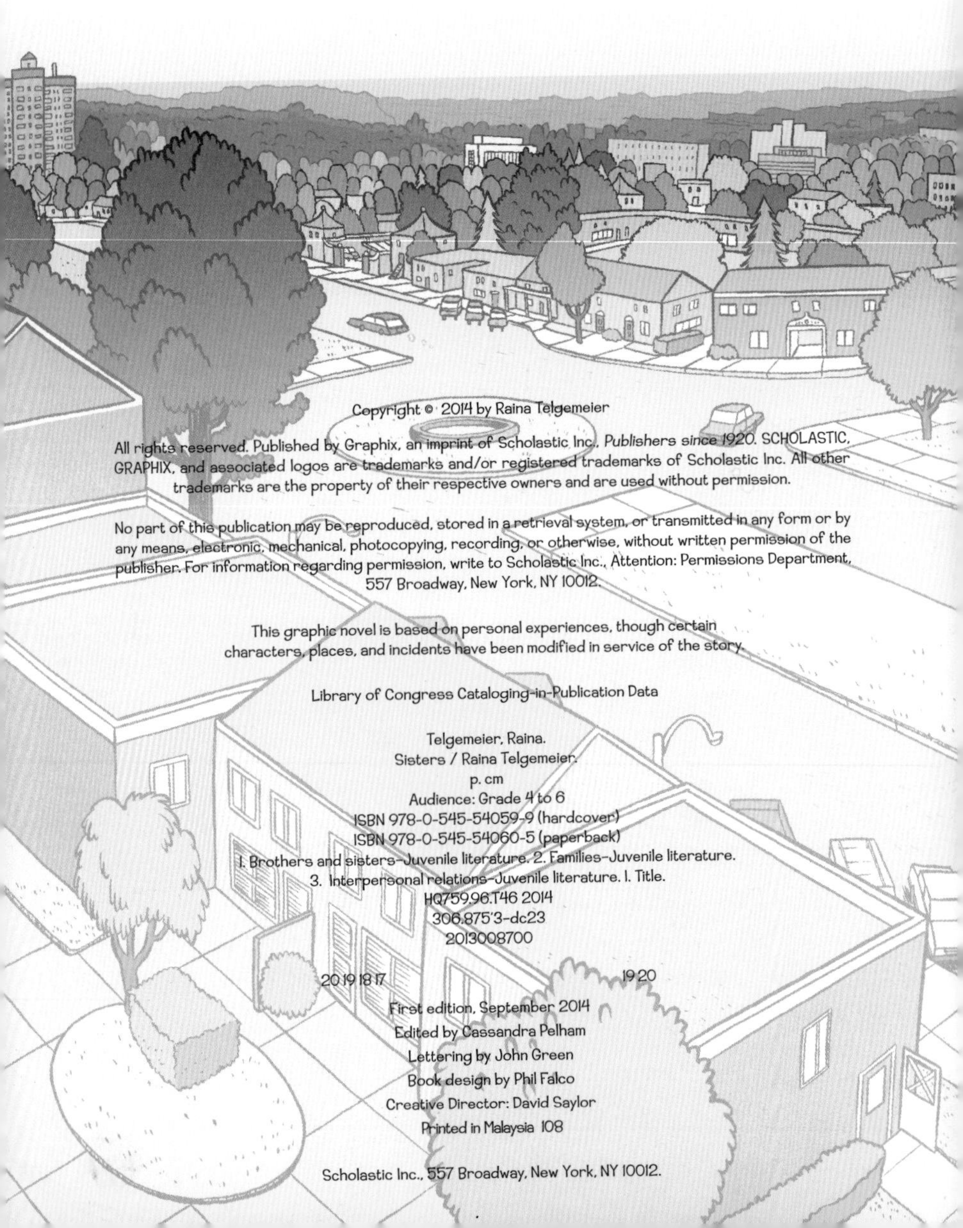

This graphic novel is based on personal experiences, though certain characters, places, and incidents have been modified in service of the story.

Library of Congress Cataloging-in-Publication Data

Telgemeier, Raina.
Sisters / Raina Telgemeier.
p. cm
Audience: Grade 4 to 6
ISBN 978-0-545-54059-9 (hardcover)
ISBN 978-0-545-54060-5 (paperback)
1. Brothers and sisters–Juvenile literature. 2. Families–Juvenile literature.
3. Interpersonal relations–Juvenile literature. I. Title.
HQ759.96.T46 2014
306.875'3–dc23
2013008700

20 19 18 17 19 20

First edition, September 2014
Edited by Cassandra Pelham
Lettering by John Green
Book design by Phil Falco
Creative Director: David Saylor
Printed in Malaysia 108

Scholastic Inc., 557 Broadway, New York, NY 10012.

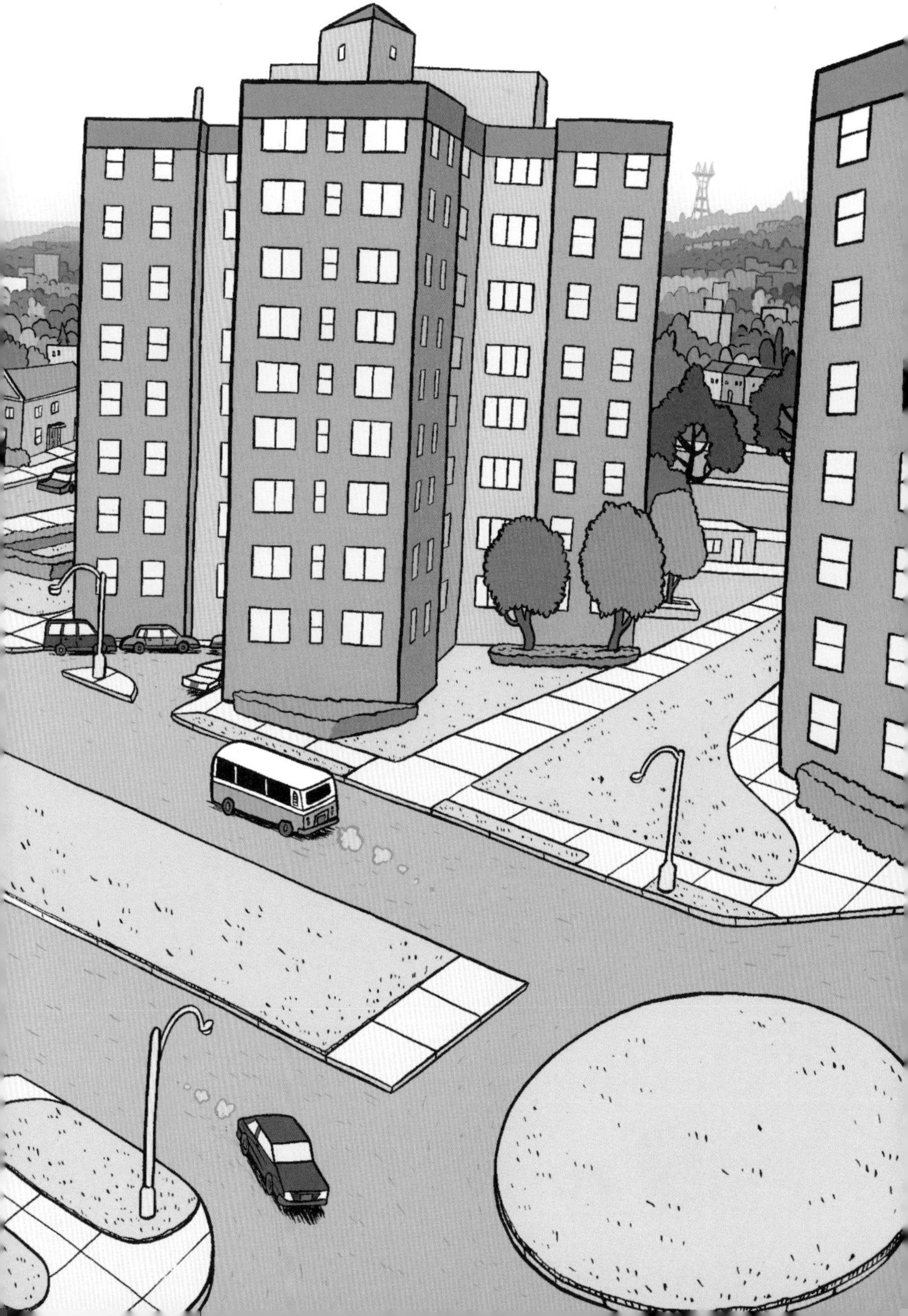

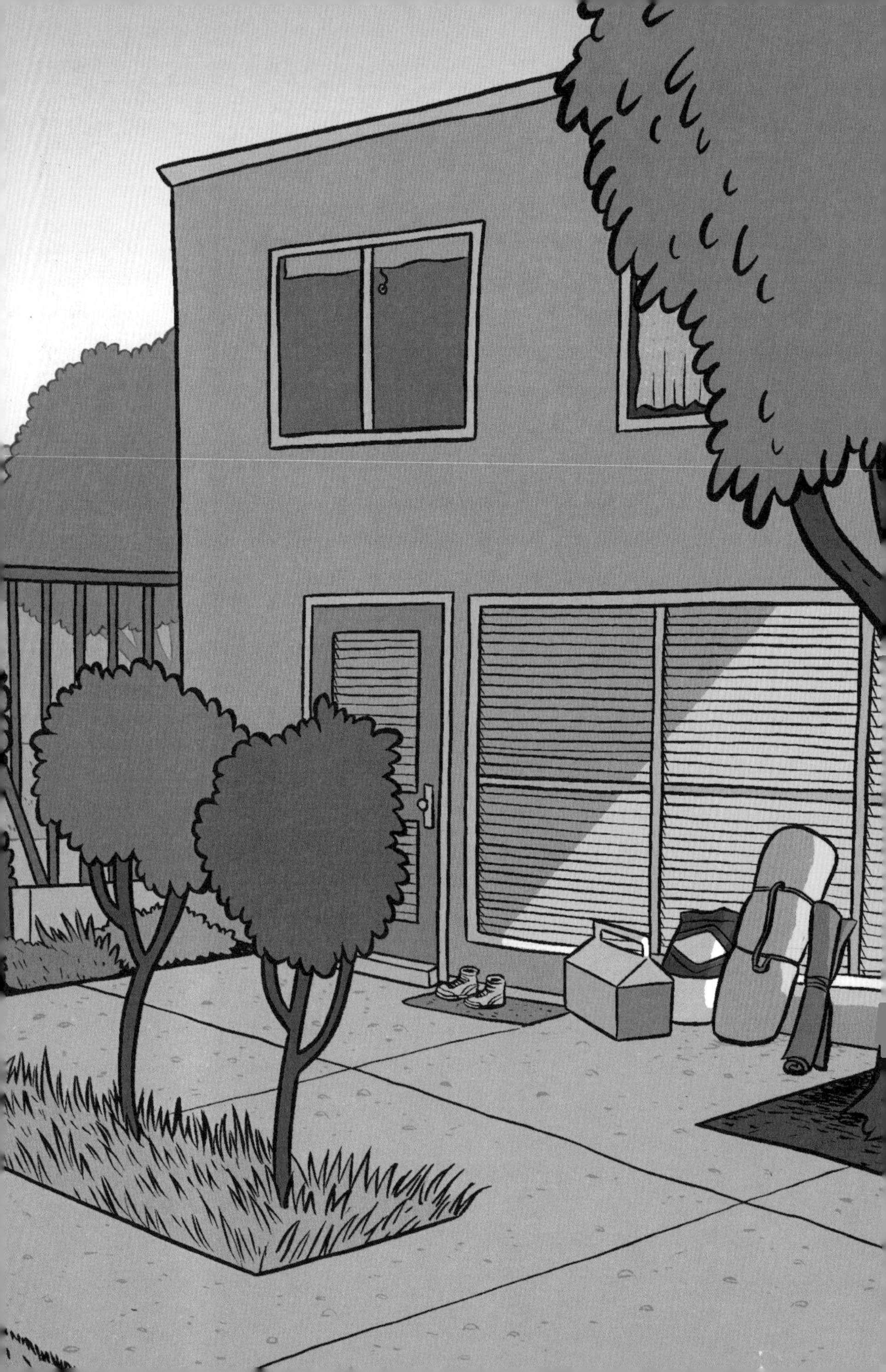

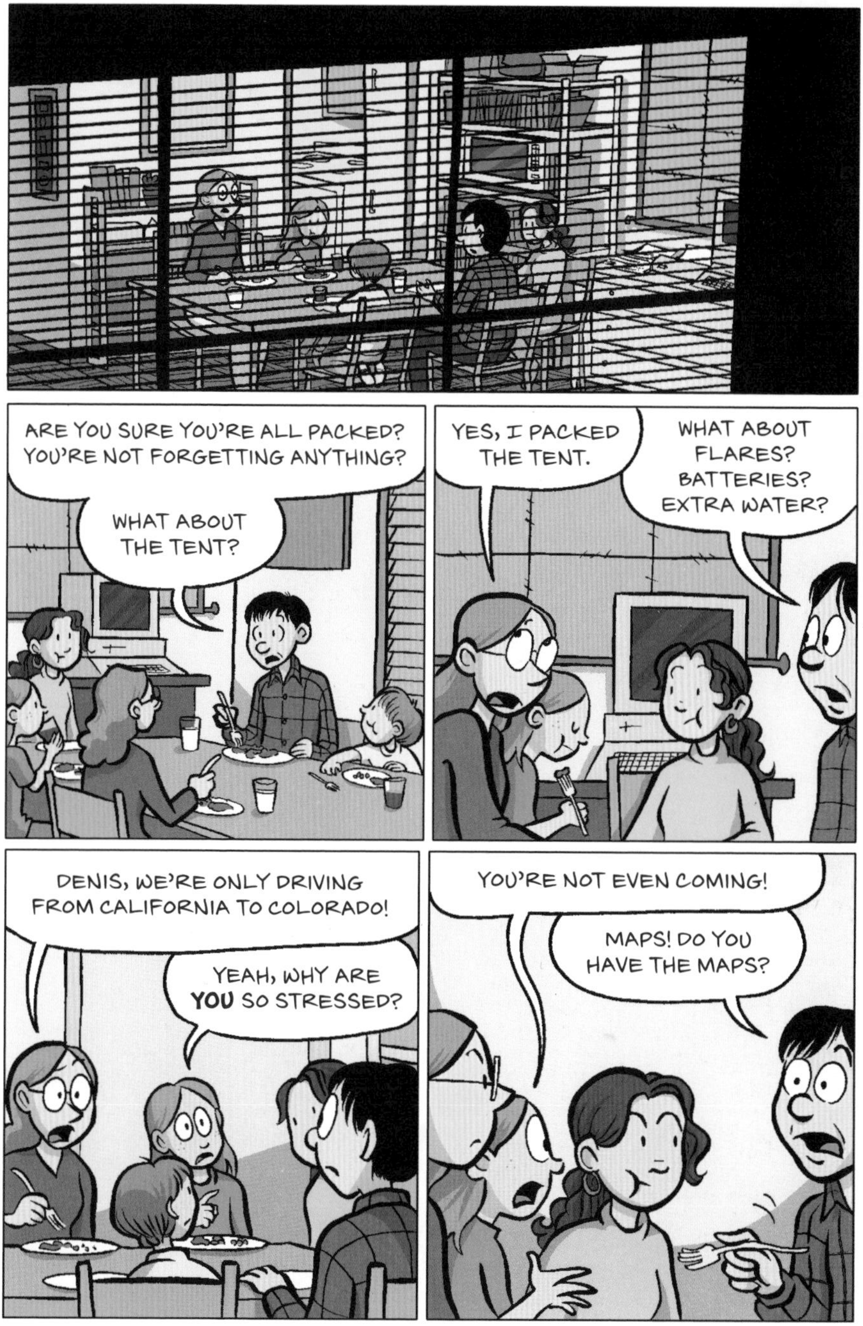
ARE YOU SURE YOU'RE ALL PACKED? YOU'RE NOT FORGETTING ANYTHING?
WHAT ABOUT THE TENT?
YES, I PACKED THE TENT.
WHAT ABOUT FLARES? BATTERIES? EXTRA WATER?
DENIS, WE'RE ONLY DRIVING FROM CALIFORNIA TO COLORADO!
YEAH, WHY ARE **YOU** SO STRESSED?
YOU'RE NOT EVEN COMING!
MAPS! DO YOU HAVE THE MAPS?

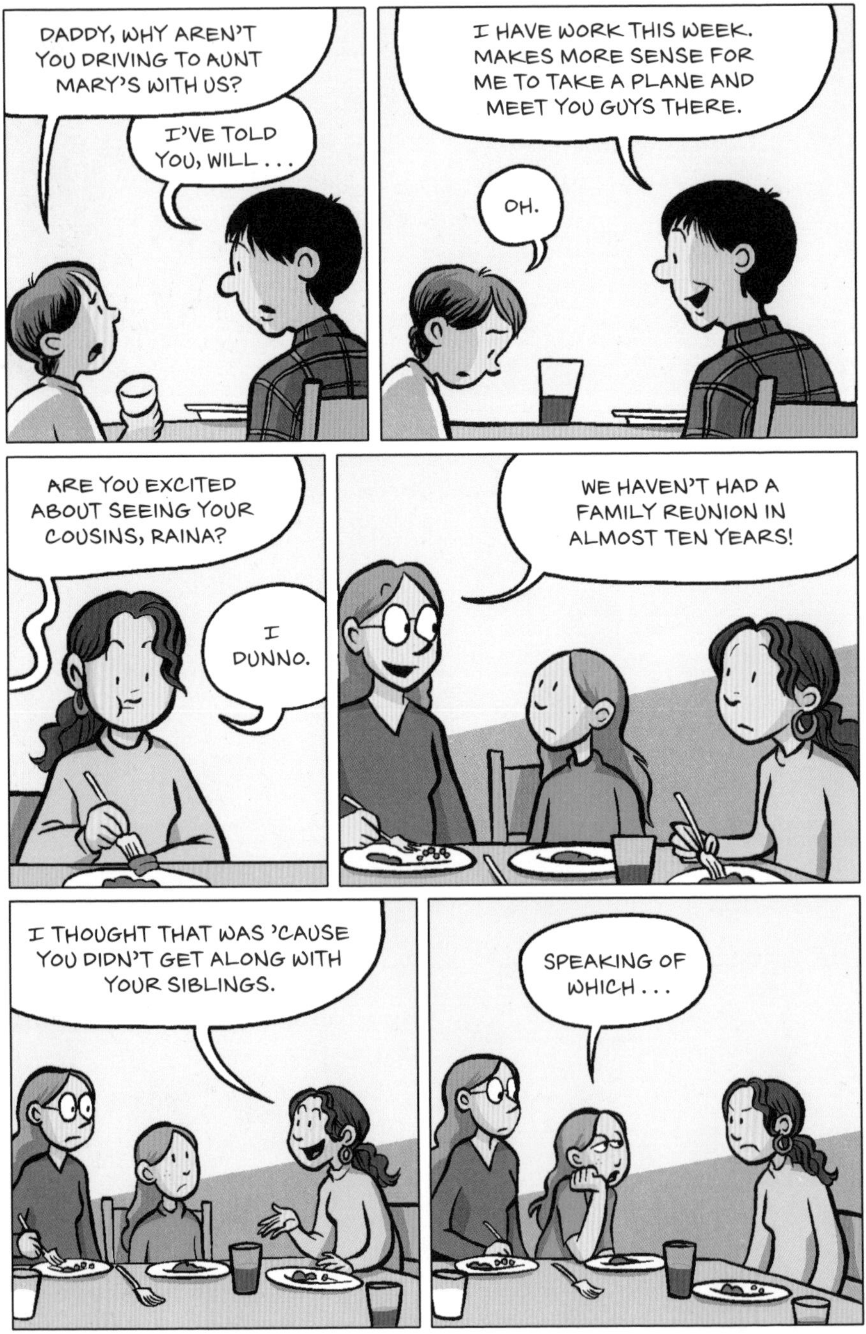
DADDY, WHY AREN'T YOU DRIVING TO AUNT MARY'S WITH US?
I'VE TOLD YOU, WILL . . .
I HAVE WORK THIS WEEK. MAKES MORE SENSE FOR ME TO TAKE A PLANE AND MEET YOU GUYS THERE.
OH.
ARE YOU EXCITED ABOUT SEEING YOUR COUSINS, RAINA?
I DUNNO.
WE HAVEN'T HAD A FAMILY REUNION IN ALMOST TEN YEARS!
I THOUGHT THAT WAS 'CAUSE YOU DIDN'T GET ALONG WITH YOUR SIBLINGS.
SPEAKING OF WHICH . . .

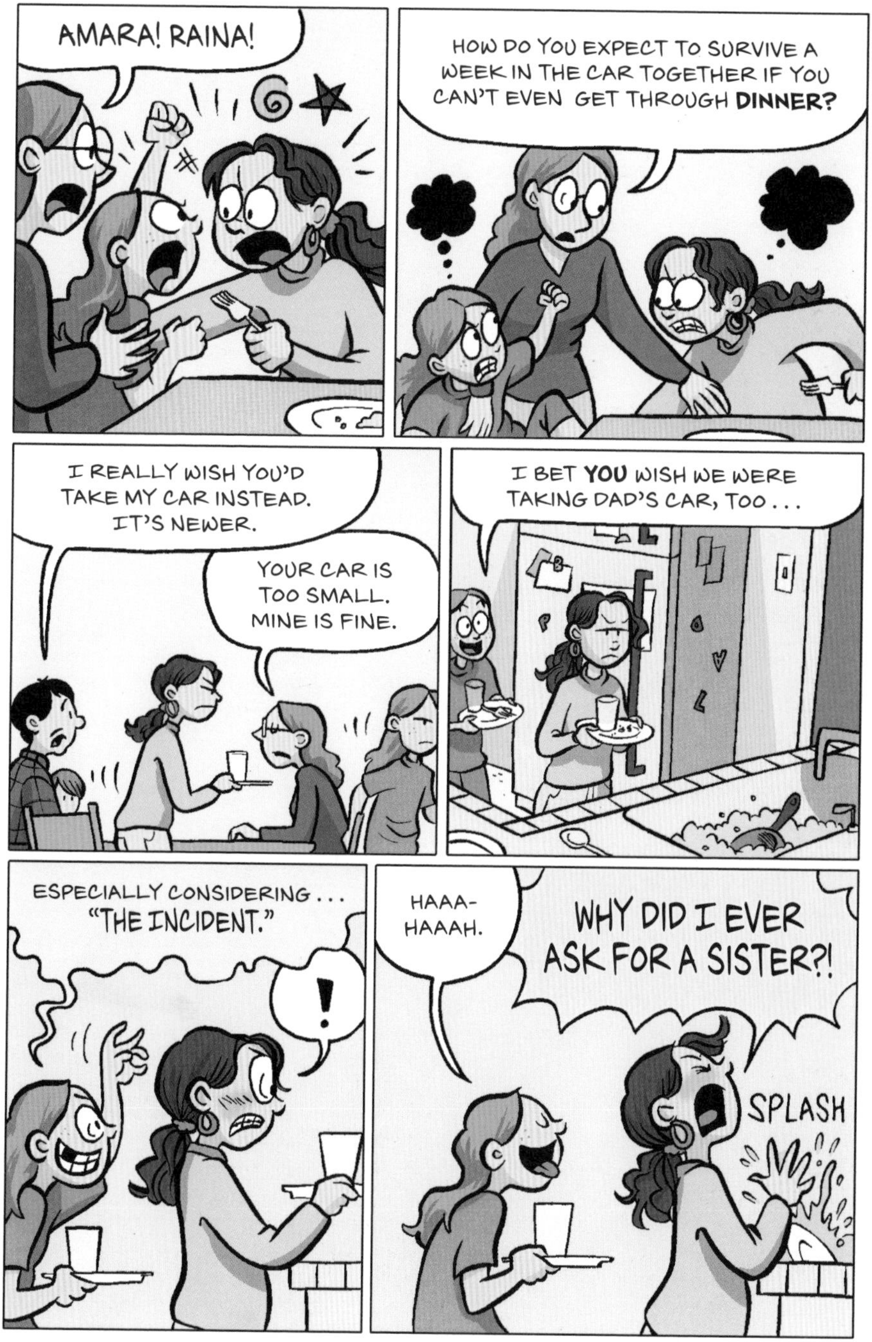
AMARA! RAINA!
HOW DO YOU EXPECT TO SURVIVE A WEEK IN THE CAR TOGETHER IF YOU CAN'T EVEN GET THROUGH DINNER?
I REALLY WISH YOU'D TAKE MY CAR INSTEAD. IT'S NEWER.
YOUR CAR IS TOO SMALL. MINE IS FINE.
I BET YOU WISH WE WERE TAKING DAD'S CAR, TOO . . .
ESPECIALLY CONSIDERING . . . "THE INCIDENT."
!
HAAA-HAAAH.
WHY DID I EVER ASK FOR A SISTER?!
SPLASH

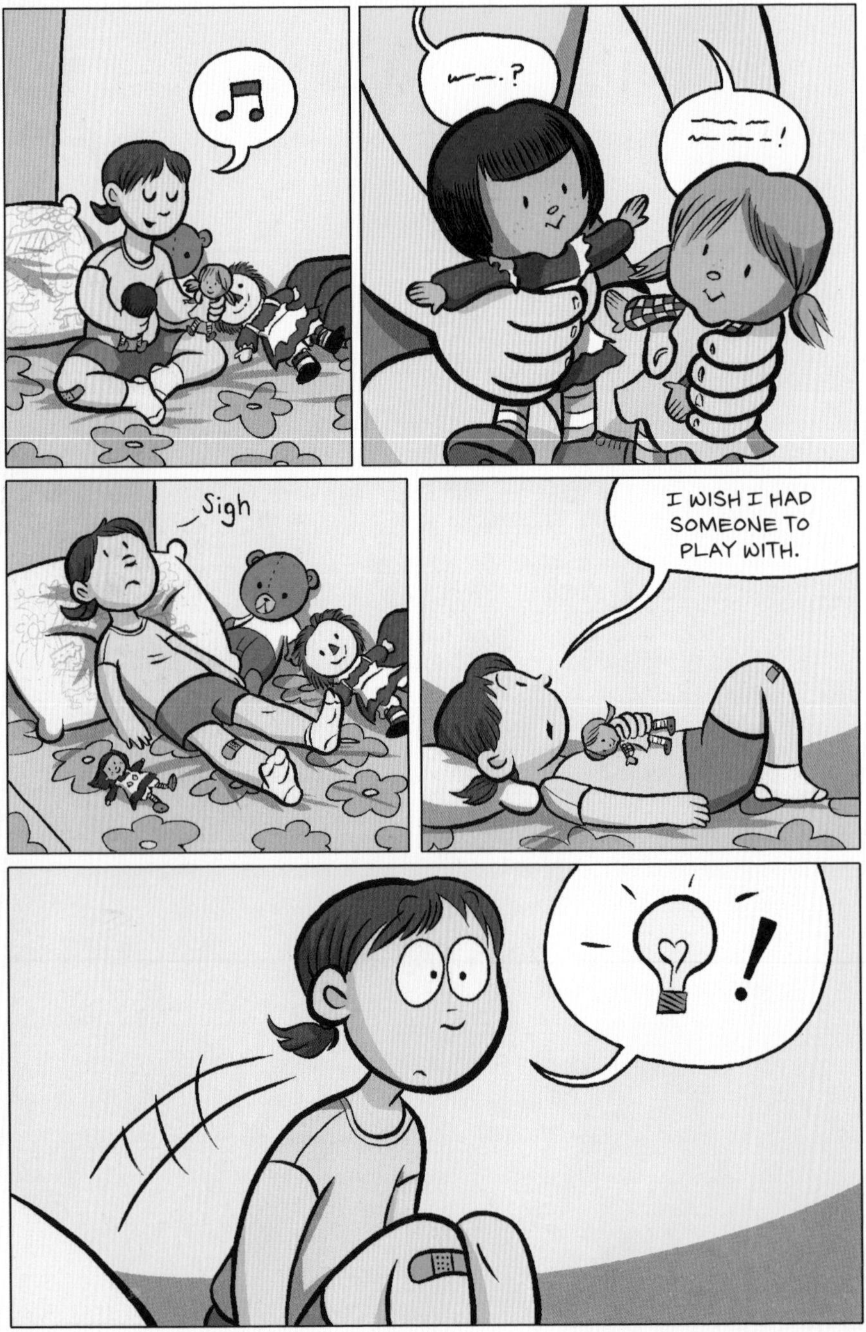

Sigh
I WISH I HAD SOMEONE TO PLAY WITH.
!

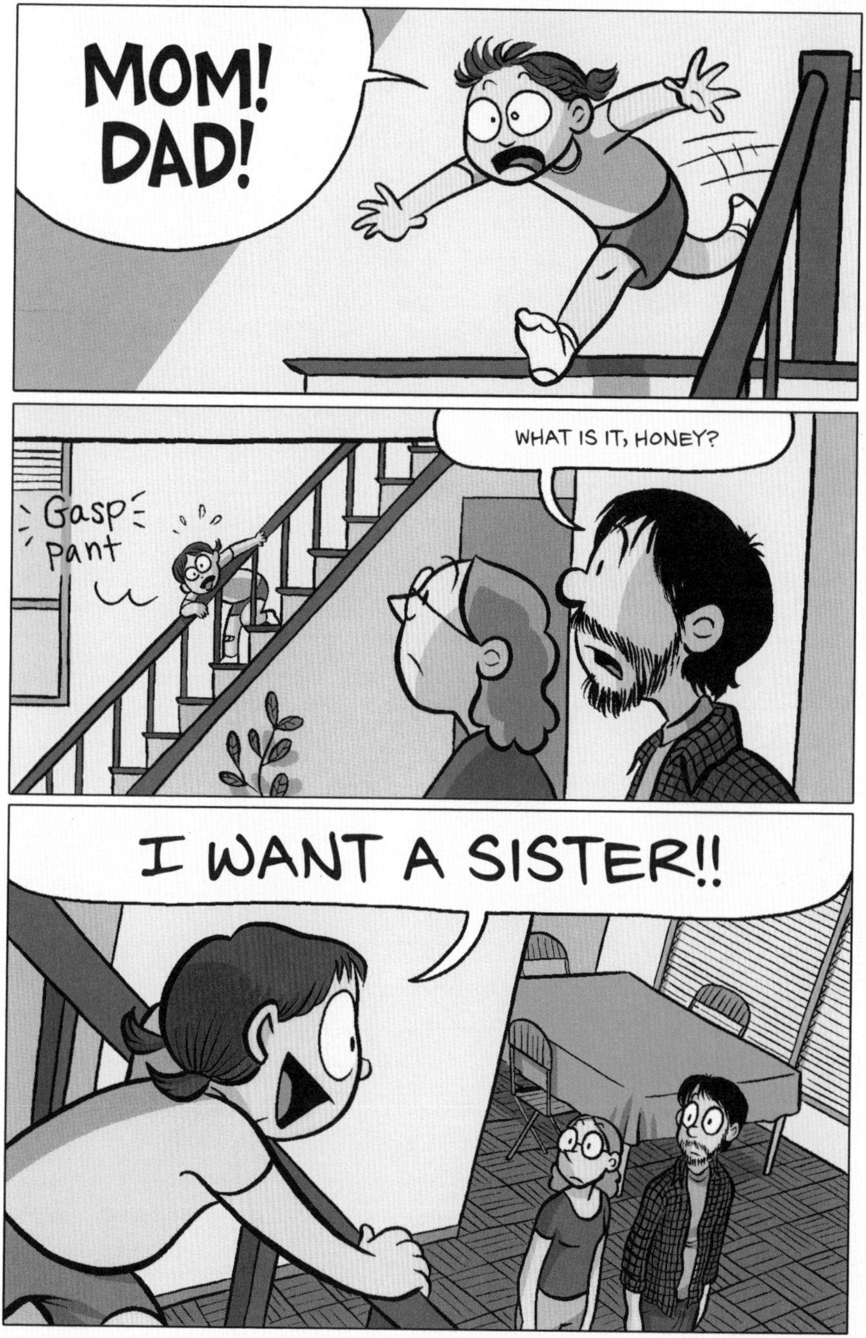
MOM! DAD!
WHAT IS IT, HONEY?
Gasp pant
I WANT A SISTER!!

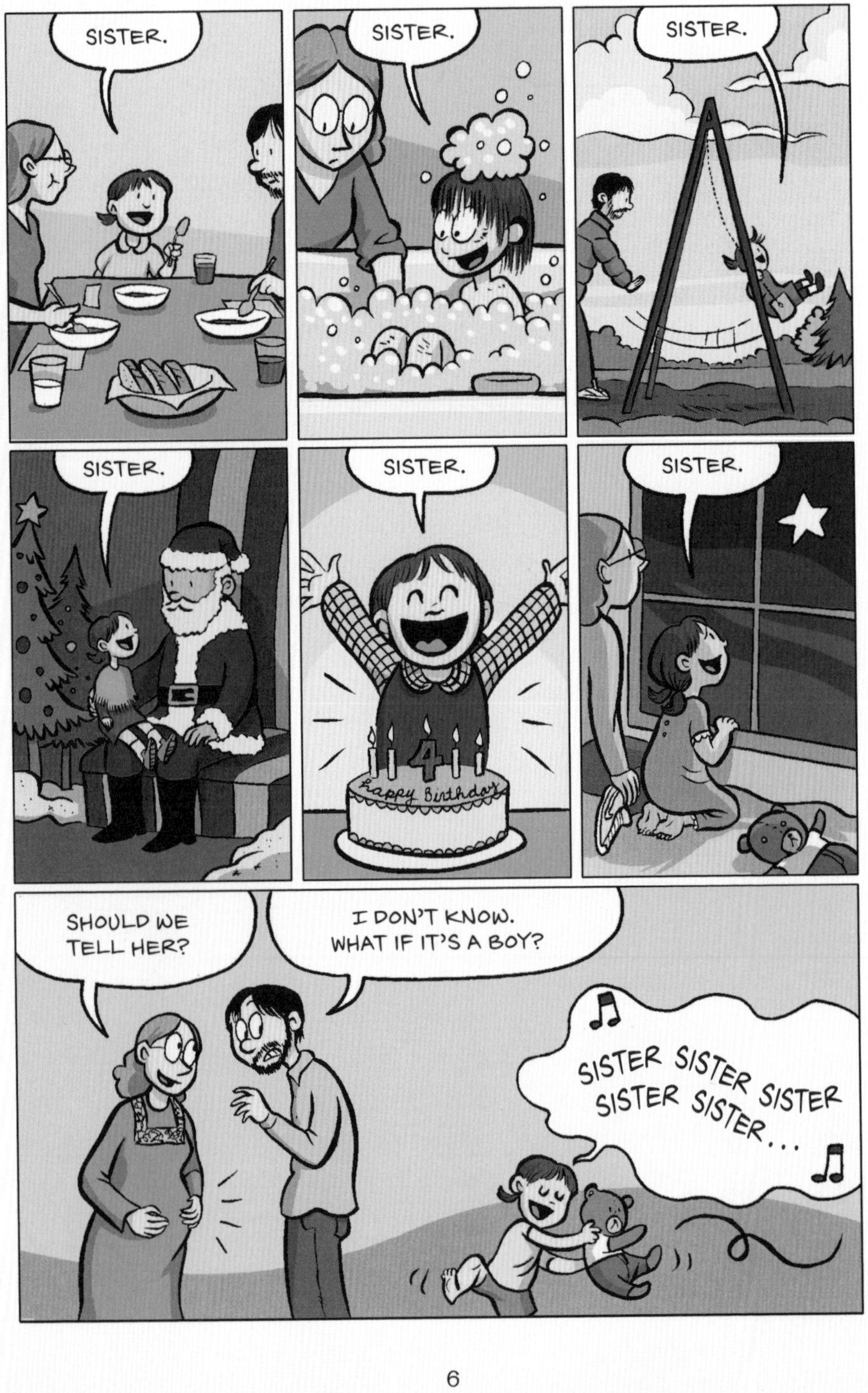
SISTER.
SISTER.
SISTER.
SISTER.
SISTER.
SISTER.
happy Birthday
SHOULD WE TELL HER?
I DON'T KNOW. WHAT IF IT'S A BOY?
SISTER SISTER SISTER SISTER SISTER...

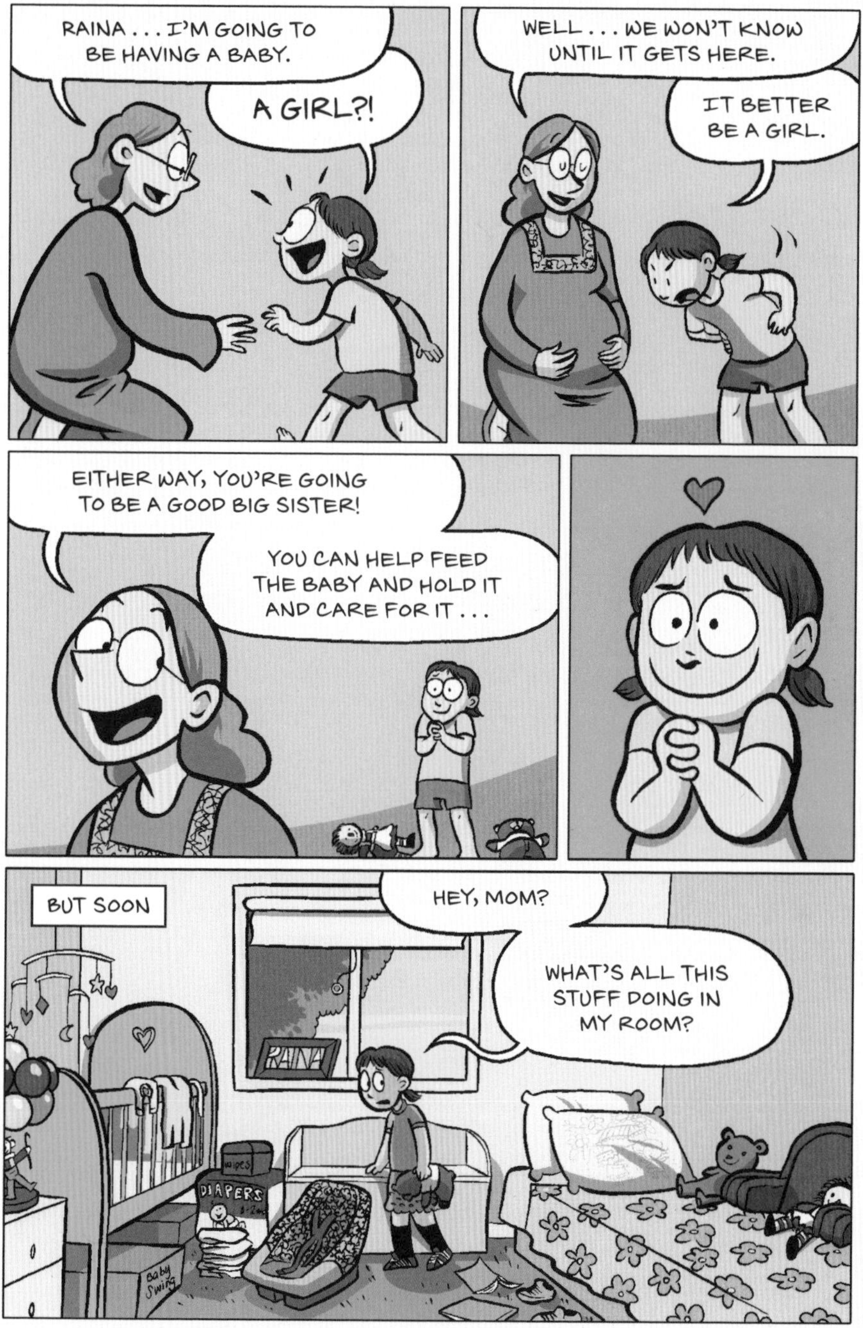
RAINA . . . I'M GOING TO BE HAVING A BABY.
A GIRL?!
WELL . . . WE WON'T KNOW UNTIL IT GETS HERE.
IT BETTER BE A GIRL.
EITHER WAY, YOU'RE GOING TO BE A GOOD BIG SISTER!
YOU CAN HELP FEED THE BABY AND HOLD IT AND CARE FOR IT . . .
BUT SOON
HEY, MOM?
WHAT'S ALL THIS STUFF DOING IN MY ROOM?
RAINA
WIPES
DIAPERS
Baby Swing

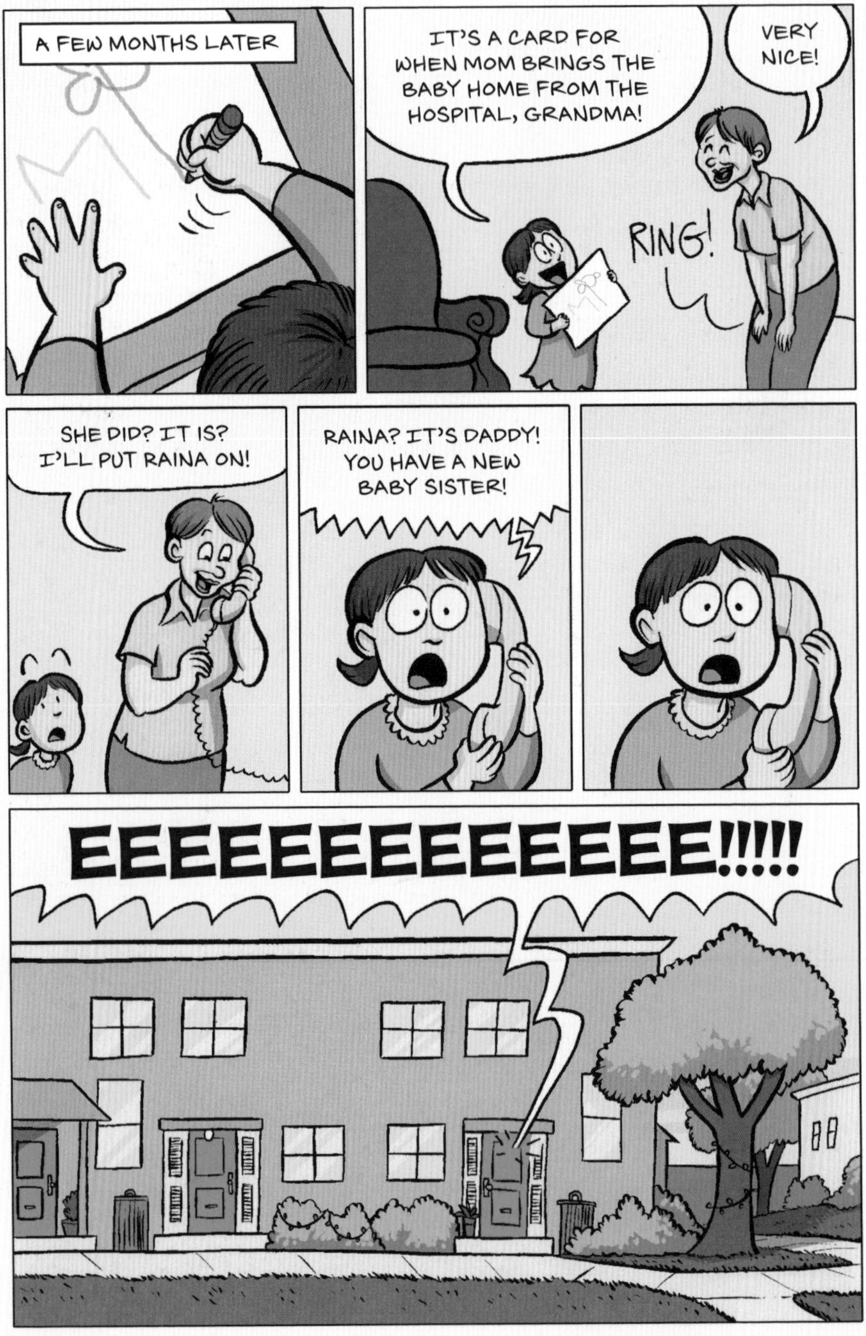
A FEW MONTHS LATER
IT'S A CARD FOR WHEN MOM BRINGS THE BABY HOME FROM THE HOSPITAL, GRANDMA!
VERY NICE!
RING!
SHE DID? IT IS? I'LL PUT RAINA ON!
RAINA? IT'S DADDY! YOU HAVE A NEW BABY SISTER!
EEEEEEEEEEEEEE!!!!!

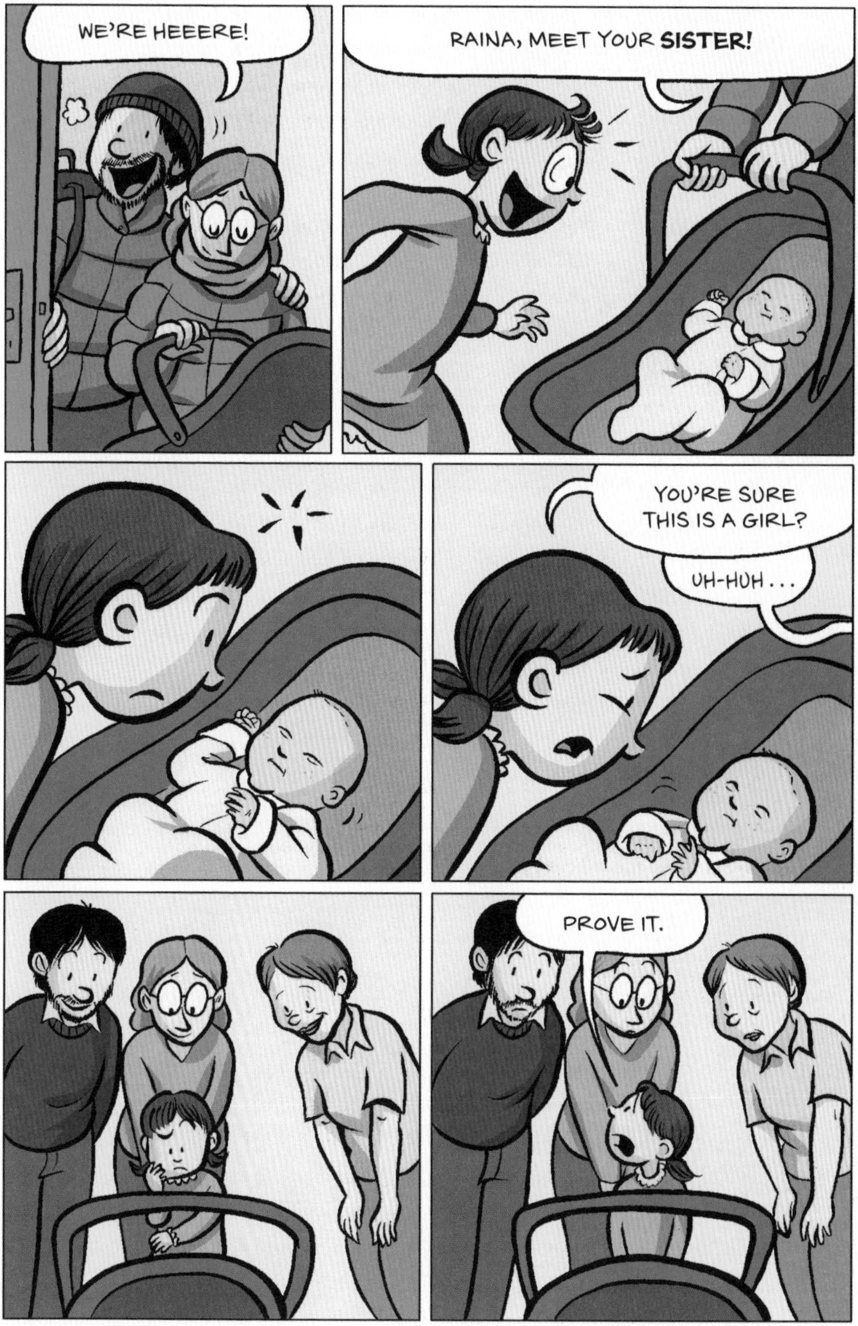

WE'RE HEEERE!
RAINA, MEET YOUR **SISTER!**
YOU'RE SURE THIS IS A GIRL?
UH-HUH . . .
PROVE IT.

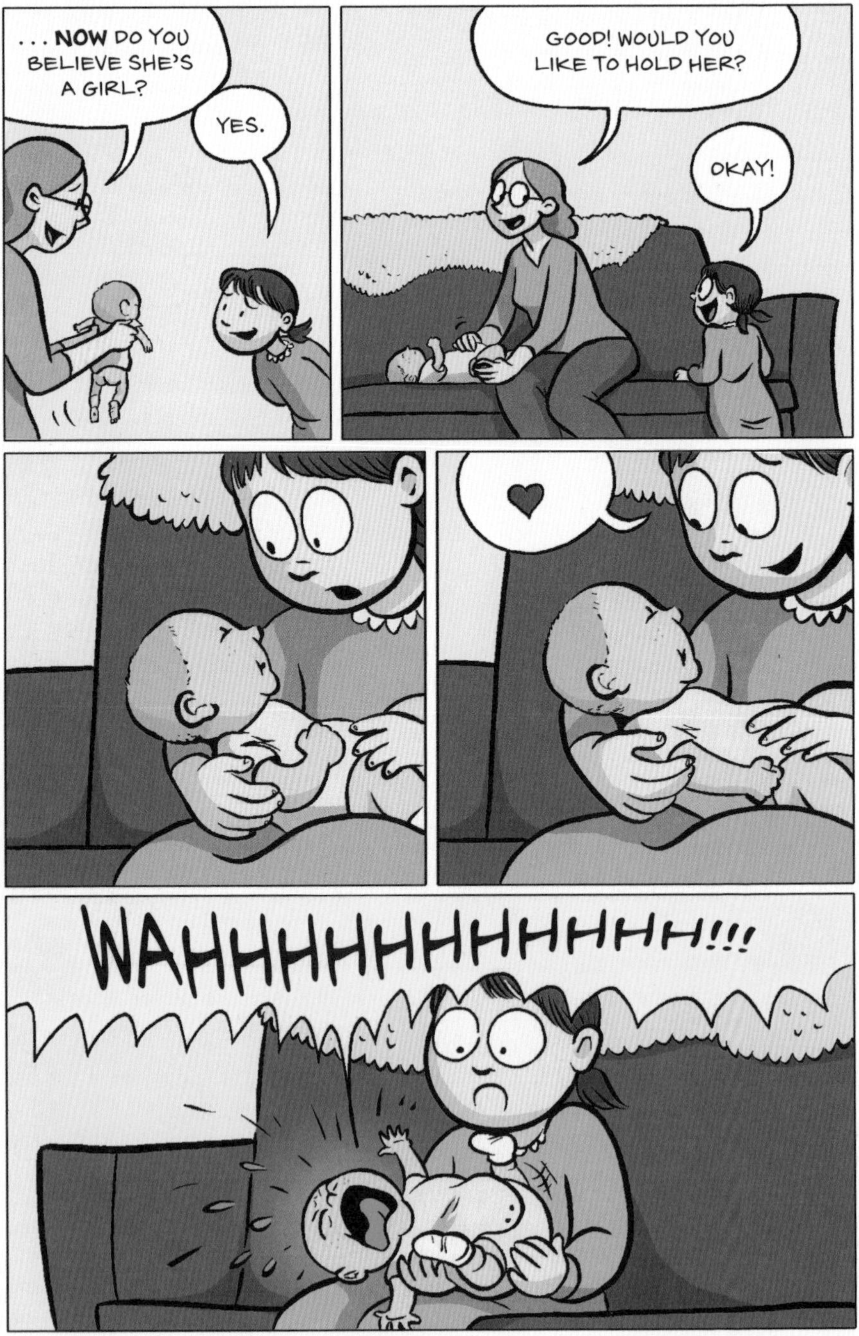
. . . **NOW** DO YOU BELIEVE SHE'S A GIRL?
YES.
GOOD! WOULD YOU LIKE TO HOLD HER?
OKAY!
WAHHHHHHHHHHH!!!

IT'S OKAY, SHHH...

WAAAAAA AAAAAAA AAA AAAAAA AAH HHHHHHH

pat pat

SO YOU'RE NAMING HER **DANA**, RIGHT? TO RHYME WITH RAINA? SO WE MATCH?

ACTUALLY...

... I'D LIKE TO CALL HER **AMARA**.

WHAT? WHAT KIND OF NAME IS **THAT?!**

IT MEANS "IMMORTAL" IN SANSKRIT, AND "LOVE" IN LATIN.

IT ALSO MEANS "BITTER ONE," BUT YOUR MOM LIKES IT, SO THAT'S THAT.

pat pat

cough

hic

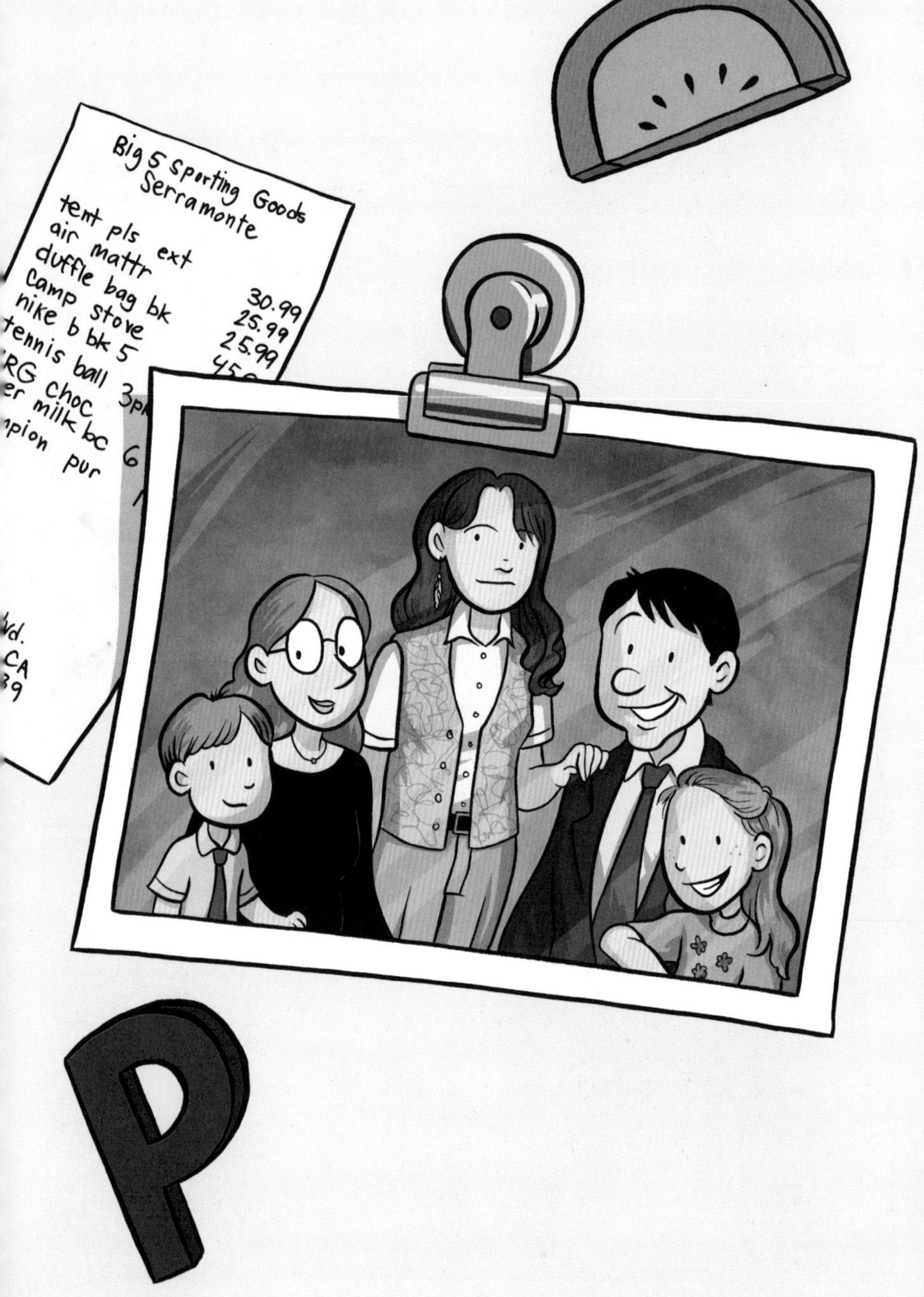

Big 5 Sporting Goods
Serramonte
tent pls ext
air mattr
duffle bag bk 30.99
camp stove 25.99
nike b bk 5 25.99
tennis ball 3pk
RG choc
er milk bc
npion pur

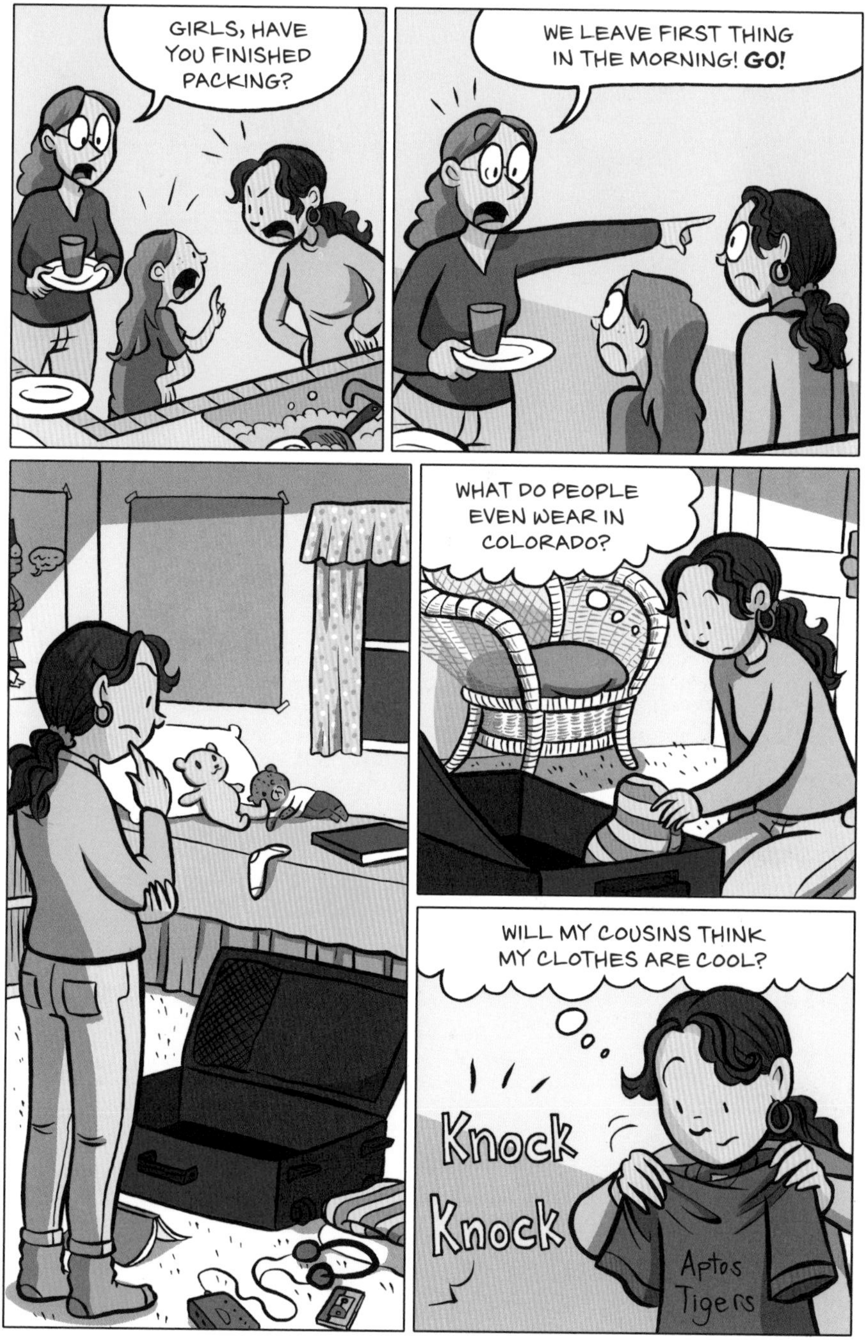
GIRLS, HAVE YOU FINISHED PACKING?
WE LEAVE FIRST THING IN THE MORNING! **GO!**
WHAT DO PEOPLE EVEN WEAR IN COLORADO?
WILL MY COUSINS THINK MY CLOTHES ARE COOL?
Knock
Knock
Aptos Tigers

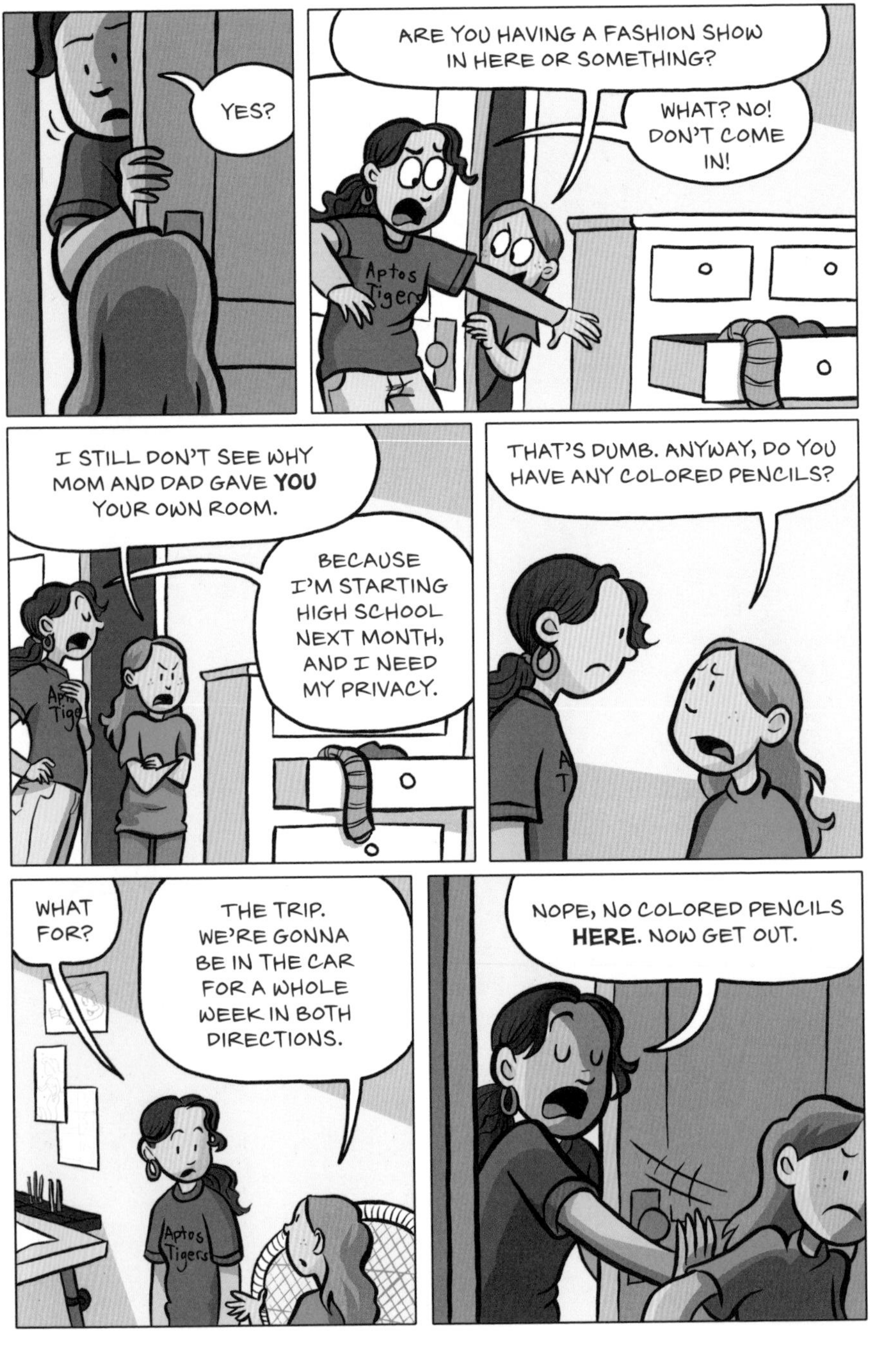
YES?
ARE YOU HAVING A FASHION SHOW IN HERE OR SOMETHING?
WHAT? NO! DON'T COME IN!
Aptos Tigers
I STILL DON'T SEE WHY MOM AND DAD GAVE **YOU** YOUR OWN ROOM.
BECAUSE I'M STARTING HIGH SCHOOL NEXT MONTH, AND I NEED MY PRIVACY.
THAT'S DUMB. ANYWAY, DO YOU HAVE ANY COLORED PENCILS?
WHAT FOR?
THE TRIP. WE'RE GONNA BE IN THE CAR FOR A WHOLE WEEK IN BOTH DIRECTIONS.
Aptos Tigers
NOPE, NO COLORED PENCILS **HERE**. NOW GET OUT.

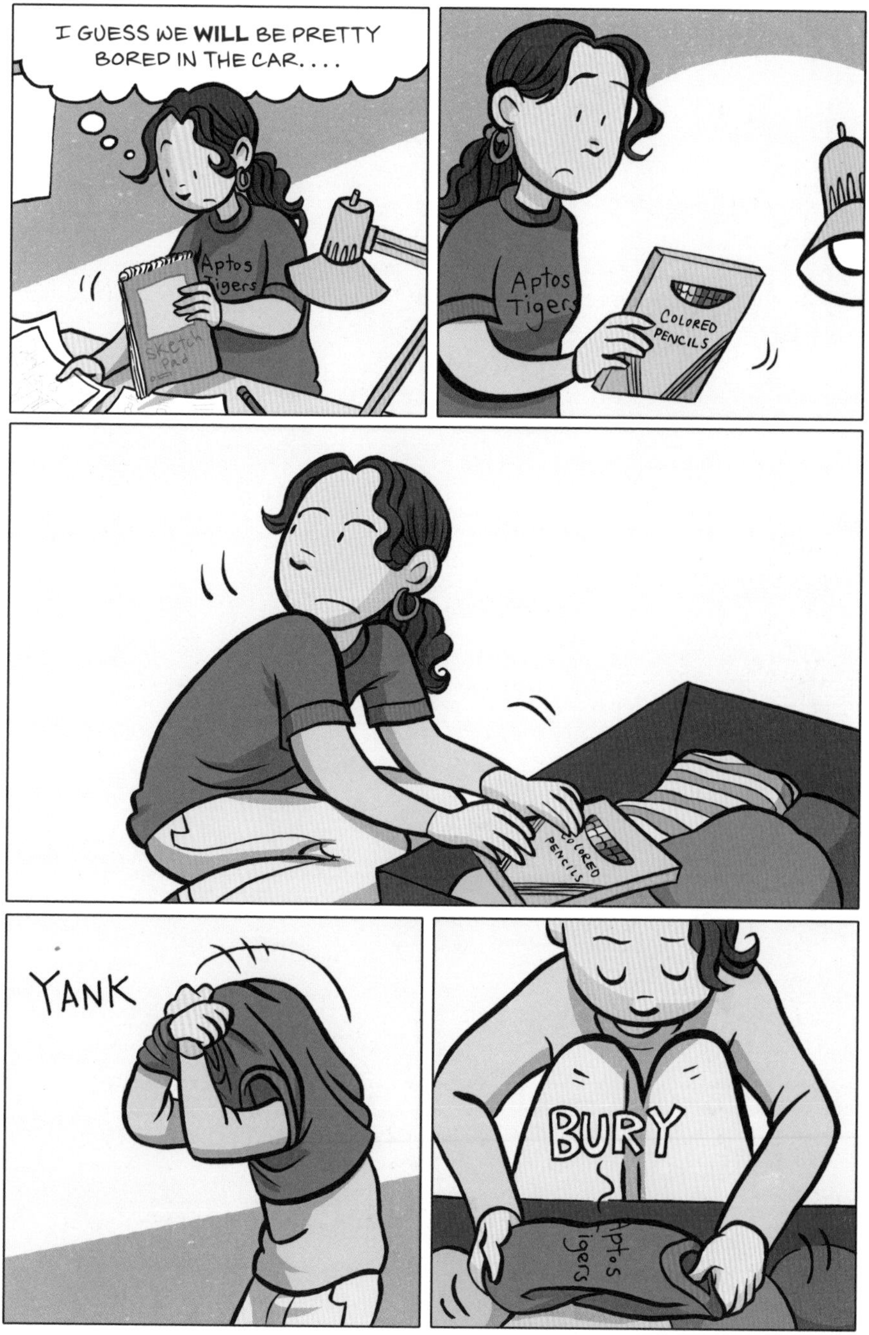

I GUESS WE **WILL** BE PRETTY BORED IN THE CAR. . . .
Aptos Tigers
SKETCH PAD
Aptos Tigers
COLORED PENCILS
COLORED PENCILS
YANK
BURY
Aptos Tigers

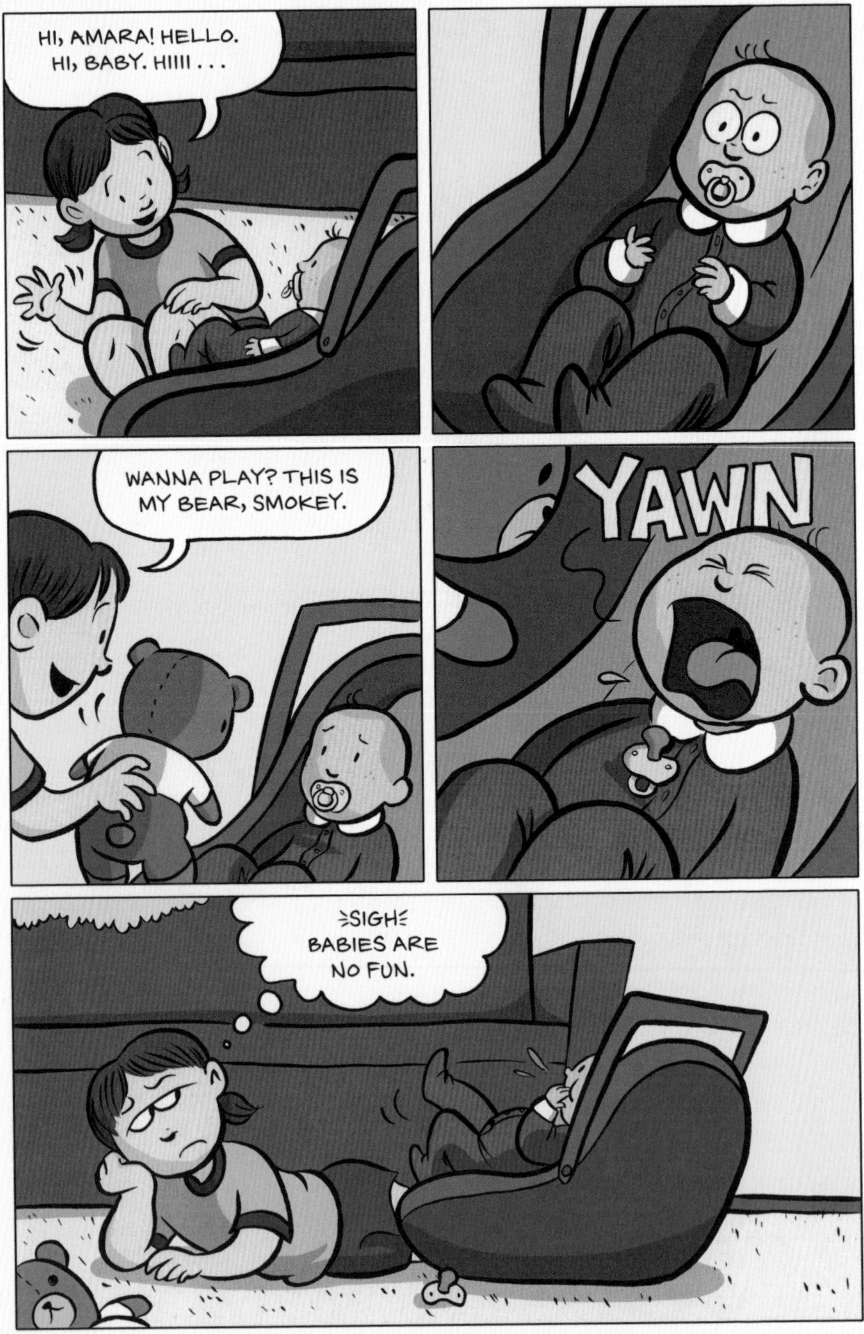

HI, AMARA! HELLO.
HI, BABY. HIIII . . .
WANNA PLAY? THIS IS MY BEAR, SMOKEY.
YAWN
SIGH
BABIES ARE NO FUN.

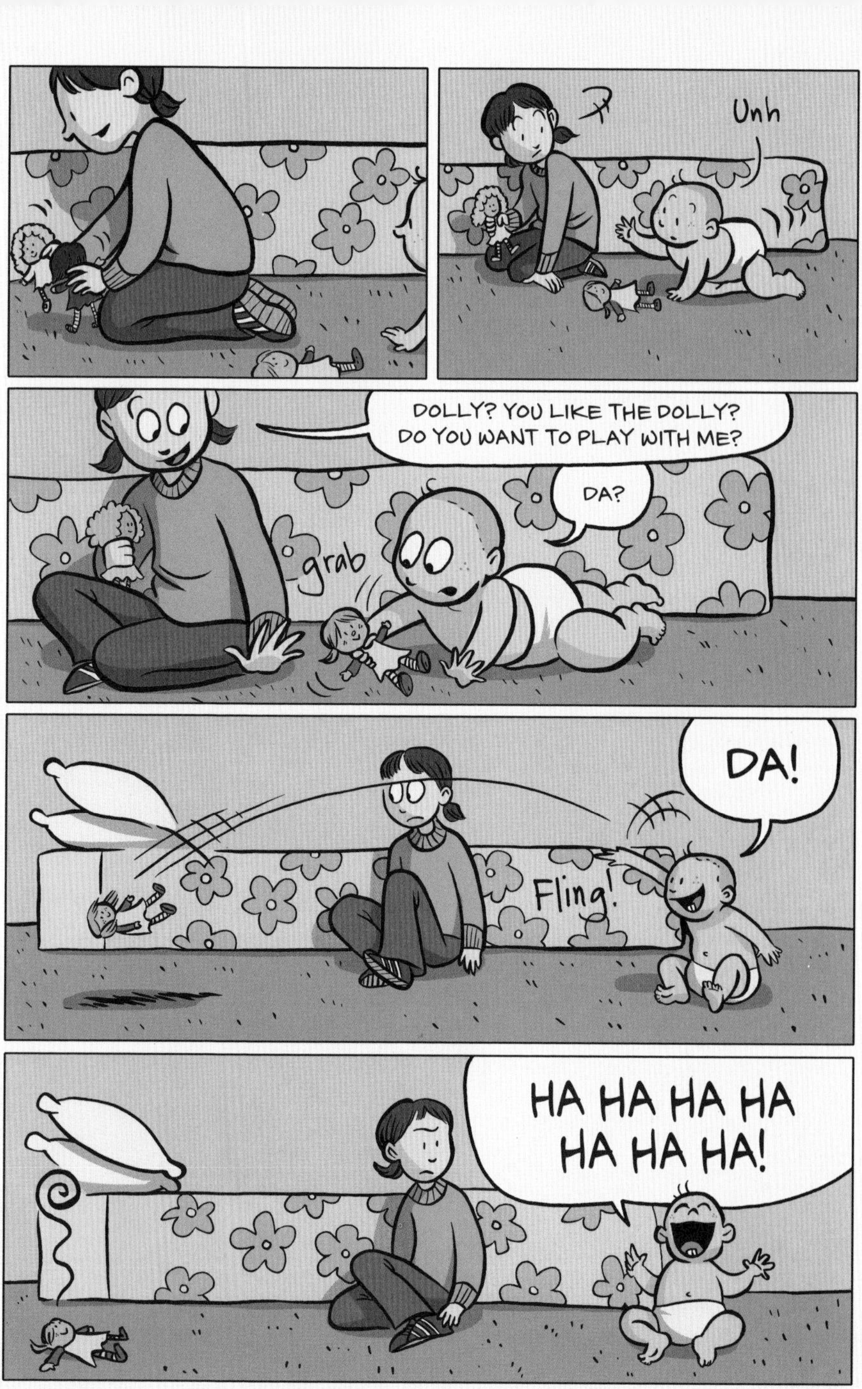

Unh
DOLLY? YOU LIKE THE DOLLY? DO YOU WANT TO PLAY WITH ME?
DA?
grab
DA!
Fling!
HA HA HA HA HA HA HA!

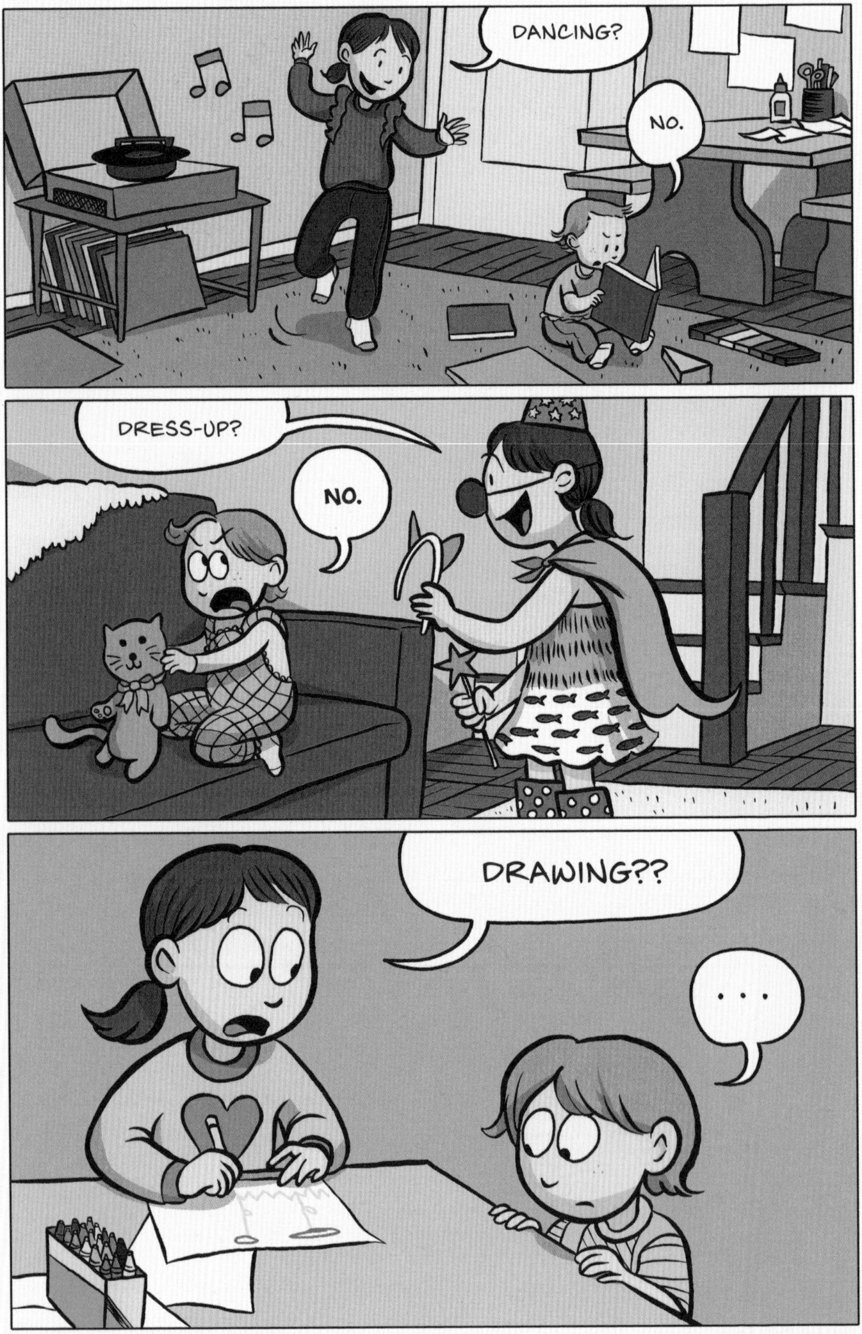
DANCING?
NO.
DRESS-UP?
NO.
DRAWING??
. . .

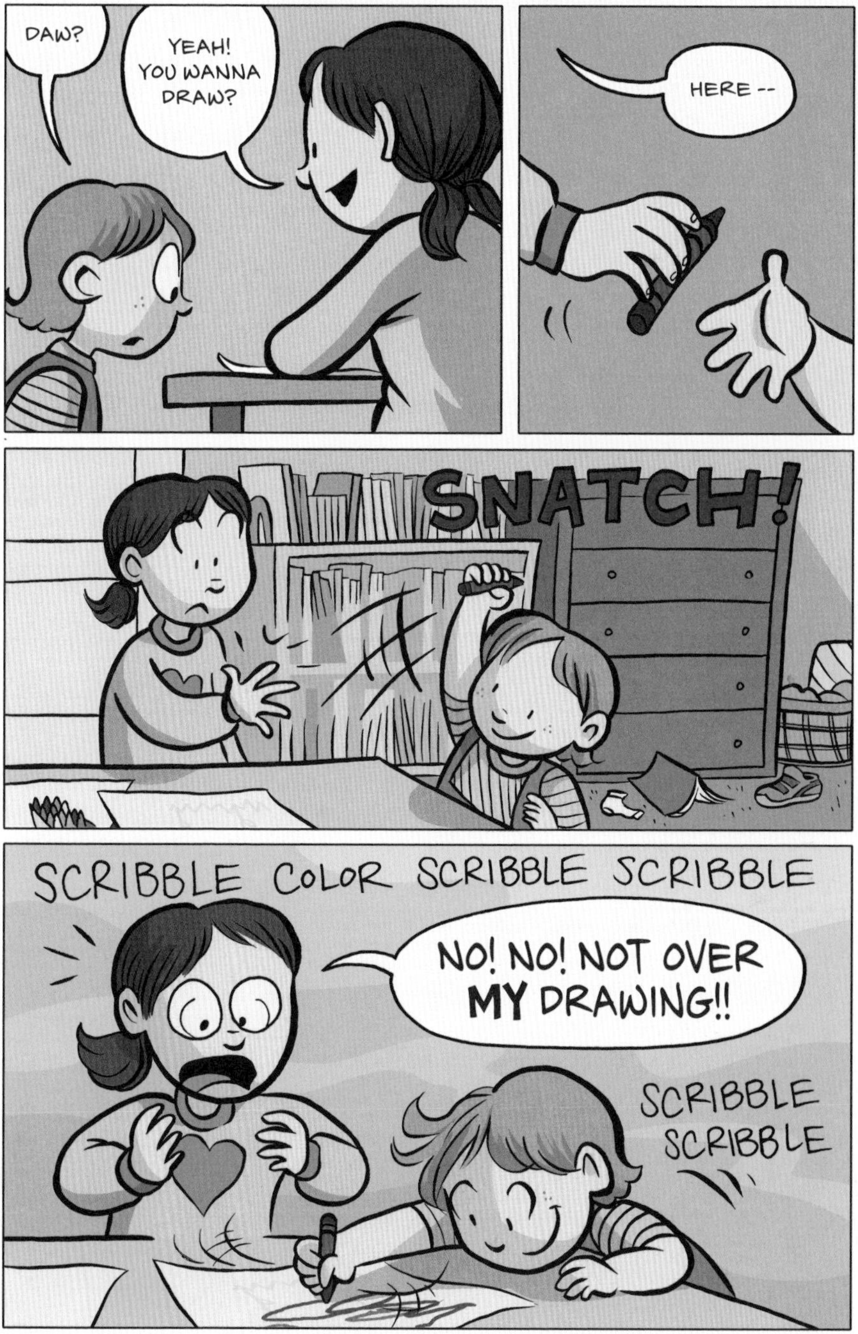
DAW?
YEAH! YOU WANNA DRAW?
HERE --
SNATCH!
SCRIBBLE COLOR SCRIBBLE SCRIBBLE
NO! NO! NOT OVER MY DRAWING!!
SCRIBBLE SCRIBBLE

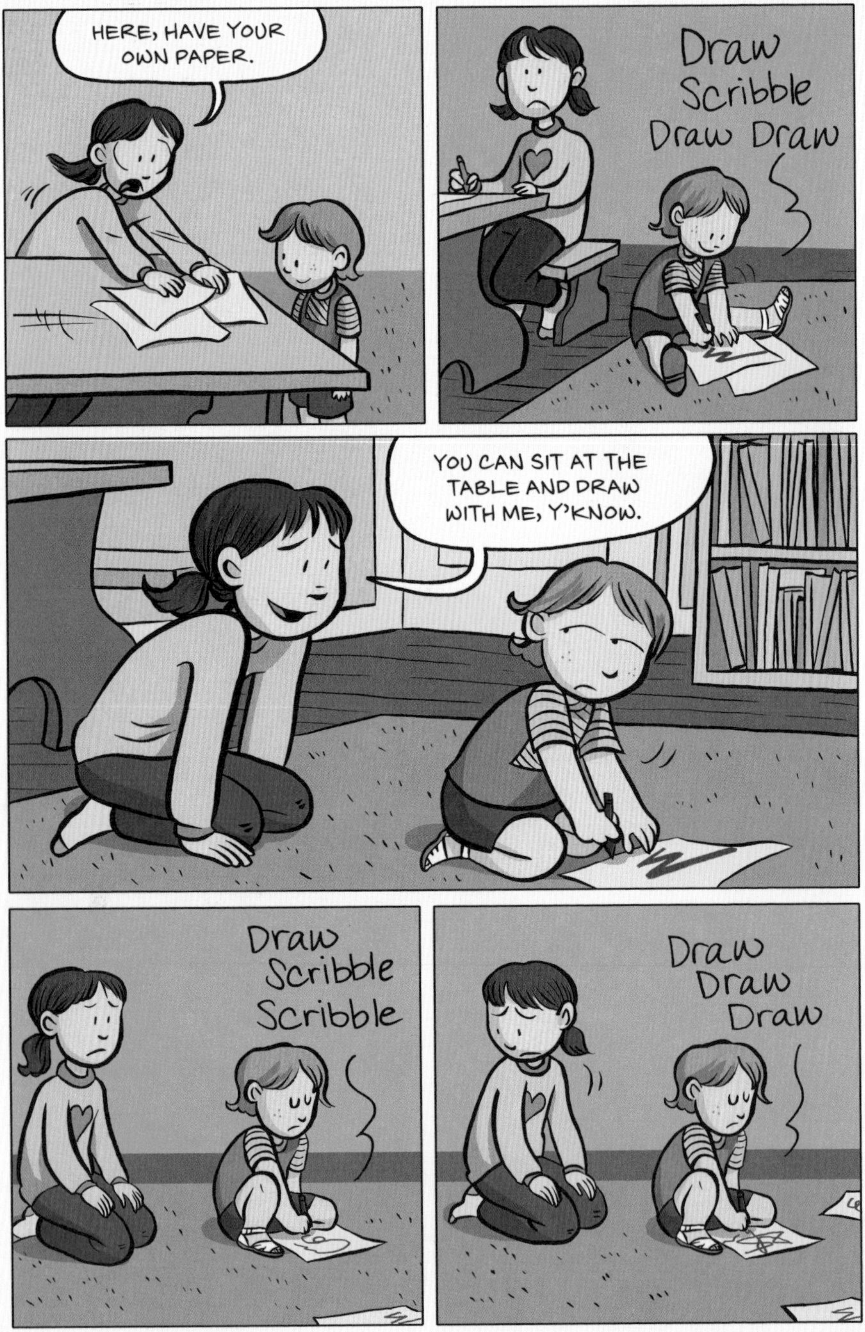
HERE, HAVE YOUR OWN PAPER.
Draw Scribble Draw Draw
YOU CAN SIT AT THE TABLE AND DRAW WITH ME, Y'KNOW.
Draw Scribble Scribble
Draw Draw Draw

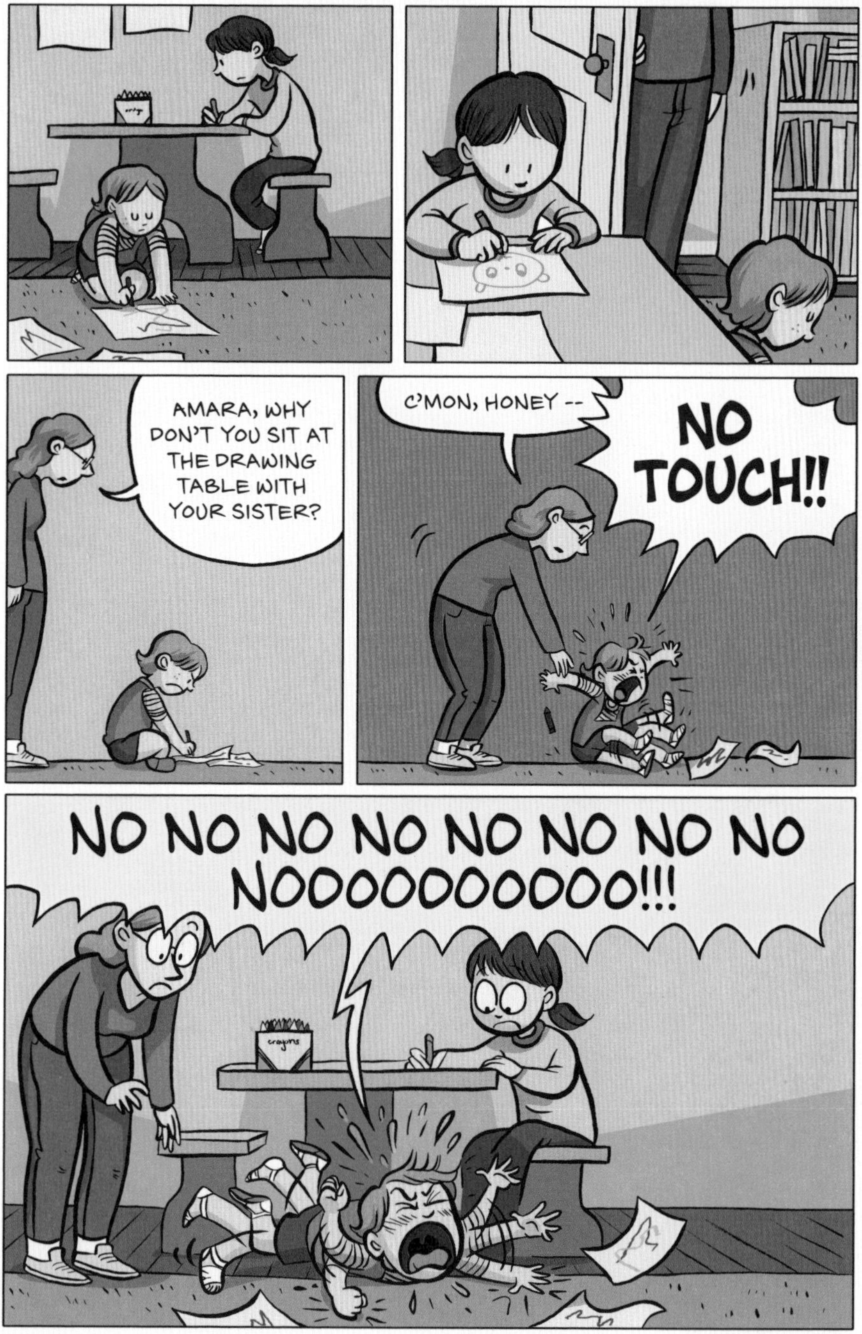
AMARA, WHY DON'T YOU SIT AT THE DRAWING TABLE WITH YOUR SISTER?
C'MON, HONEY --
NO TOUCH!!
NO NO NO NO NO NO NO NO NOOOOOOOOOO!!!
crayons

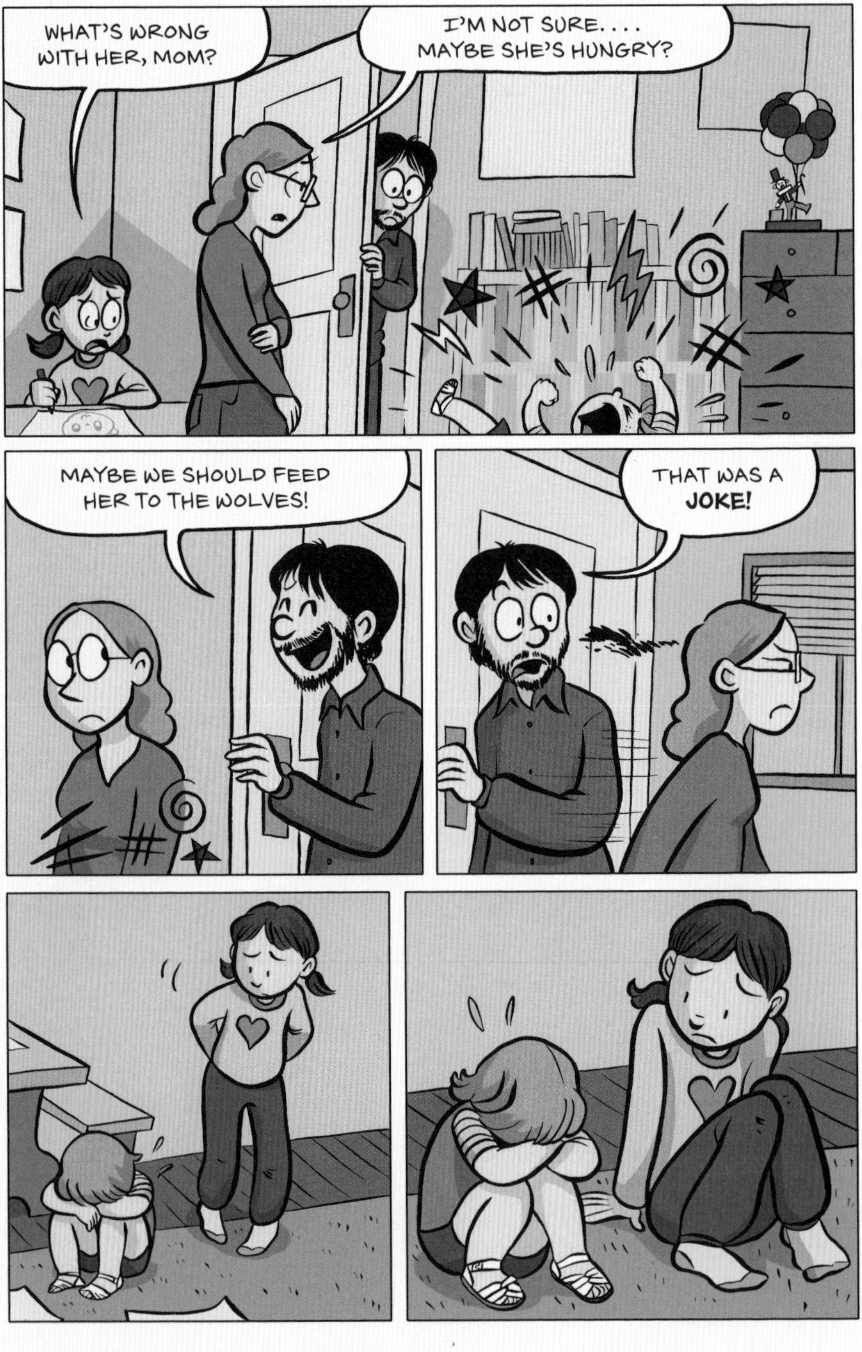
WHAT'S WRONG WITH HER, MOM?
I'M NOT SURE. . . . MAYBE SHE'S HUNGRY?
MAYBE WE SHOULD FEED HER TO THE WOLVES!
THAT WAS A **JOKE!**

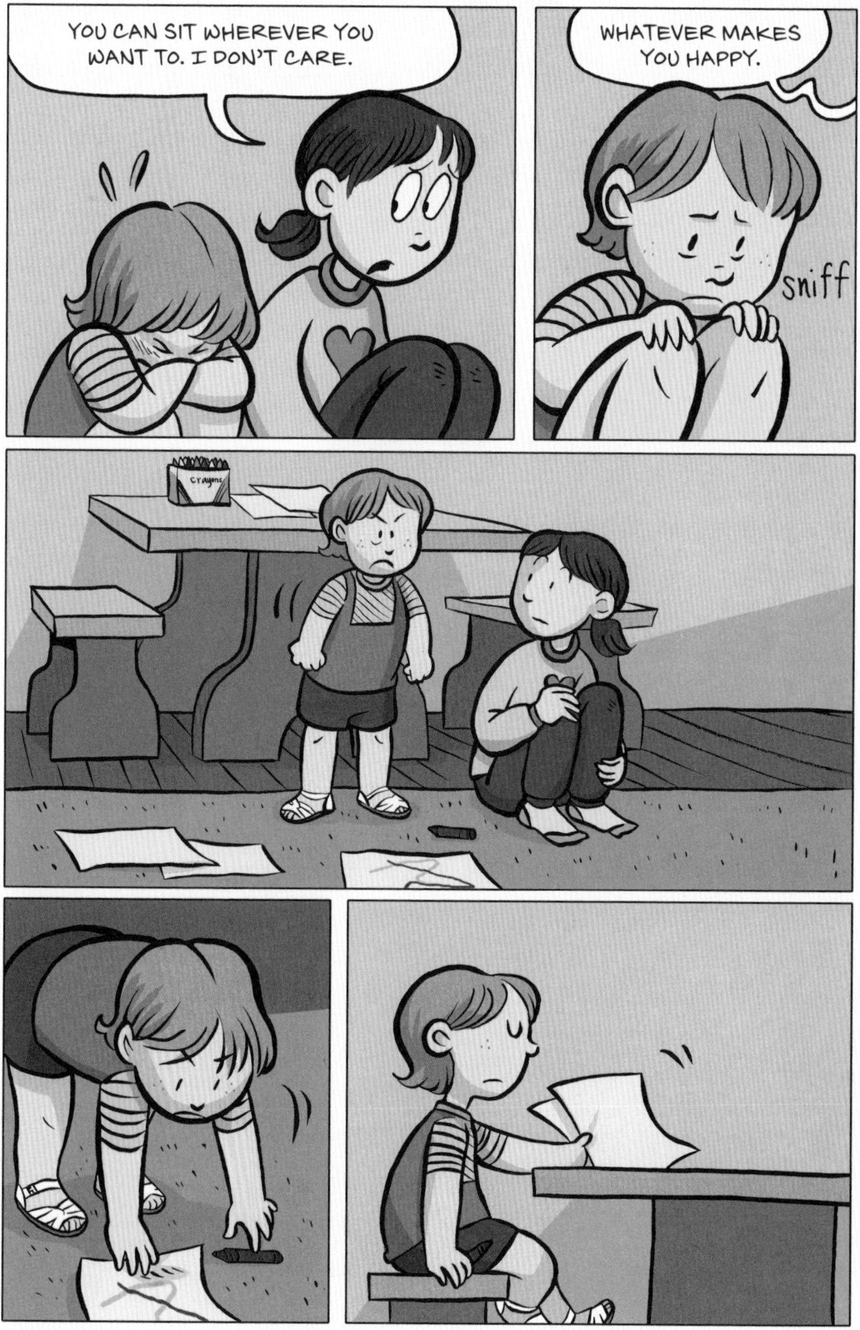
YOU CAN SIT WHEREVER YOU WANT TO. I DON'T CARE.
WHATEVER MAKES YOU HAPPY.
sniff
crayons

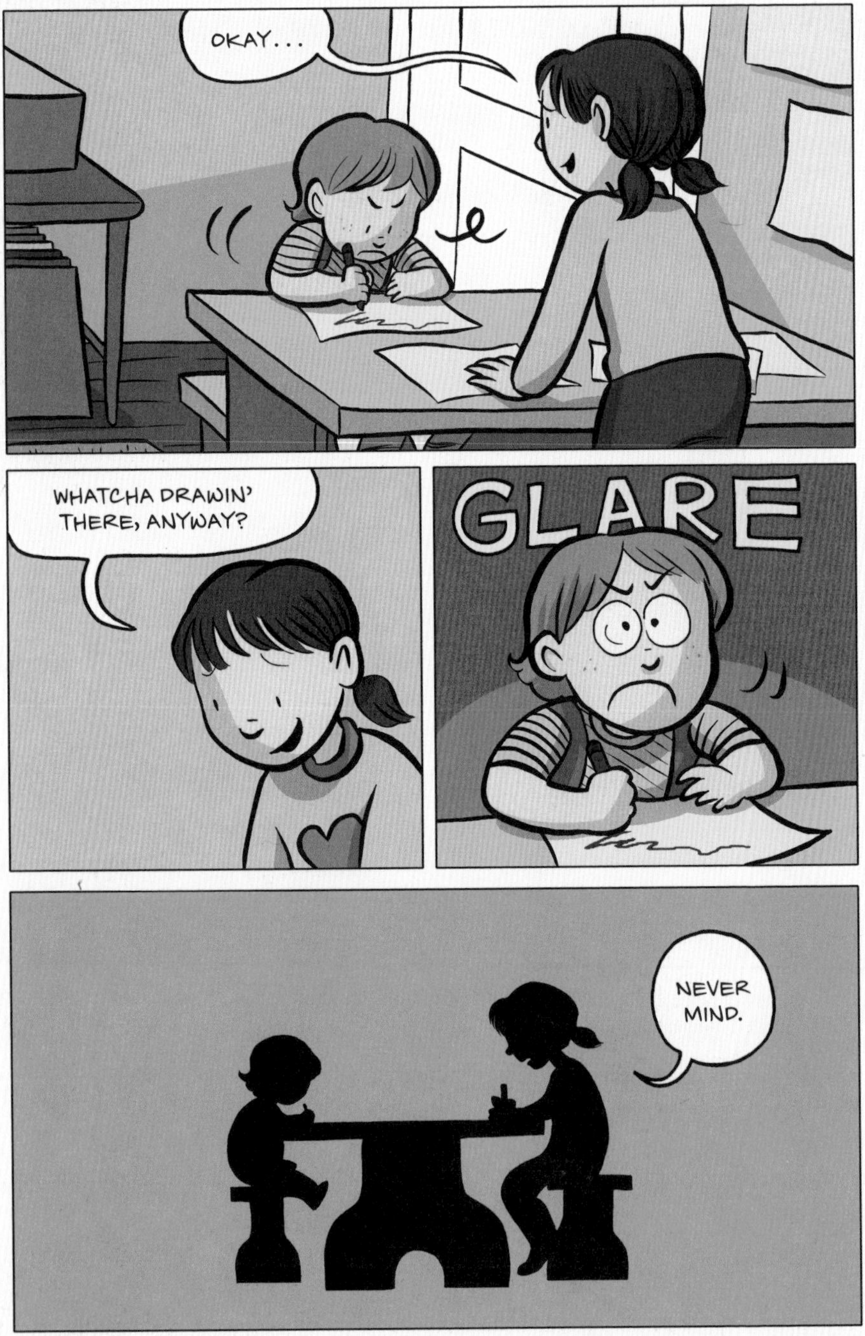
OKAY...
WHATCHA DRAWIN' THERE, ANYWAY?
GLARE
NEVER MIND.

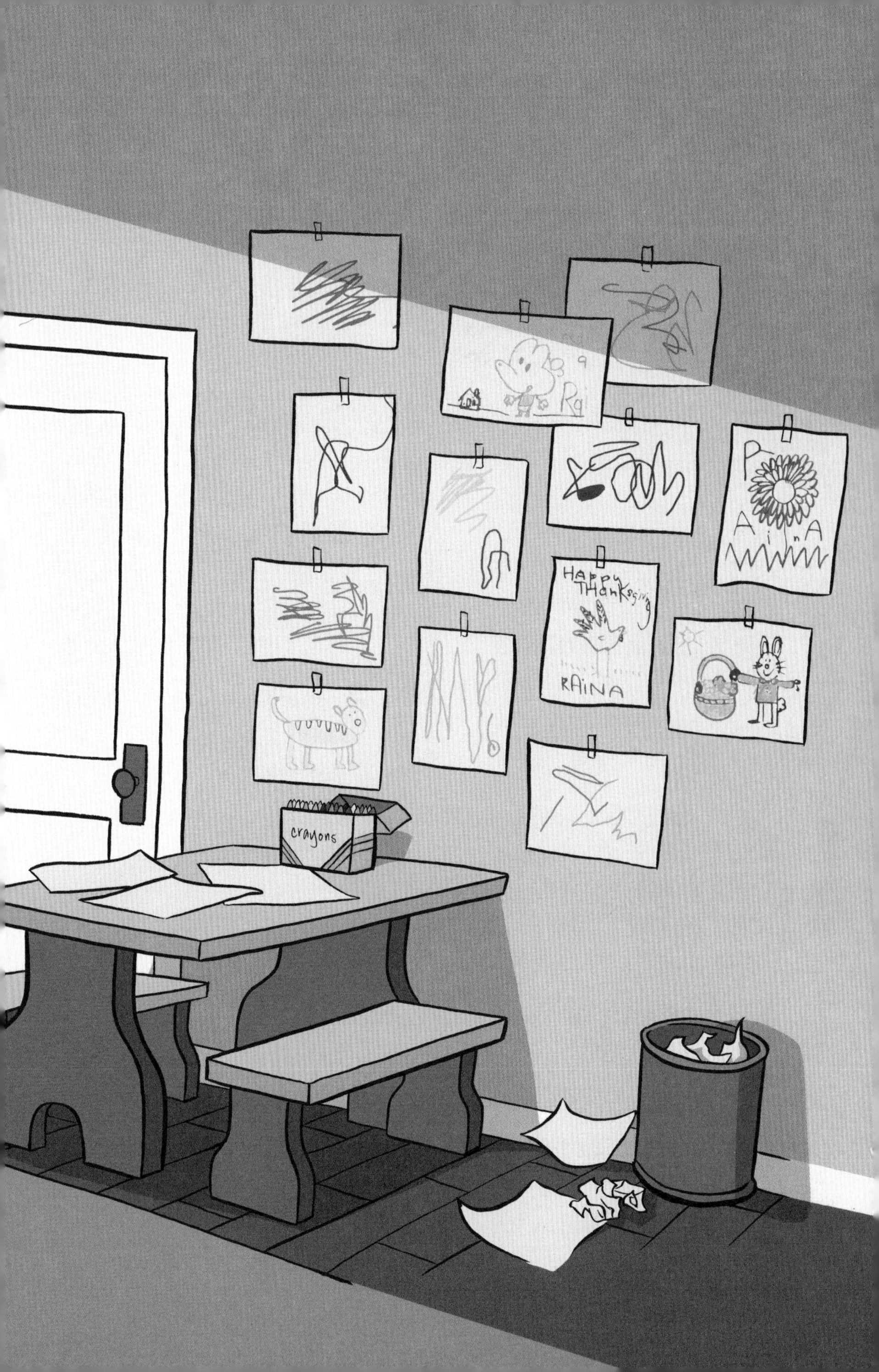
HAPPY THAnksgiving
RAINA
crayons

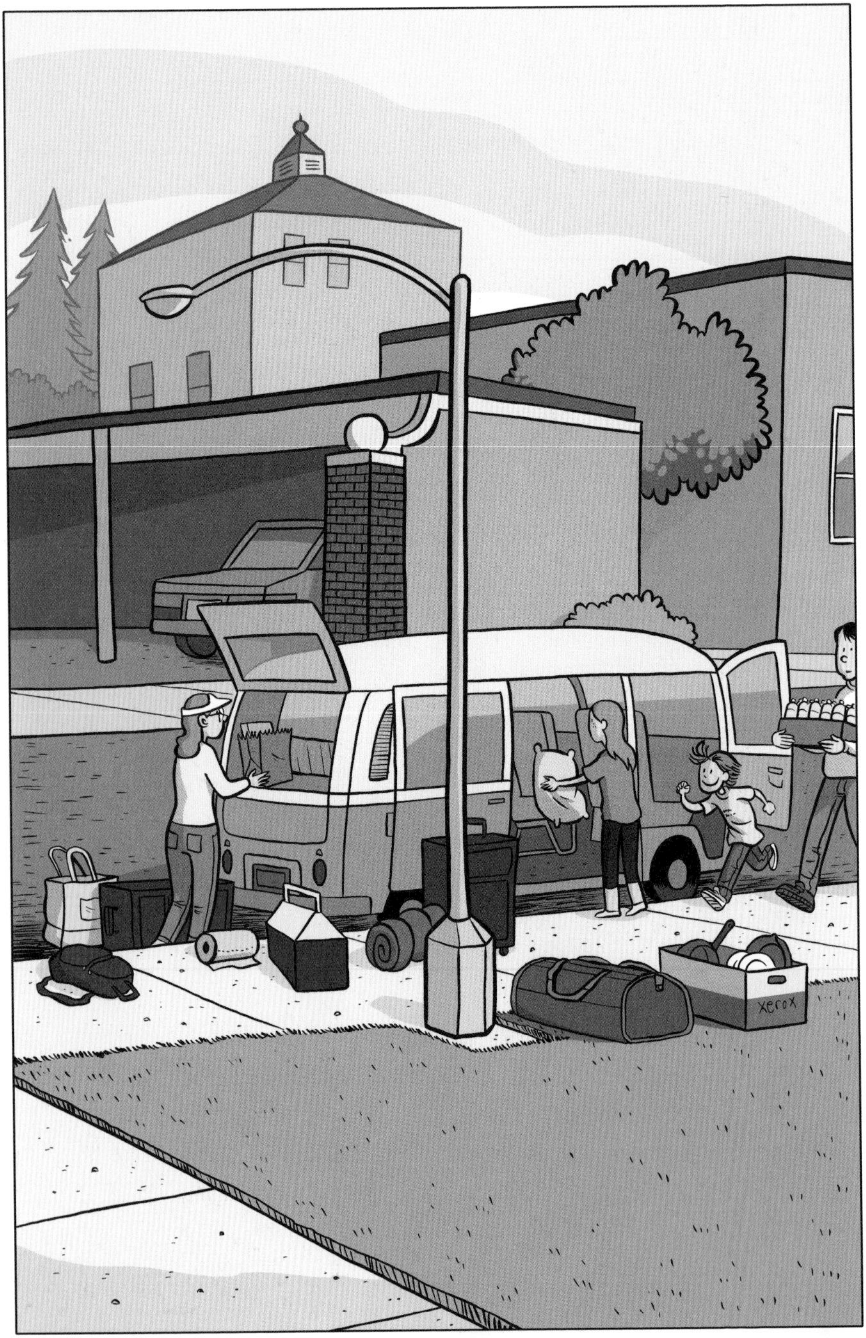
xerox

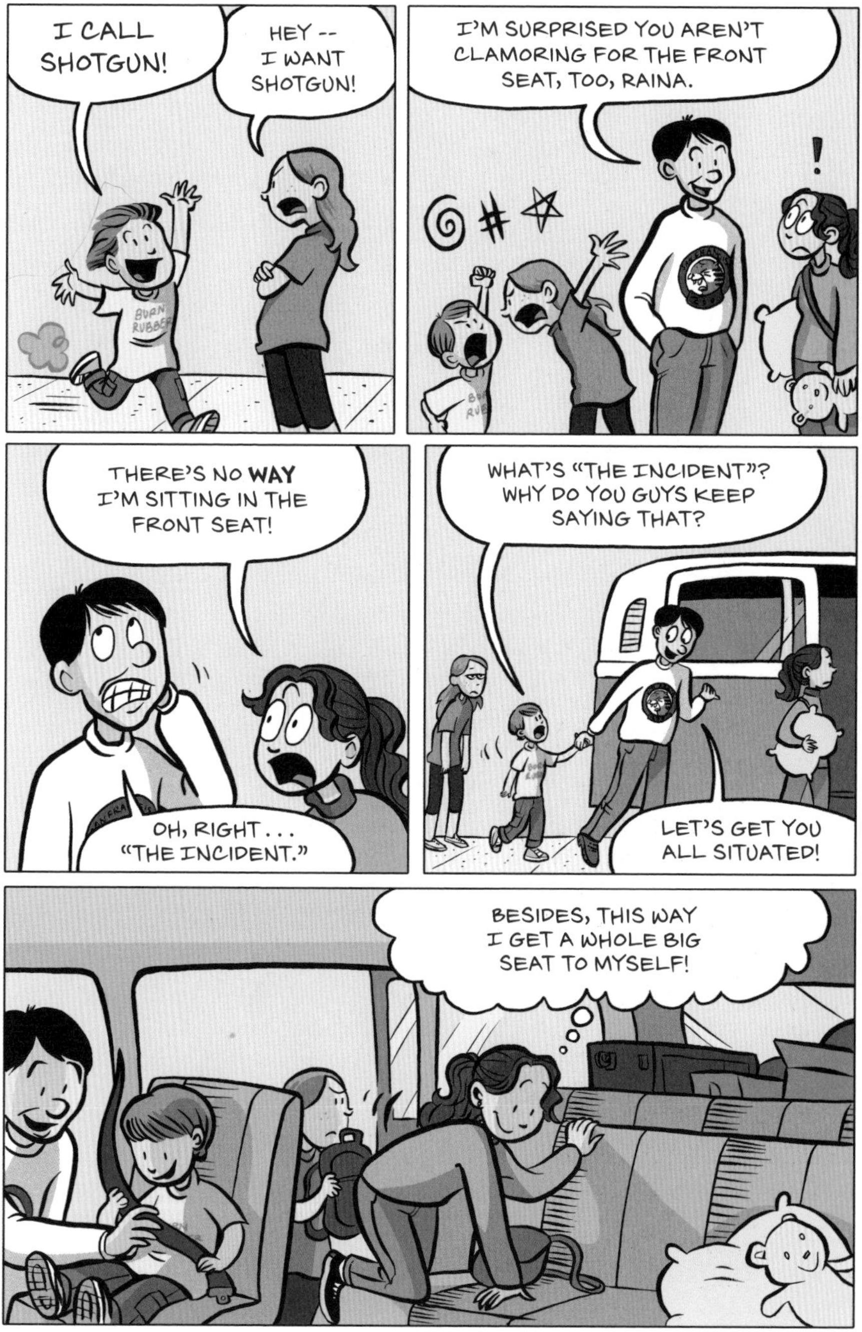
I CALL SHOTGUN!
HEY -- I WANT SHOTGUN!
I'M SURPRISED YOU AREN'T CLAMORING FOR THE FRONT SEAT, TOO, RAINA.
!
BURN RUBBER
THERE'S NO **WAY** I'M SITTING IN THE FRONT SEAT!
OH, RIGHT . . . "THE INCIDENT."
WHAT'S "THE INCIDENT"? WHY DO YOU GUYS KEEP SAYING THAT?
LET'S GET YOU ALL SITUATED!
BESIDES, THIS WAY I GET A WHOLE BIG SEAT TO MYSELF!

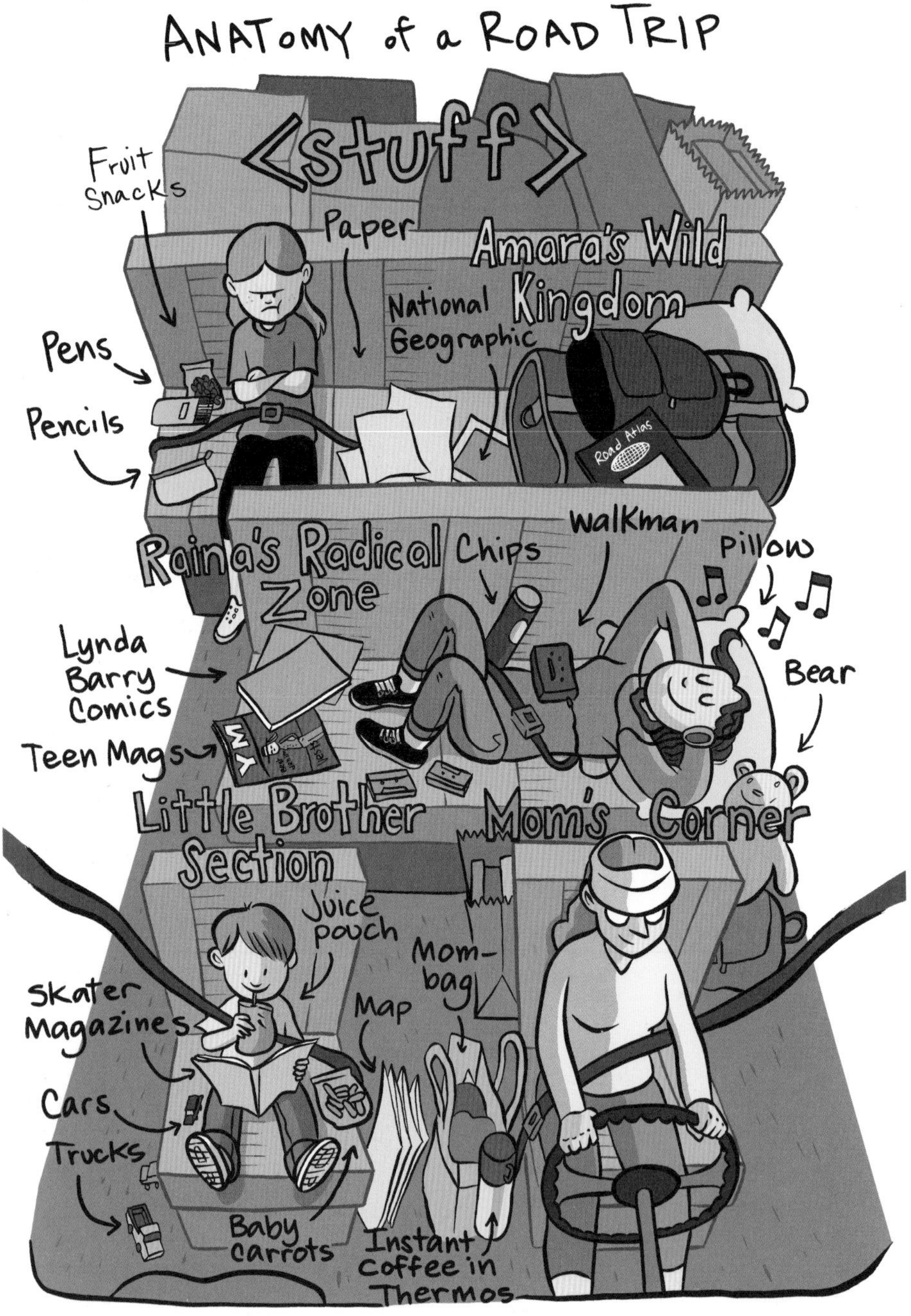
ANATOMY of a ROAD TRIP
<stuff>
Fruit Snacks
Paper
Amara's Wild Kingdom
National Geographic
Pens
Pencils
Road Atlas
Raina's Radical Zone
Chips
Walkman
Pillow
Lynda Barry Comics
Bear
Teen Mags
YM
Little Brother Section
Mom's Corner
Juice pouch
Mom-bag
Skater Magazines
Map
Cars
Trucks
Baby carrots
Instant Coffee in Thermos

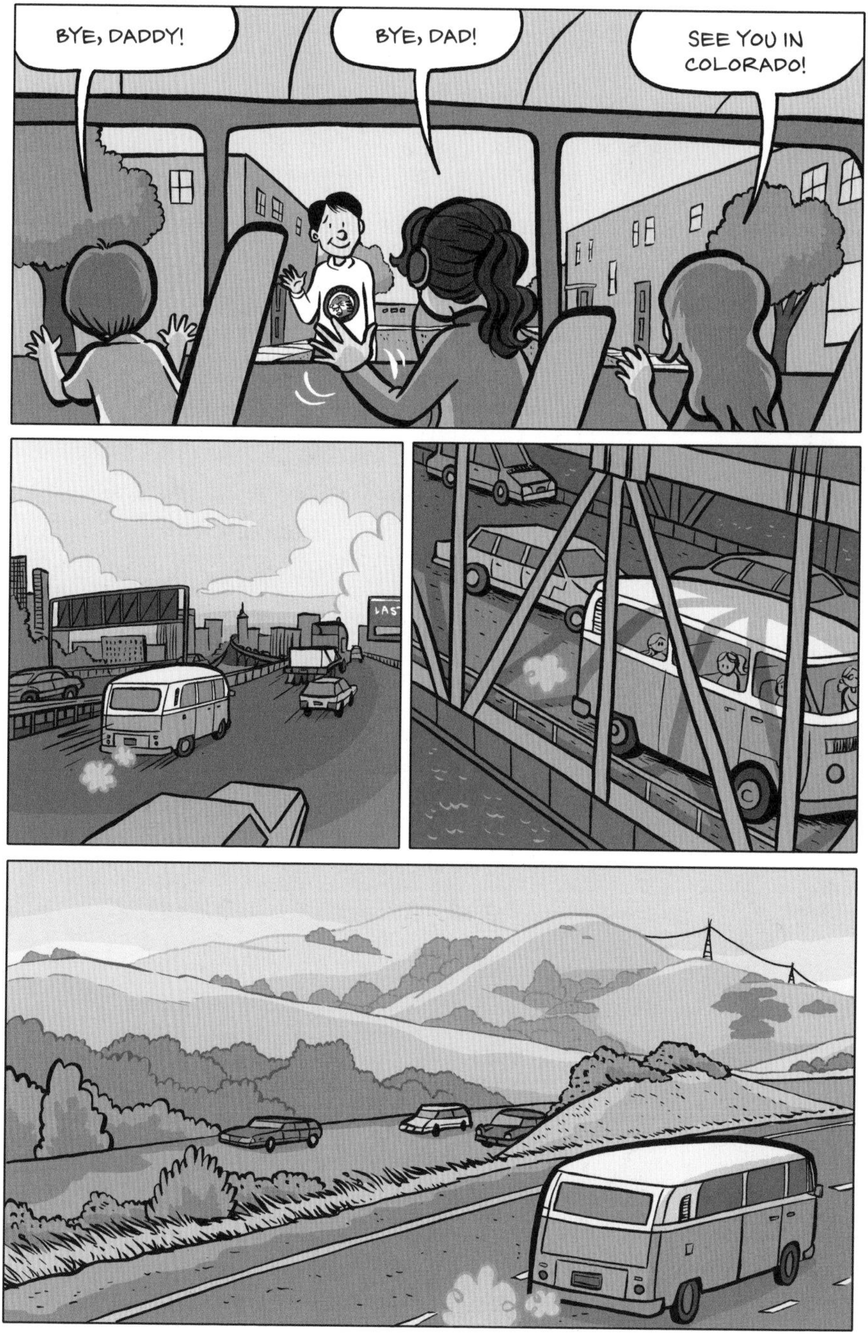
BYE, DADDY!
BYE, DAD!
SEE YOU IN COLORADO!

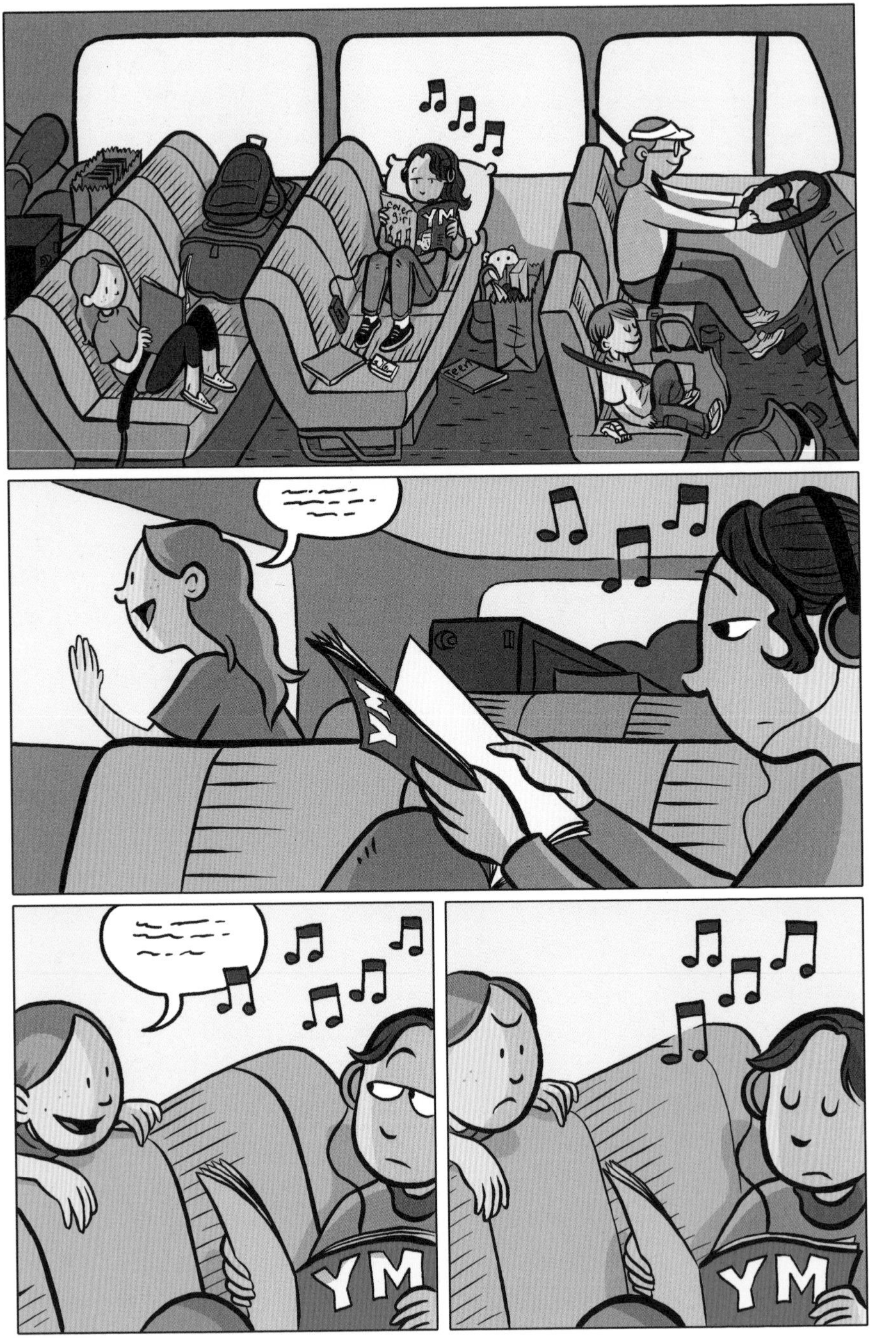
Cover girl
YM
Teen
YM
YM
YM

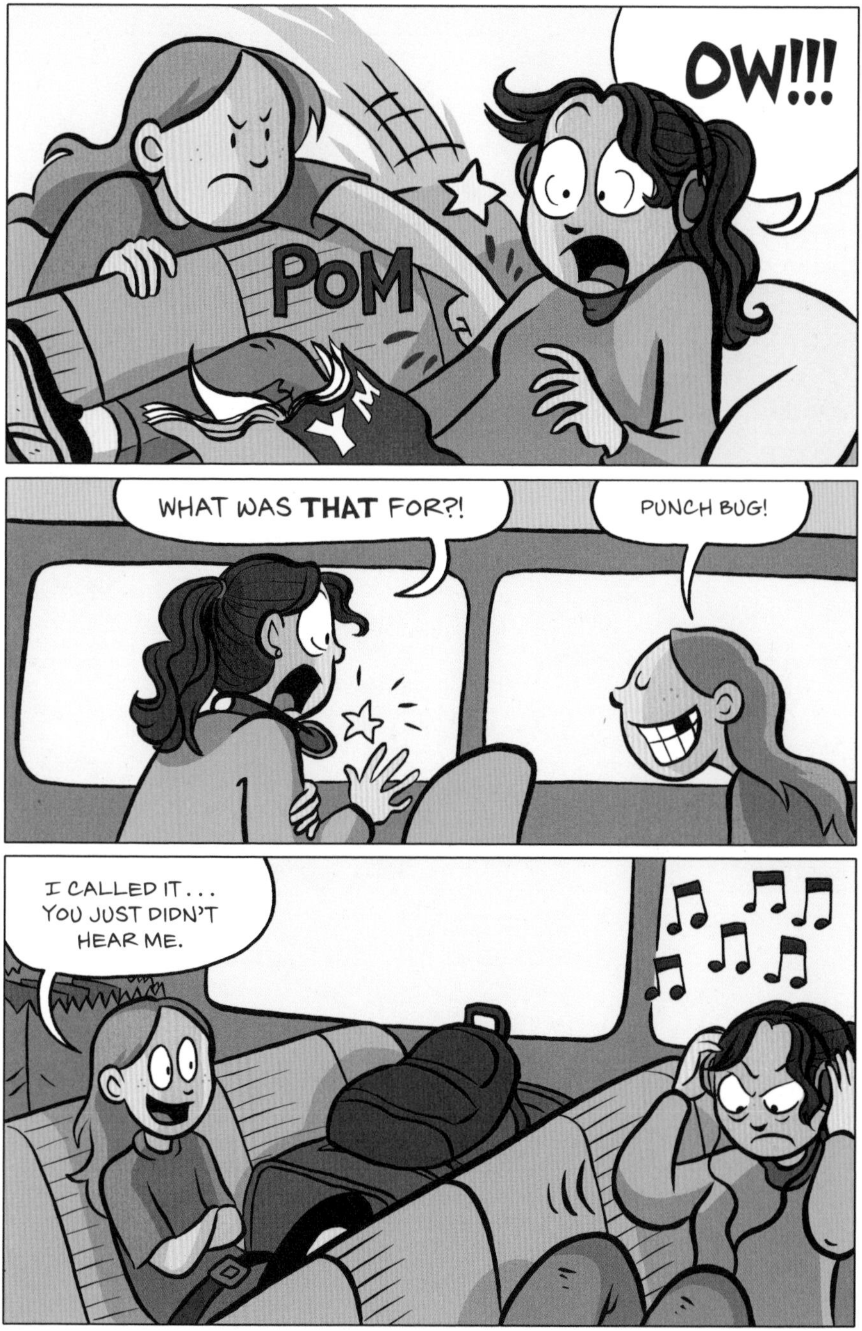
OW!!!
POM
YM
WHAT WAS **THAT** FOR?!
PUNCH BUG!
I CALLED IT . . . YOU JUST DIDN'T HEAR ME.

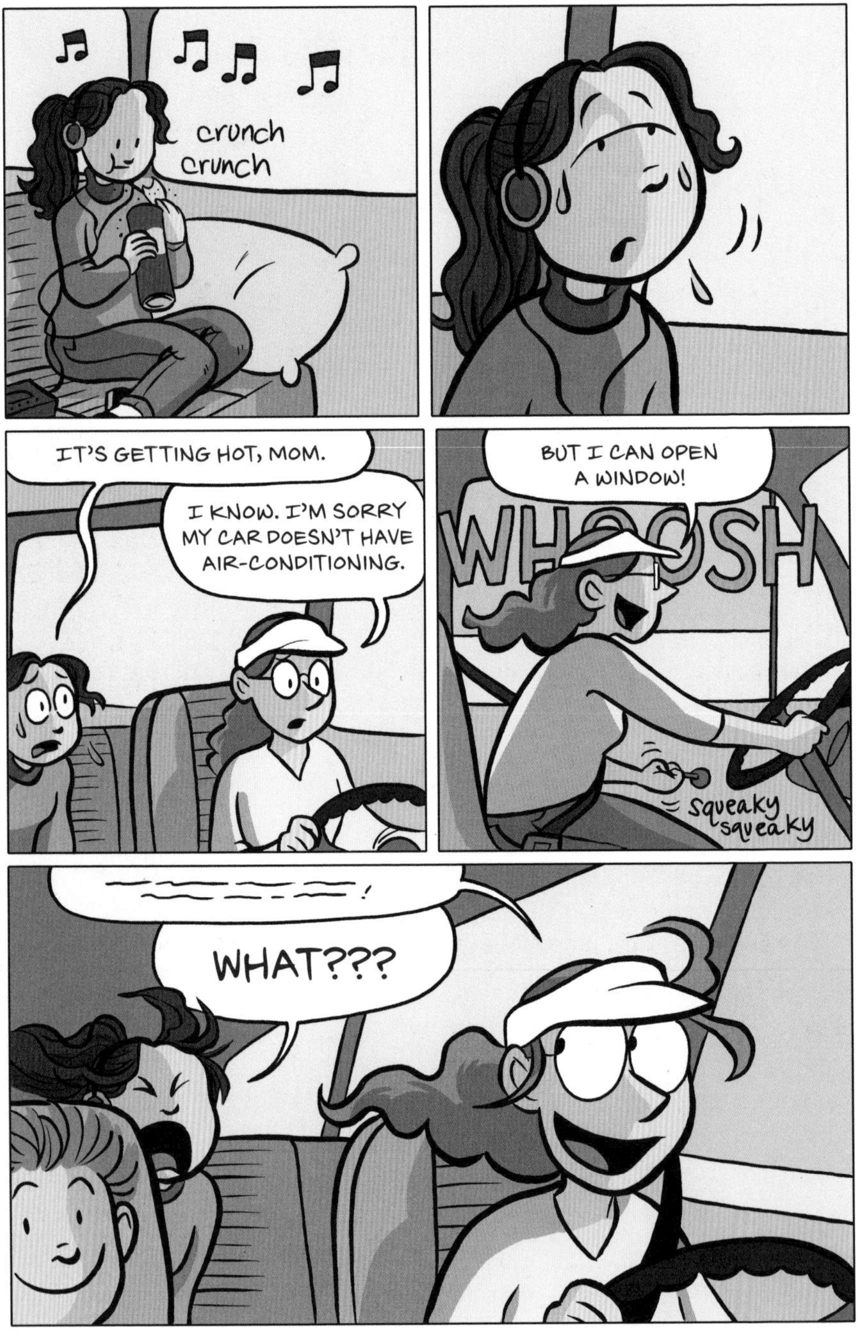
crunch
crunch
IT'S GETTING HOT, MOM.
I KNOW. I'M SORRY MY CAR DOESN'T HAVE AIR-CONDITIONING.
BUT I CAN OPEN A WINDOW!
WHOOSH
squeaky
squeaky
WHAT???

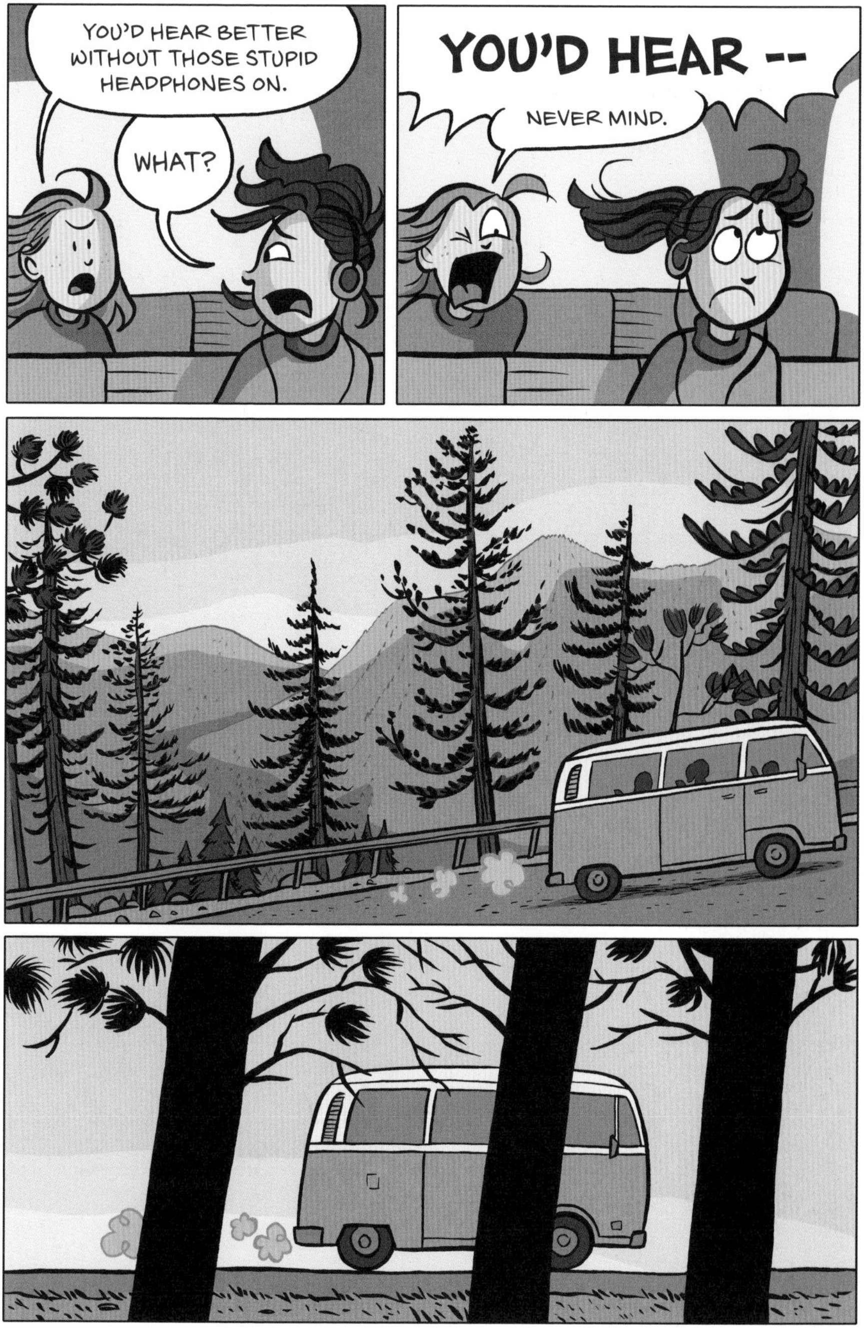
YOU'D HEAR BETTER WITHOUT THOSE STUPID HEADPHONES ON.
WHAT?
YOU'D HEAR --
NEVER MIND.

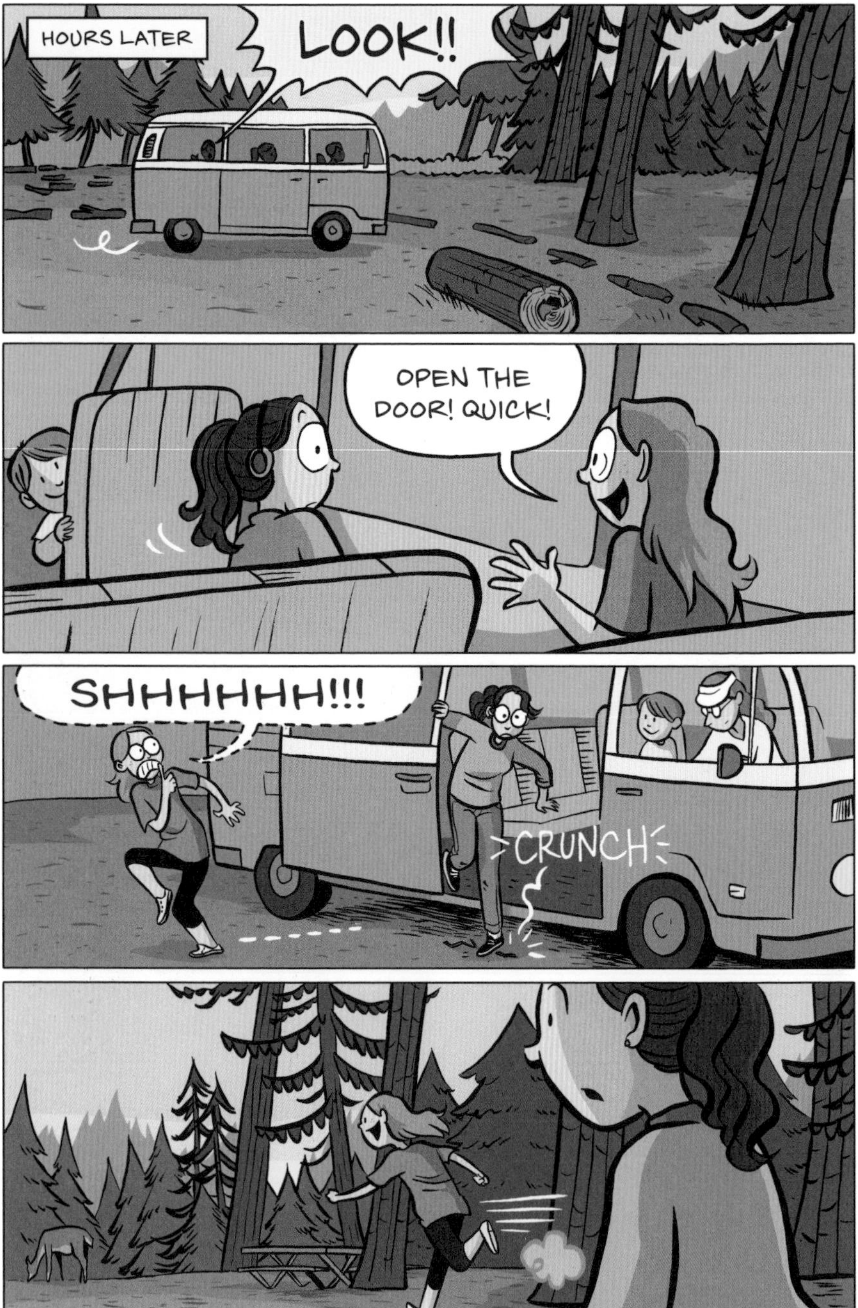
HOURS LATER
LOOK!!
OPEN THE DOOR! QUICK!
SHHHHHH!!!
CRUNCH

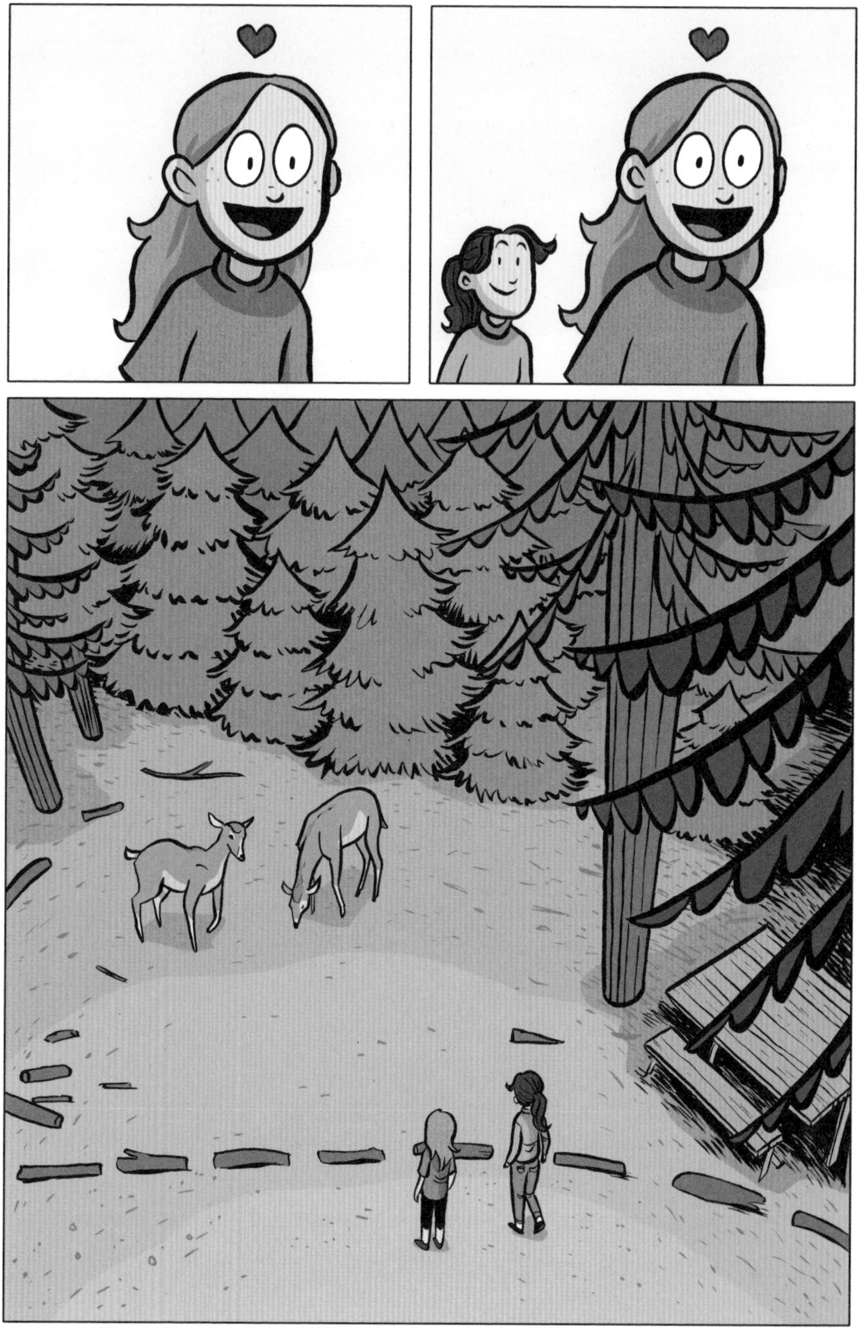

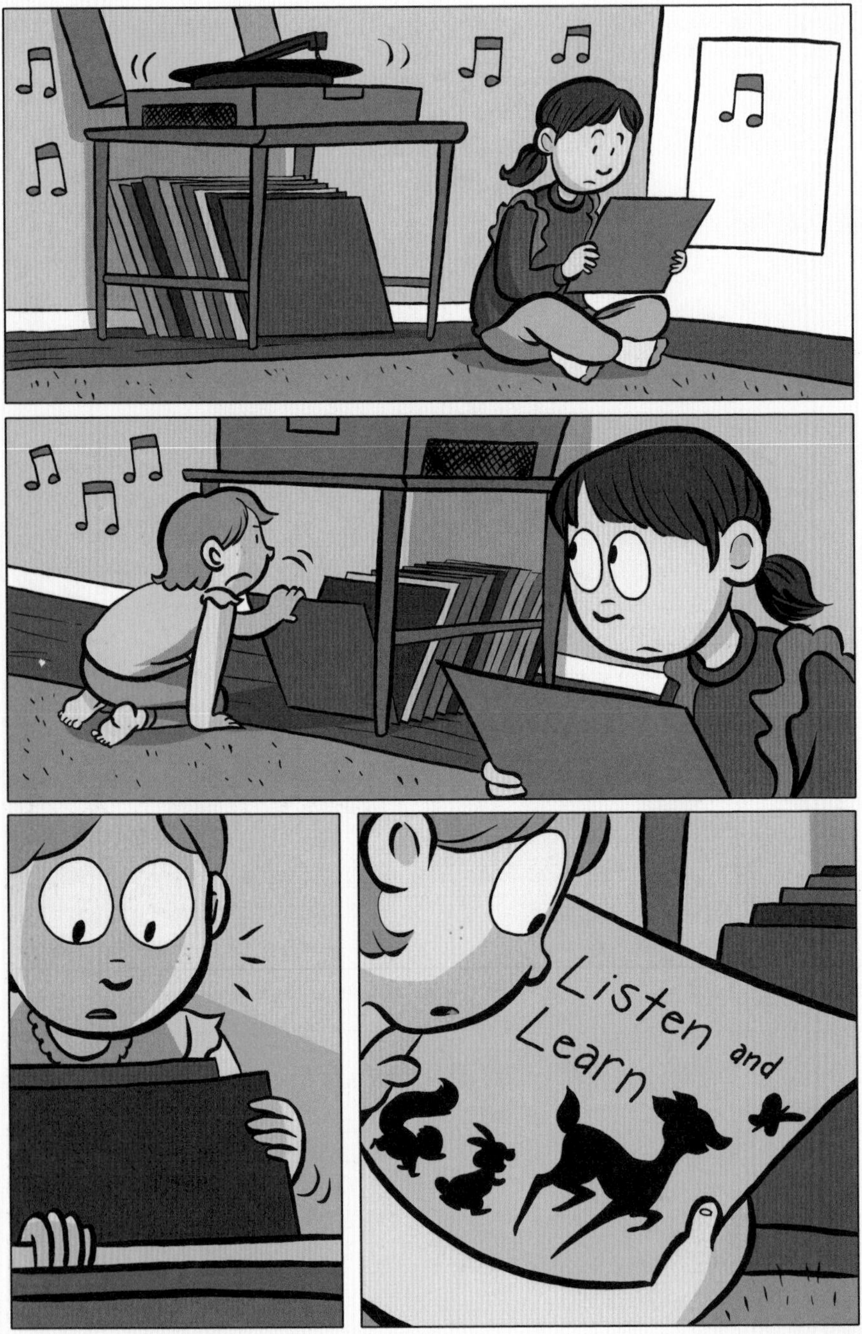
Listen and Learn

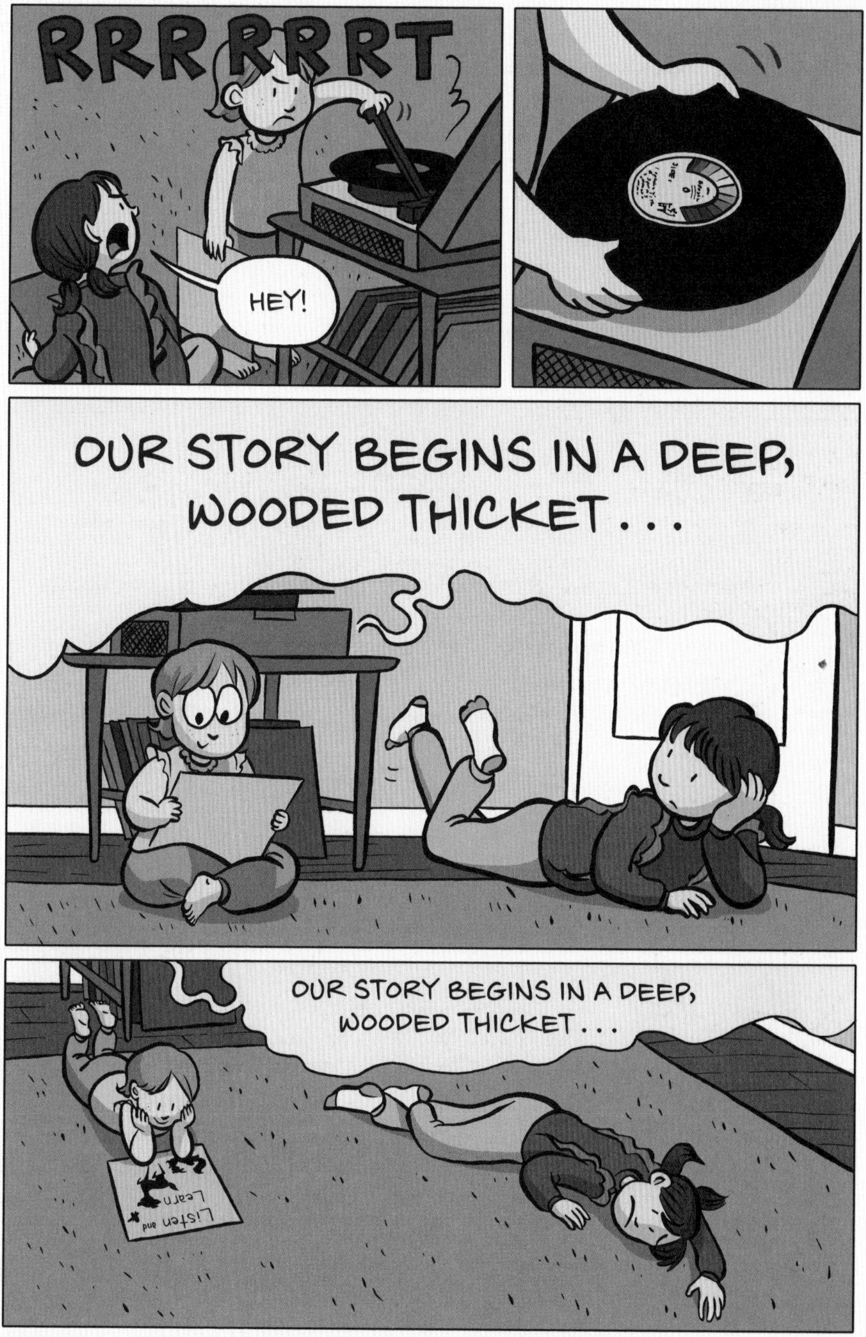
RRRRRRT
HEY!
OUR STORY BEGINS IN A DEEP, WOODED THICKET . . .
OUR STORY BEGINS IN A DEEP, WOODED THICKET . . .
Listen and Learn

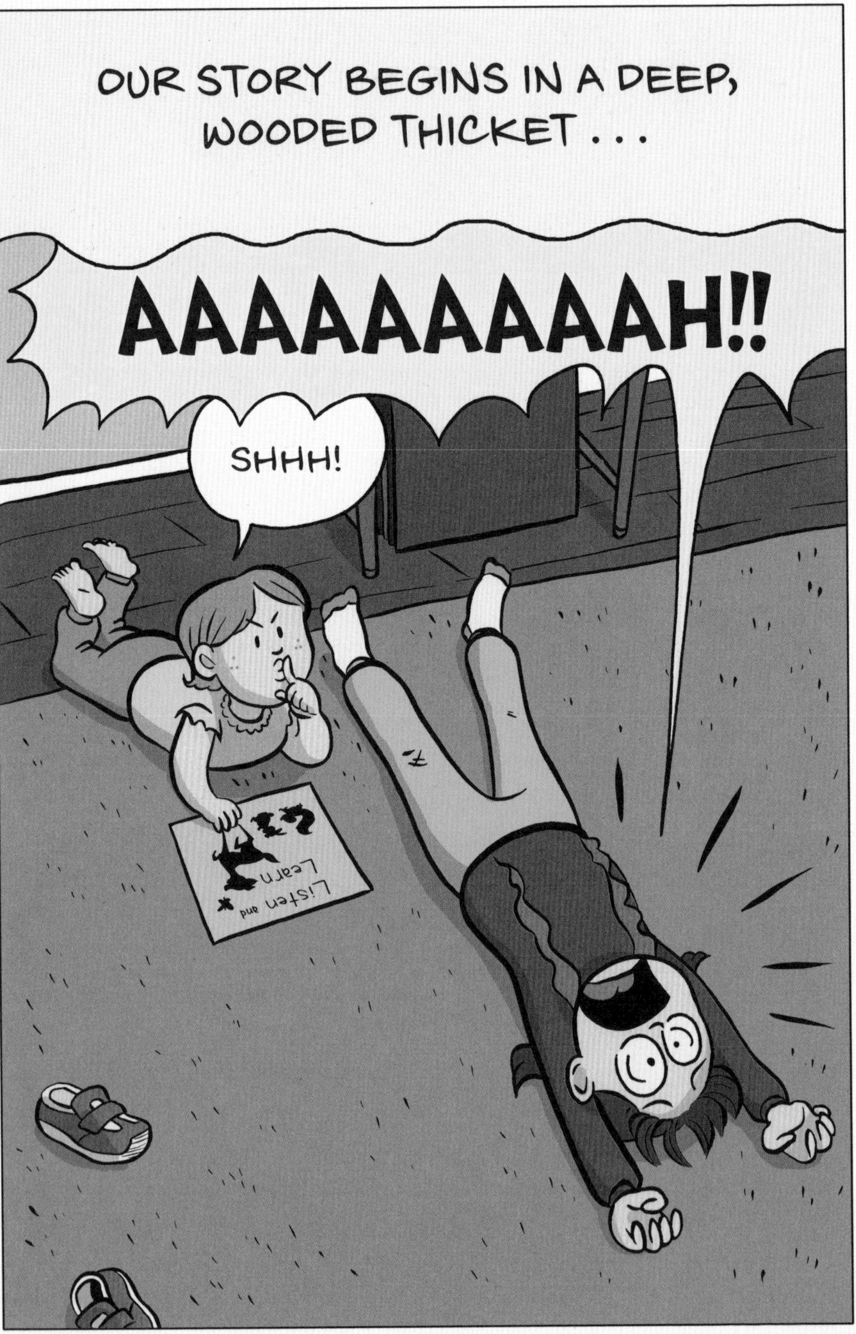
OUR STORY BEGINS IN A DEEP, WOODED THICKET . . .
AAAAAAAAAAH!!
SHHH!
Listen and Learn

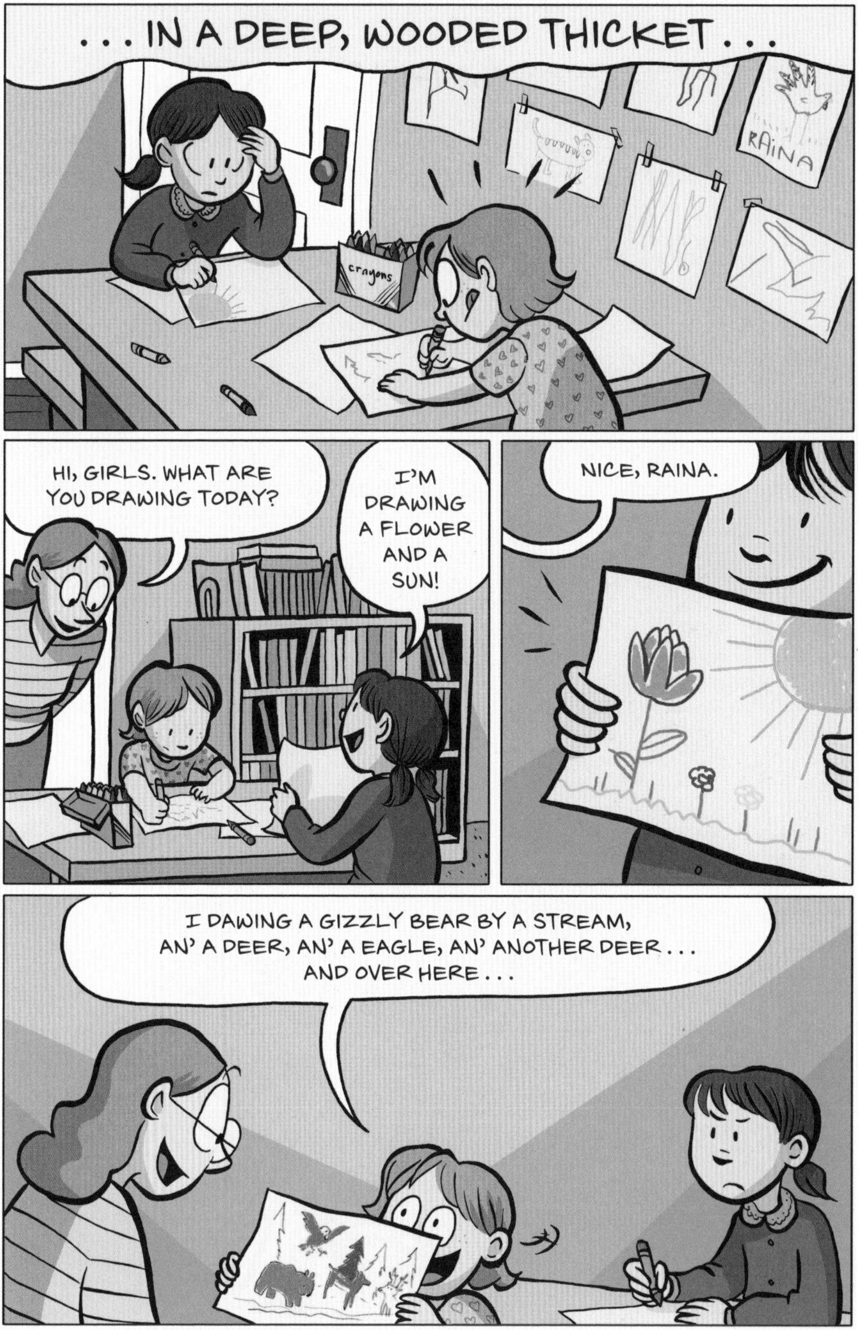
. . . IN A DEEP, WOODED THICKET . . .
crayons
RAINA
HI, GIRLS. WHAT ARE YOU DRAWING TODAY?
I'M DRAWING A FLOWER AND A SUN!
NICE, RAINA.
I DAWING A GIZZLY BEAR BY A STREAM, AN' A DEER, AN' A EAGLE, AN' ANOTHER DEER . . . AND OVER HERE . . .

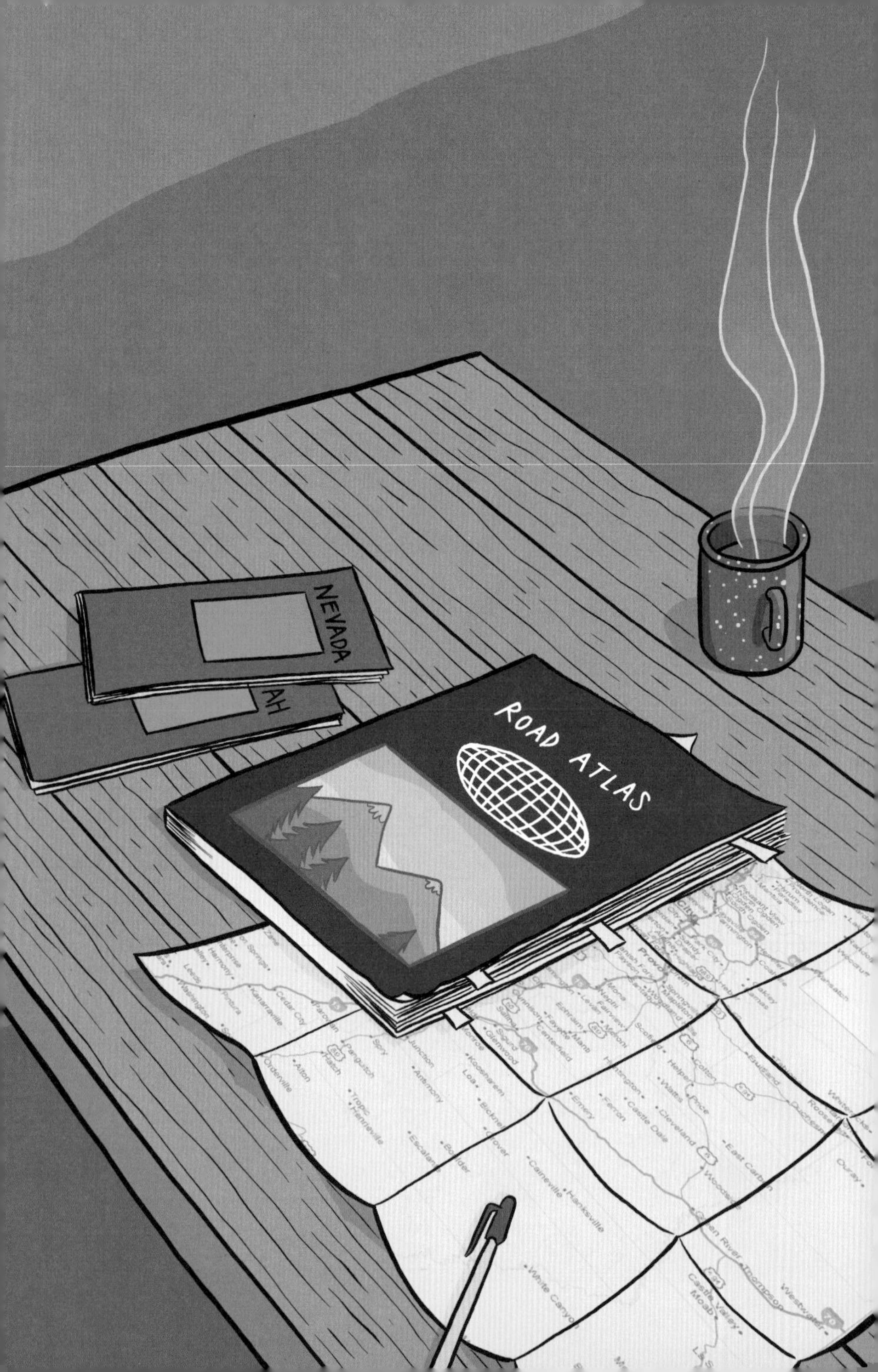
NEVADA
ROAD ATLAS

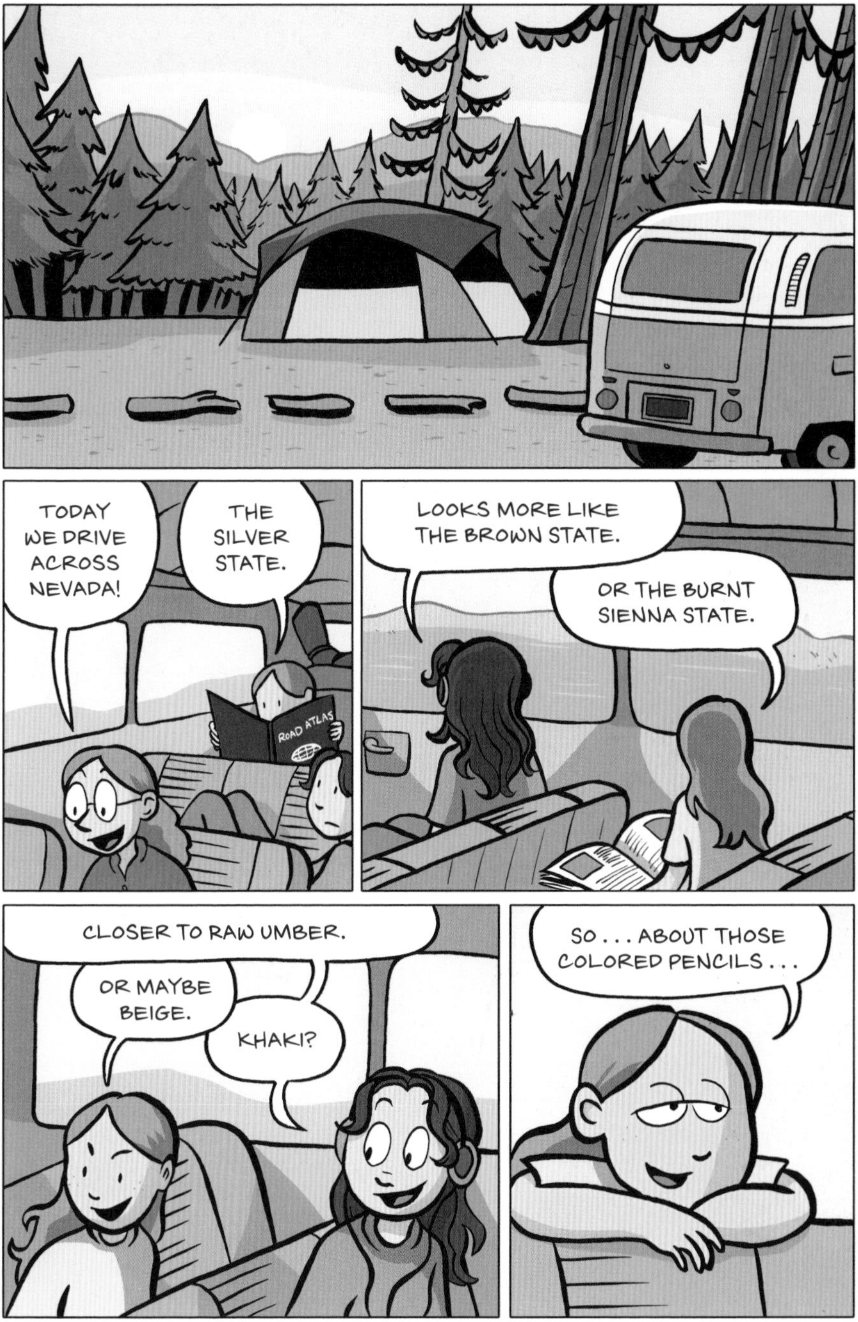
TODAY WE DRIVE ACROSS NEVADA!
THE SILVER STATE.
ROAD ATLAS
LOOKS MORE LIKE THE BROWN STATE.
OR THE BURNT SIENNA STATE.
CLOSER TO RAW UMBER.
OR MAYBE BEIGE.
KHAKI?
SO . . . ABOUT THOSE COLORED PENCILS . . .

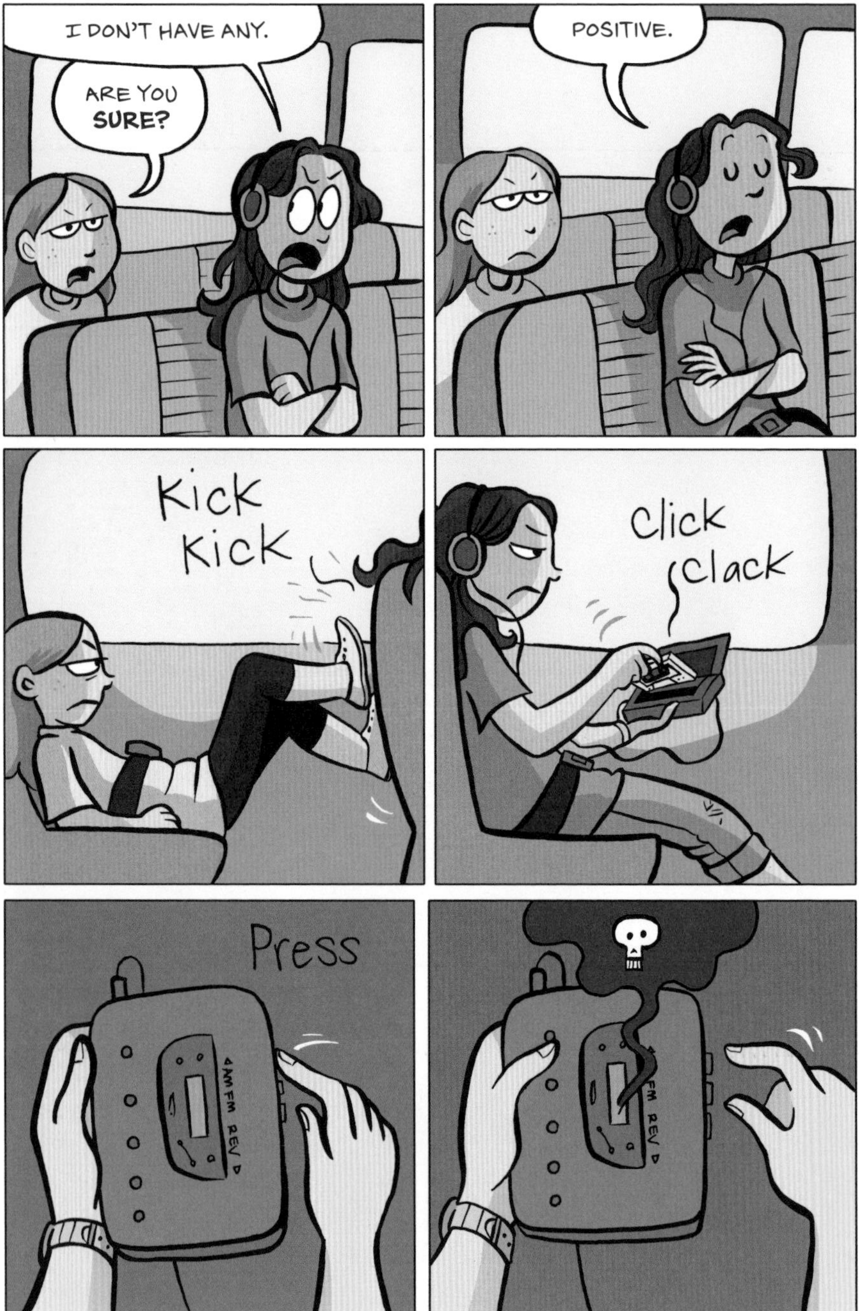
I DON'T HAVE ANY.
ARE YOU SURE?
POSITIVE.
Kick kick
Click clack
Press
◁AM FM REV▷
FM REV▷

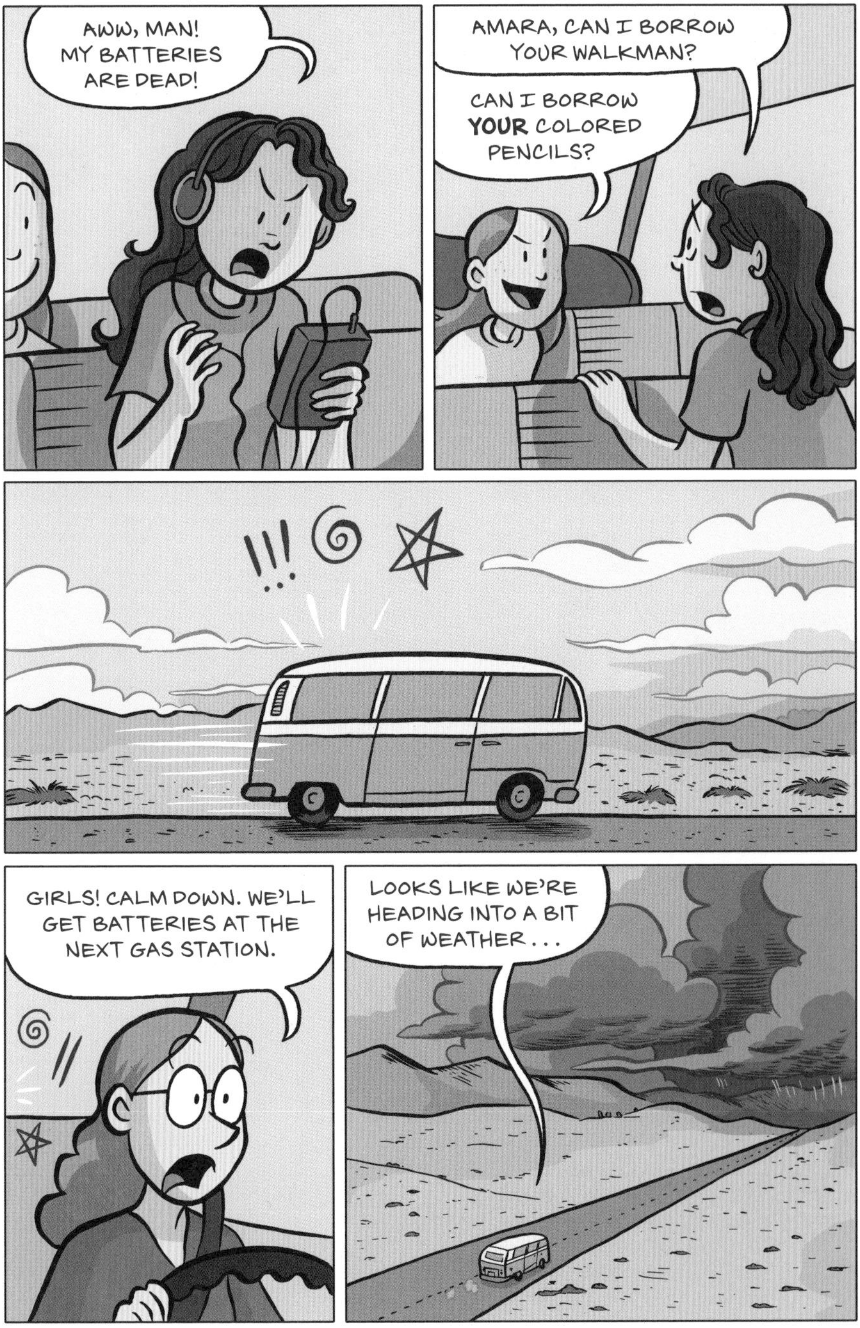
AWW, MAN! MY BATTERIES ARE DEAD!
AMARA, CAN I BORROW YOUR WALKMAN?
CAN I BORROW **YOUR** COLORED PENCILS?
!!!
GIRLS! CALM DOWN. WE'LL GET BATTERIES AT THE NEXT GAS STATION.
LOOKS LIKE WE'RE HEADING INTO A BIT OF WEATHER . . .

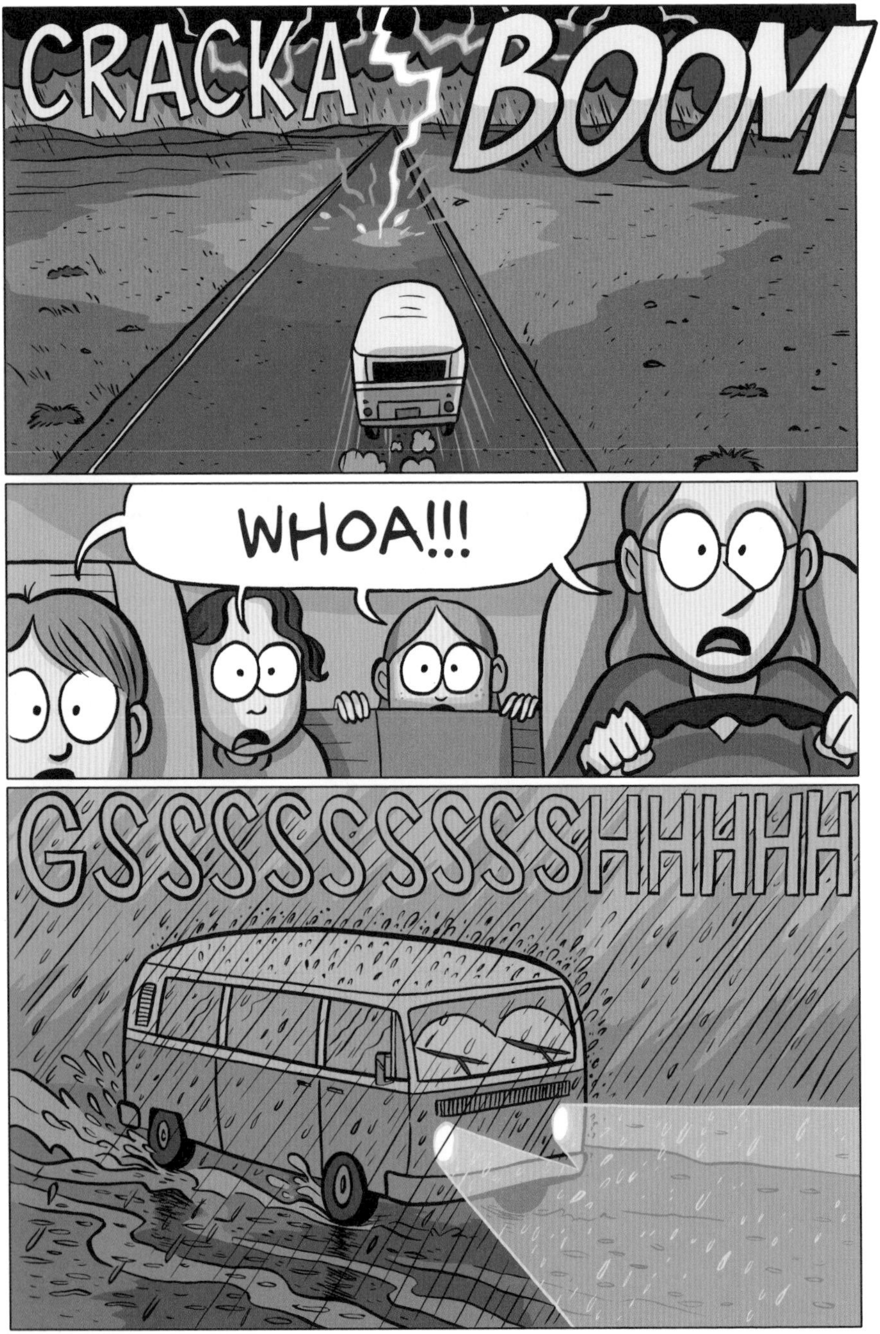
CRACKA
BOOM
WHOA!!!
GSSSSSSSSHHHHH

THE WIND REALLY PICKED UP!!

AND THE ROAD'S SO SLICK, I HAVE TO BE CAREFUL WE DON'T --

Squeak Squeak

HYDROPLANE!!!

AHHHHH!!

SLIIIIIIIIIIIIIIIIIDE~

≷GASP≷ I CAN BARELY SEE FIVE FEET AHEAD!

WE'RE GOING TO PULL OVER AND WAIT THIS STORM OUT.

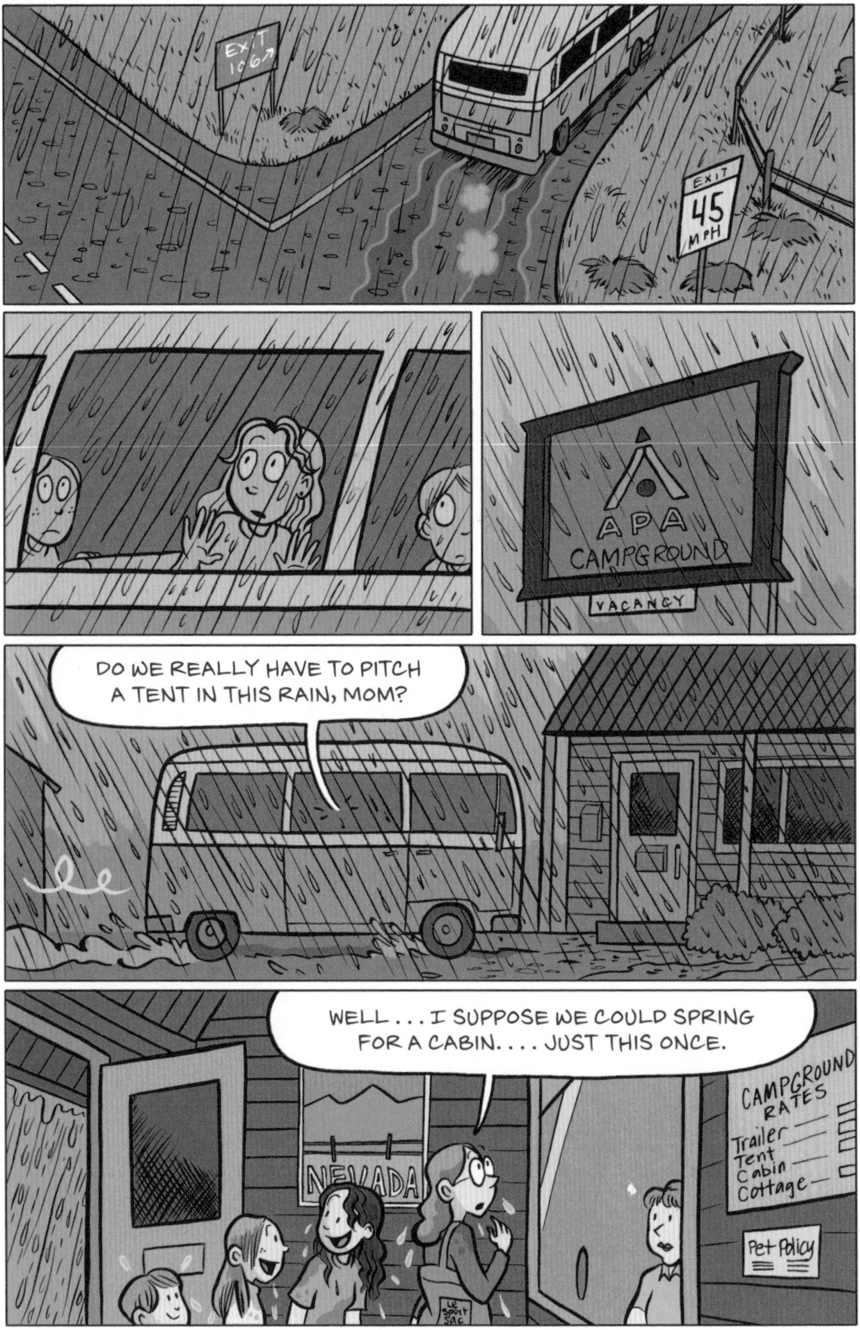
EXIT 106
EXIT 45 MPH
APA CAMPGROUND
VACANCY
DO WE REALLY HAVE TO PITCH A TENT IN THIS RAIN, MOM?
WELL . . . I SUPPOSE WE COULD SPRING FOR A CABIN. . . . JUST THIS ONCE.
NEVADA
CAMPGROUND RATES
Trailer
Tent
Cabin
Cottage
Pet Policy
LE SPORT SAC

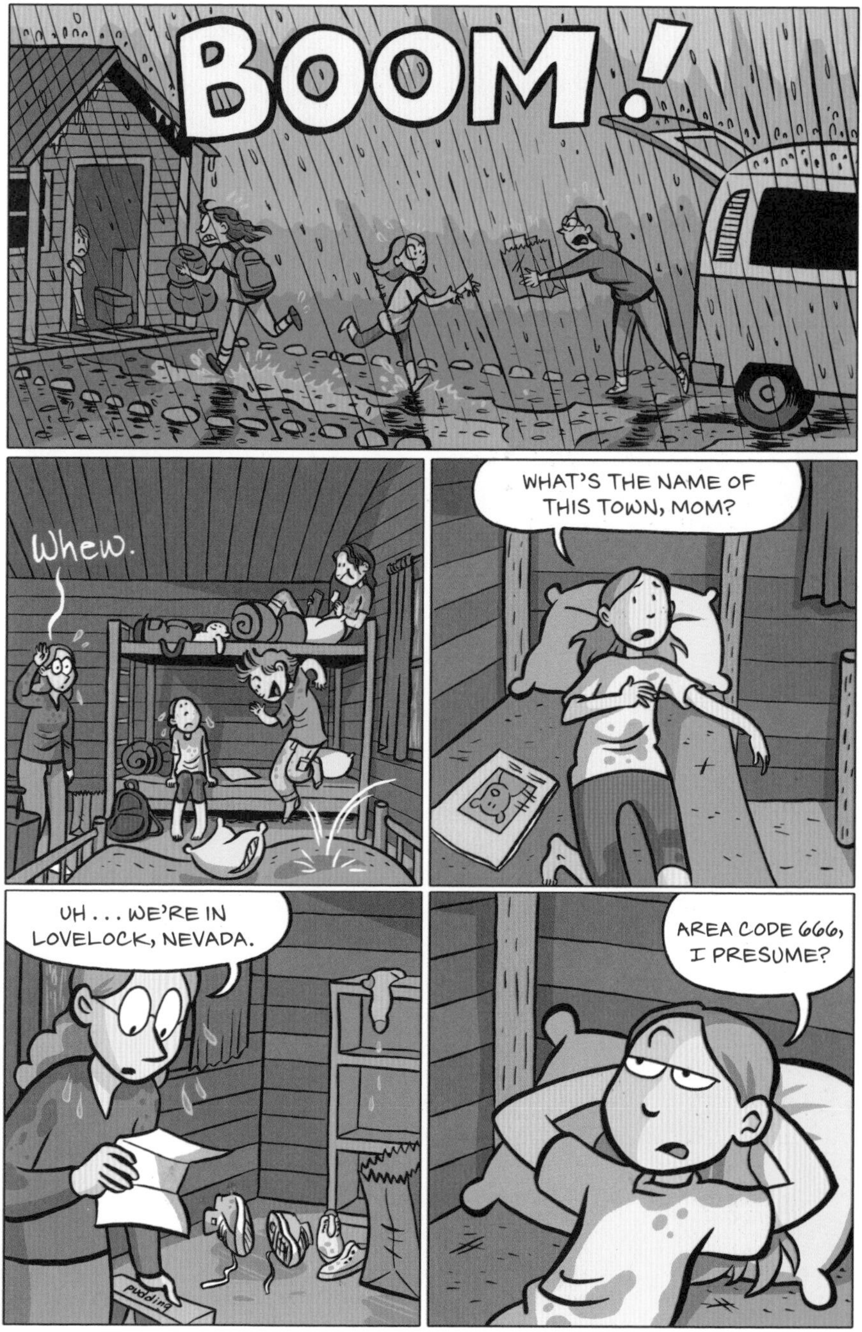
BOOM!
Whew.
WHAT'S THE NAME OF THIS TOWN, MOM?
UH . . . WE'RE IN LOVELOCK, NEVADA.
pudding
AREA CODE 666, I PRESUME?

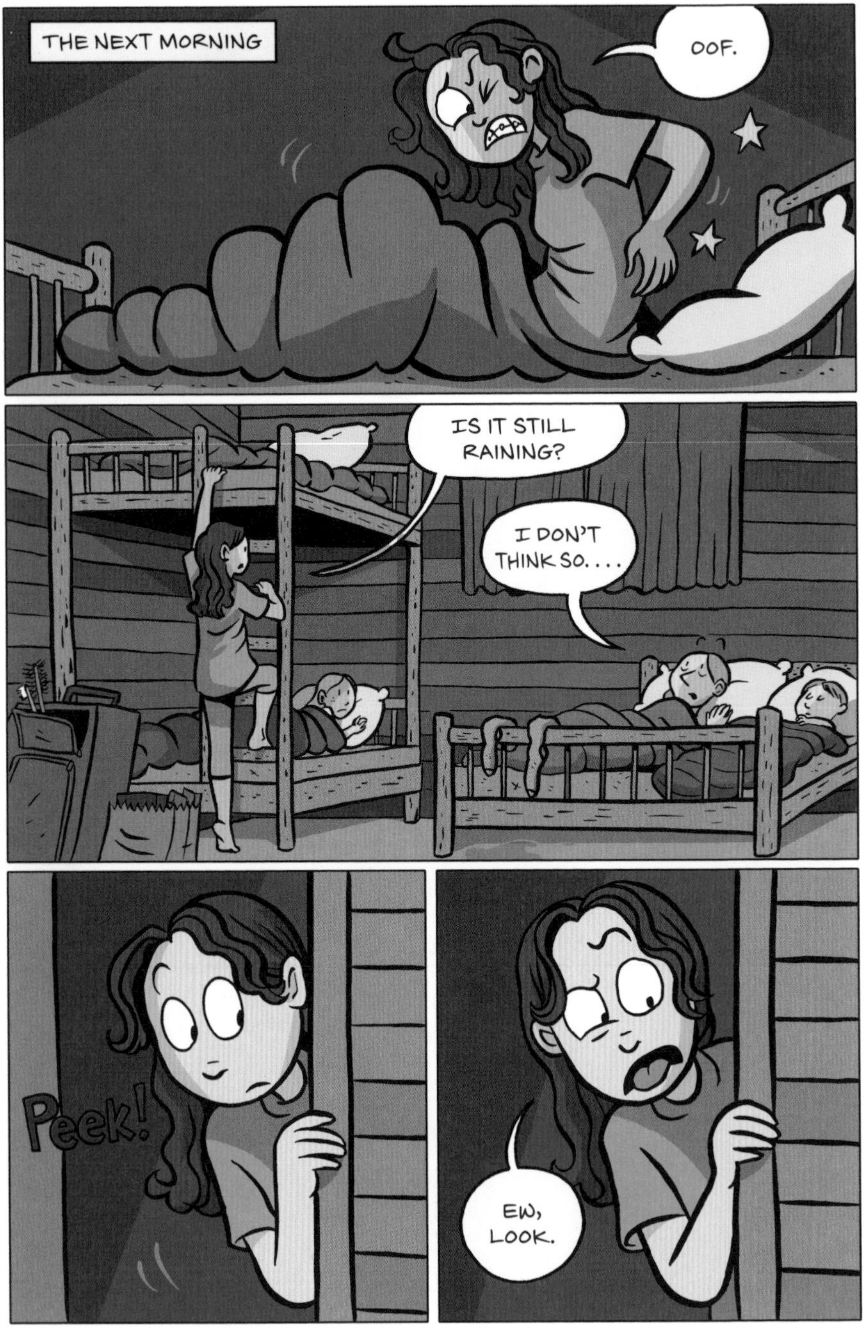
THE NEXT MORNING
OOF.
IS IT STILL RAINING?
I DON'T THINK SO....
Peek!
EW, LOOK.

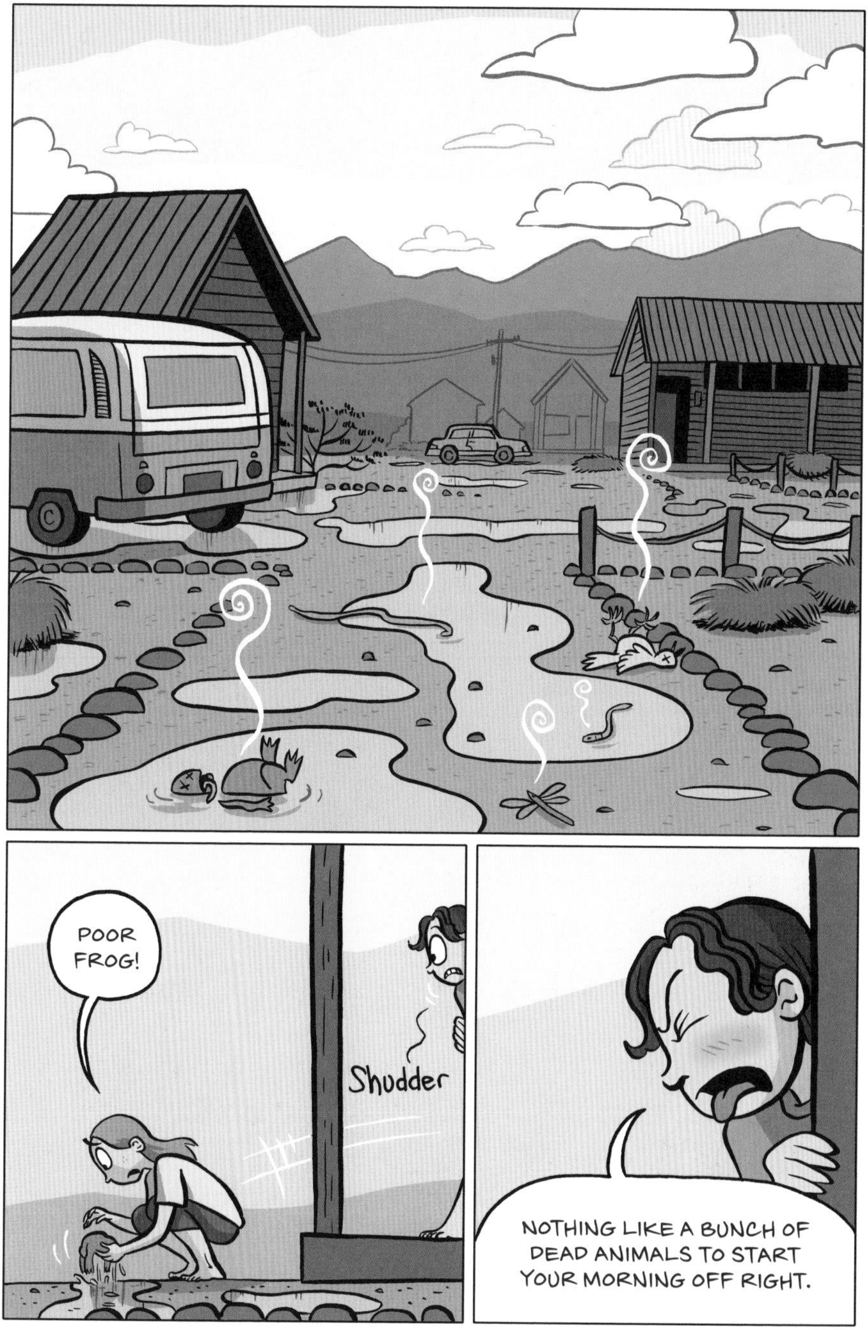
POOR FROG!
Shudder
NOTHING LIKE A BUNCH OF DEAD ANIMALS TO START YOUR MORNING OFF RIGHT.

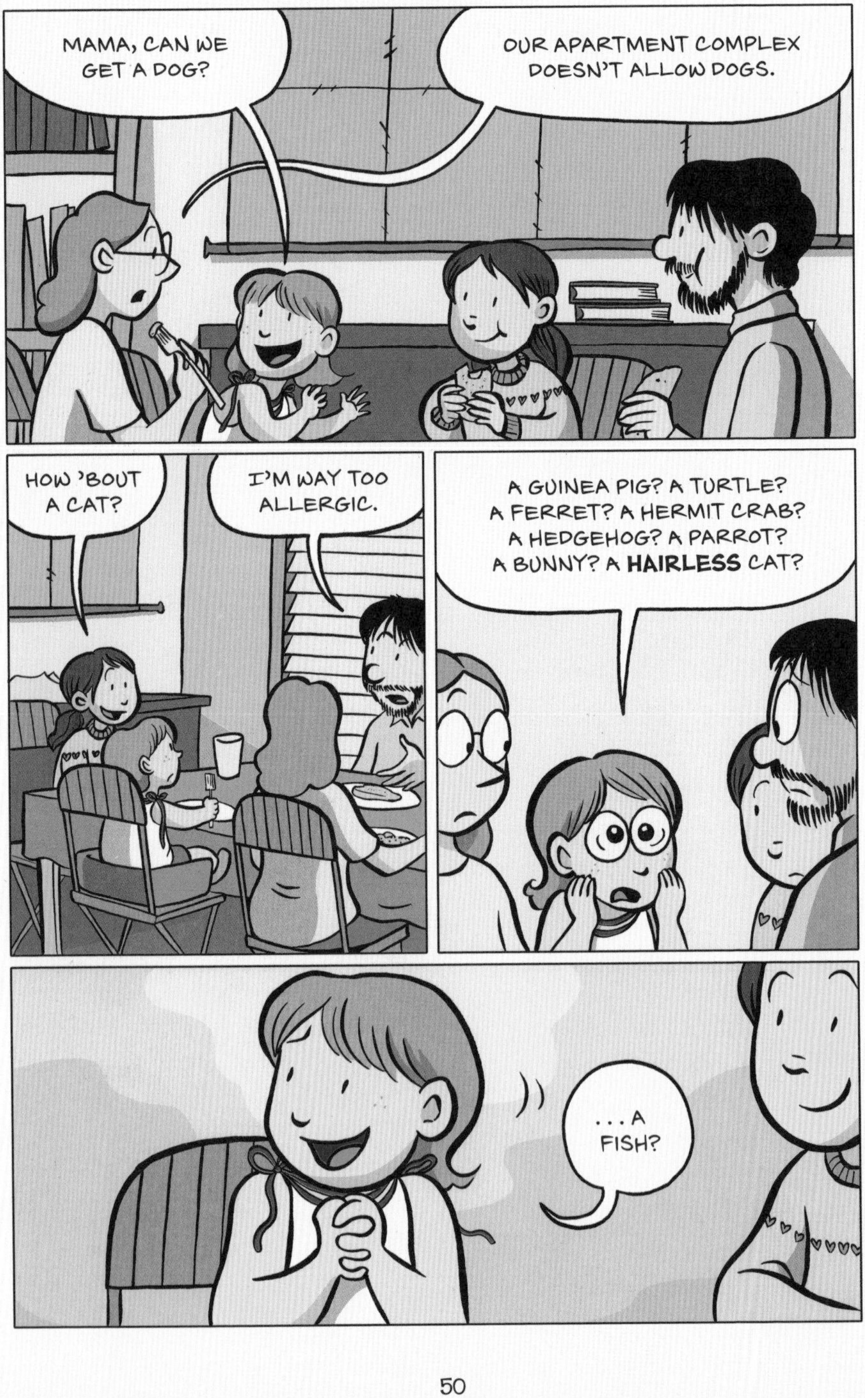
MAMA, CAN WE GET A DOG?
OUR APARTMENT COMPLEX DOESN'T ALLOW DOGS.
HOW 'BOUT A CAT?
I'M WAY TOO ALLERGIC.
A GUINEA PIG? A TURTLE? A FERRET? A HERMIT CRAB? A HEDGEHOG? A PARROT? A BUNNY? A **HAIRLESS** CAT?
. . . A FISH?

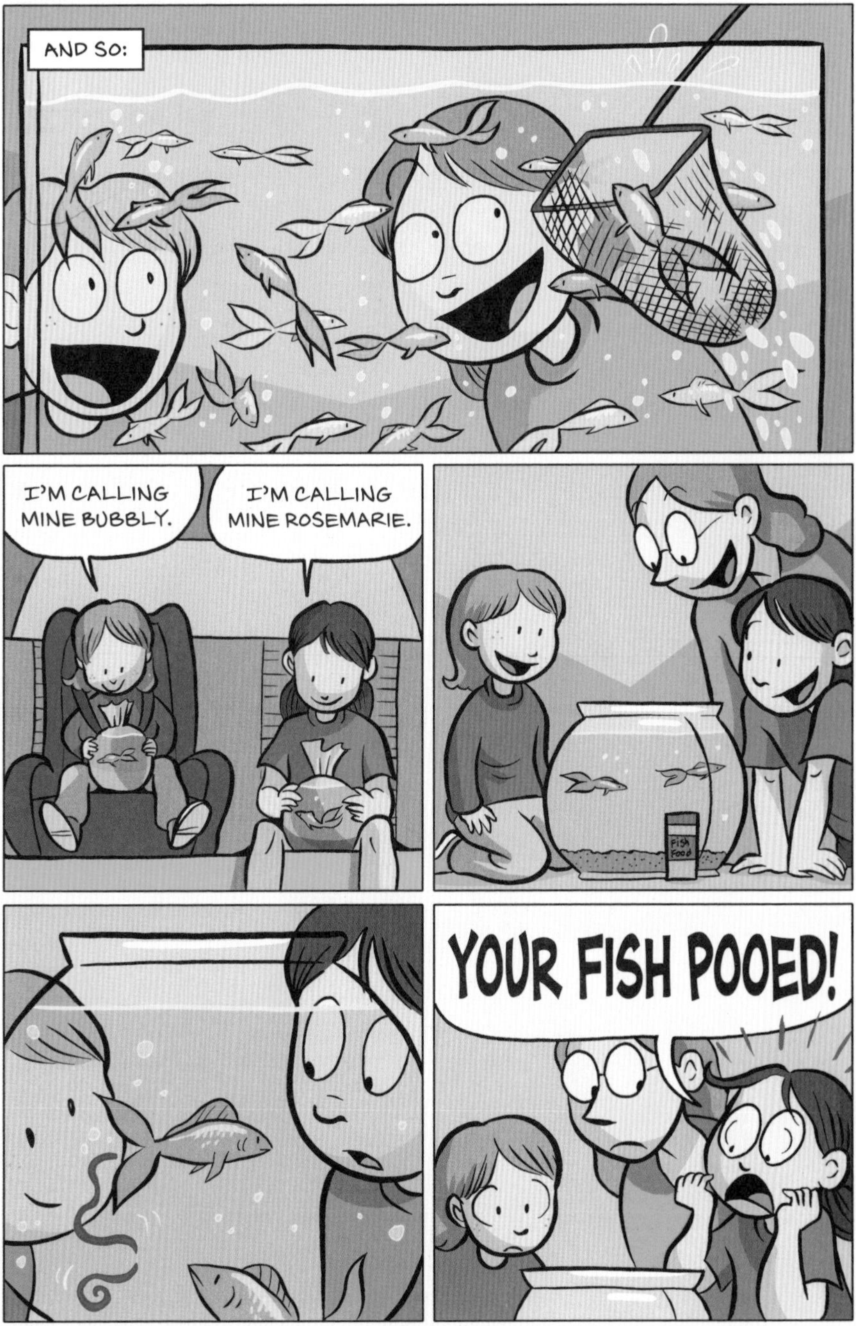
AND SO:
I'M CALLING MINE BUBBLY.
I'M CALLING MINE ROSEMARIE.
FISH FOOD
YOUR FISH POOED!

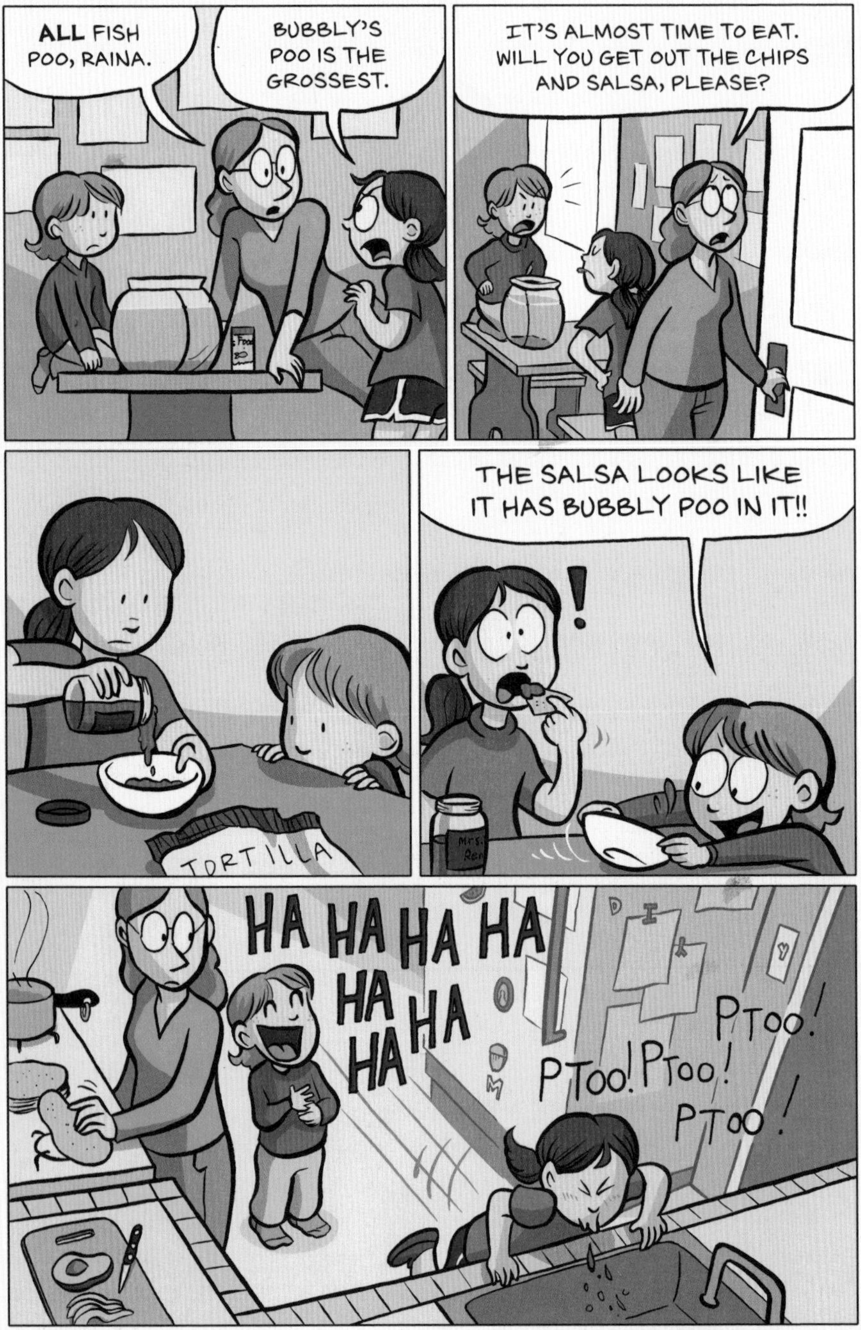
ALL FISH POO, RAINA.
BUBBLY'S POO IS THE GROSSEST.
IT'S ALMOST TIME TO EAT. WILL YOU GET OUT THE CHIPS AND SALSA, PLEASE?
TORTILLA
THE SALSA LOOKS LIKE IT HAS BUBBLY POO IN IT!!
!
HA HA HA HA HA HA HA HA
PTOO! PTOO! PTOO! PTOO!

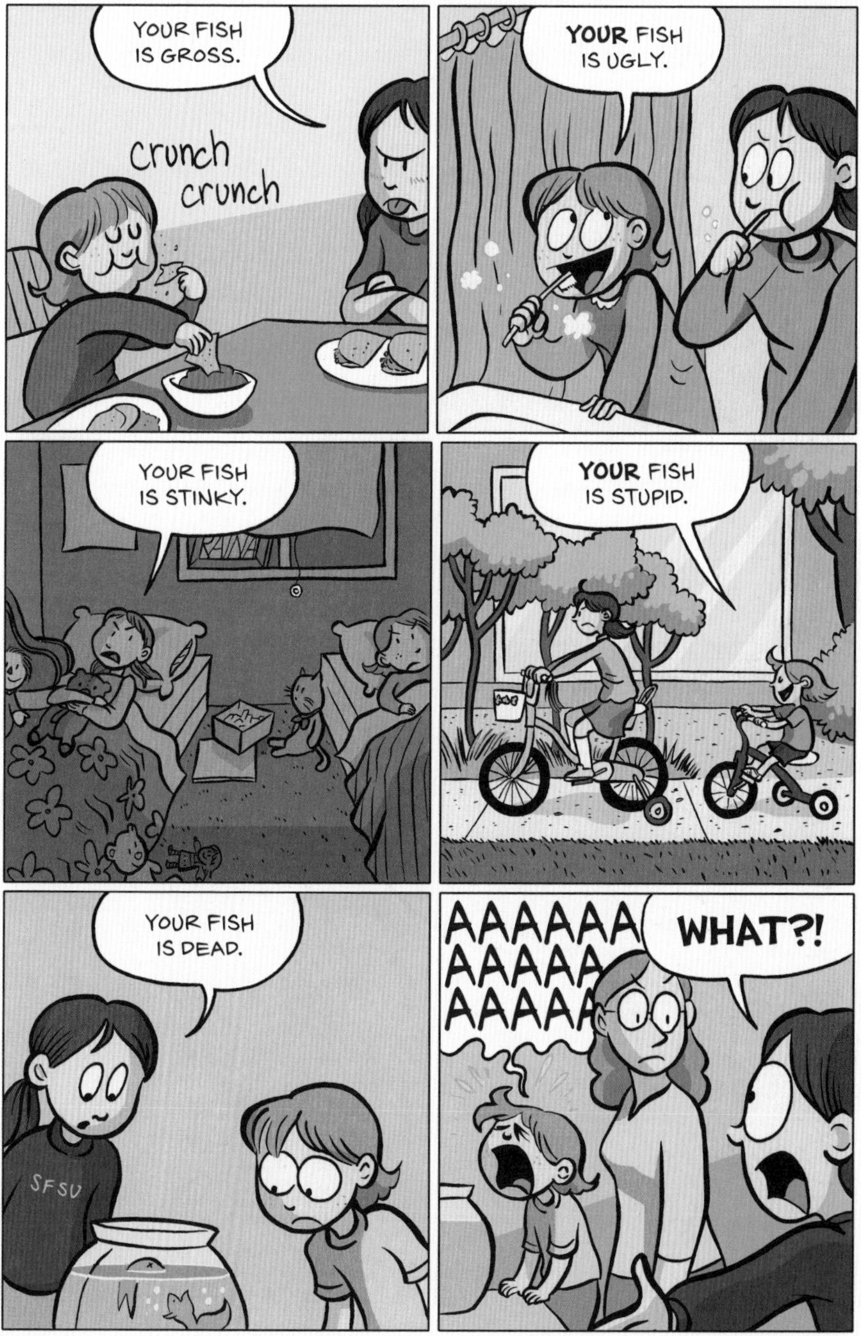
YOUR FISH IS GROSS.
crunch crunch
YOUR FISH IS UGLY.
YOUR FISH IS STINKY.
YOUR FISH IS STUPID.
YOUR FISH IS DEAD.
SFSU
AAAAAA AAAAAA AAAAAA
WHAT?!

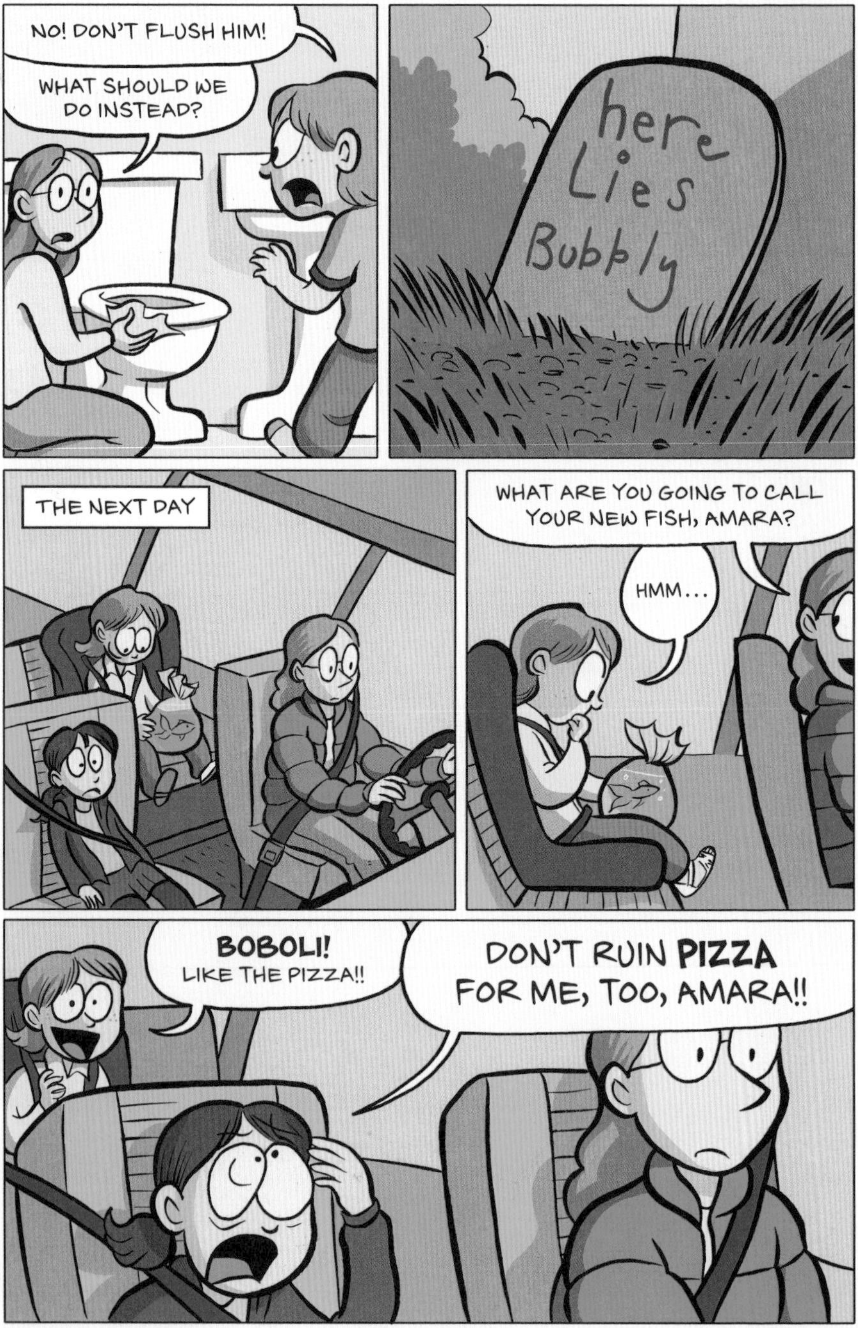
NO! DON'T FLUSH HIM!
WHAT SHOULD WE DO INSTEAD?
here Lies Bubbly
THE NEXT DAY
WHAT ARE YOU GOING TO CALL YOUR NEW FISH, AMARA?
HMM...
BOBOLI! LIKE THE PIZZA!!
DON'T RUIN PIZZA FOR ME, TOO, AMARA!!

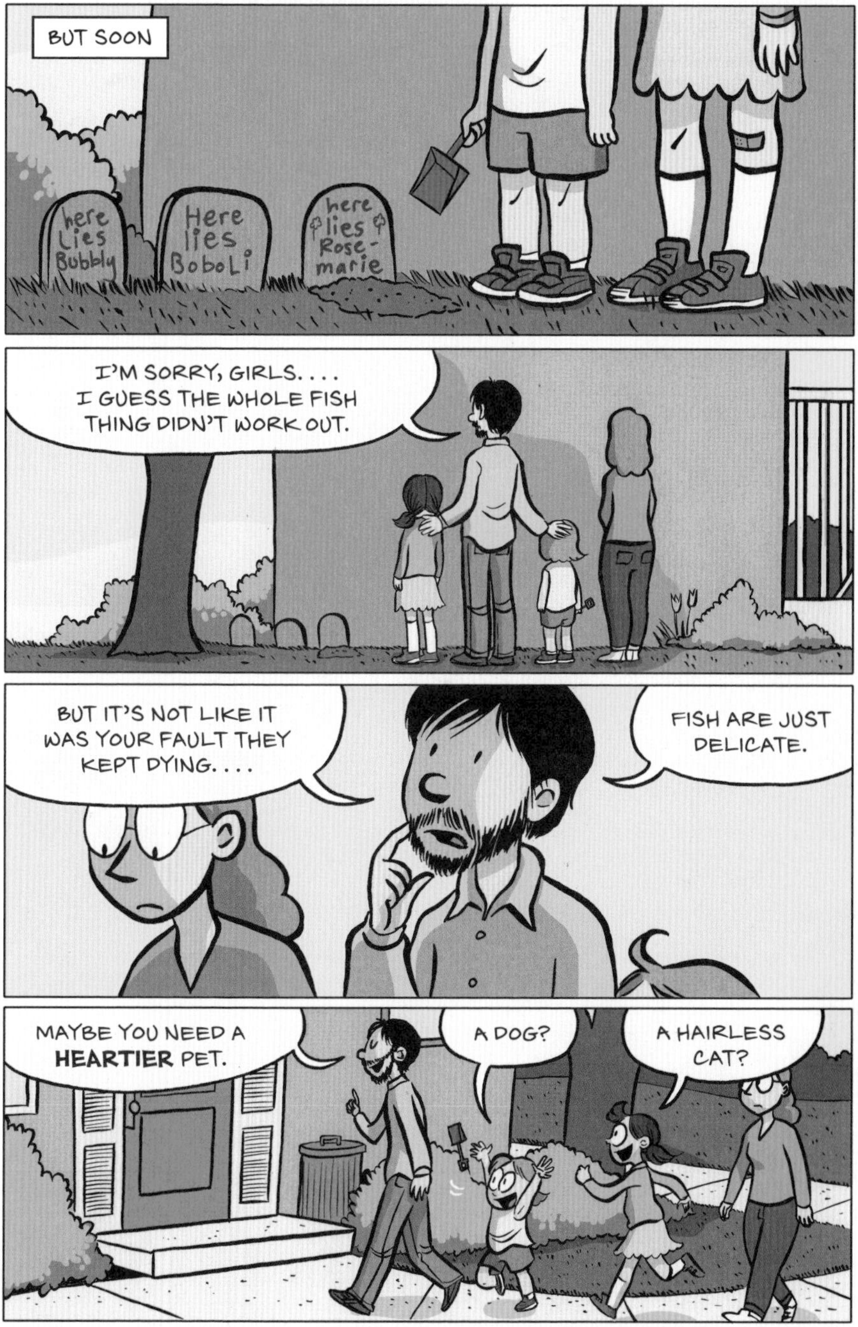
BUT SOON
here Lies Bubbly
Here lies BoboLi
here lies Rose-marie
I'M SORRY, GIRLS. . . . I GUESS THE WHOLE FISH THING DIDN'T WORK OUT.
BUT IT'S NOT LIKE IT WAS YOUR FAULT THEY KEPT DYING. . . .
FISH ARE JUST DELICATE.
MAYBE YOU NEED A **HEARTIER** PET.
A DOG?
A HAIRLESS CAT?

... A CHAMELEON??

COOOOOOL!!

DON'T WORRY! MY BUDDY FRANK BREEDS 'EM. HE SAYS THEY'RE PRETTY INDESTRUCTIBLE.

Veterans Upward Bound

AT THE PET STORE

THEY EAT CRICKETS??

UH-HUH, AND WE'RE HAVING A SALE! FIVE DOLLARS FOR TWENTY!

Flea Flea   Flea

Rabbit Feed   Bunny Chow   Hop Fuel

THIS SEEMS LIKE A LOT OF CRICKETS, DAD....

chirp chirp chirp chir chirp chirp chirp chirp chirp ch chirp chir chirp chirp chirp ch chirp chir

YEP! LELAND'S GONNA BE IN FOODIE PARADISE!

chirp chirp chirp Ch chirp chirp Chir chirp chirp chi

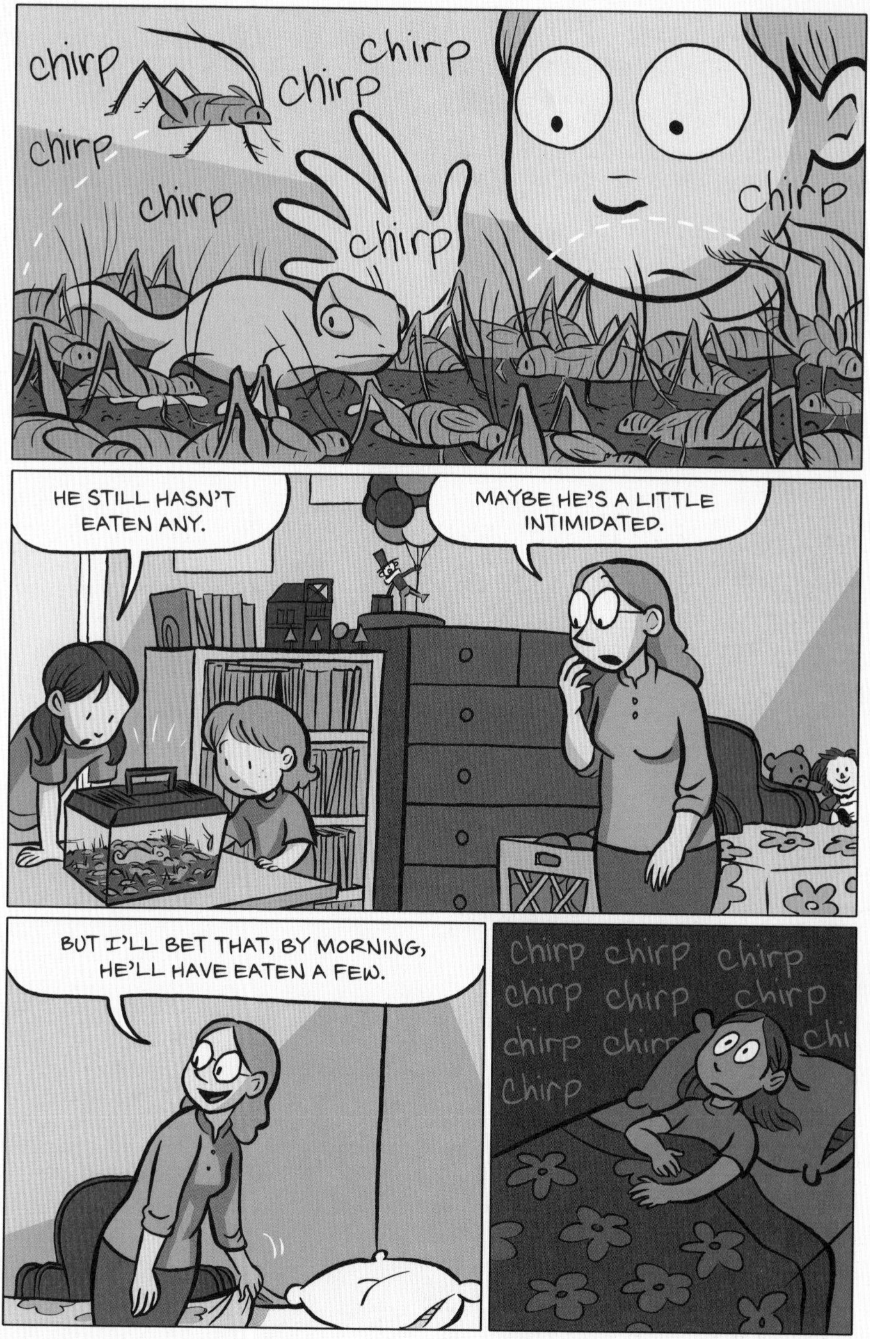
chirp
chirp
chirp
chirp
chirp
chirp
chirp
HE STILL HASN'T EATEN ANY.
MAYBE HE'S A LITTLE INTIMIDATED.
BUT I'LL BET THAT, BY MORNING, HE'LL HAVE EATEN A FEW.
chirp chirp chirp
chirp chirp chirp
chirp
chirp

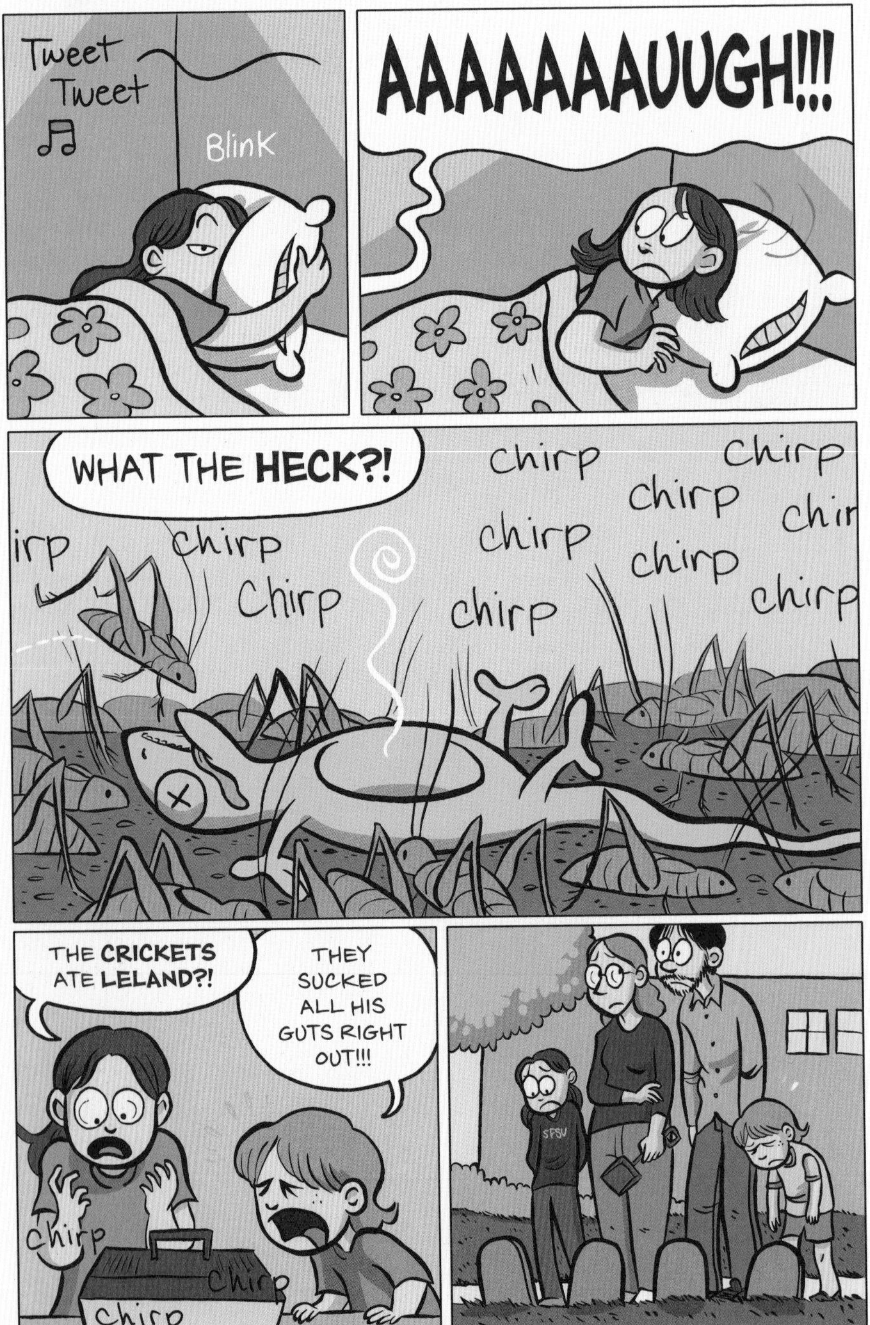

Tweet
Tweet
Blink
AAAAAAAUUGH!!!
WHAT THE HECK?!
chirp
chirp
chirp
chirp
chirp
chirp
chirp
chirp
chirp
THE CRICKETS ATE LELAND?!
THEY SUCKED ALL HIS GUTS RIGHT OUT!!!
chirp
chirp
chirp
SFSU

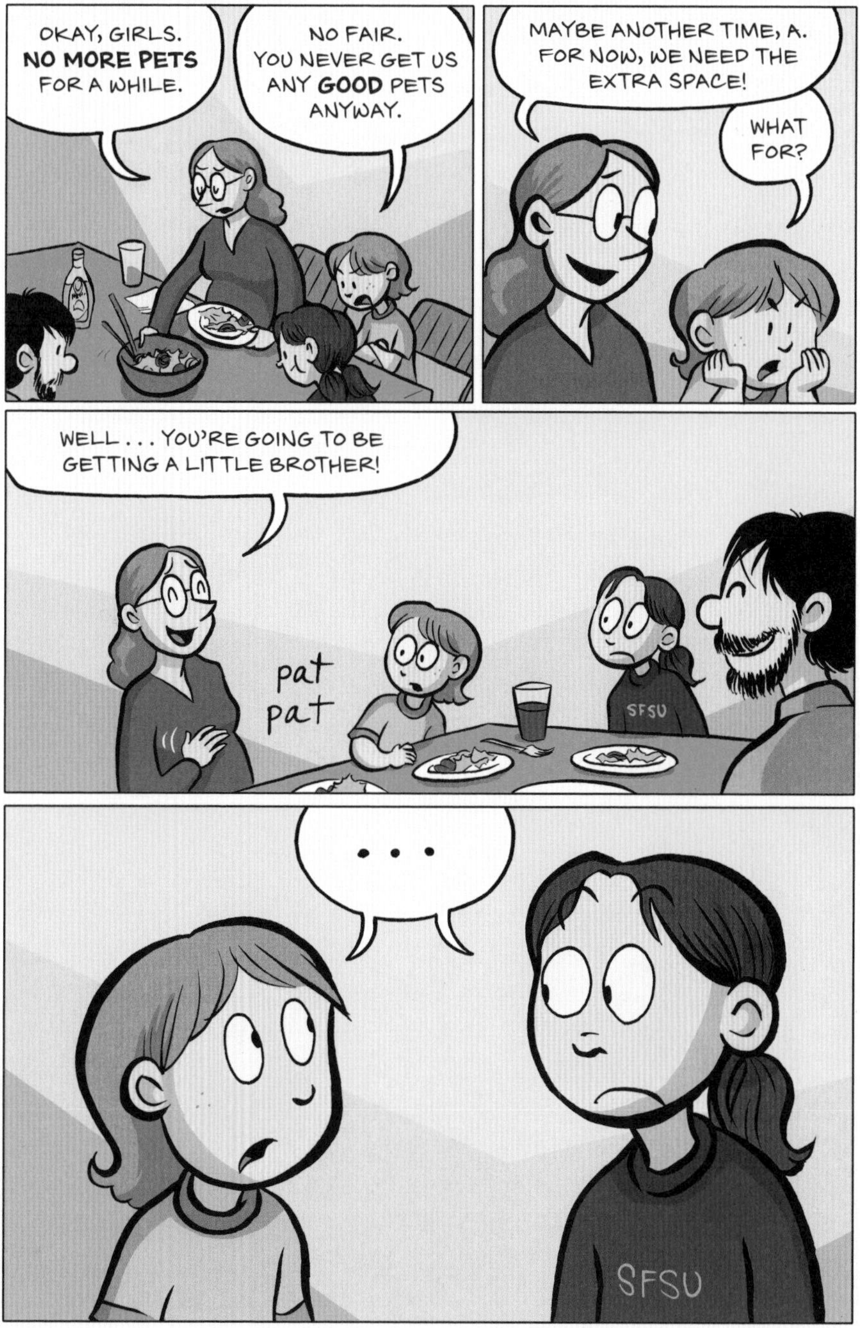
OKAY, GIRLS. **NO MORE PETS** FOR A WHILE.
NO FAIR. YOU NEVER GET US ANY **GOOD** PETS ANYWAY.
MAYBE ANOTHER TIME, A. FOR NOW, WE NEED THE EXTRA SPACE!
WHAT FOR?
WELL . . . YOU'RE GOING TO BE GETTING A LITTLE BROTHER!
pat pat
SFSU
. . .
SFSU

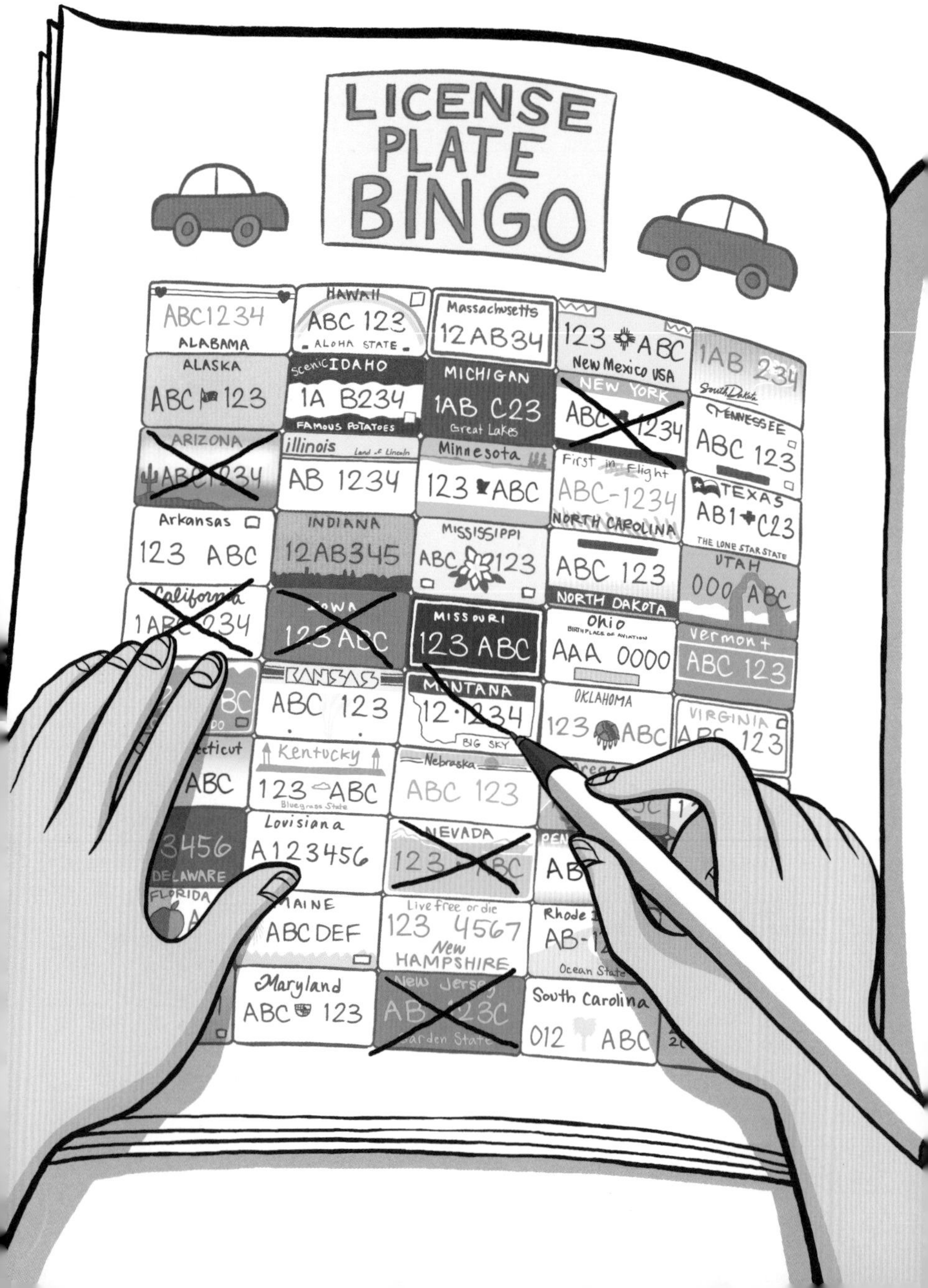
LICENSE PLATE BINGO
ABC1234 ALABAMA
HAWAII ABC 123 ALOHA STATE
Massachusetts 12AB34
123 ABC New Mexico USA
1AB 234 South Dakota
ALASKA ABC 123
Scenic IDAHO 1A B234 FAMOUS POTATOES
MICHIGAN 1AB C23 Great Lakes
NEW YORK ABC 1234
TENNESSEE ABC 123
ARIZONA ABC1234
illinois Land of Lincoln AB 1234
Minnesota 123 ABC
First in Flight ABC-1234 NORTH CAROLINA
TEXAS AB1 C23 THE LONE STAR STATE
Arkansas 123 ABC
INDIANA 12AB345
MISSISSIPPI ABC 123
ABC 123 NORTH DAKOTA
UTAH 000 ABC
California 1ABC234
IOWA 123 ABC
MISSOURI 123 ABC
Ohio BIRTHPLACE OF AVIATION AAA 0000
Vermont ABC 123
KANSAS ABC 123
MONTANA 12-1234 BIG SKY
OKLAHOMA 123 ABC
VIRGINIA ABC 123
Kentucky 123 ABC Bluegrass State
Nebraska ABC 123
3456 DELAWARE
Louisiana A123456
NEVADA 123 ABC
FLORIDA
MAINE ABCDEF
Live free or die 123 4567 New HAMPSHIRE
Ocean State
Maryland ABC 123
New Jersey AB 123C Garden State
South Carolina 012 ABC

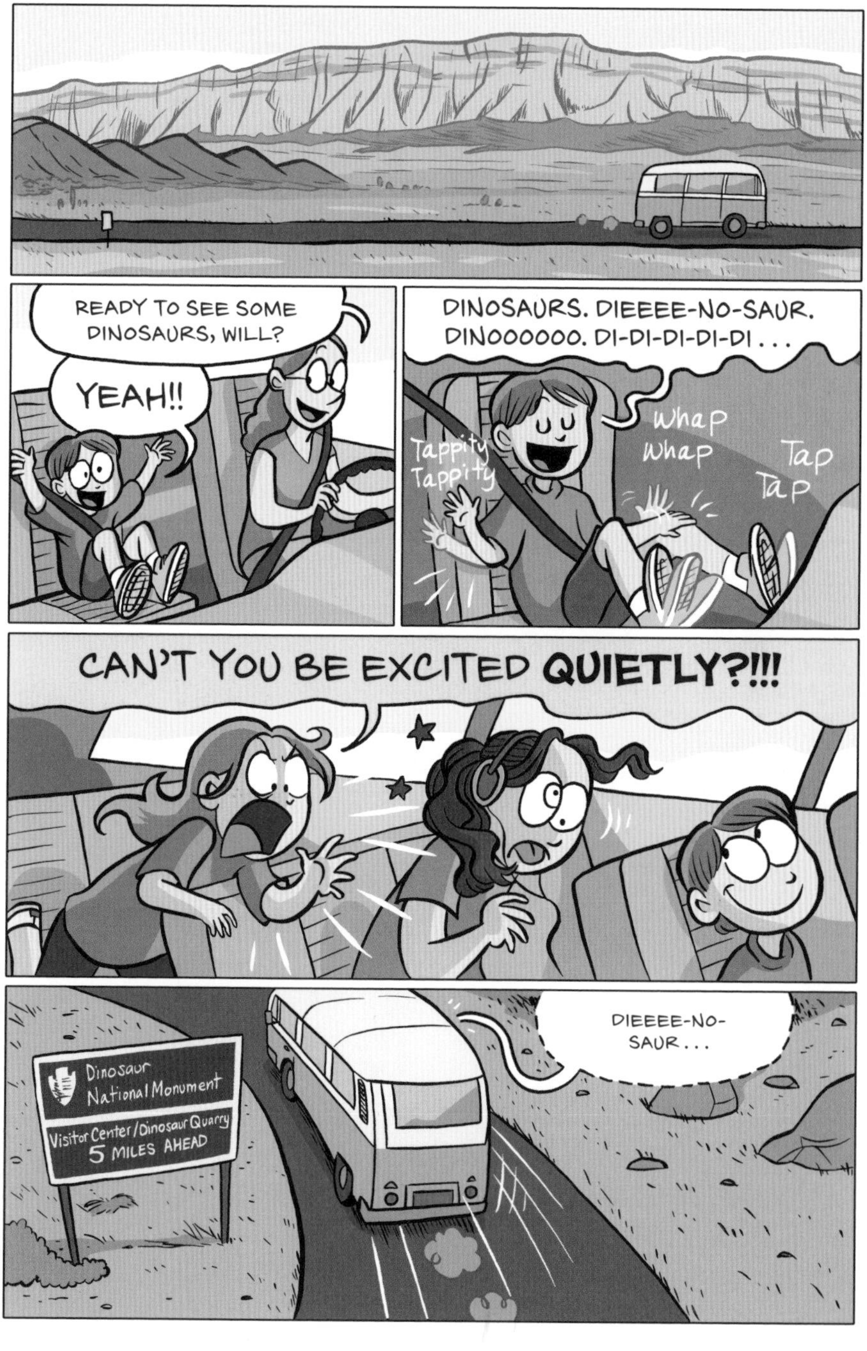
READY TO SEE SOME DINOSAURS, WILL?
YEAH!!
DINOSAURS. DIEEEE-NO-SAUR. DINOOOOOO. DI-DI-DI-DI-DI . . .
Tappity Tappity
Whap Whap
Tap Tap
CAN'T YOU BE EXCITED **QUIETLY?!!!**
Dinosaur National Monument
Visitor Center / Dinosaur Quarry 5 MILES AHEAD
DIEEEE-NO-SAUR . . .

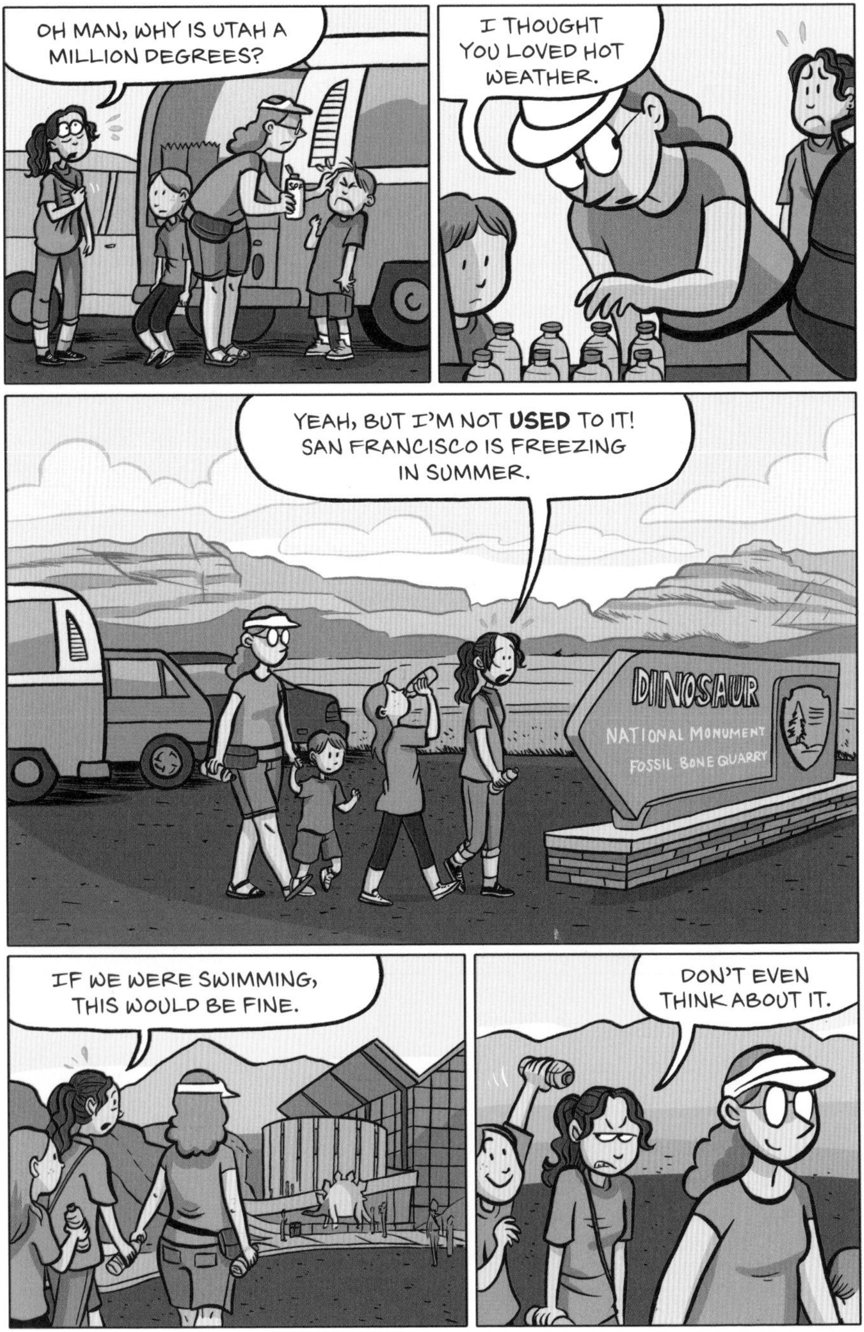
OH MAN, WHY IS UTAH A MILLION DEGREES?
SPF
I THOUGHT YOU LOVED HOT WEATHER.
YEAH, BUT I'M NOT **USED** TO IT! SAN FRANCISCO IS FREEZING IN SUMMER.
DINOSAUR
NATIONAL MONUMENT
FOSSIL BONE QUARRY
IF WE WERE SWIMMING, THIS WOULD BE FINE.
DON'T EVEN THINK ABOUT IT.

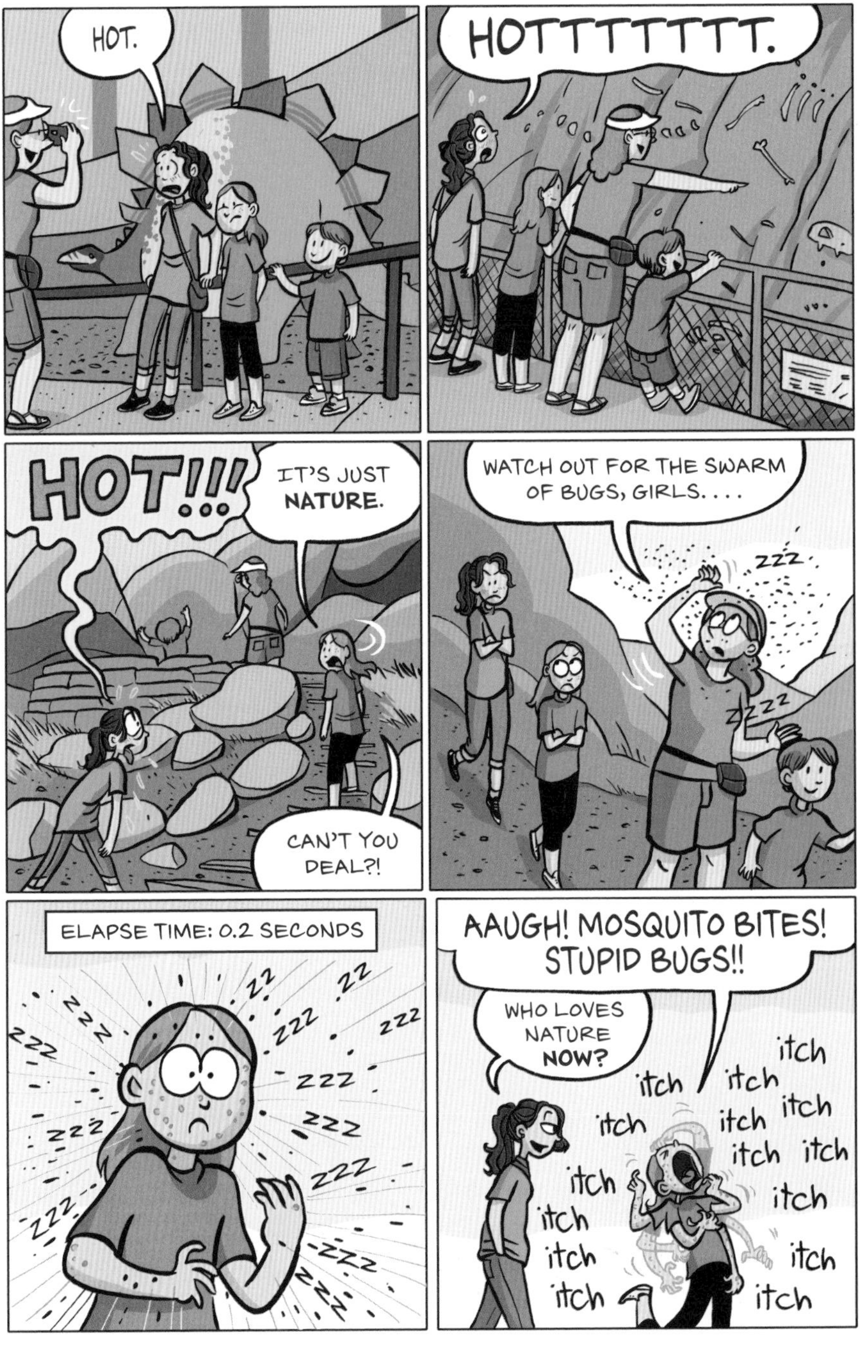
HOT.
HOTTTTTTT.
HOT!!!
IT'S JUST NATURE.
CAN'T YOU DEAL?!
WATCH OUT FOR THE SWARM OF BUGS, GIRLS. . . .
ZZZ
ELAPSE TIME: 0.2 SECONDS
ZZZ
AAUGH! MOSQUITO BITES! STUPID BUGS!!
WHO LOVES NATURE NOW?
itch itch itch itch itch itch itch itch itch itch itch itch itch itch itch

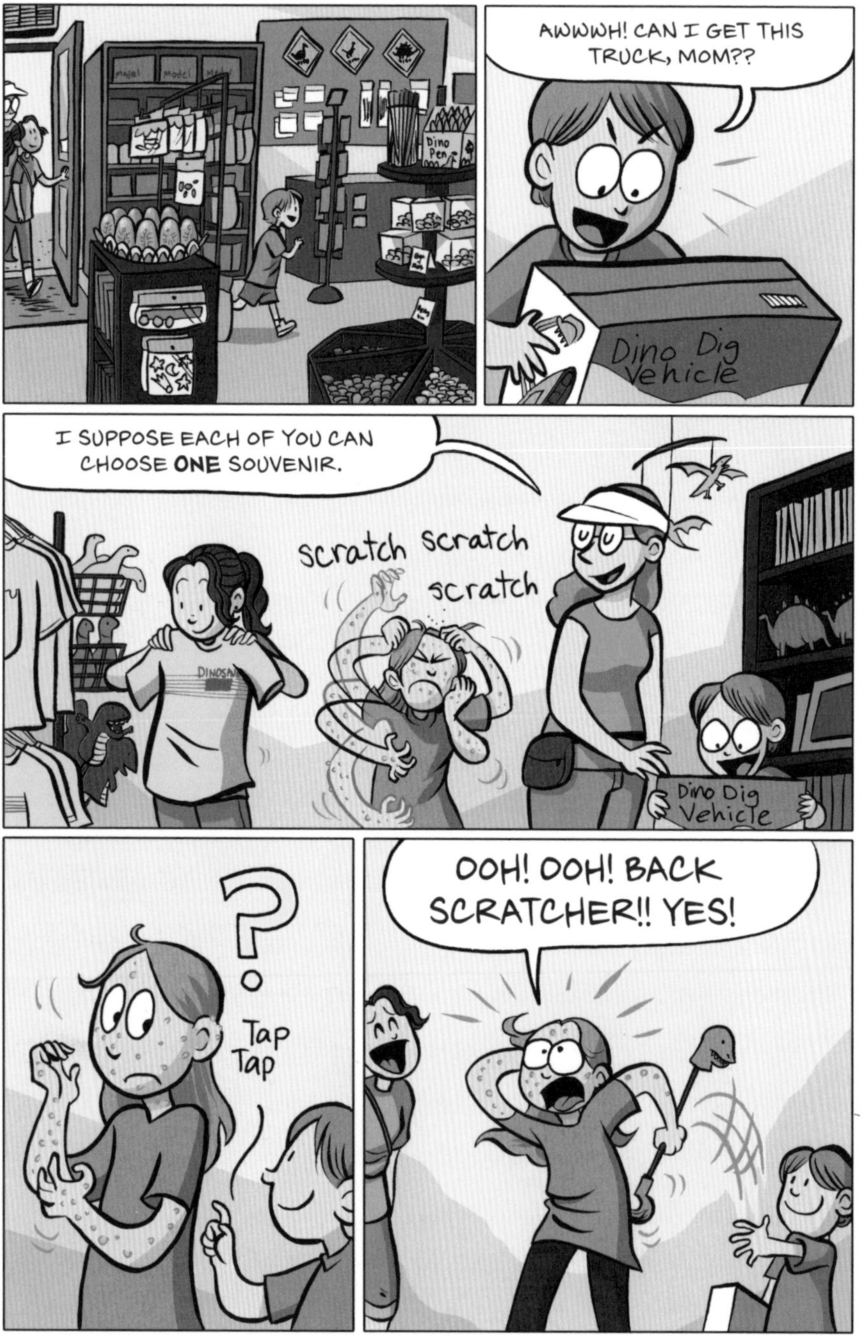

model
model
Dino Pen
AWWWH! CAN I GET THIS TRUCK, MOM??
Dino Dig Vehicle
I SUPPOSE EACH OF YOU CAN CHOOSE **ONE** SOUVENIR.
scratch scratch scratch
Dino Dig Vehicle
Tap Tap
OOH! OOH! BACK SCRATCHER!! YES!

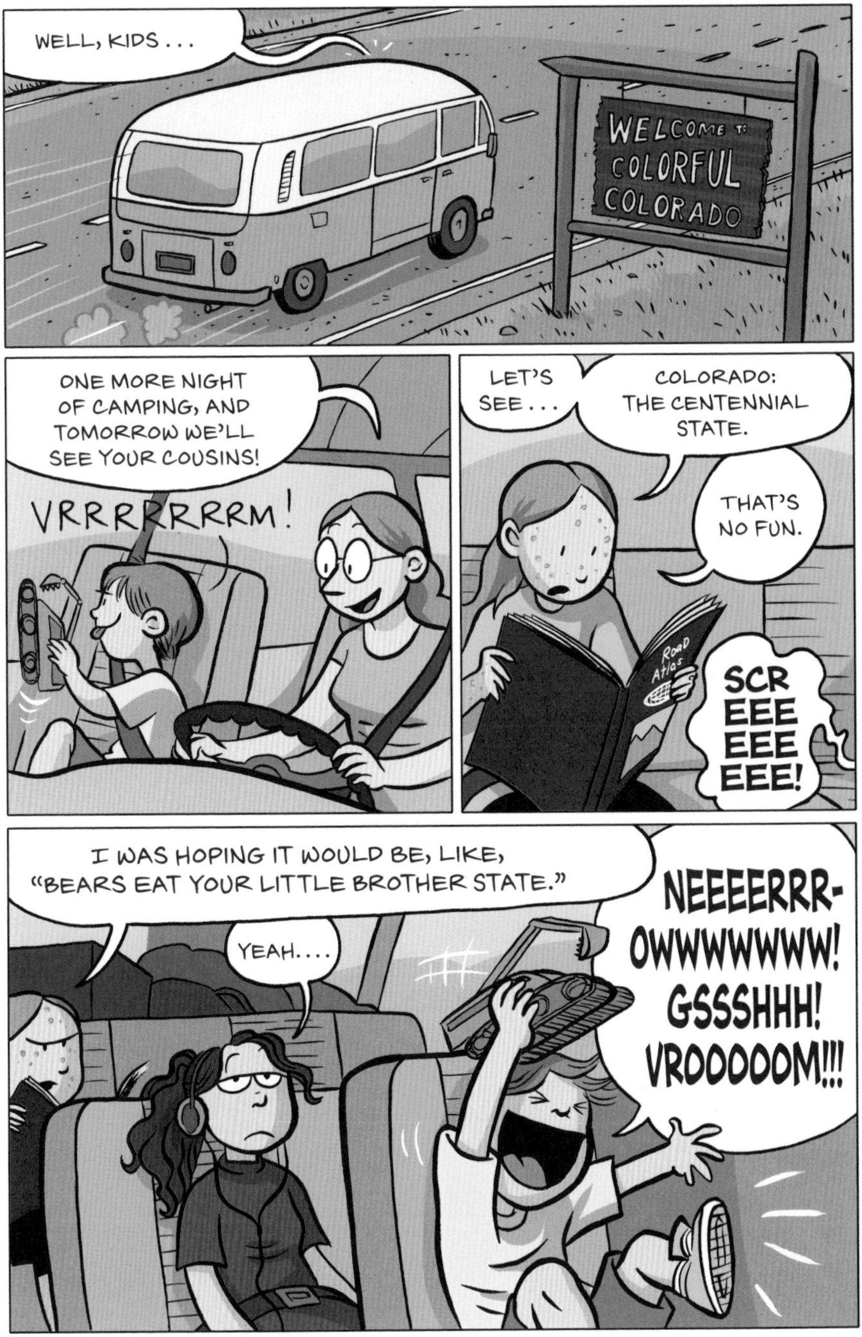
WELL, KIDS . . .
WELCOME TO COLORFUL COLORADO
ONE MORE NIGHT OF CAMPING, AND TOMORROW WE'LL SEE YOUR COUSINS!
VRRRRRRRM!
LET'S SEE . . .
COLORADO: THE CENTENNIAL STATE.
THAT'S NO FUN.
ROAD Atlas
SCREEEEEEEEE!
I WAS HOPING IT WOULD BE, LIKE, "BEARS EAT YOUR LITTLE BROTHER STATE."
YEAH. . . .
NEEEERRR-OWWWWWWW! GSSSHHH! VROOOOOM!!!

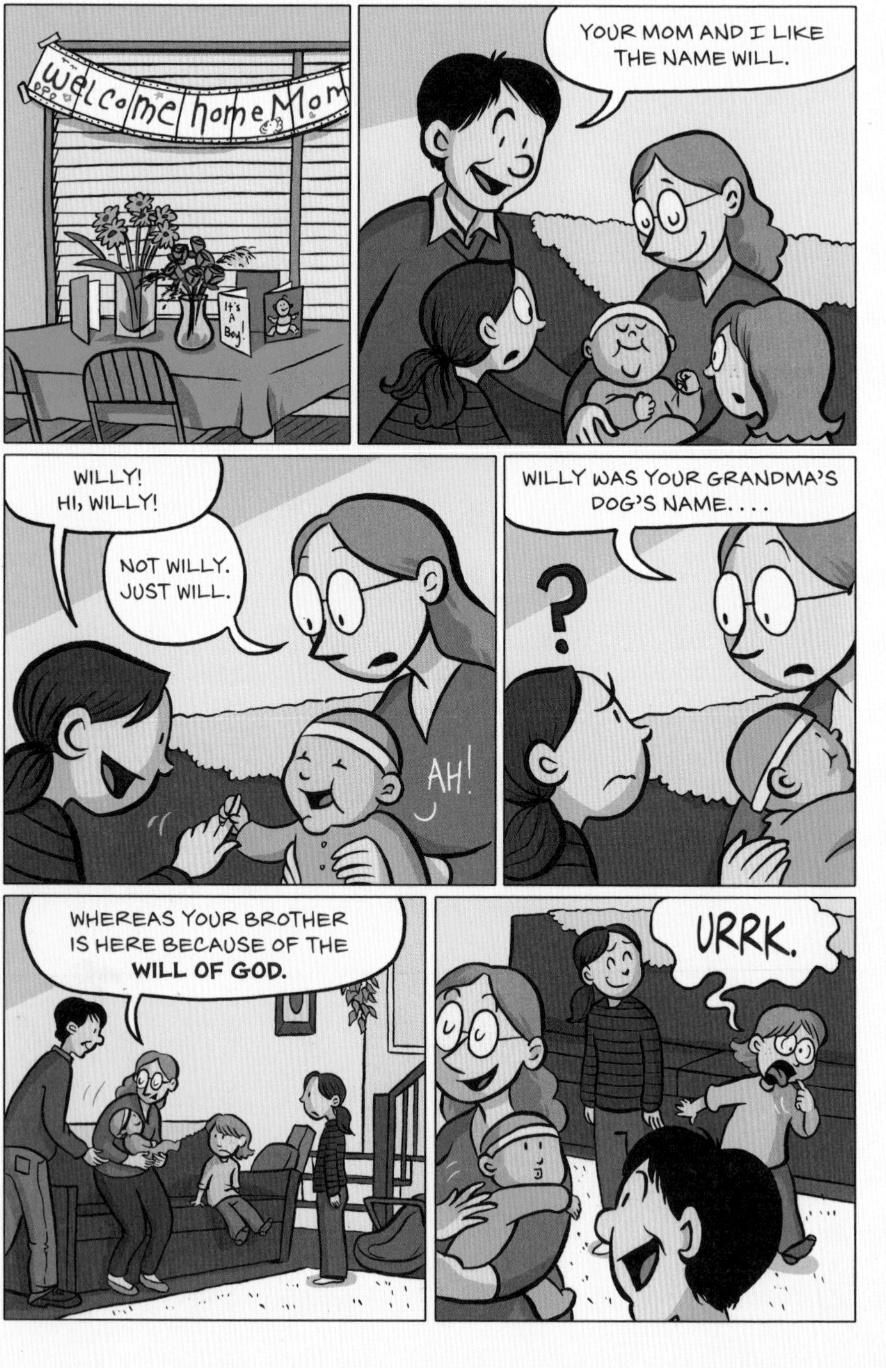
welcome home Mom
It's A Boy!
YOUR MOM AND I LIKE THE NAME WILL.
WILLY! HI, WILLY!
NOT WILLY. JUST WILL.
AH!
WILLY WAS YOUR GRANDMA'S DOG'S NAME. . . .
?
WHEREAS YOUR BROTHER IS HERE BECAUSE OF THE **WILL OF GOD.**
URRK.

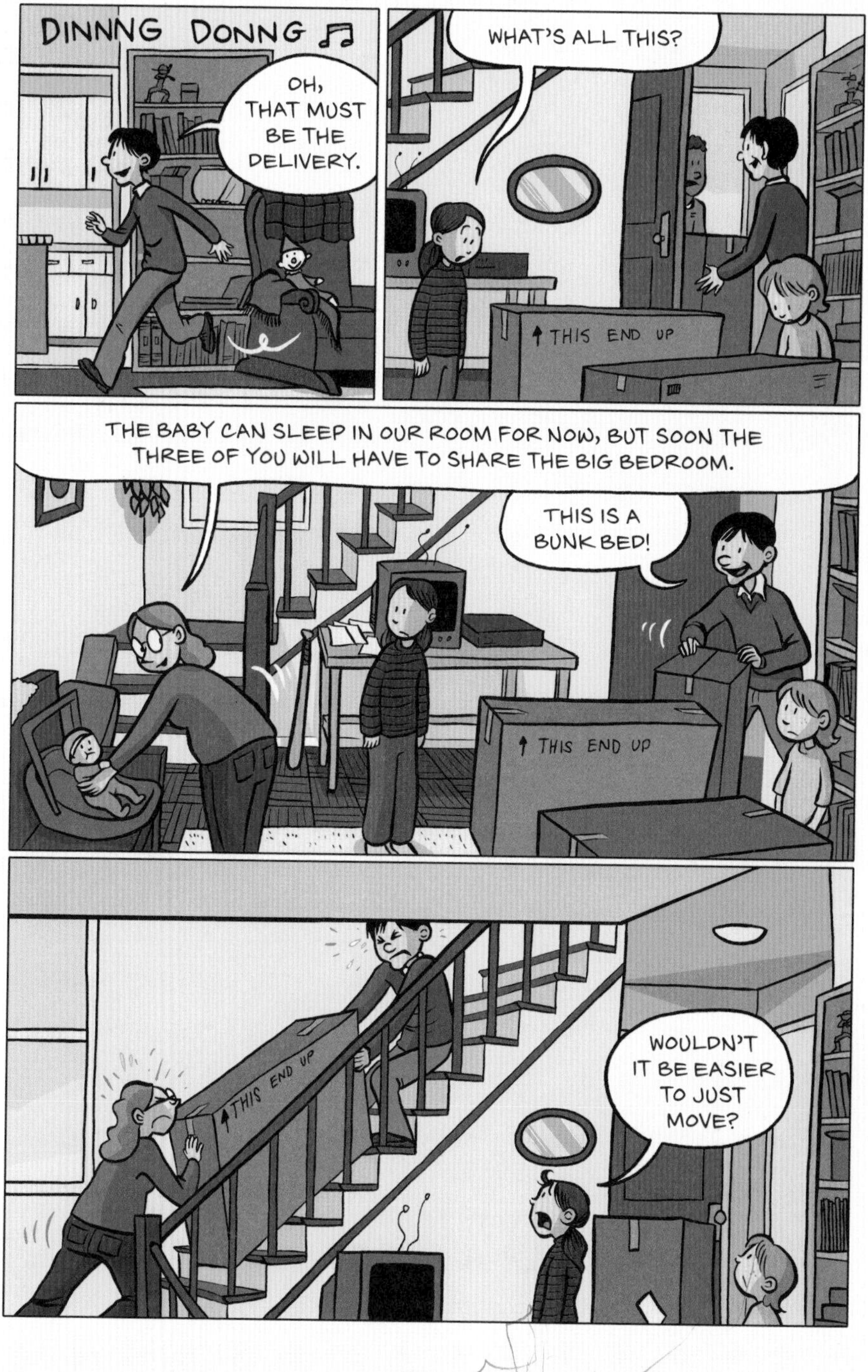
DINNNG DONNG
OH, THAT MUST BE THE DELIVERY.
WHAT'S ALL THIS?
THIS END UP
THE BABY CAN SLEEP IN OUR ROOM FOR NOW, BUT SOON THE THREE OF YOU WILL HAVE TO SHARE THE BIG BEDROOM.
THIS IS A BUNK BED!
THIS END UP
THIS END UP
WOULDN'T IT BE EASIER TO JUST MOVE?

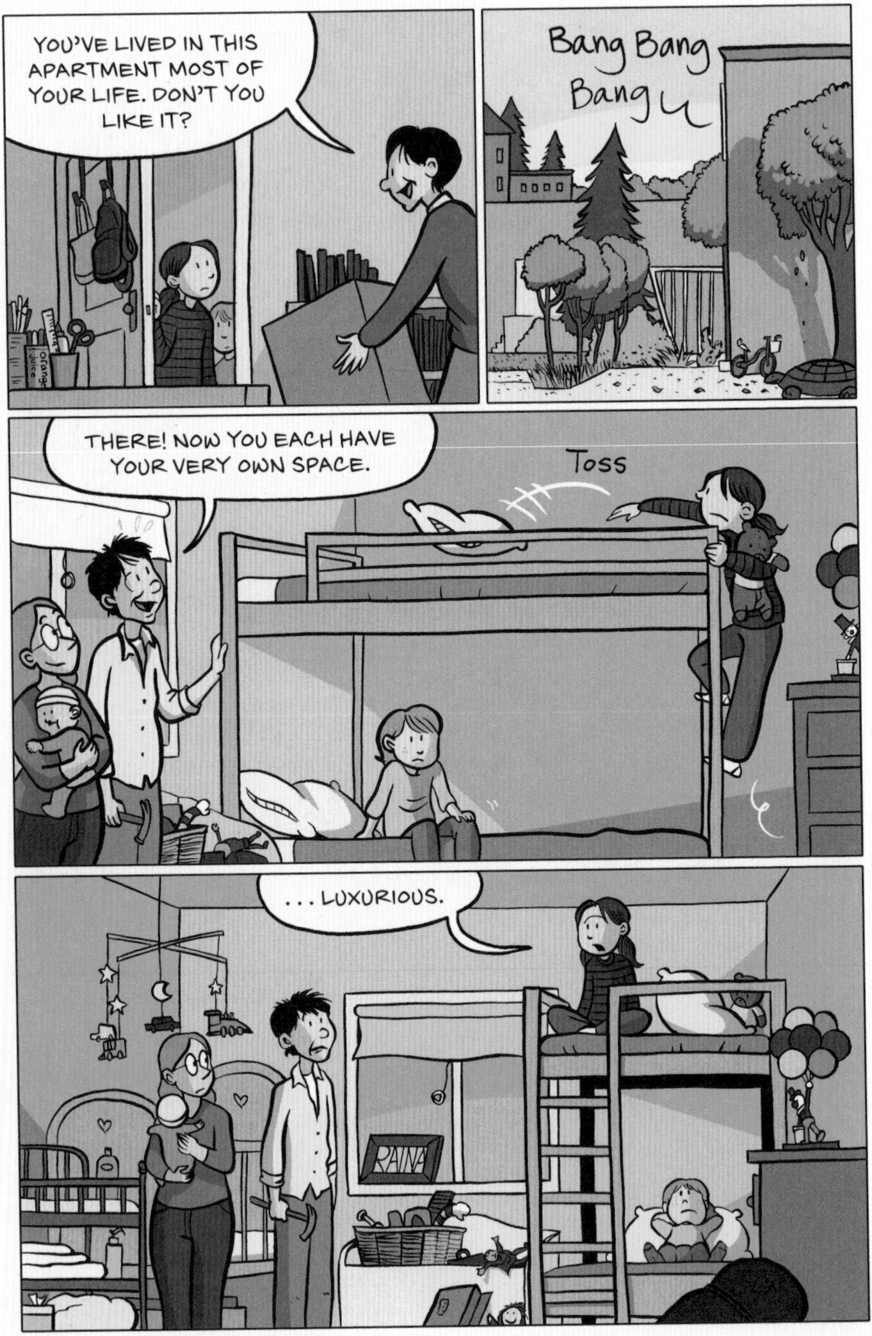
YOU'VE LIVED IN THIS APARTMENT MOST OF YOUR LIFE. DON'T YOU LIKE IT?
Bang Bang Bang
THERE! NOW YOU EACH HAVE YOUR VERY OWN SPACE.
Toss
. . . LUXURIOUS.
RAINA

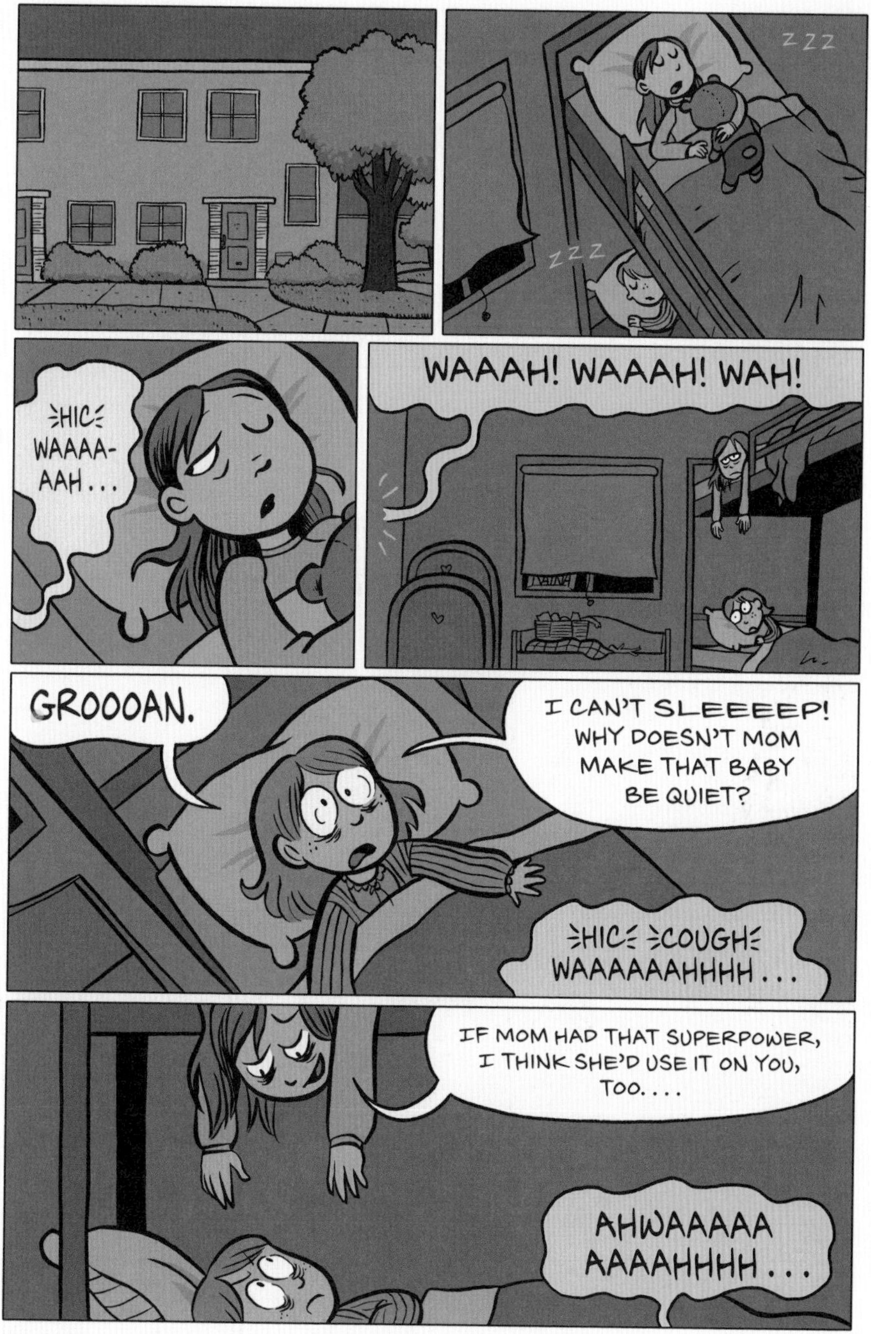

Z Z Z
Z Z Z
HIC WAAAA-AAH . . .
WAAAH! WAAAH! WAH!
GROOOAN.
I CAN'T SLEEEEP! WHY DOESN'T MOM MAKE THAT BABY BE QUIET?
HIC COUGH WAAAAAAHHHH . . .
IF MOM HAD THAT SUPERPOWER, I THINK SHE'D USE IT ON YOU, TOO. . . .
AHWAAAAA AAAAHHHH . . .

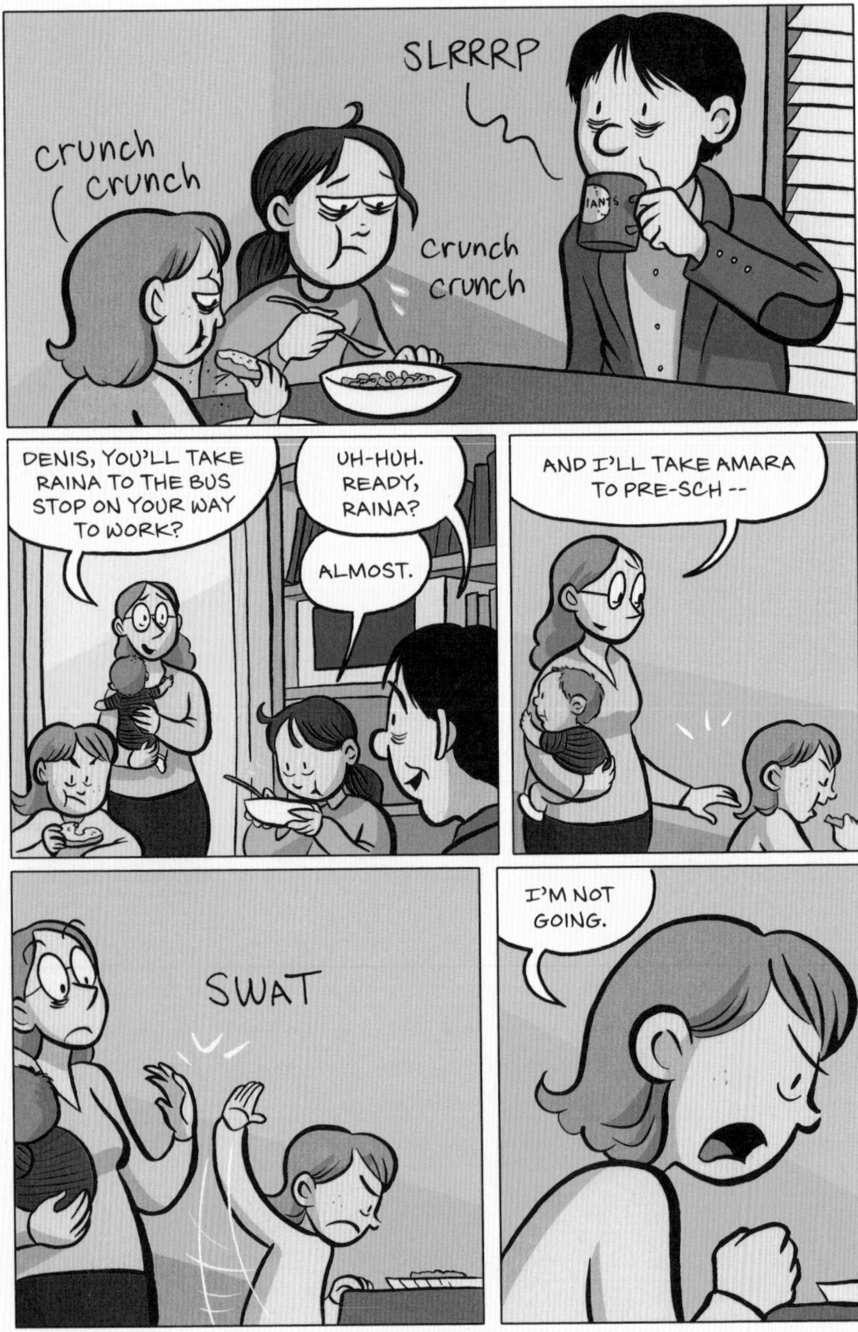
crunch crunch
SLRRRP
crunch crunch
DENIS, YOU'LL TAKE RAINA TO THE BUS STOP ON YOUR WAY TO WORK?
UH-HUH. READY, RAINA?
ALMOST.
AND I'LL TAKE AMARA TO PRE-SCH --
SWAT
I'M NOT GOING.

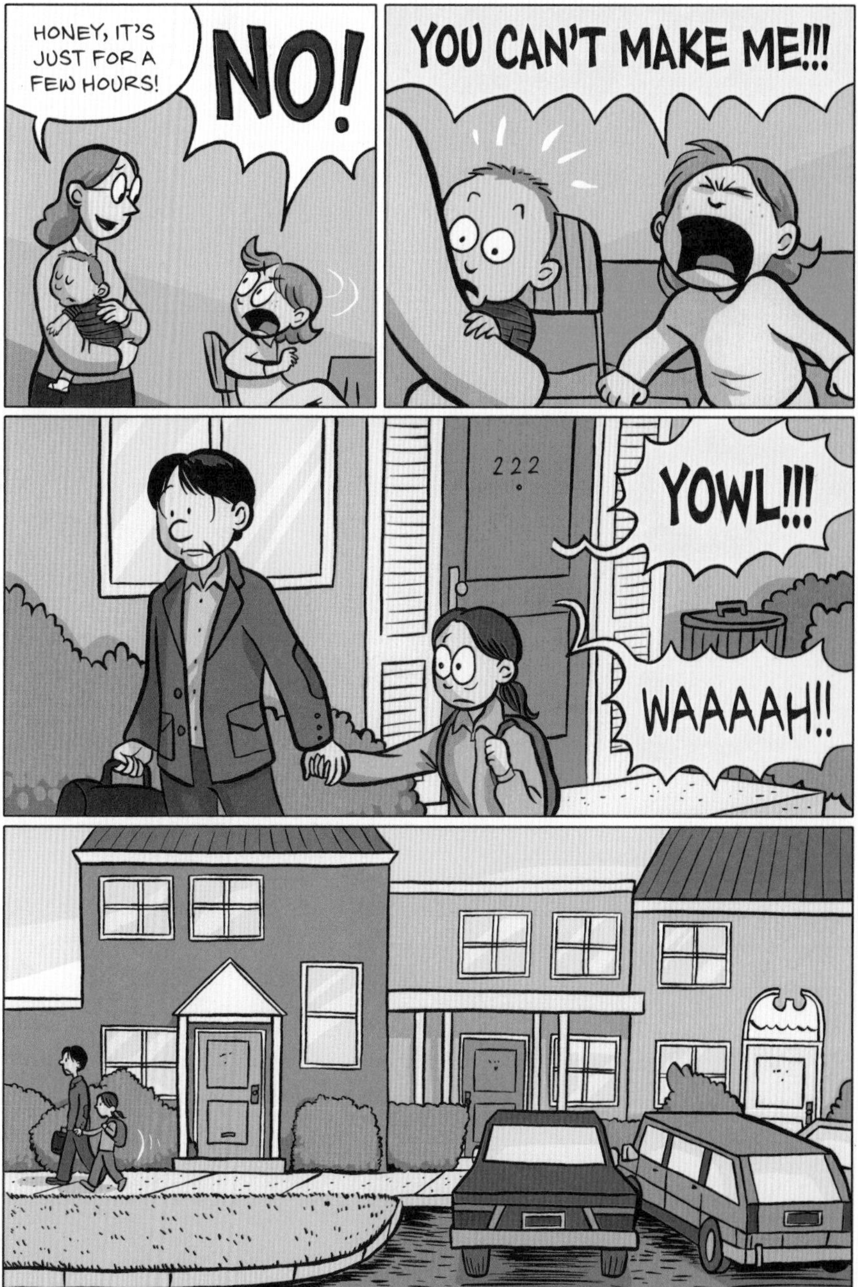
HONEY, IT'S JUST FOR A FEW HOURS!
NO!
YOU CAN'T MAKE ME!!!
222
YOWL!!!
WAAAAH!!

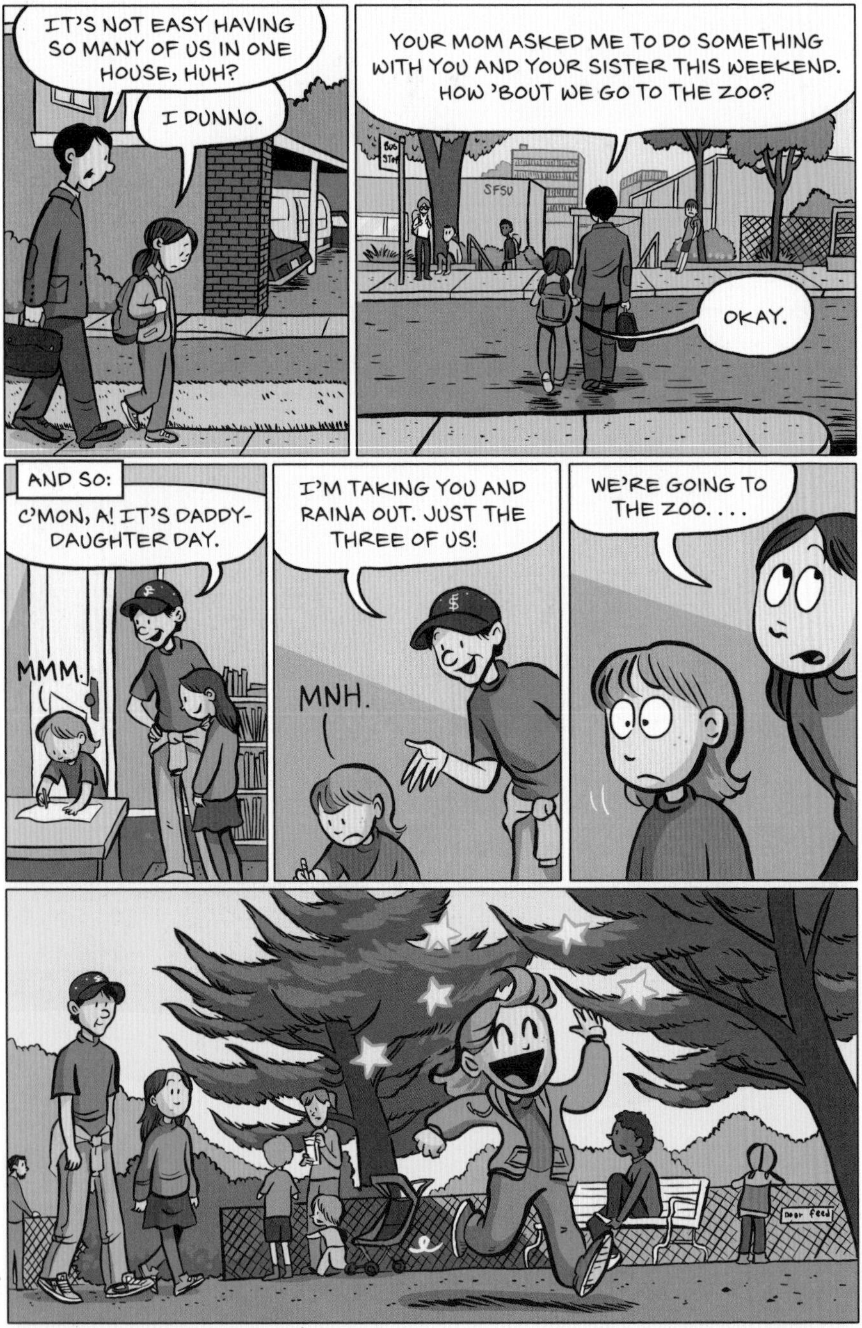
IT'S NOT EASY HAVING SO MANY OF US IN ONE HOUSE, HUH?
I DUNNO.
YOUR MOM ASKED ME TO DO SOMETHING WITH YOU AND YOUR SISTER THIS WEEKEND. HOW 'BOUT WE GO TO THE ZOO?
SFSU
OKAY.
AND SO:
C'MON, A! IT'S DADDY-DAUGHTER DAY.
MMM.
I'M TAKING YOU AND RAINA OUT. JUST THE THREE OF US!
MNH.
WE'RE GOING TO THE ZOO. . . .

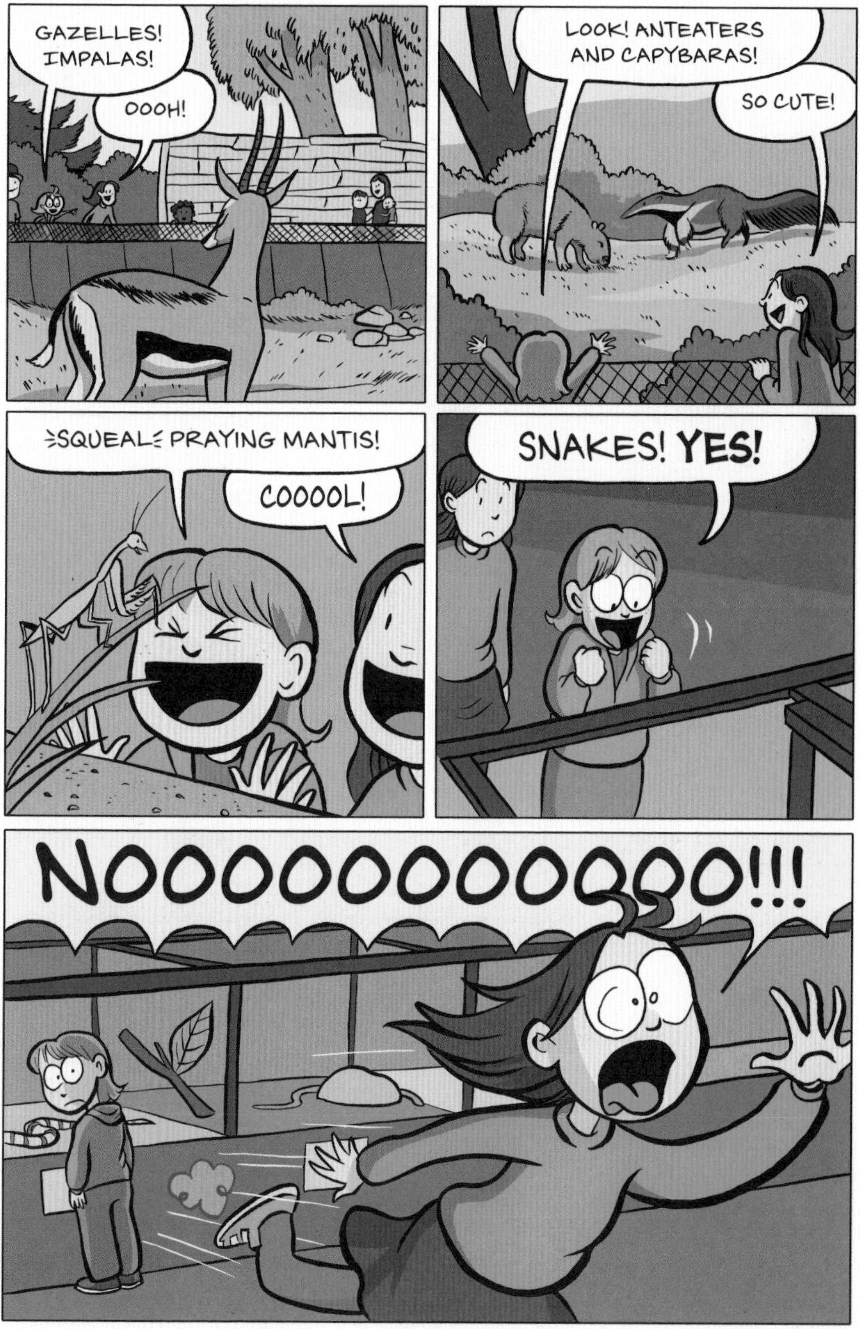
GAZELLES! IMPALAS!
OOOH!
LOOK! ANTEATERS AND CAPYBARAS!
SO CUTE!
SQUEAL PRAYING MANTIS!
COOOOL!
SNAKES! YES!
NOOOOOOOOOOO!!!

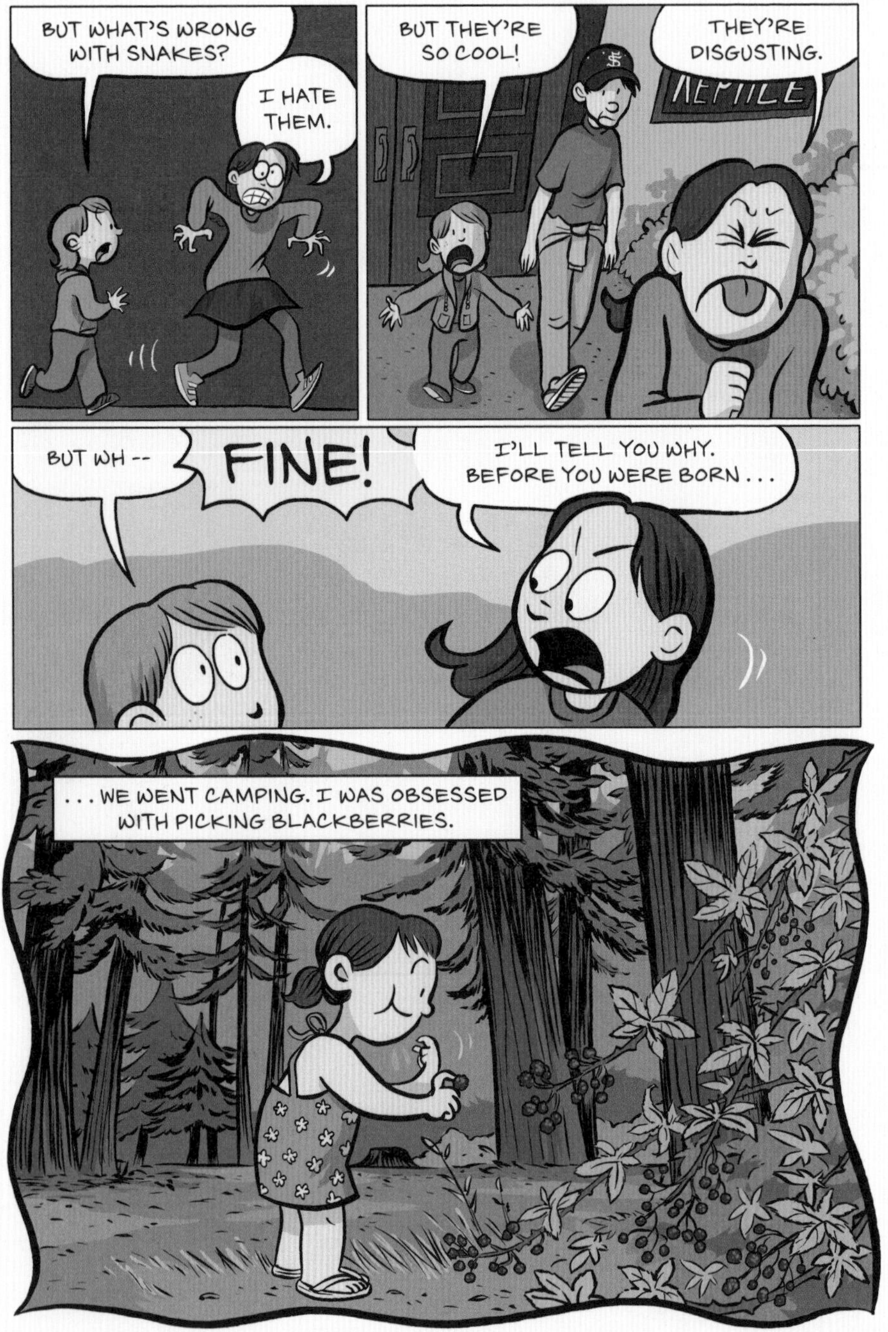
BUT WHAT'S WRONG WITH SNAKES?
I HATE THEM.
BUT THEY'RE SO COOL!
THEY'RE DISGUSTING.
BUT WH --
FINE!
I'LL TELL YOU WHY. BEFORE YOU WERE BORN . . .
. . . WE WENT CAMPING. I WAS OBSESSED WITH PICKING BLACKBERRIES.

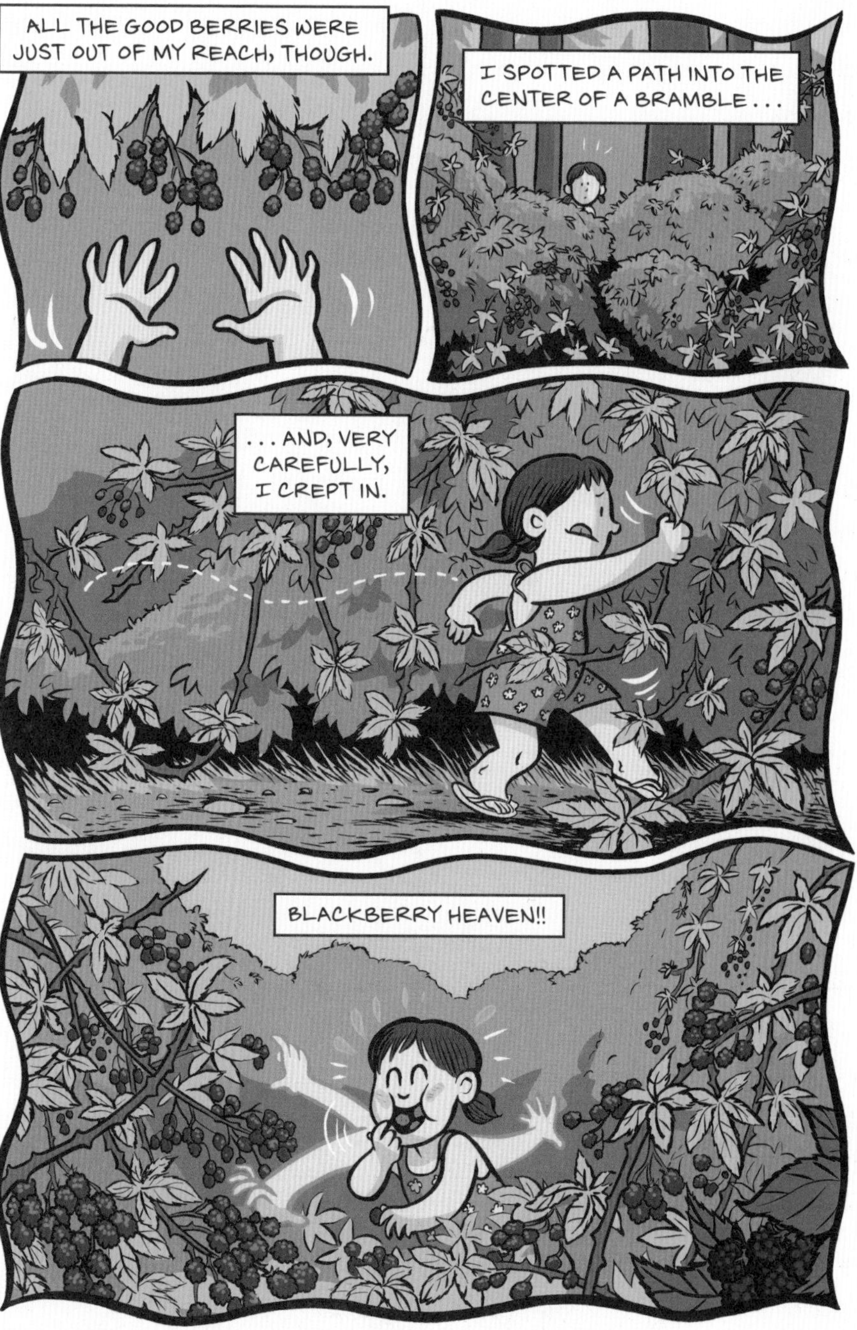
ALL THE GOOD BERRIES WERE JUST OUT OF MY REACH, THOUGH.
I SPOTTED A PATH INTO THE CENTER OF A BRAMBLE . . .
. . . AND, VERY CAREFULLY, I CREPT IN.
BLACKBERRY HEAVEN!!

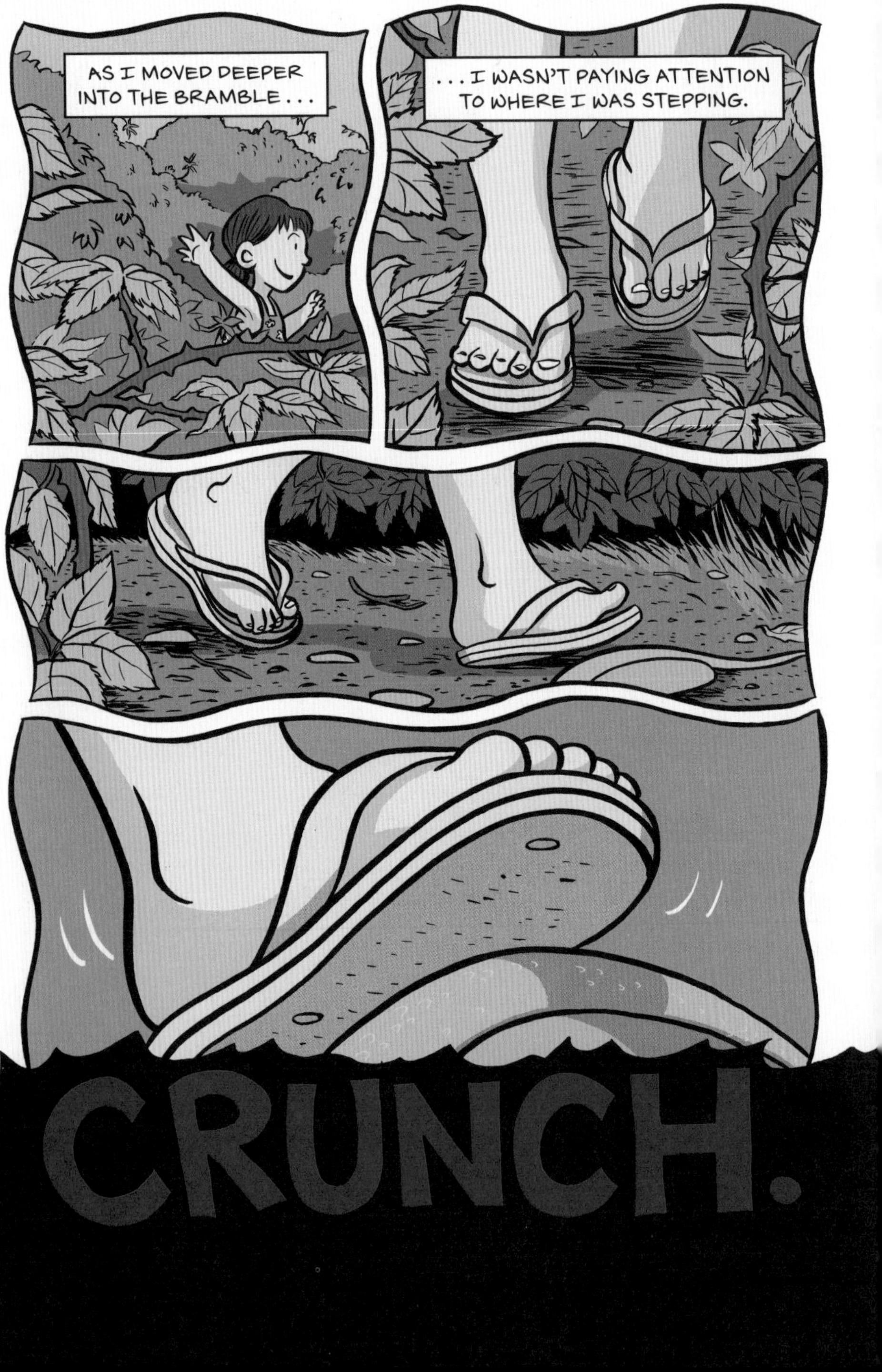
AS I MOVED DEEPER INTO THE BRAMBLE . . .
. . . I WASN'T PAYING ATTENTION TO WHERE I WAS STEPPING.
CRUNCH.

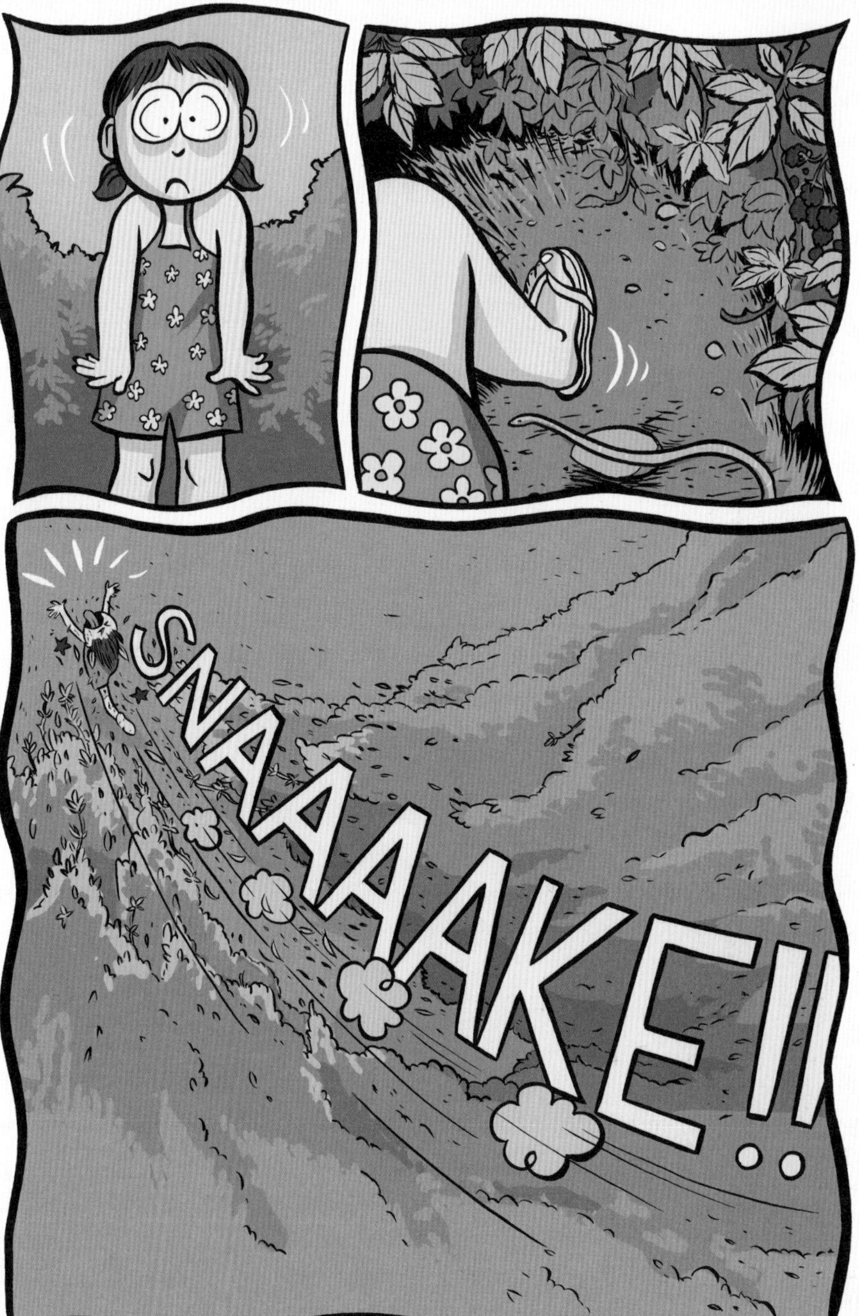
SNAAAAKE!!

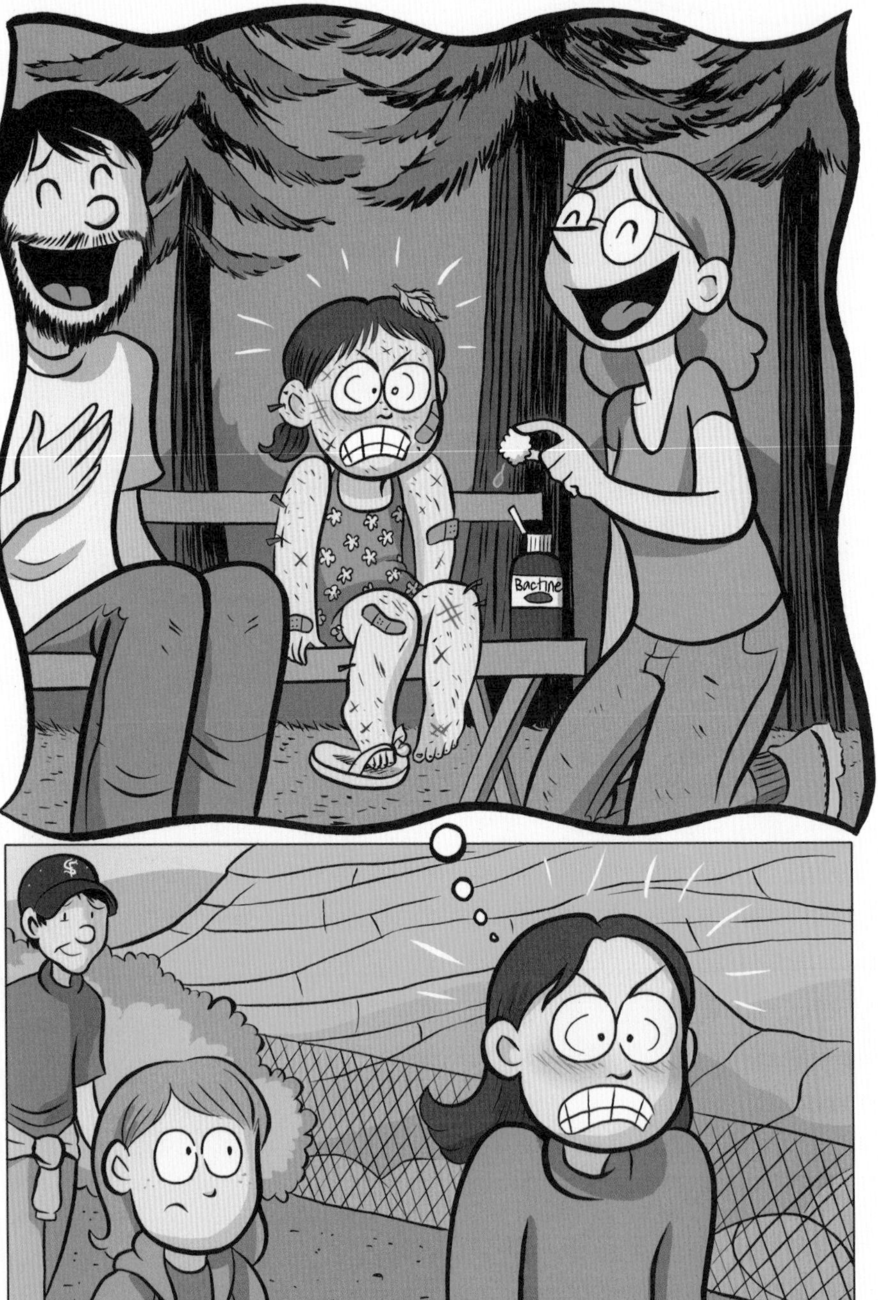
Bactine

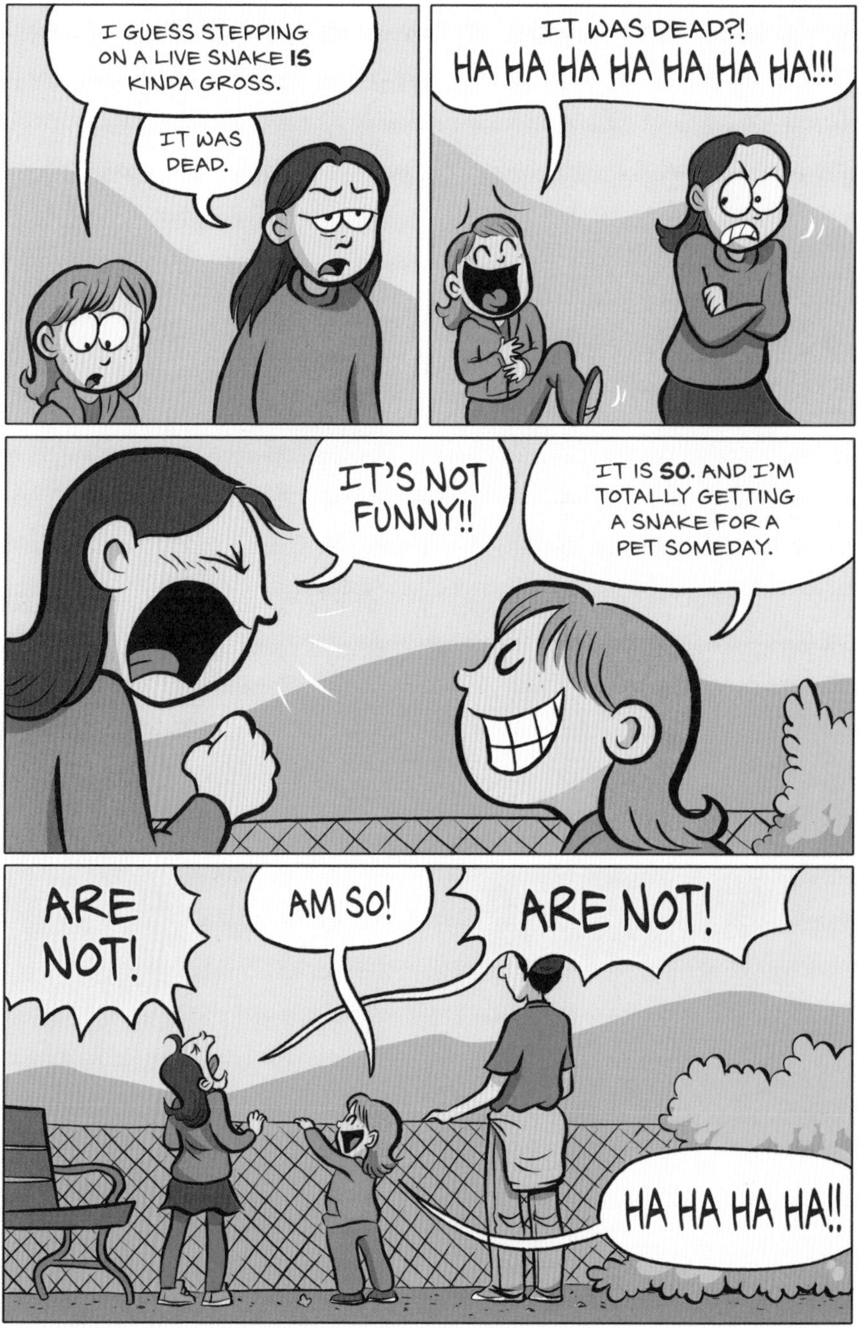
I GUESS STEPPING ON A LIVE SNAKE **IS** KINDA GROSS.
IT WAS DEAD.
IT WAS DEAD?!
HA HA HA HA HA HA HA!!!
IT'S NOT FUNNY!!
IT IS **SO**. AND I'M TOTALLY GETTING A SNAKE FOR A PET SOMEDAY.
ARE NOT!
AM SO!
ARE NOT!
HA HA HA HA!!

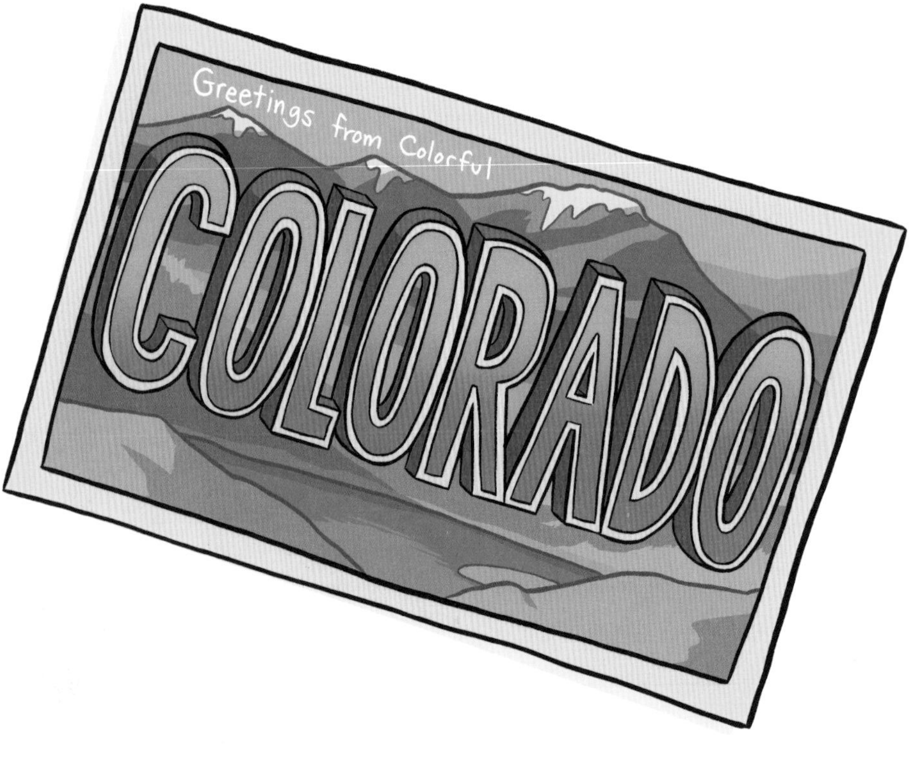
Greetings from Colorful
COLORADO

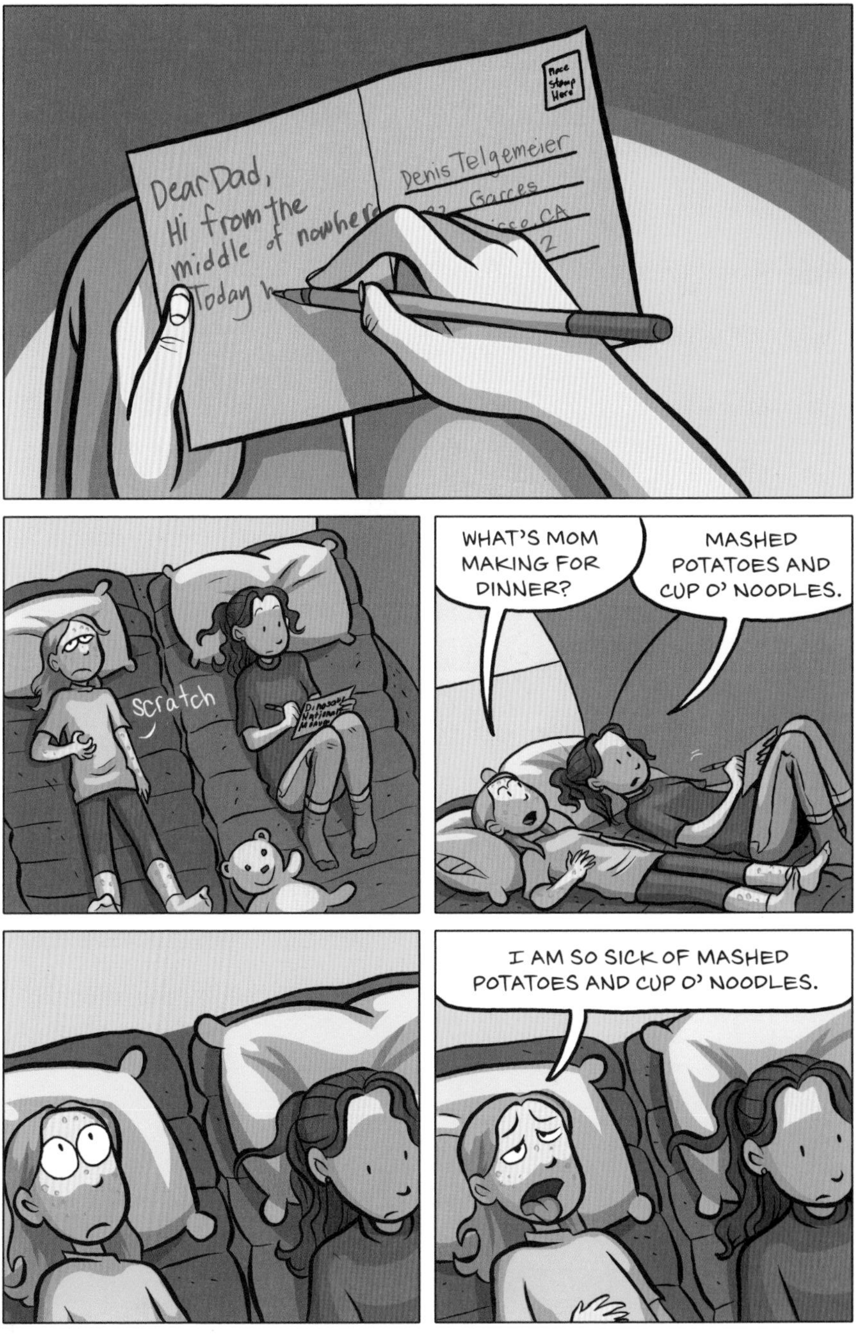
Place Stamp Here
Dear Dad,
Hi from the
middle of nowhe
Today
Denis Telgemeier
Garces
CA
scratch
WHAT'S MOM MAKING FOR DINNER?
MASHED POTATOES AND CUP O' NOODLES.
I AM SO SICK OF MASHED POTATOES AND CUP O' NOODLES.

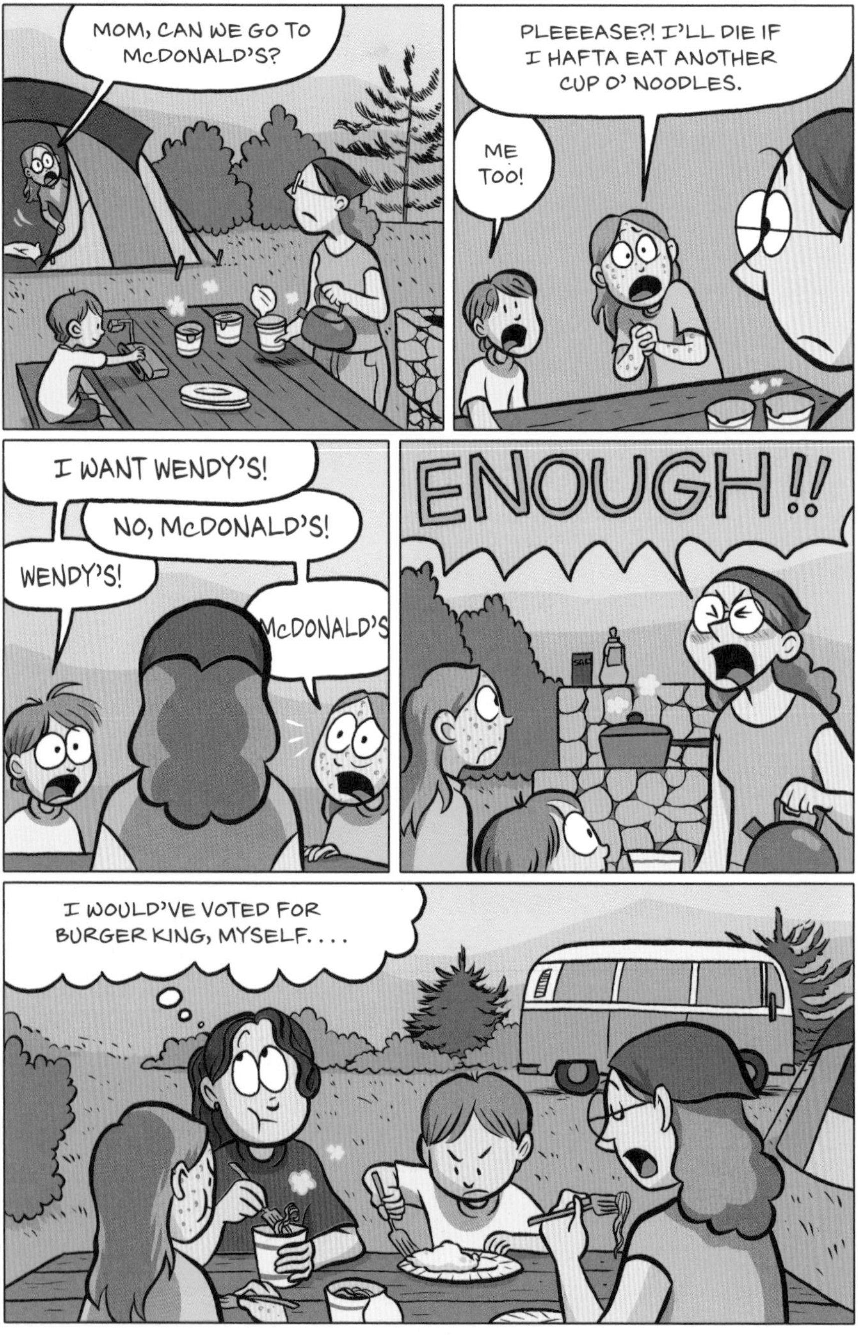
MOM, CAN WE GO TO McDONALD'S?
PLEEEEASE?! I'LL DIE IF I HAFTA EAT ANOTHER CUP O' NOODLES.
ME TOO!
I WANT WENDY'S!
NO, McDONALD'S!
WENDY'S!
McDONALD'S
ENOUGH!!
I WOULD'VE VOTED FOR BURGER KING, MYSELF. . . .

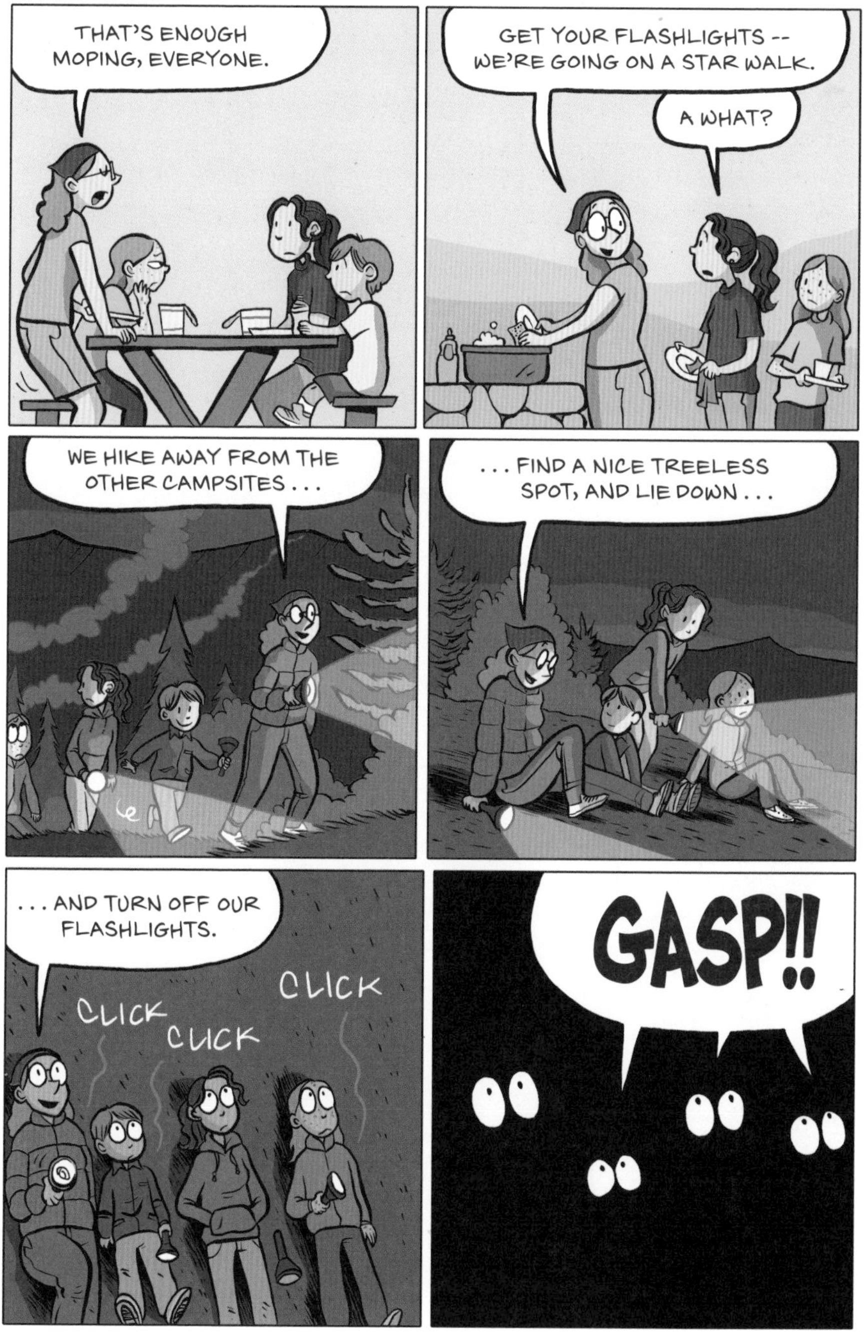
THAT'S ENOUGH MOPING, EVERYONE.
GET YOUR FLASHLIGHTS -- WE'RE GOING ON A STAR WALK.
A WHAT?
WE HIKE AWAY FROM THE OTHER CAMPSITES . . .
. . . FIND A NICE TREELESS SPOT, AND LIE DOWN . . .
. . . AND TURN OFF OUR FLASHLIGHTS.
CLICK
CLICK
CLICK
GASP!!

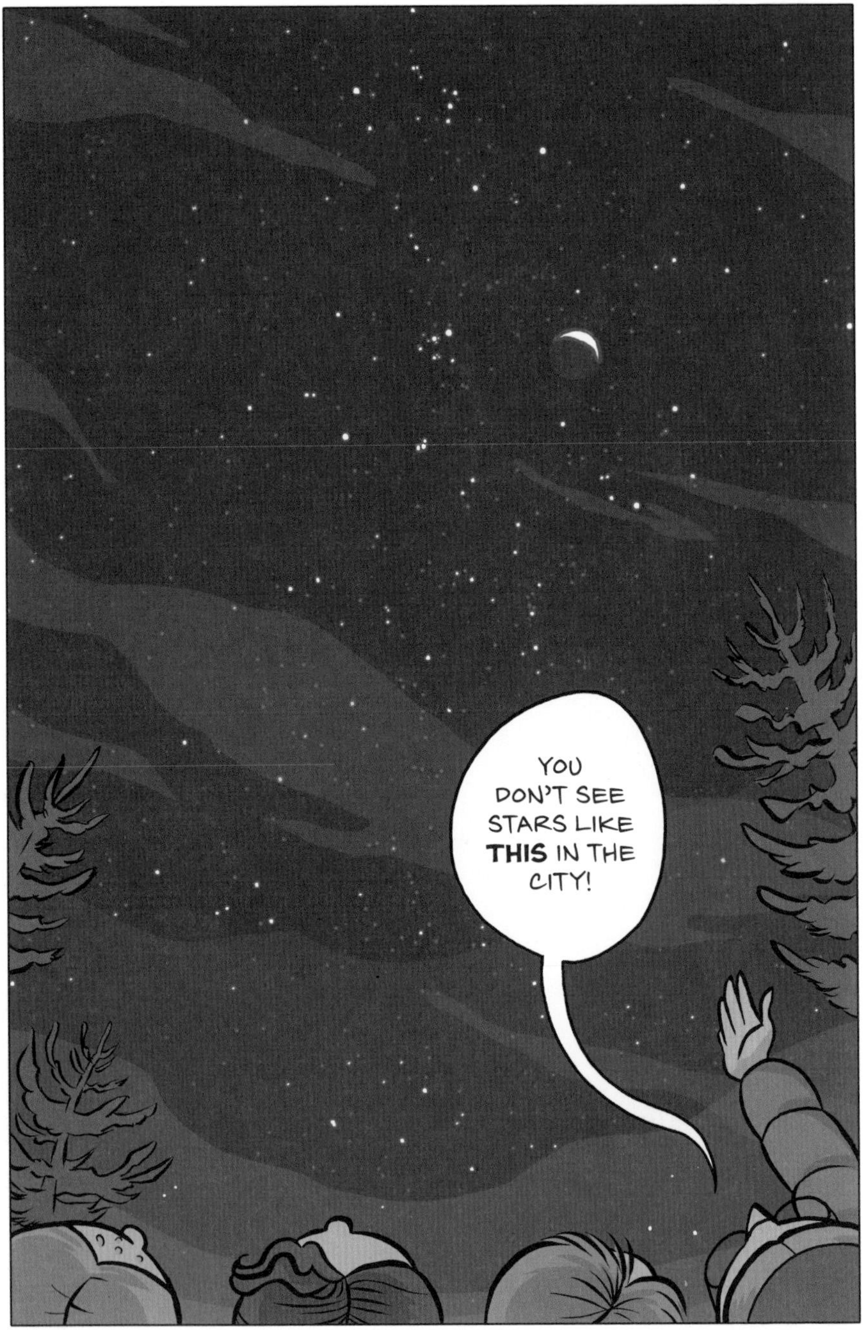
YOU DON'T SEE STARS LIKE **THIS** IN THE CITY!

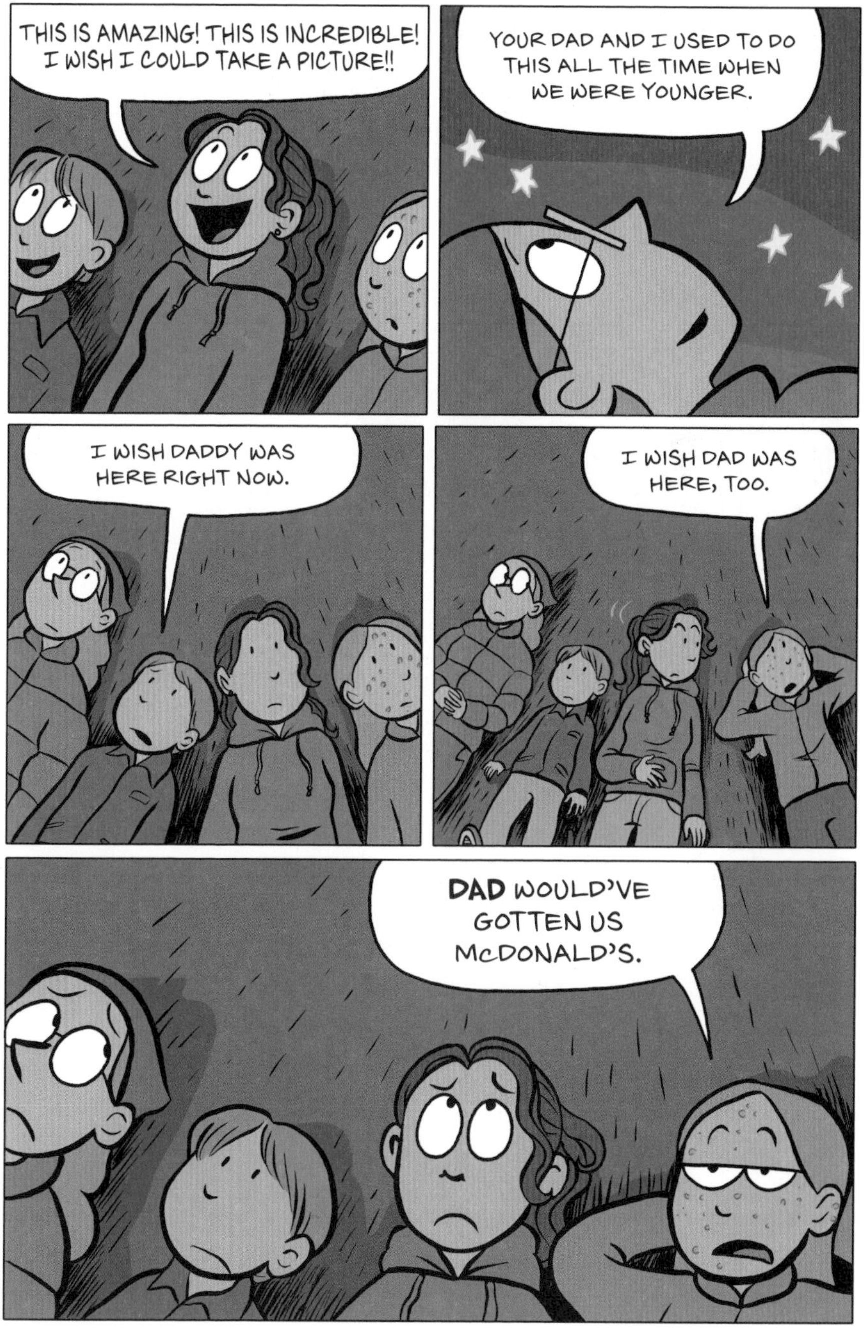
THIS IS AMAZING! THIS IS INCREDIBLE! I WISH I COULD TAKE A PICTURE!!
YOUR DAD AND I USED TO DO THIS ALL THE TIME WHEN WE WERE YOUNGER.
I WISH DADDY WAS HERE RIGHT NOW.
I WISH DAD WAS HERE, TOO.
DAD WOULD'VE GOTTEN US McDONALD'S.

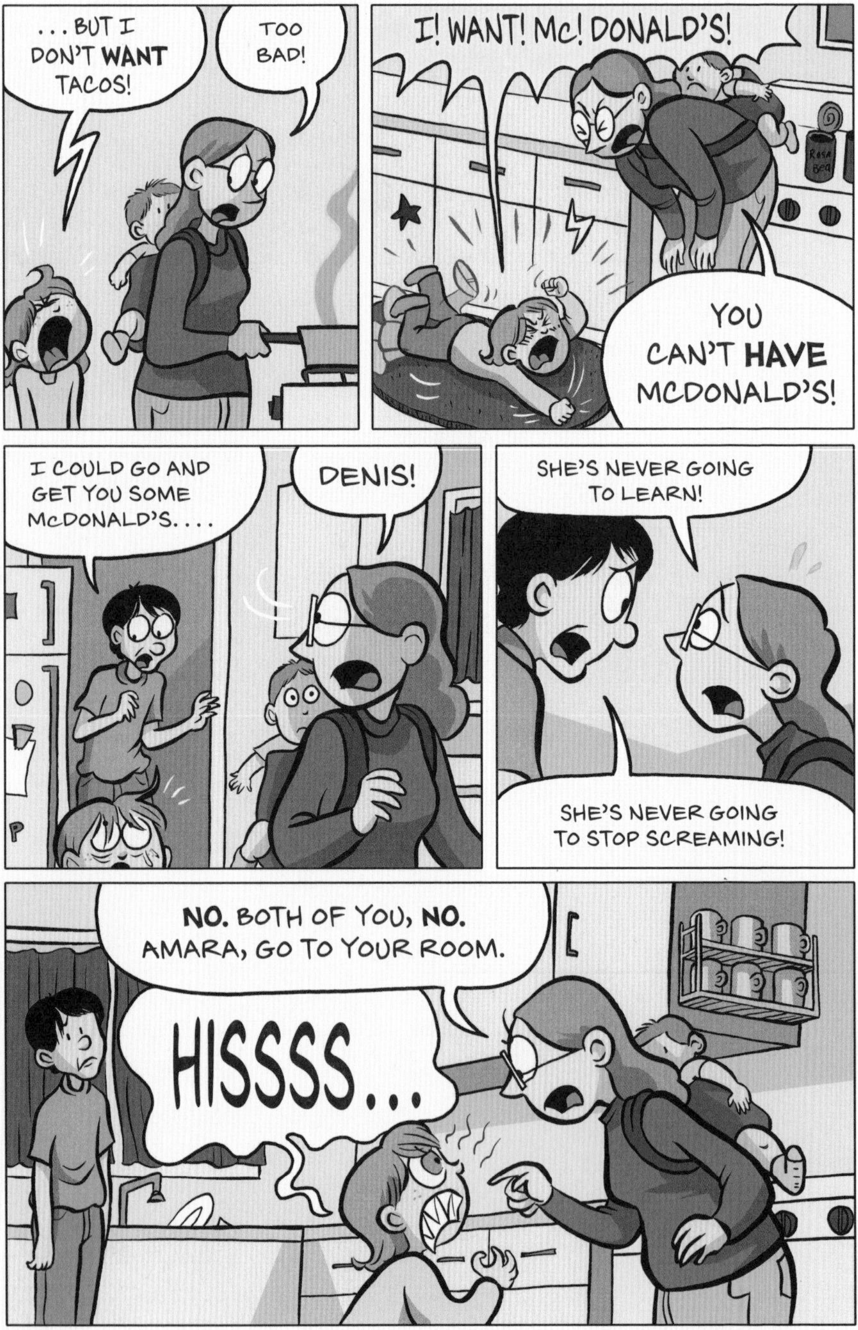
. . . BUT I DON'T **WANT** TACOS!
TOO BAD!
I! WANT! Mc! DONALD'S!
YOU CAN'T **HAVE** MCDONALD'S!
I COULD GO AND GET YOU SOME McDONALD'S. . . .
DENIS!
SHE'S NEVER GOING TO LEARN!
SHE'S NEVER GOING TO STOP SCREAMING!
NO. BOTH OF YOU, **NO.** AMARA, GO TO YOUR ROOM.
HISSSS . . .

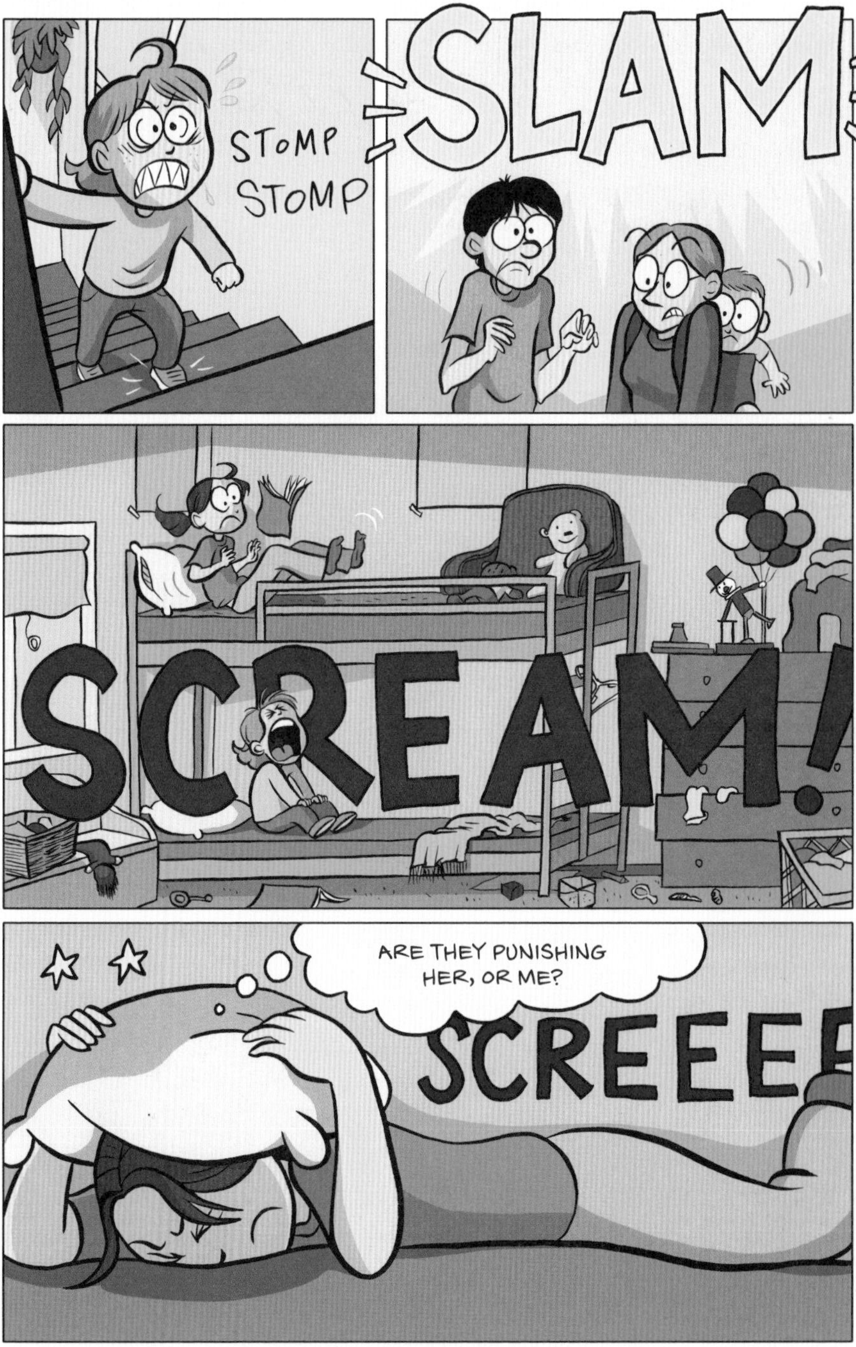
STOMP
STOMP
SLAM
SCREAM!
ARE THEY PUNISHING HER, OR ME?
SCREEE

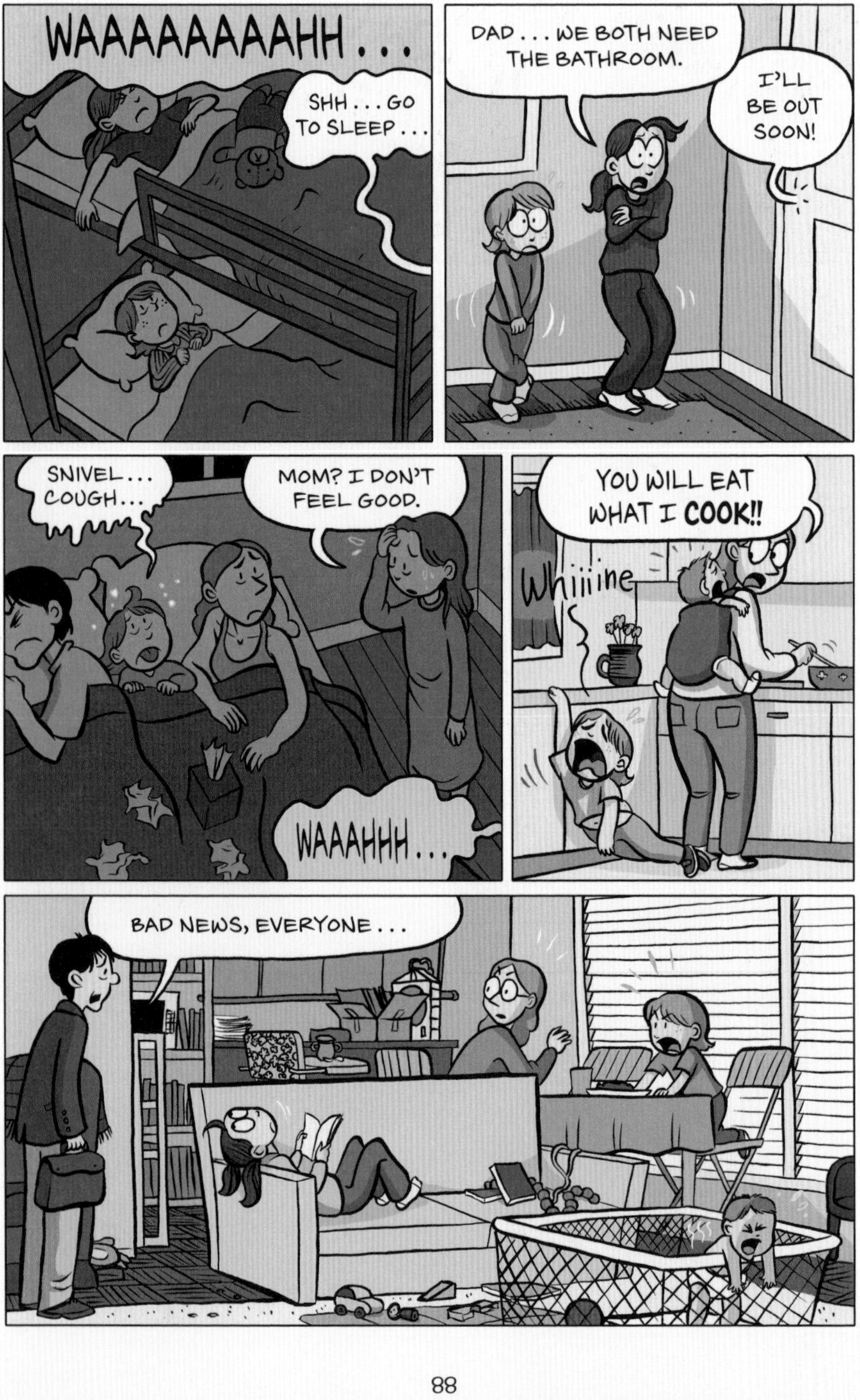
WAAAAAAAAHH . . .
SHH . . . GO TO SLEEP . . .
DAD . . . WE BOTH NEED THE BATHROOM.
I'LL BE OUT SOON!
SNIVEL . . . COUGH . . .
MOM? I DON'T FEEL GOOD.
WAAAHHH . . .
YOU WILL EAT WHAT I COOK!!
Whiiiine
BAD NEWS, EVERYONE . . .

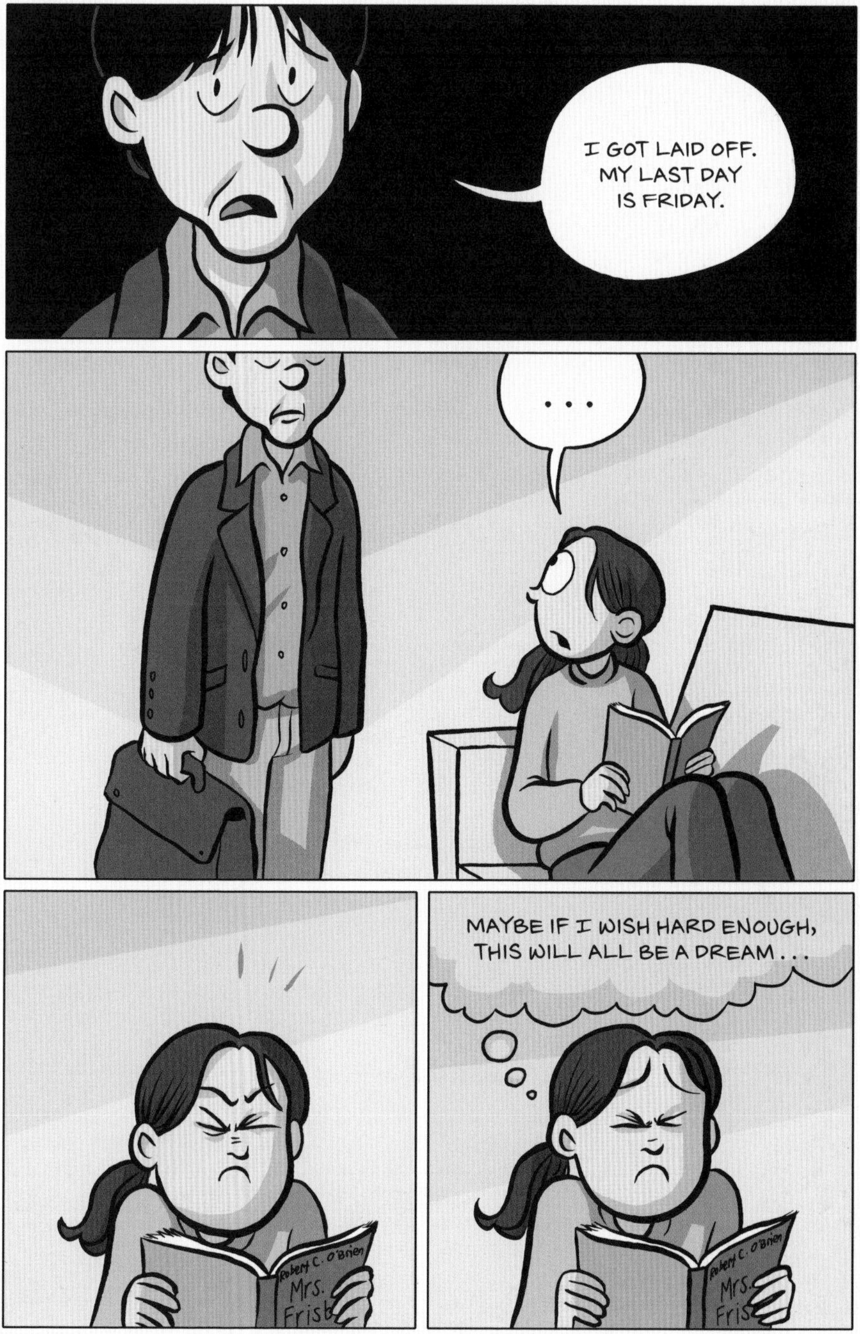
I GOT LAID OFF. MY LAST DAY IS FRIDAY.
. . .
MAYBE IF I WISH HARD ENOUGH, THIS WILL ALL BE A DREAM . . .
Robert C. O'Brien
Mrs. Frisb
Robert C. O'Brien
Mrs. Fris

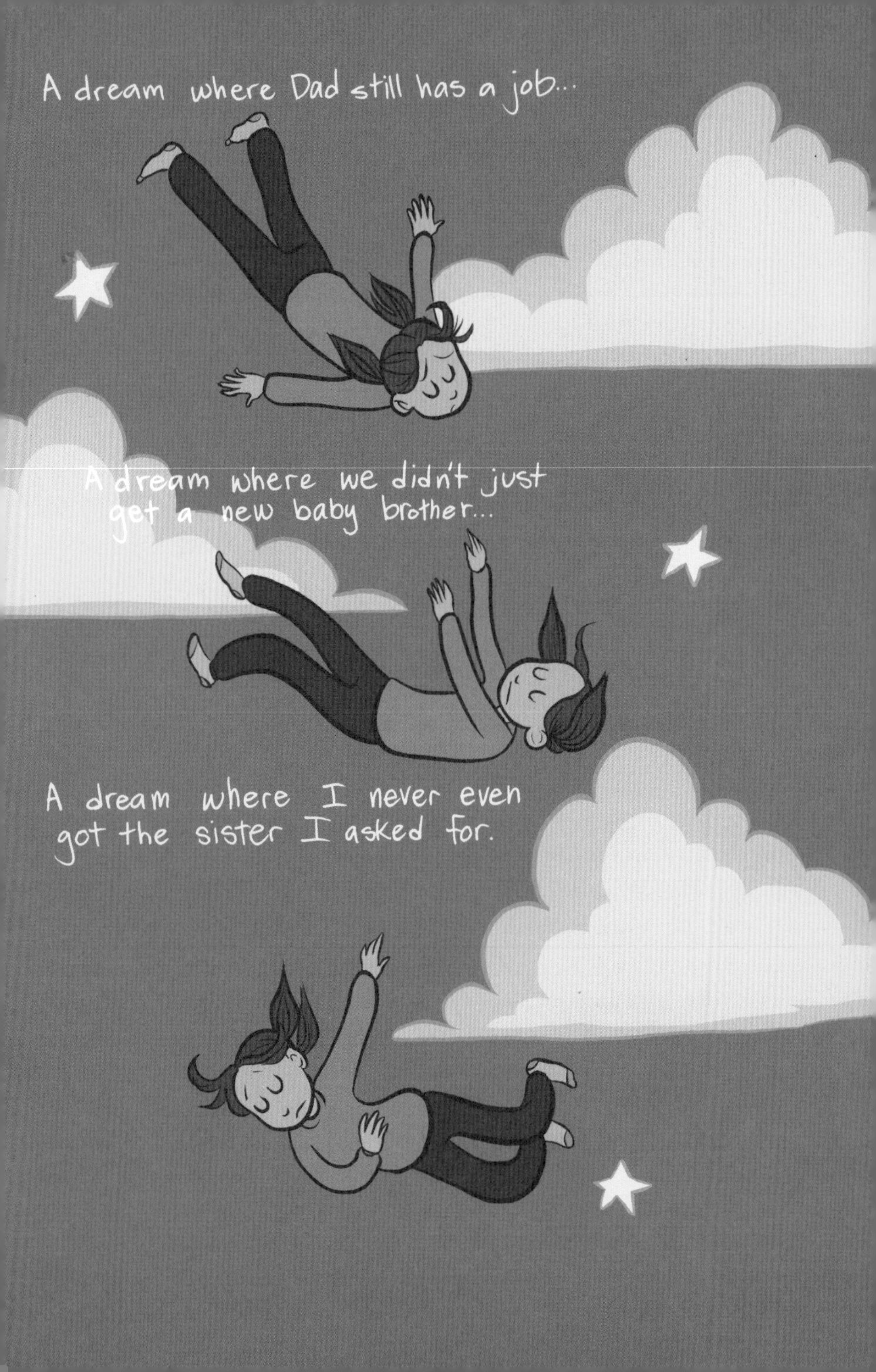
A dream where Dad still has a job...
A dream where we didn't just get a new baby brother...
A dream where I never even got the sister I asked for.

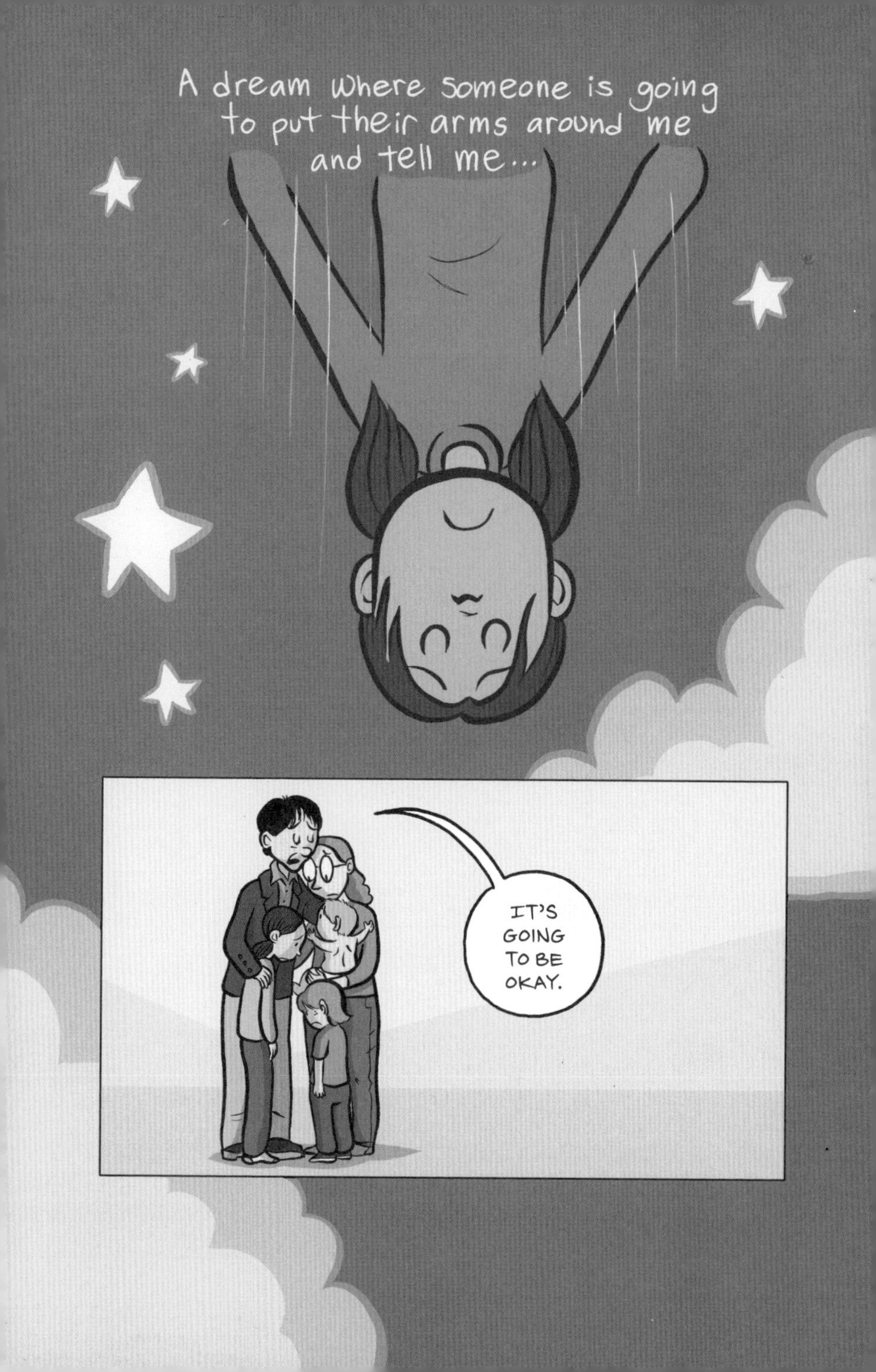
A dream where someone is going to put their arms around me and tell me...
IT'S GOING TO BE OKAY.

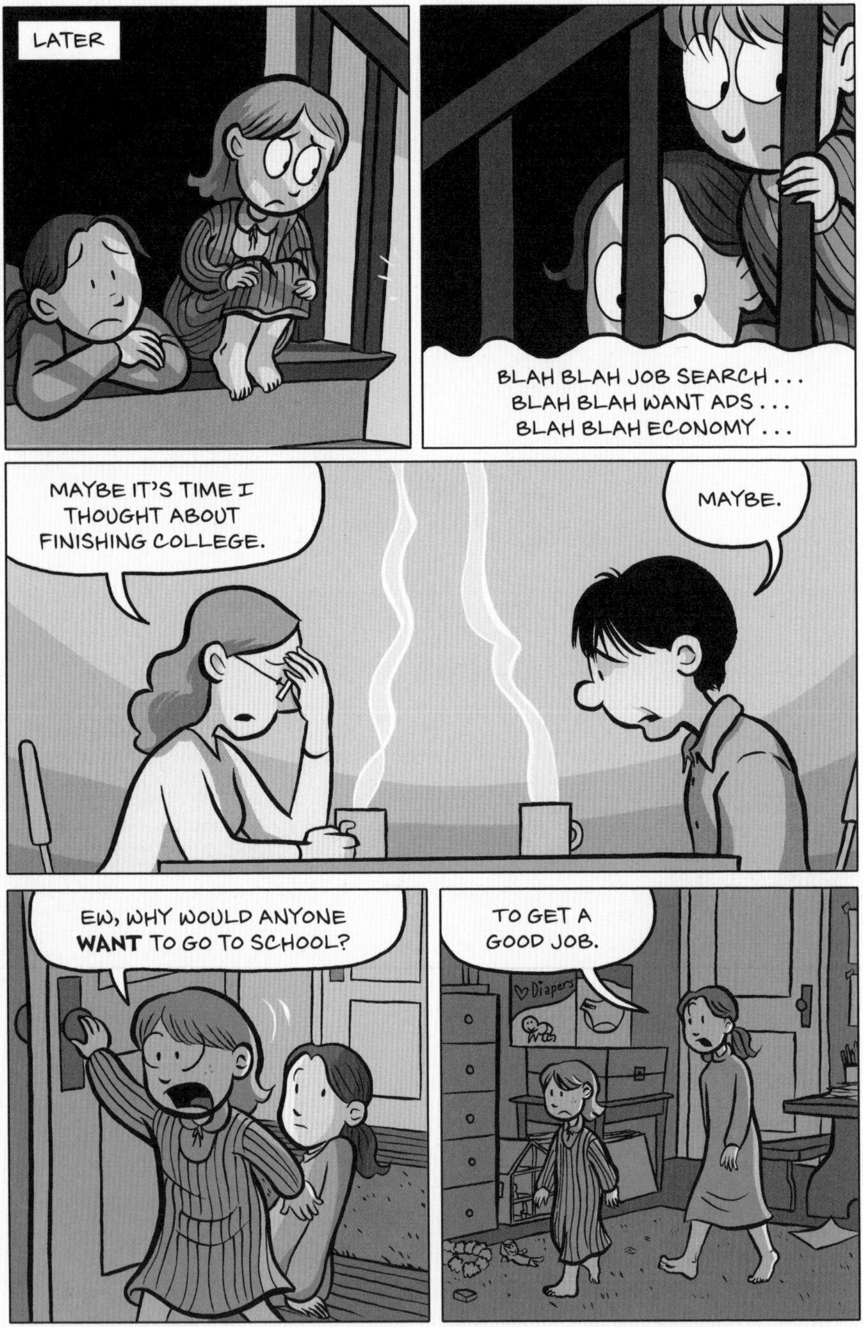
LATER
BLAH BLAH JOB SEARCH . . .
BLAH BLAH WANT ADS . . .
BLAH BLAH ECONOMY . . .
MAYBE IT'S TIME I THOUGHT ABOUT FINISHING COLLEGE.
MAYBE.
EW, WHY WOULD ANYONE **WANT** TO GO TO SCHOOL?
TO GET A GOOD JOB.
Diapers

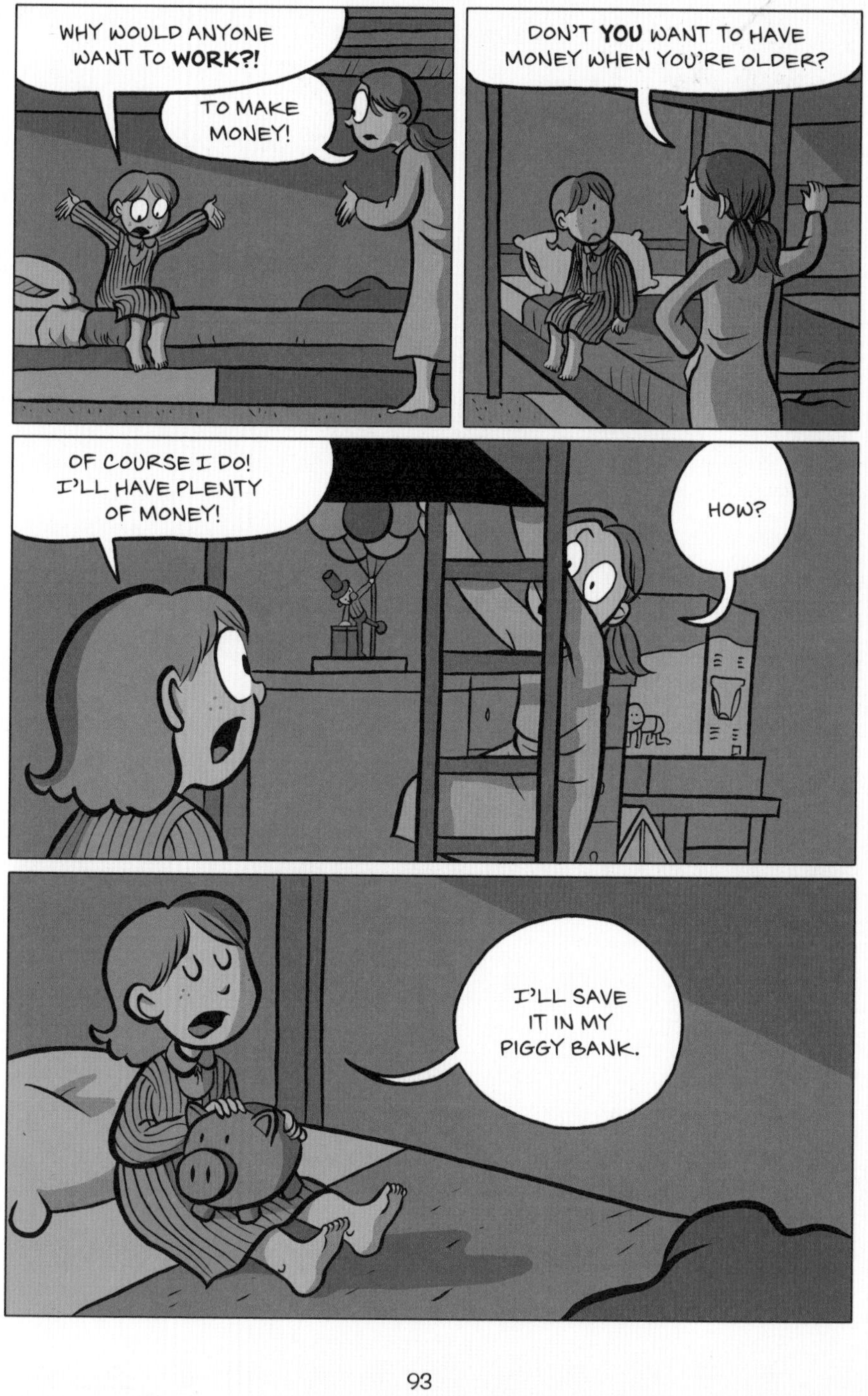
WHY WOULD ANYONE WANT TO **WORK?!**
TO MAKE MONEY!
DON'T **YOU** WANT TO HAVE MONEY WHEN YOU'RE OLDER?
OF COURSE I DO! I'LL HAVE PLENTY OF MONEY!
HOW?
I'LL SAVE IT IN MY PIGGY BANK.

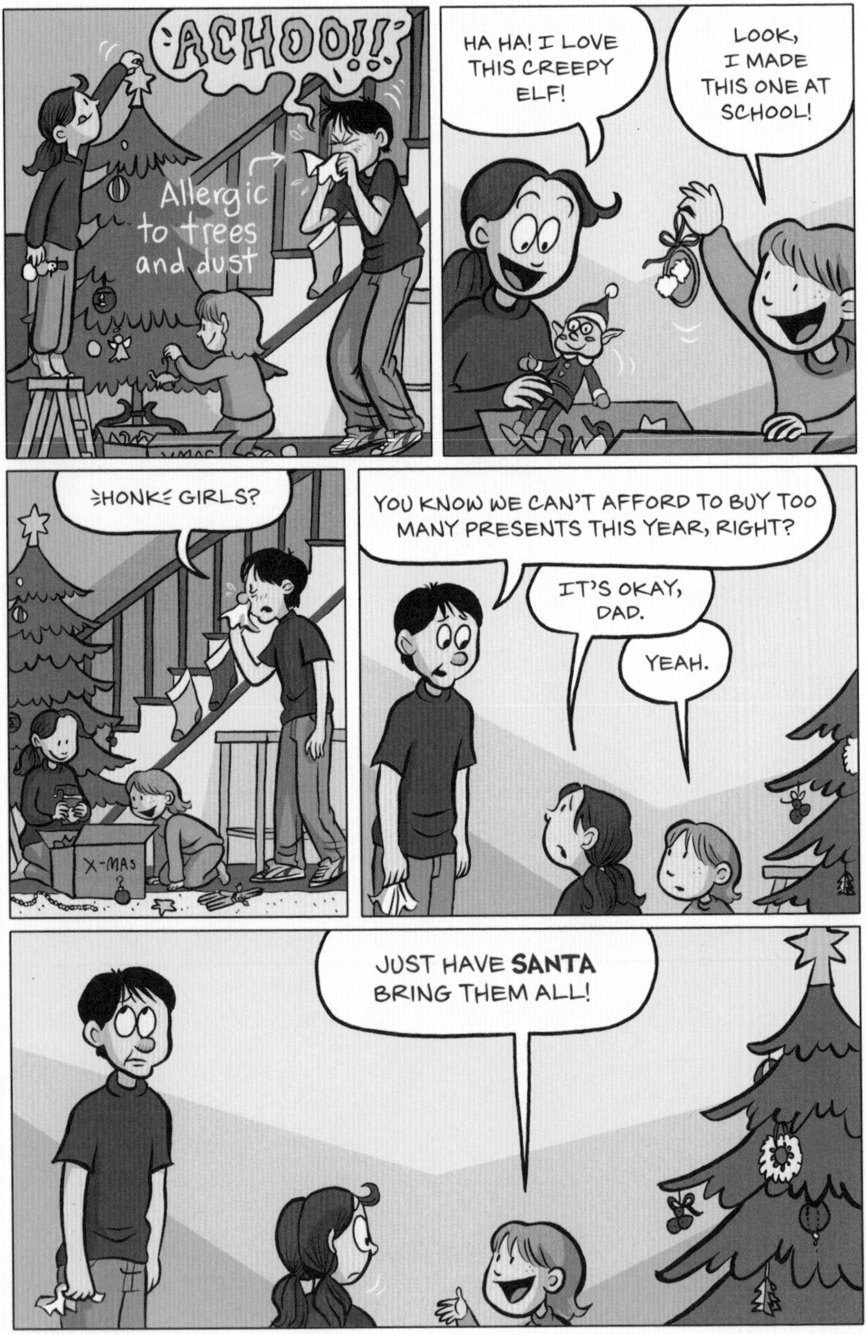
ACHOO!!
Allergic to trees and dust
HA HA! I LOVE THIS CREEPY ELF!
LOOK, I MADE THIS ONE AT SCHOOL!
X-MAS
HONK GIRLS?
X-MAS
YOU KNOW WE CAN'T AFFORD TO BUY TOO MANY PRESENTS THIS YEAR, RIGHT?
IT'S OKAY, DAD.
YEAH.
JUST HAVE **SANTA** BRING THEM ALL!

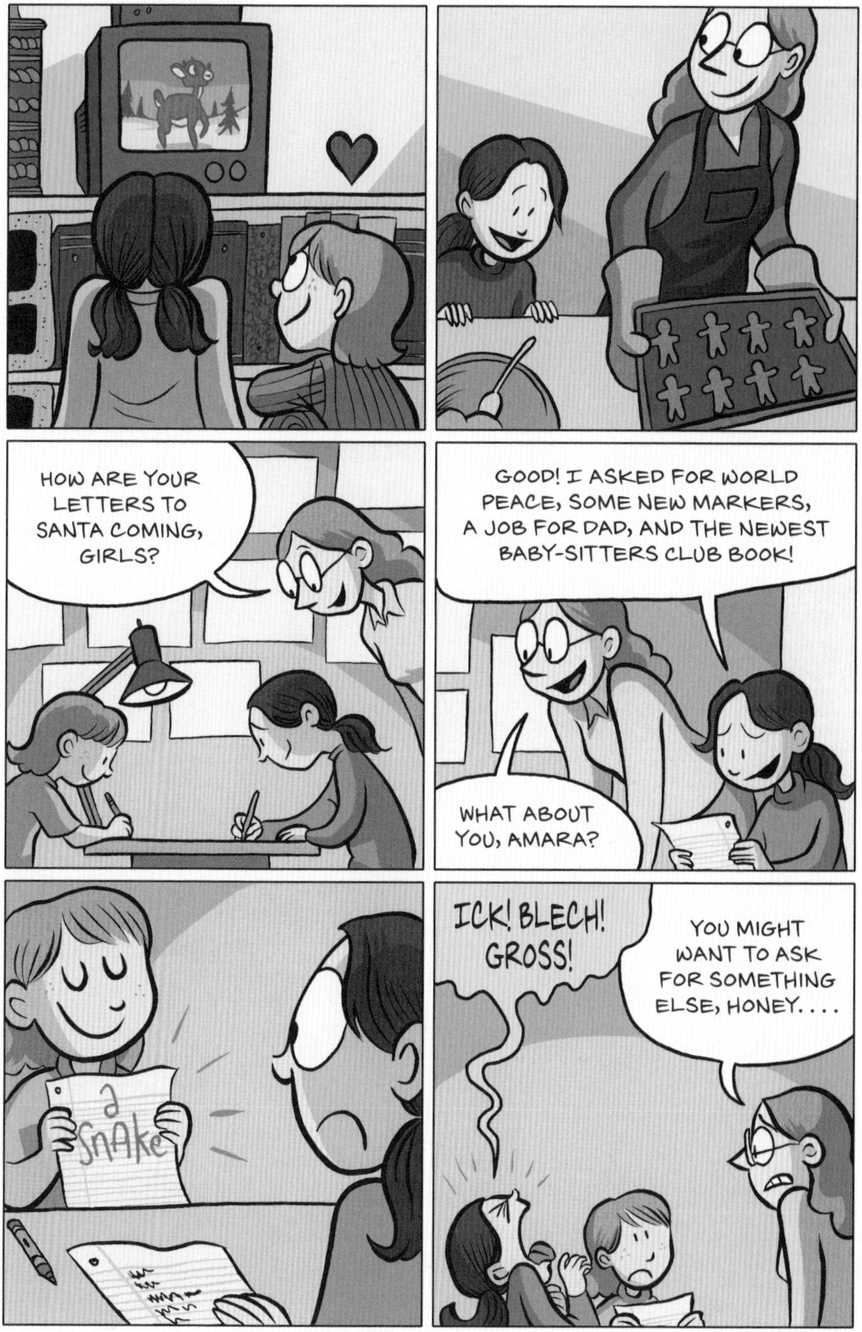
HOW ARE YOUR LETTERS TO SANTA COMING, GIRLS?
GOOD! I ASKED FOR WORLD PEACE, SOME NEW MARKERS, A JOB FOR DAD, AND THE NEWEST BABY-SITTERS CLUB BOOK!
WHAT ABOUT YOU, AMARA?
a SnAke
ICK! BLECH! GROSS!
YOU MIGHT WANT TO ASK FOR SOMETHING ELSE, HONEY. . . .

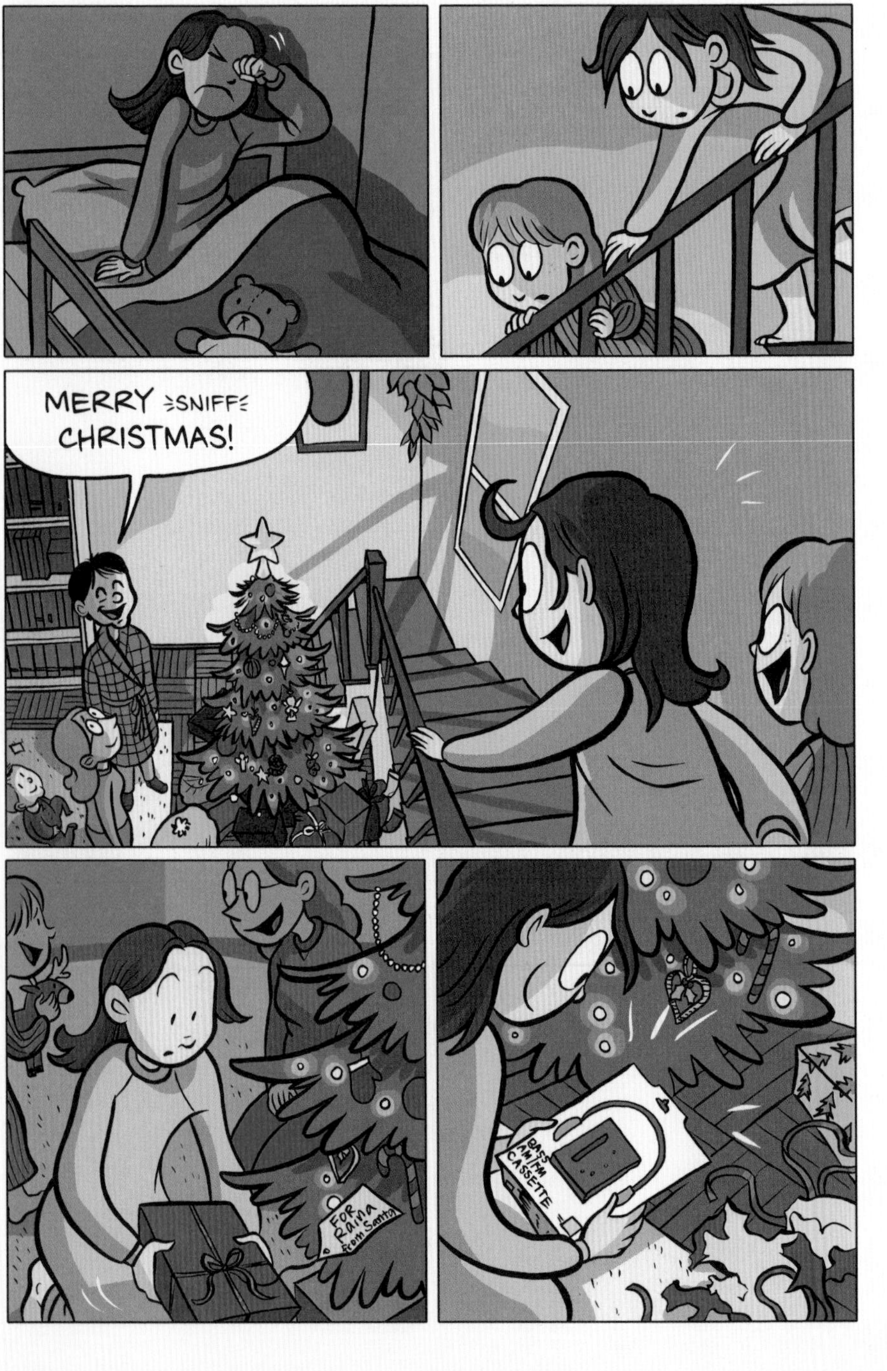

MERRY ≈SNIFF≈ CHRISTMAS!
FOR Raina From Santa
BASS
AM/FM
CASSETTE

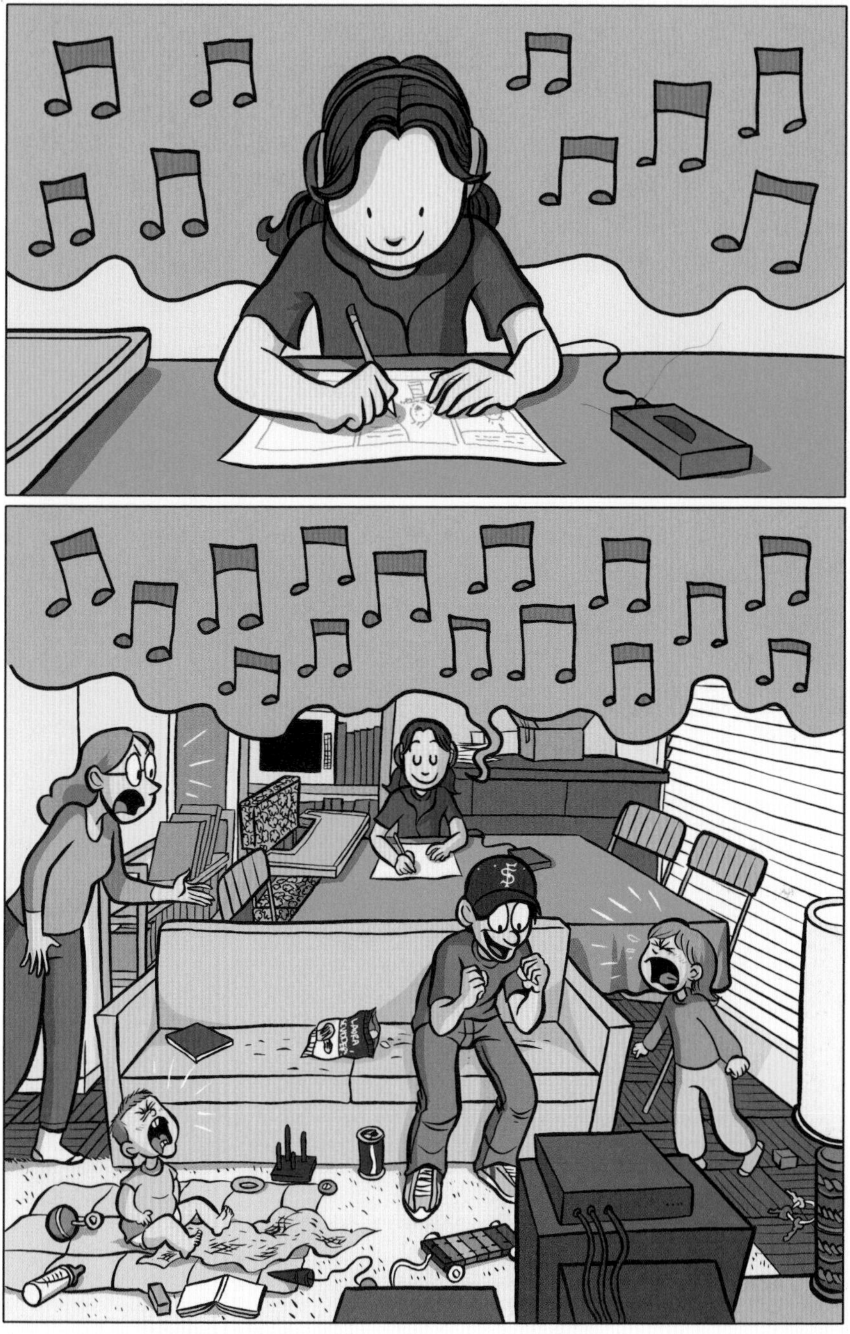

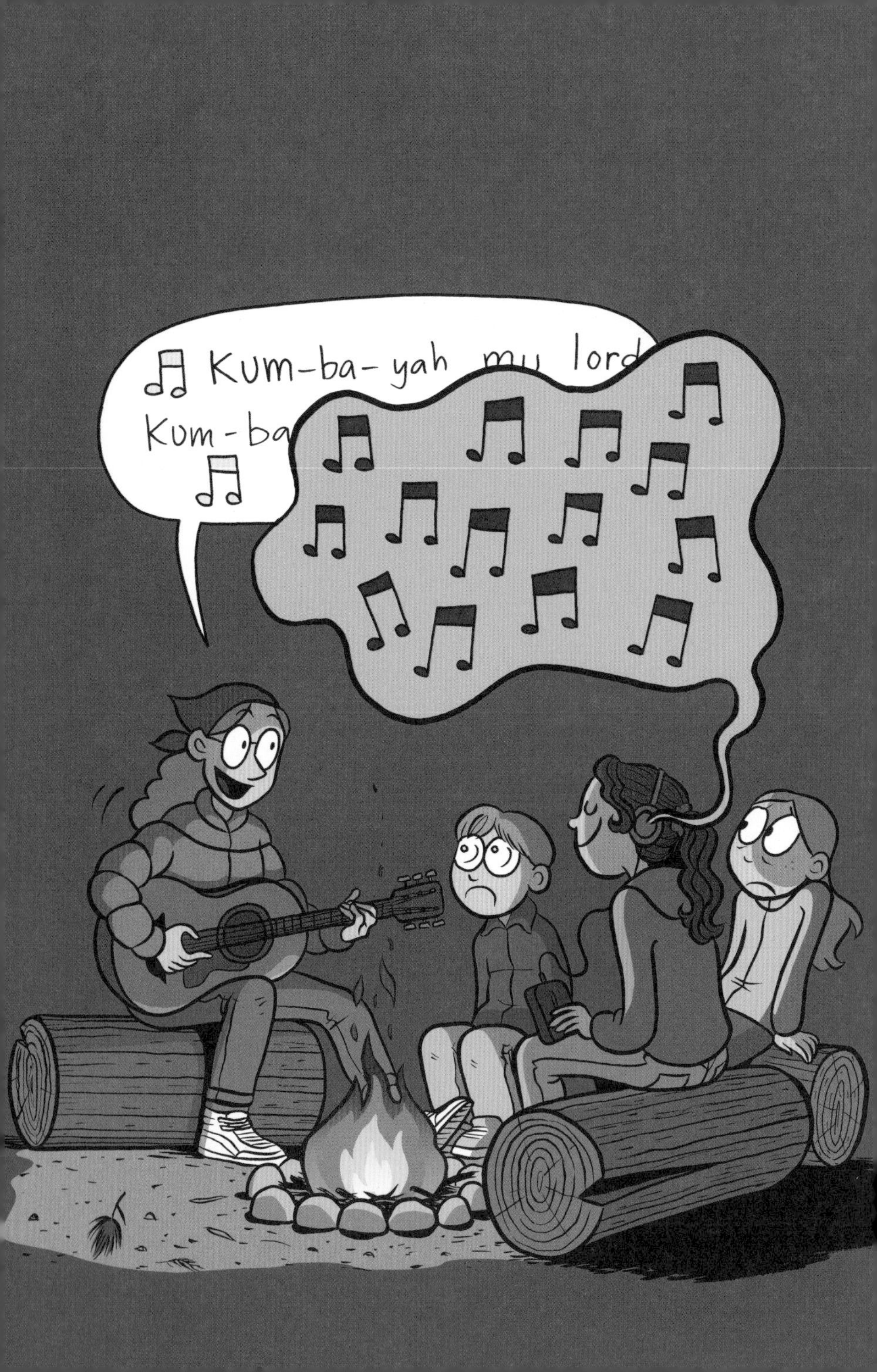
Kum-ba-yah my lord
Kum-ba

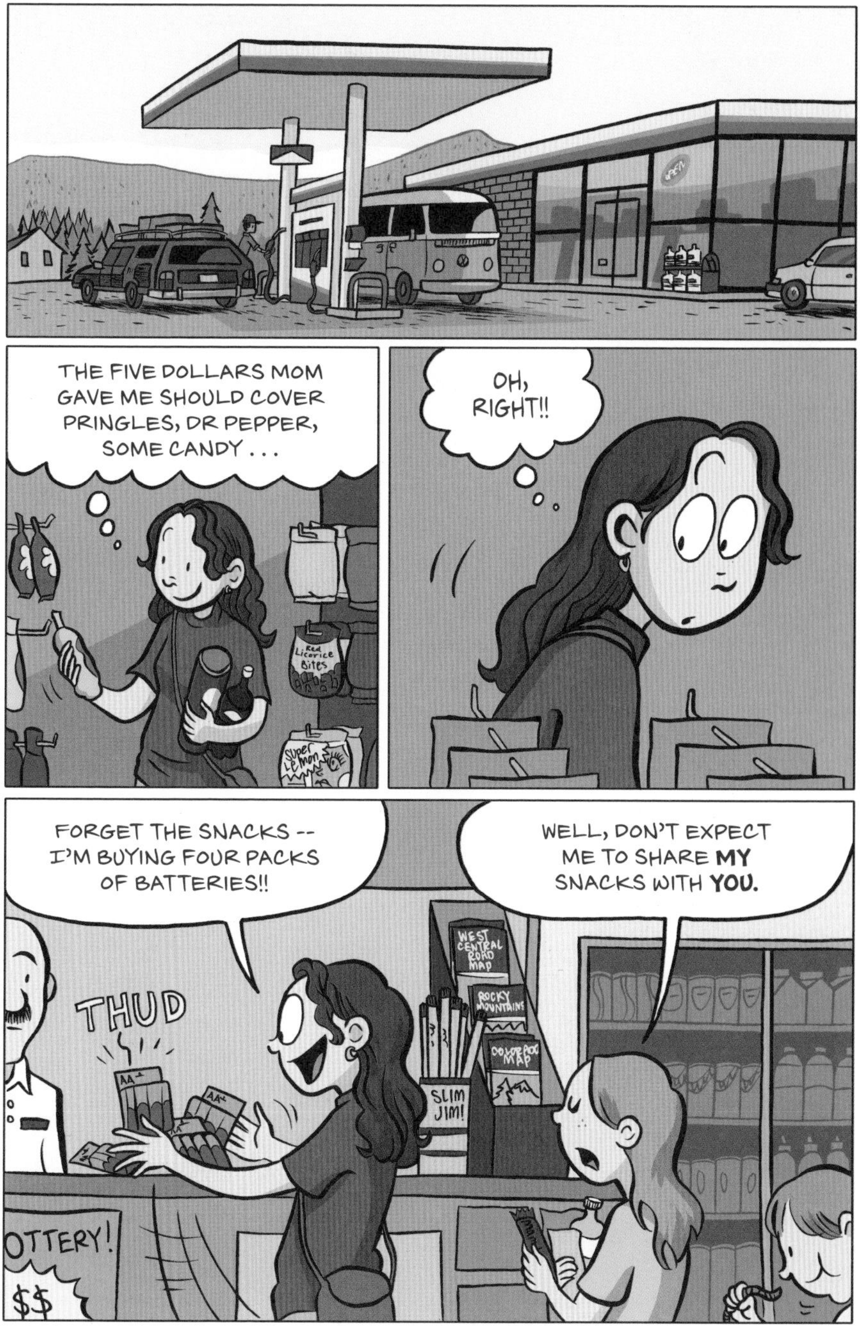
THE FIVE DOLLARS MOM GAVE ME SHOULD COVER PRINGLES, DR PEPPER, SOME CANDY . . .
Red Licorice Bites
Super Lemon
OH, RIGHT!!
FORGET THE SNACKS -- I'M BUYING FOUR PACKS OF BATTERIES!!
WELL, DON'T EXPECT ME TO SHARE **MY** SNACKS WITH **YOU.**
THUD
WEST CENTRAL ROAD MAP
ROCKY MOUNTAINS
SLIM JIM!
OTTERY!
$$

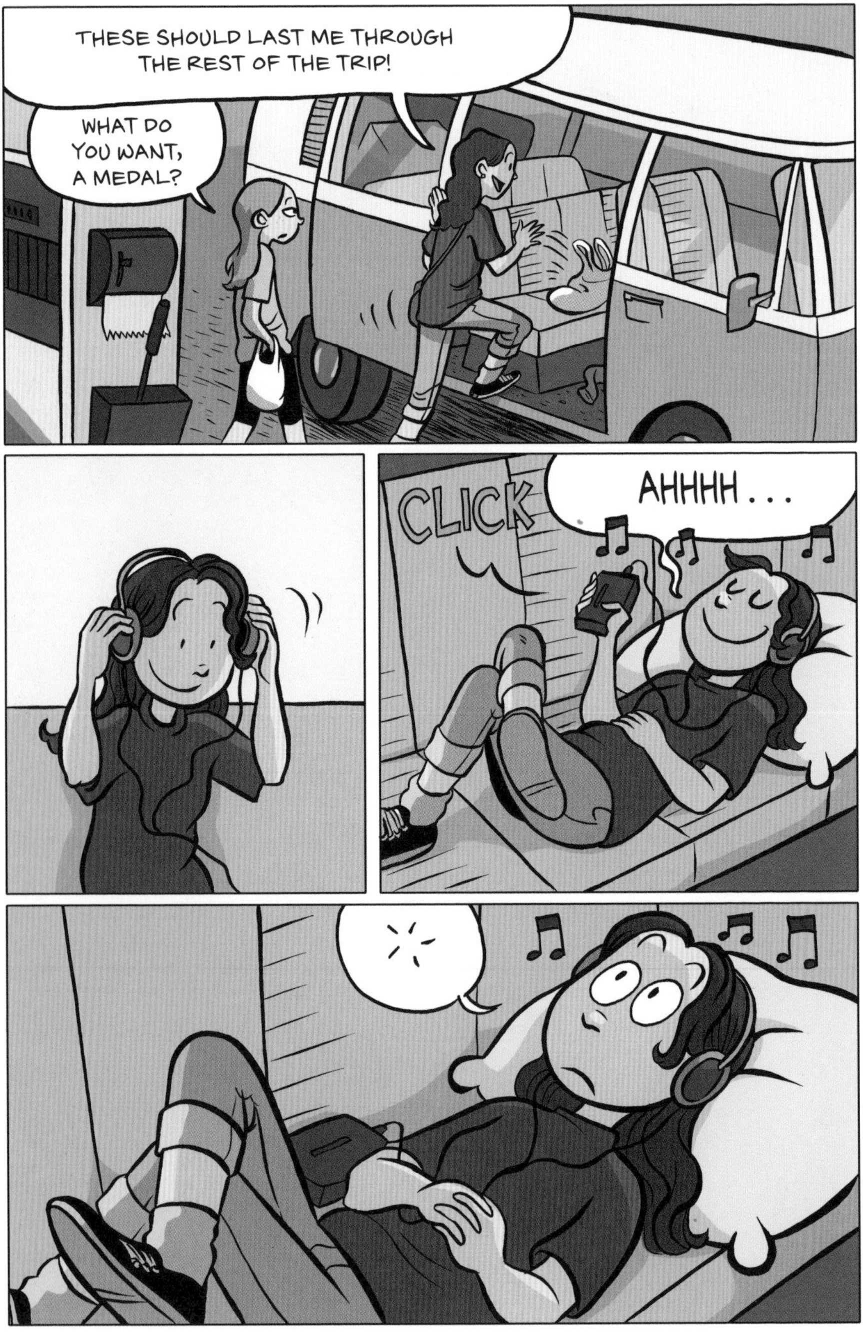
THESE SHOULD LAST ME THROUGH THE REST OF THE TRIP!
WHAT DO YOU WANT, A MEDAL?
CLICK
AHHHH . . .

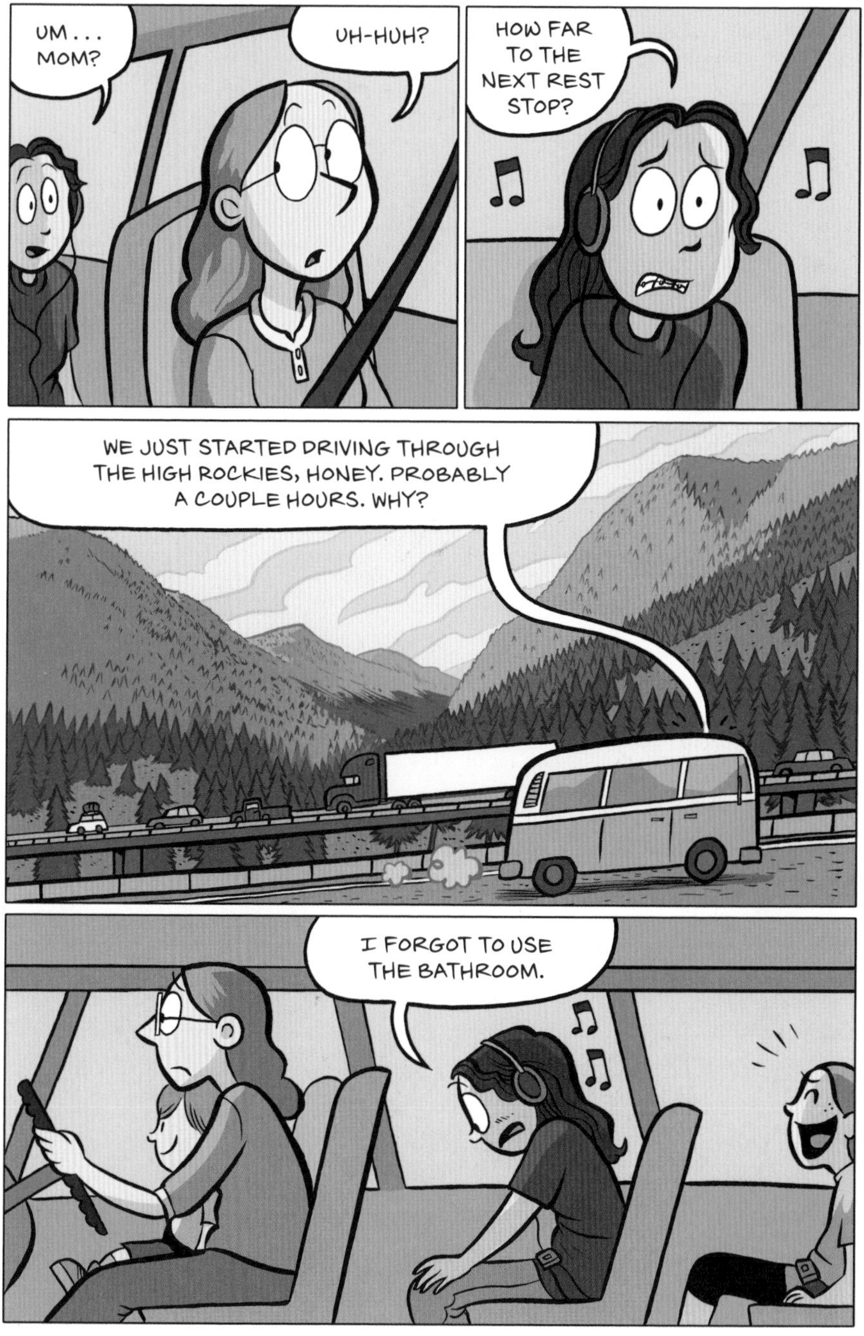
UM . . . MOM?
UH-HUH?
HOW FAR TO THE NEXT REST STOP?
WE JUST STARTED DRIVING THROUGH THE HIGH ROCKIES, HONEY. PROBABLY A COUPLE HOURS. WHY?
I FORGOT TO USE THE BATHROOM.

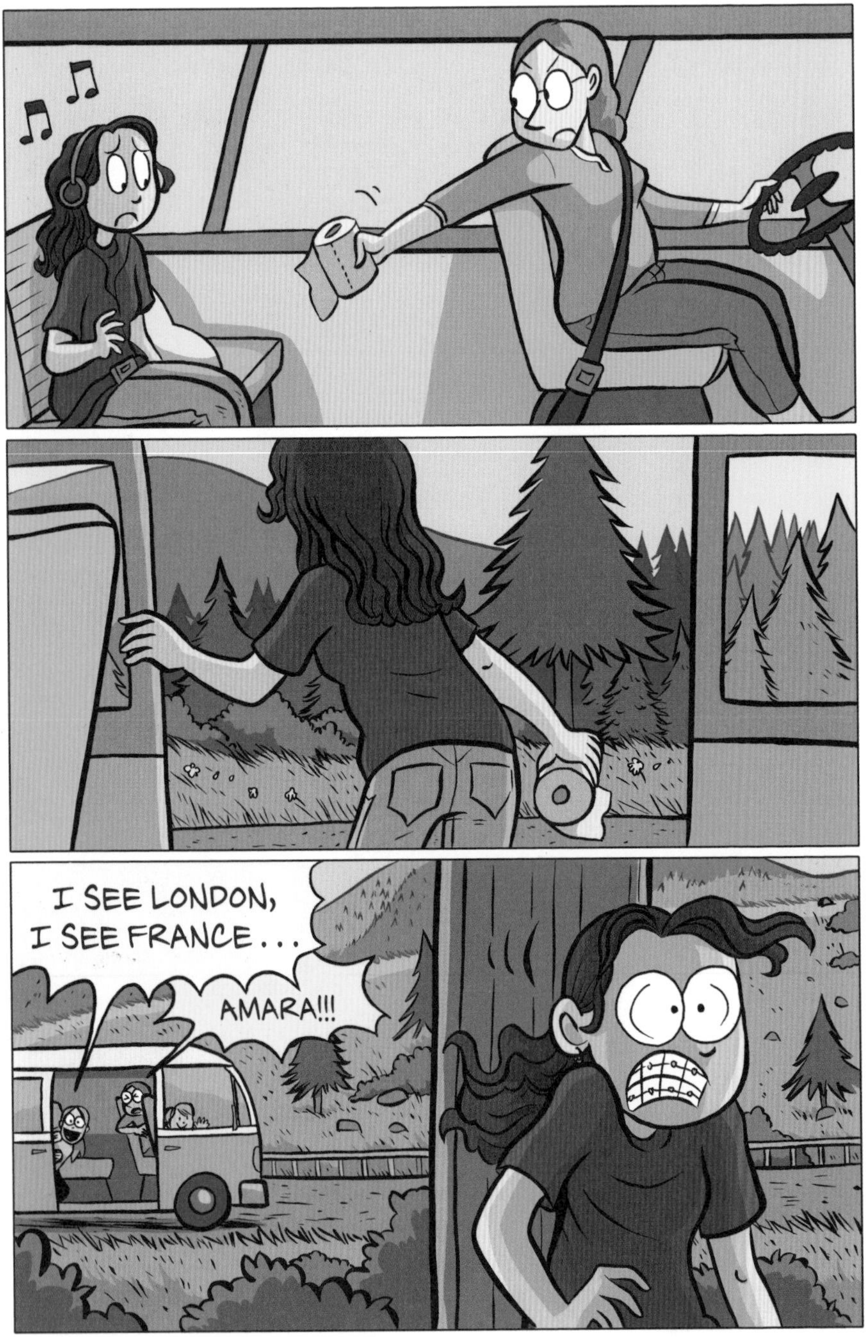

I SEE LONDON, I SEE FRANCE . . .
AMARA!!!

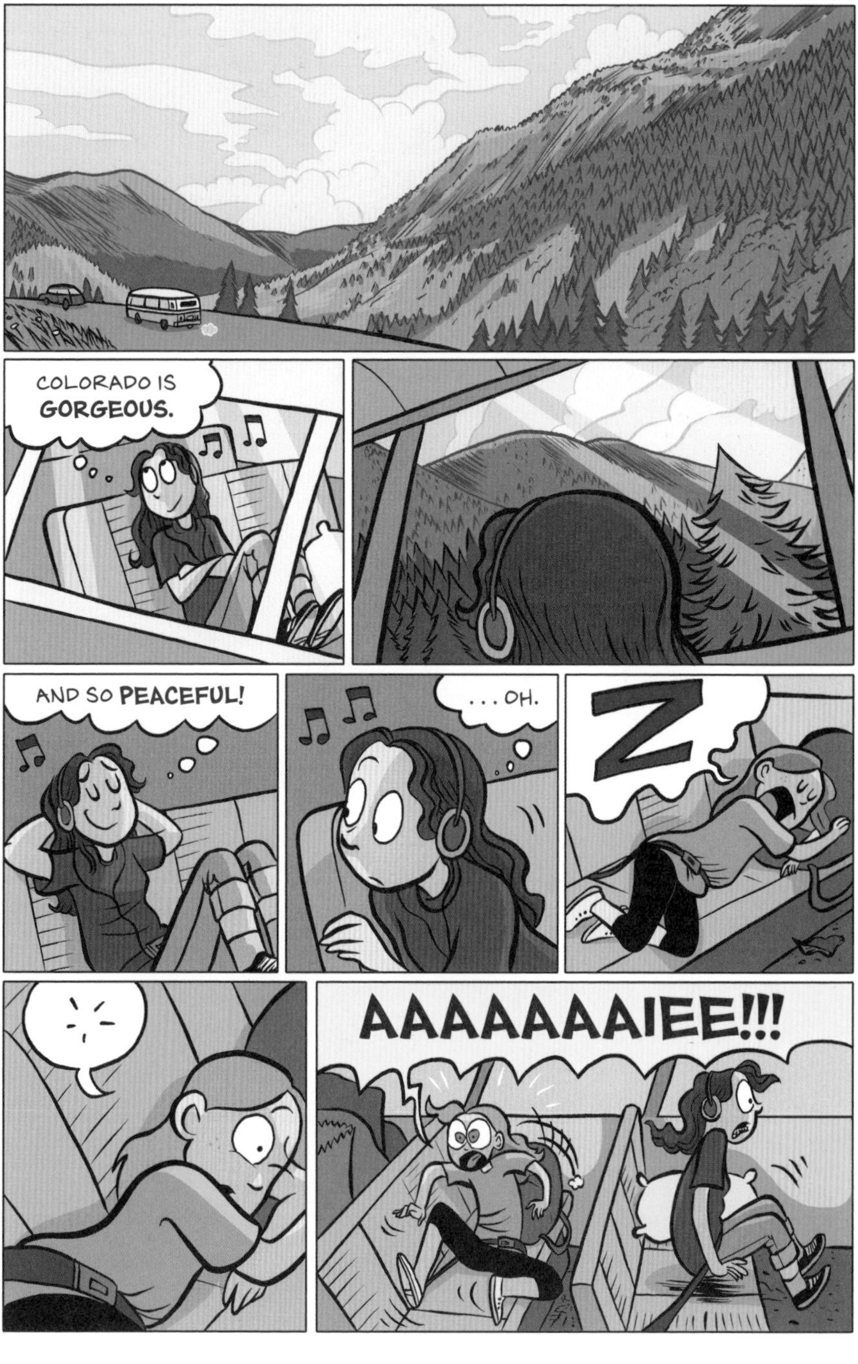
COLORADO IS GORGEOUS.
AND SO PEACEFUL!
. . . OH.
Z
AAAAAAAIEE!!!

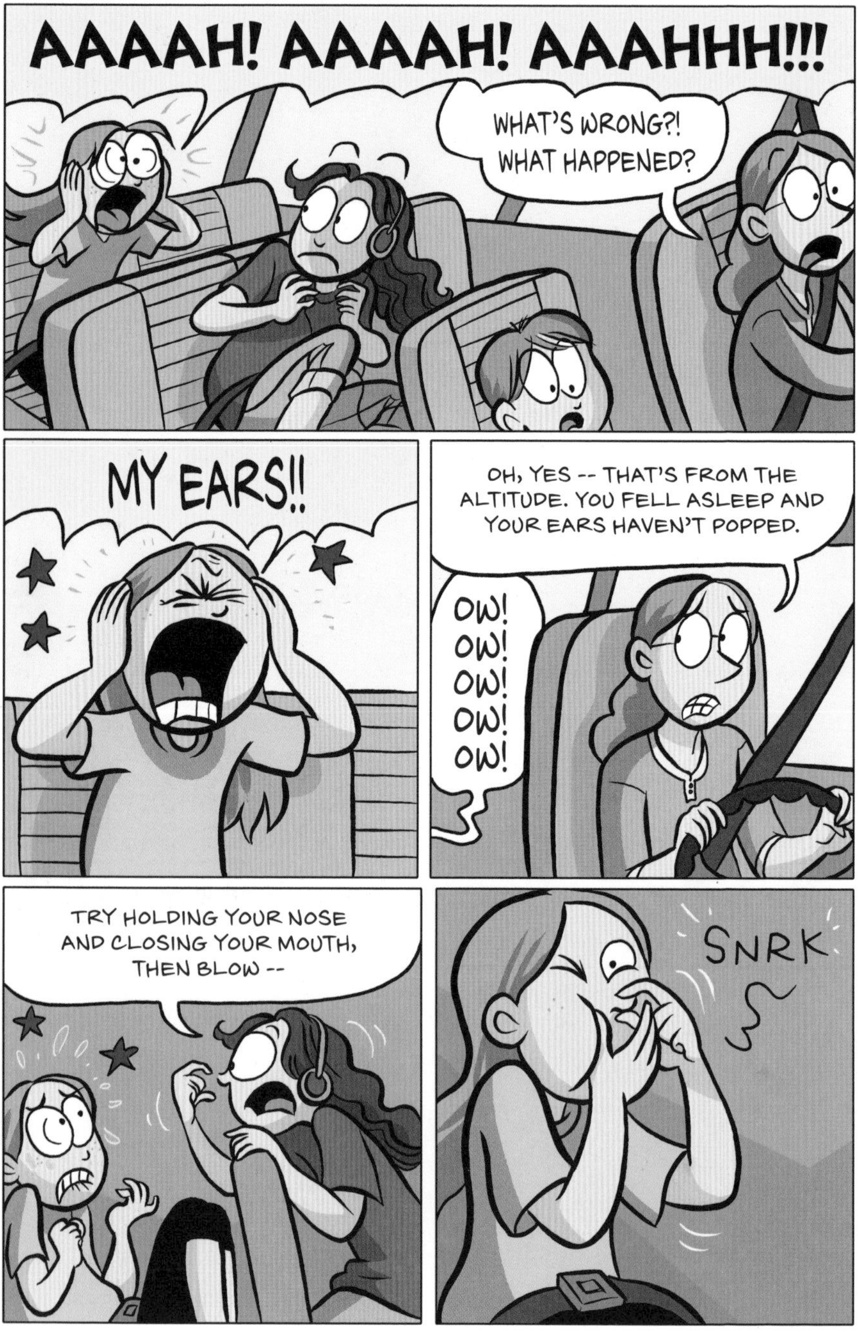
AAAAH! AAAAH! AAAHHH!!!
WHAT'S WRONG?! WHAT HAPPENED?
MY EARS!!
OH, YES -- THAT'S FROM THE ALTITUDE. YOU FELL ASLEEP AND YOUR EARS HAVEN'T POPPED.
OW! OW! OW! OW! OW!
TRY HOLDING YOUR NOSE AND CLOSING YOUR MOUTH, THEN BLOW --
SNRK

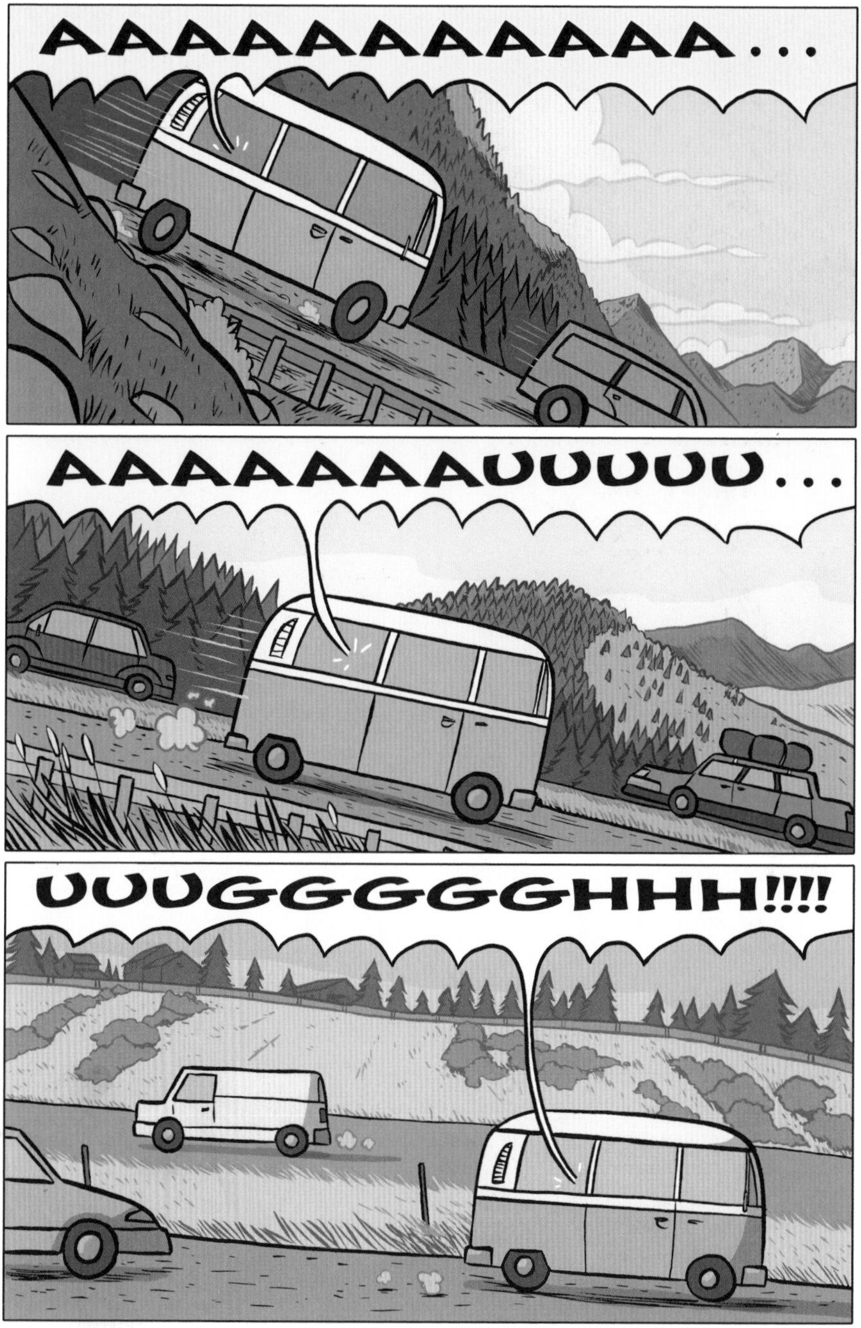
AAAAAAAAAAAA...
AAAAAAAUUUUU...
UUUGGGGGGHHH!!!!

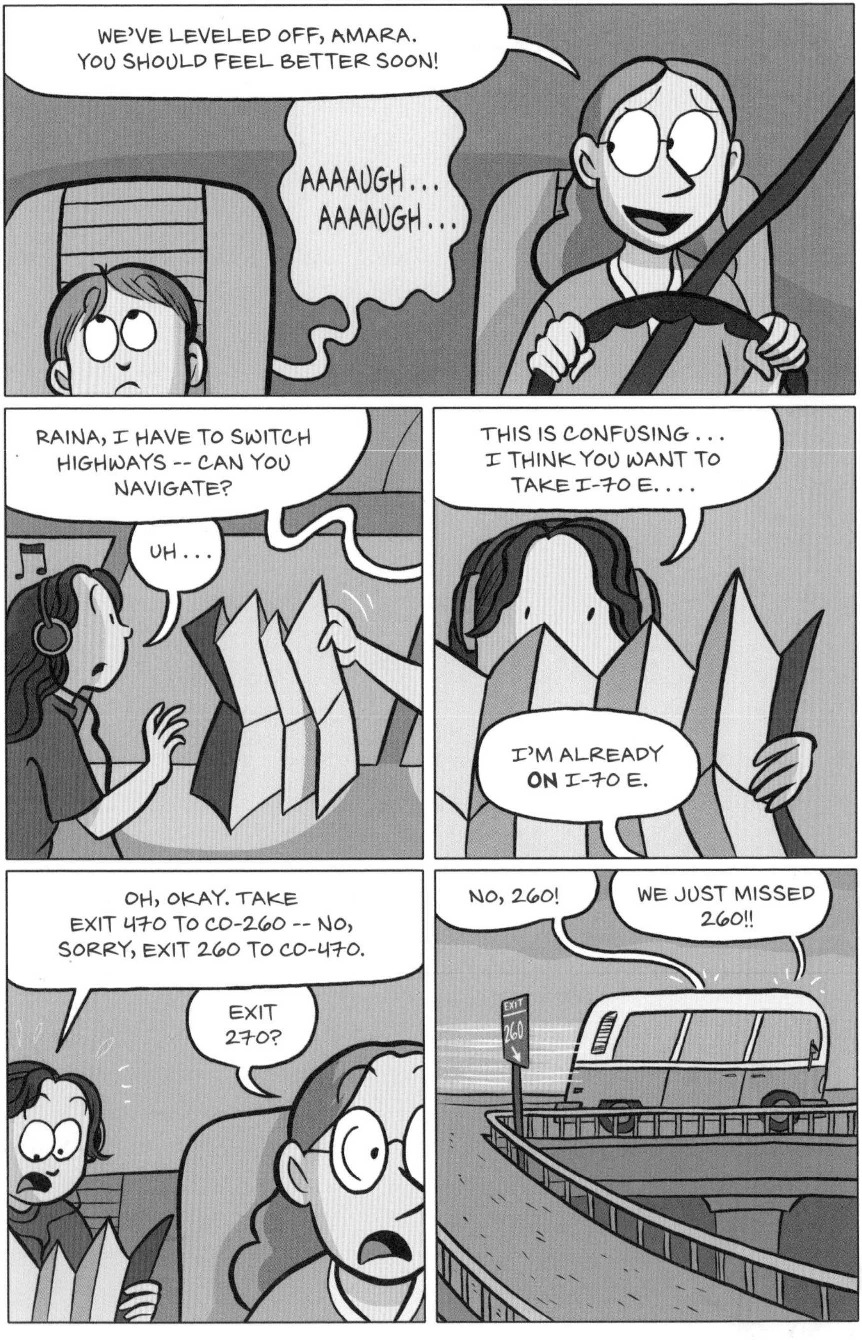
WE'VE LEVELED OFF, AMARA. YOU SHOULD FEEL BETTER SOON!
AAAAUGH... AAAAUGH...
RAINA, I HAVE TO SWITCH HIGHWAYS -- CAN YOU NAVIGATE?
UH...
THIS IS CONFUSING... I THINK YOU WANT TO TAKE I-70 E....
I'M ALREADY **ON** I-70 E.
OH, OKAY. TAKE EXIT 470 TO CO-260 -- NO, SORRY, EXIT 260 TO CO-470.
EXIT 270?
NO, 260!
WE JUST MISSED 260!!
EXIT
260

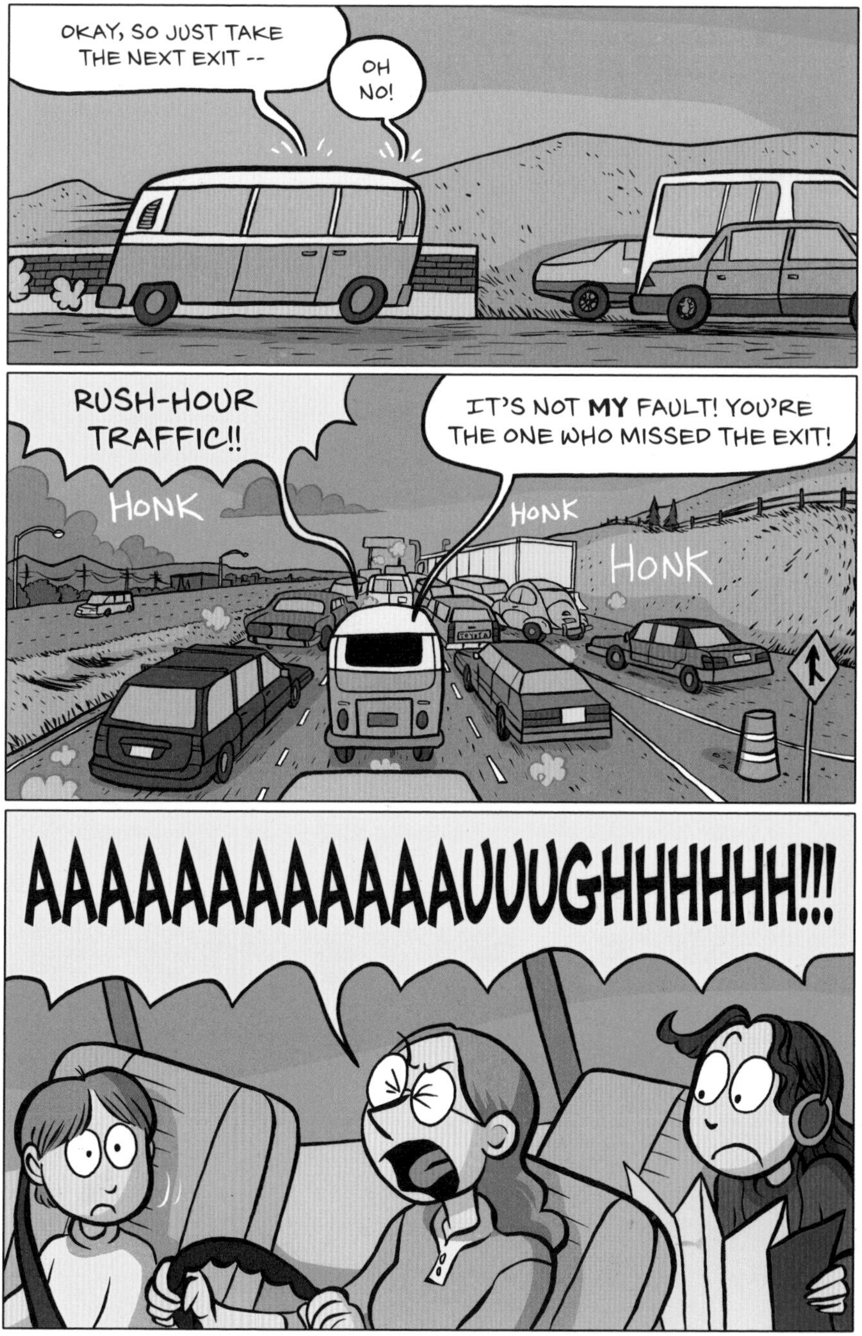
OKAY, SO JUST TAKE THE NEXT EXIT --
OH NO!
RUSH-HOUR TRAFFIC!!
IT'S NOT **MY** FAULT! YOU'RE THE ONE WHO MISSED THE EXIT!
HONK
HONK
HONK
AAAAAAAAAAAAUUUGHHHHHH!!!

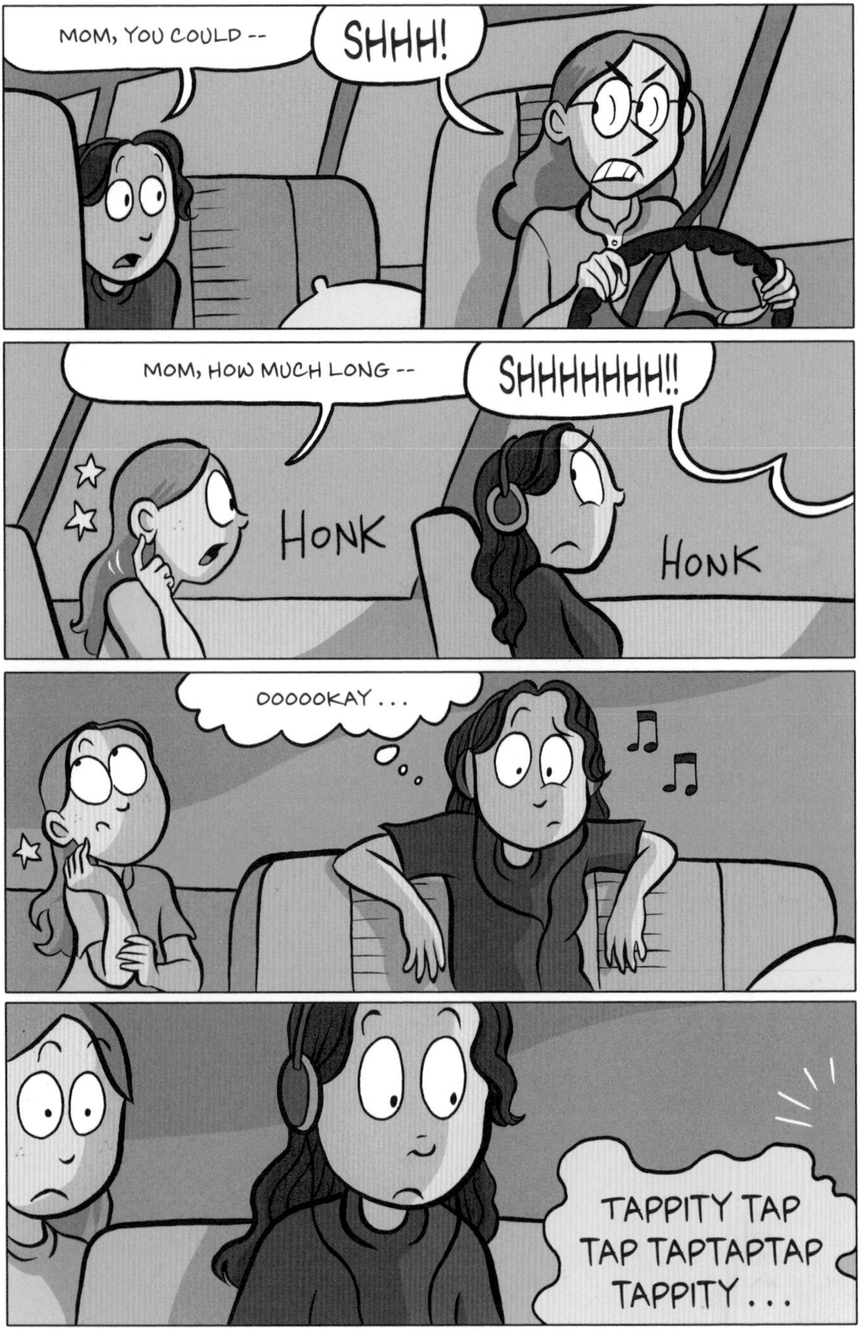
MOM, YOU COULD --
SHHH!
MOM, HOW MUCH LONG --
SHHHHHHH!!
HONK
HONK
OOOOOKAY . . .
TAPPITY TAP
TAP TAPTAPTAP
TAPPITY . . .

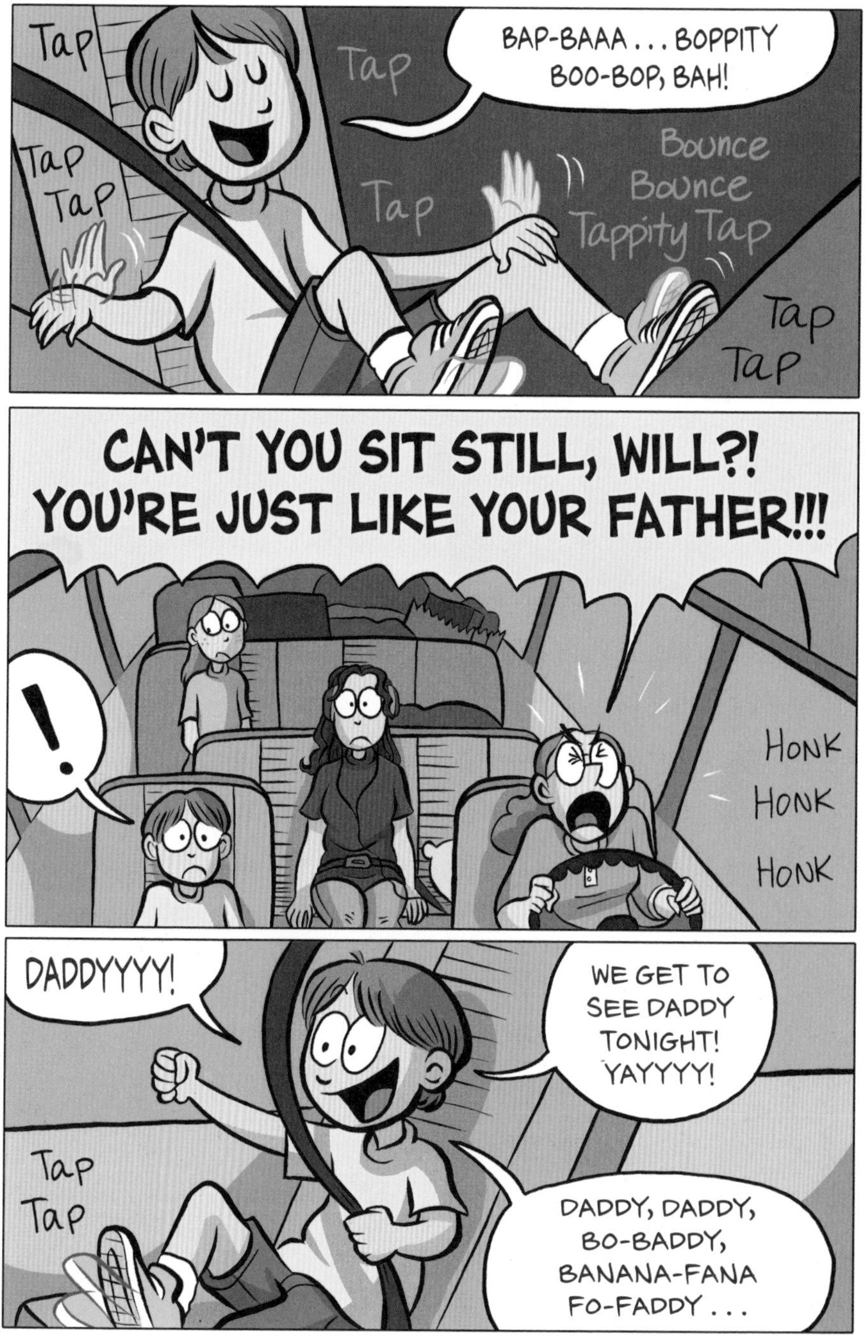
Tap
Tap
BAP-BAAA . . . BOPPITY BOO-BOP, BAH!
Tap Tap
Tap
Bounce Bounce Tappity Tap
Tap Tap
CAN'T YOU SIT STILL, WILL?! YOU'RE JUST LIKE YOUR FATHER!!!
!
HONK HONK HONK
DADDYYYY!
WE GET TO SEE DADDY TONIGHT! YAYYYY!
Tap Tap
DADDY, DADDY, BO-BADDY, BANANA-FANA FO-FADDY . . .

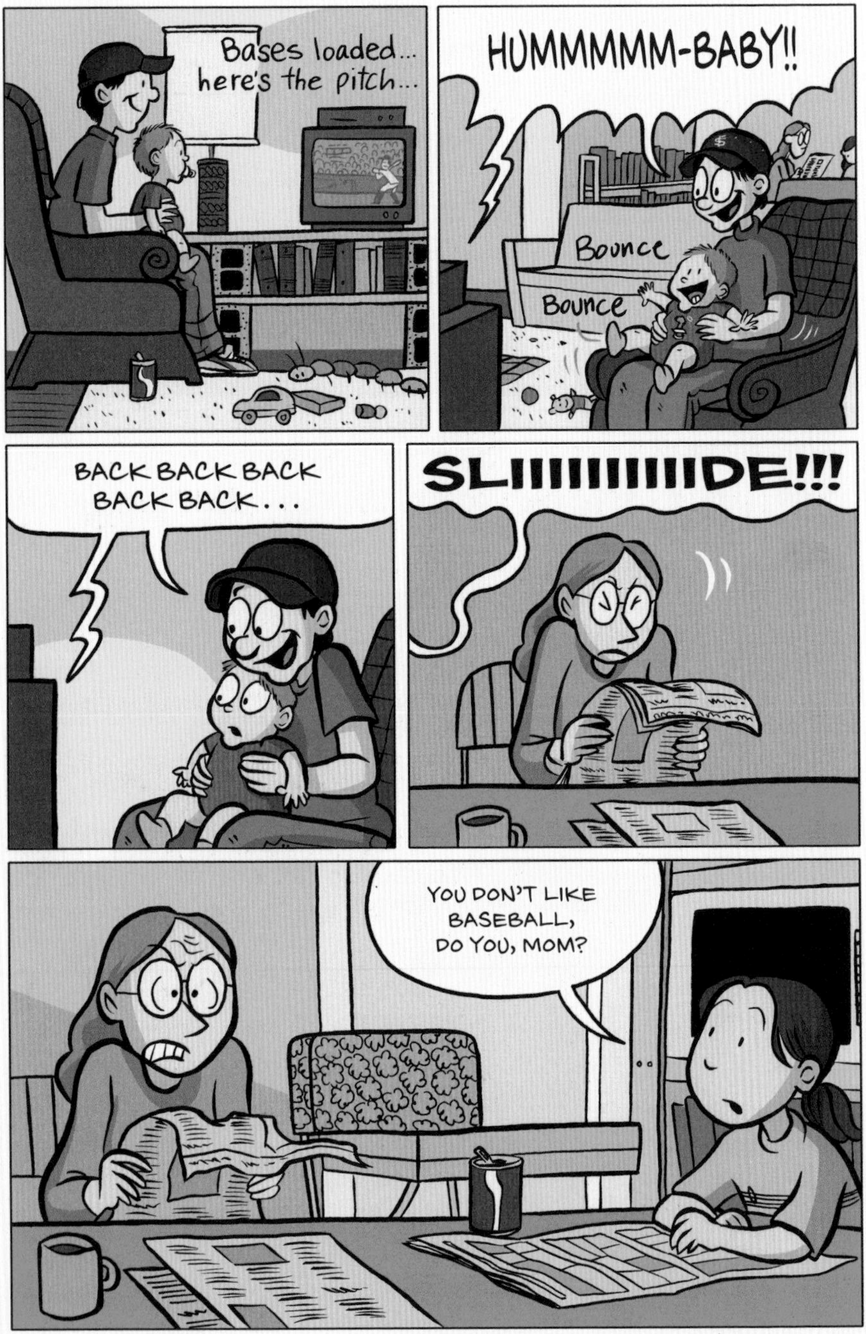

Bases loaded... here's the pitch...
HUMMMMM-BABY!!
Bounce
Bounce
BACK BACK BACK BACK BACK...
SLIIIIIIIIIDE!!!
YOU DON'T LIKE BASEBALL, DO YOU, MOM?

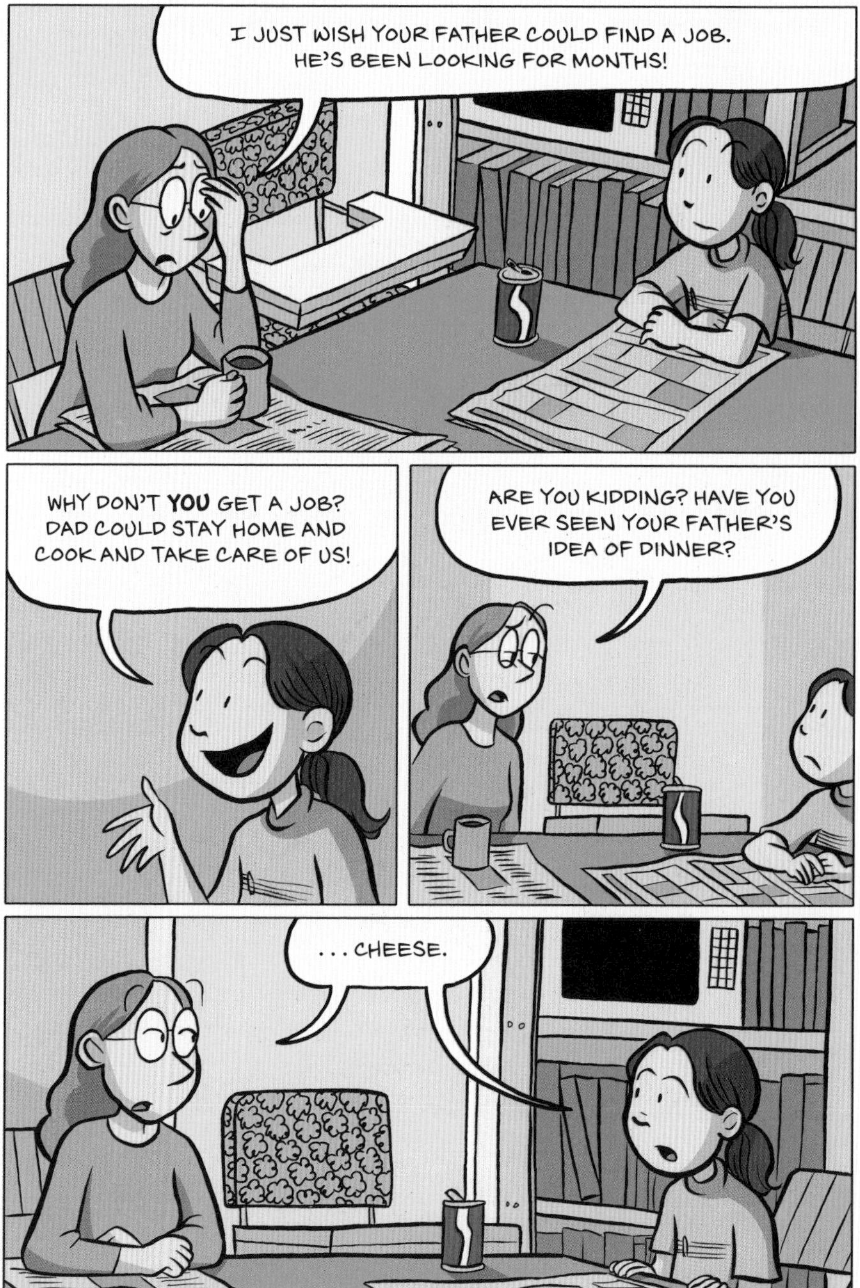
I JUST WISH YOUR FATHER COULD FIND A JOB. HE'S BEEN LOOKING FOR MONTHS!
WHY DON'T **YOU** GET A JOB? DAD COULD STAY HOME AND COOK AND TAKE CARE OF US!
ARE YOU KIDDING? HAVE YOU EVER SEEN YOUR FATHER'S IDEA OF DINNER?
. . . CHEESE.

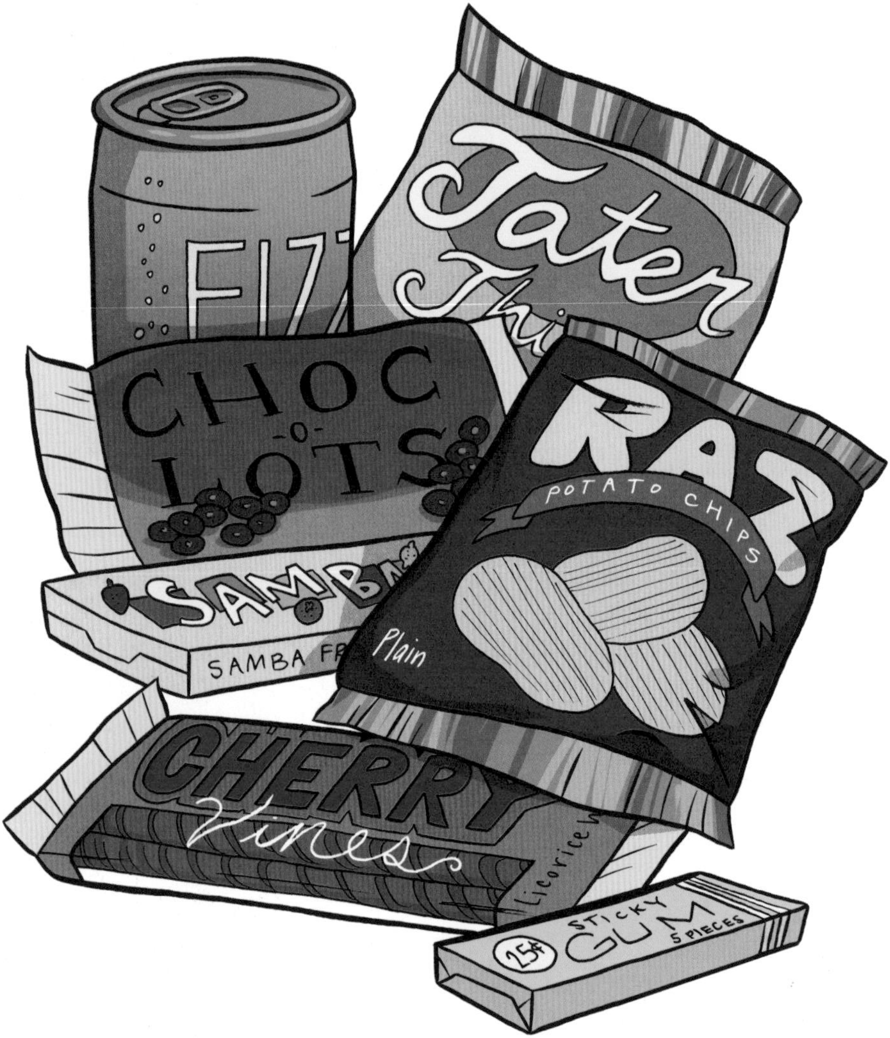
FIZZ
Tater Thi
CHOC -O- LOTS
RAZ
POTATO CHIPS
Plain
SAMBA
SAMBA FR
CHERRY
Vines
Licorice
STICKY GUM
5 PIECES
25¢

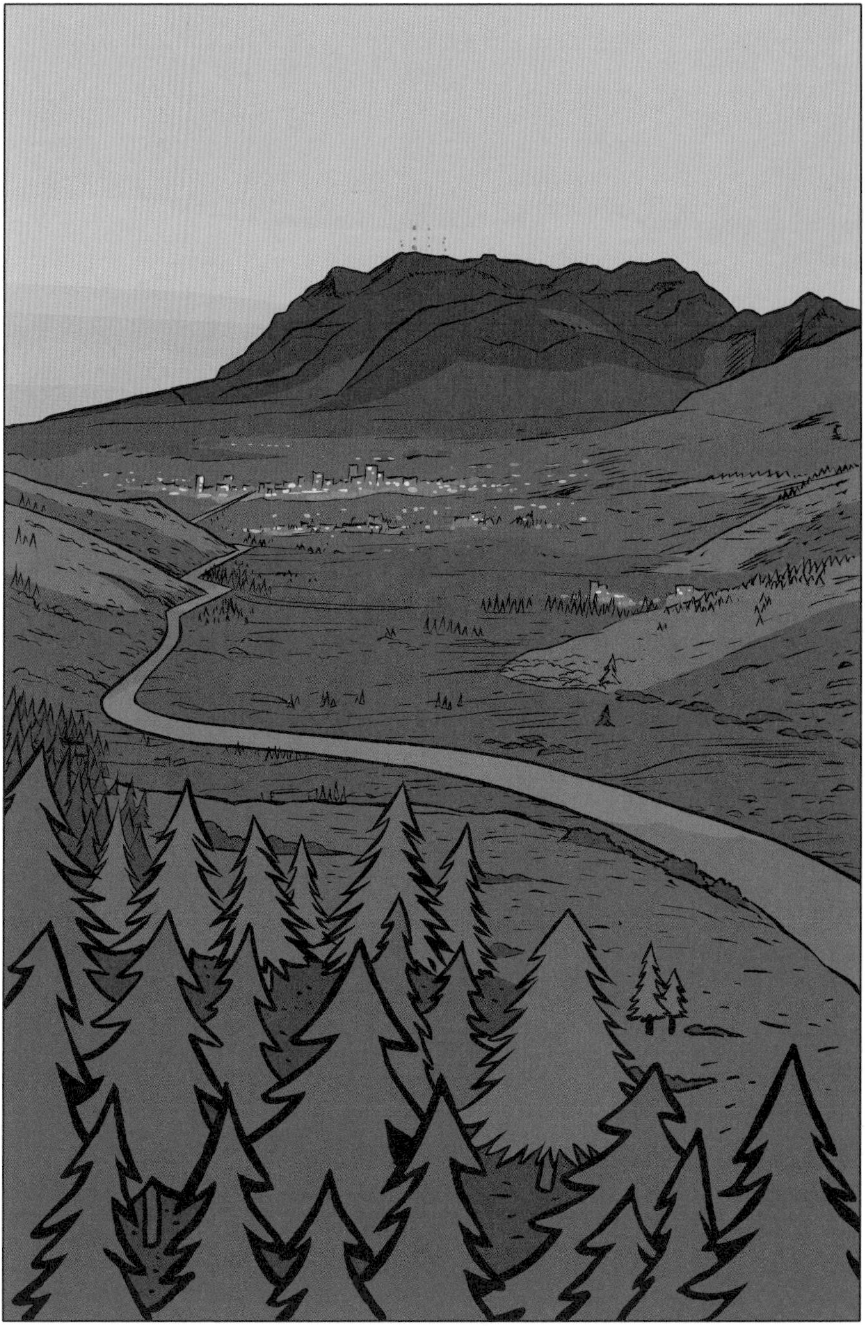

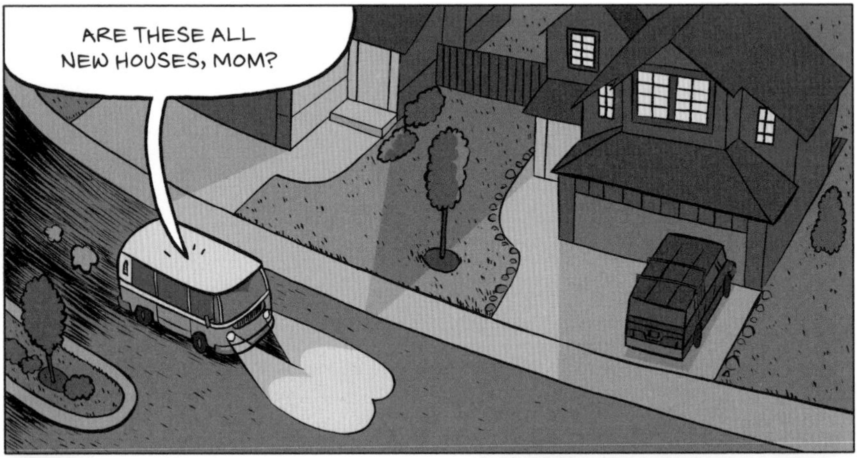
ARE THESE ALL NEW HOUSES, MOM?

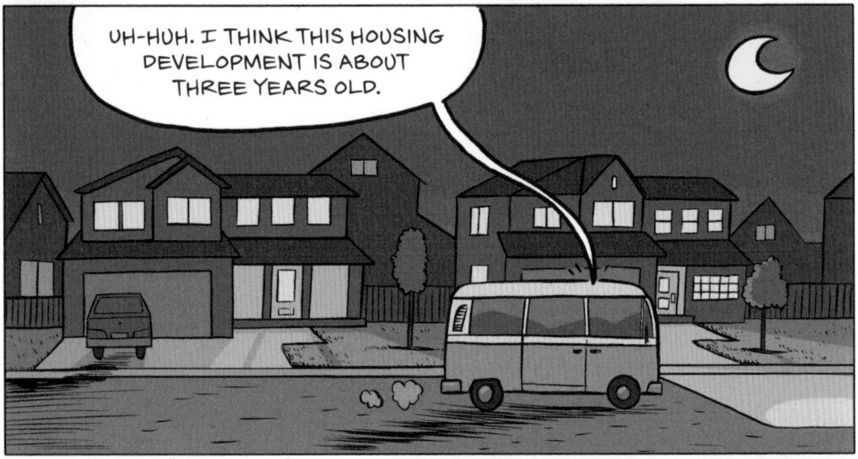
UH-HUH. I THINK THIS HOUSING DEVELOPMENT IS ABOUT THREE YEARS OLD.

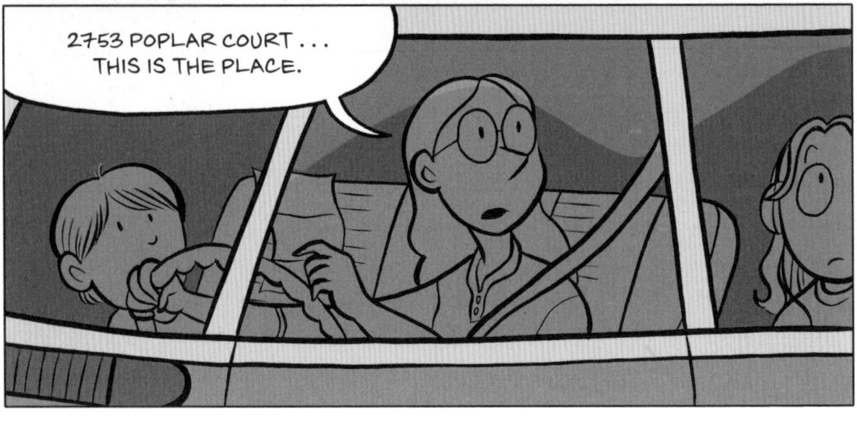
2753 POPLAR COURT . . . THIS IS THE PLACE.

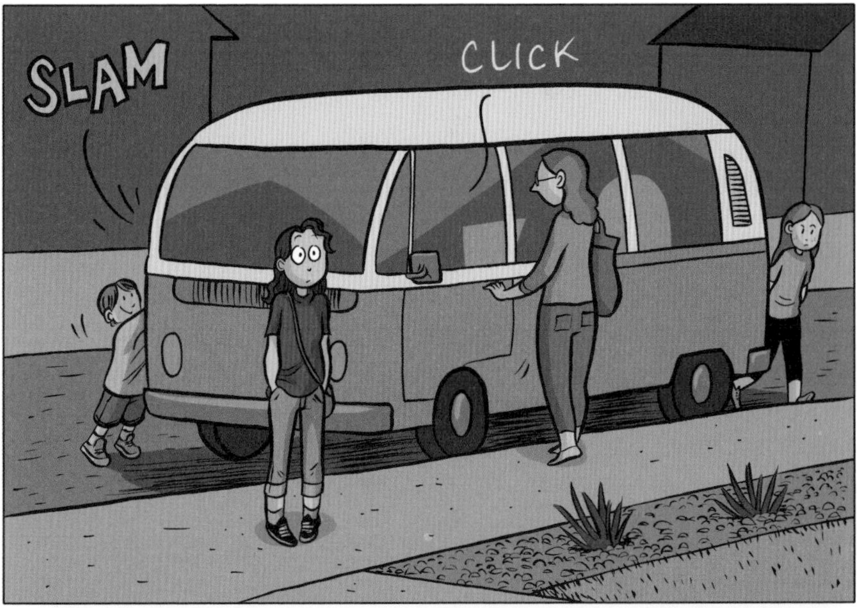
SLAM
CLICK

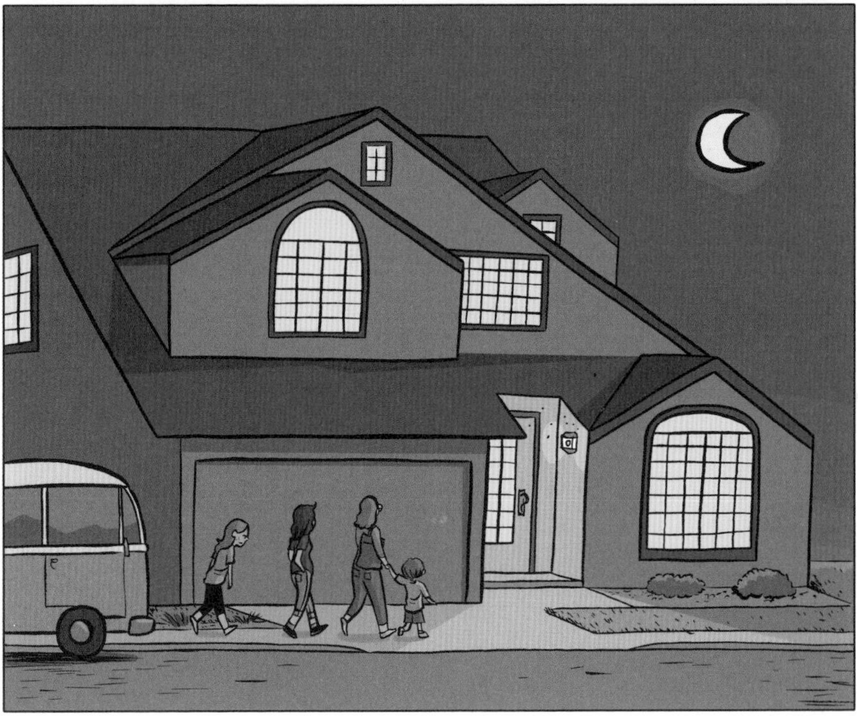

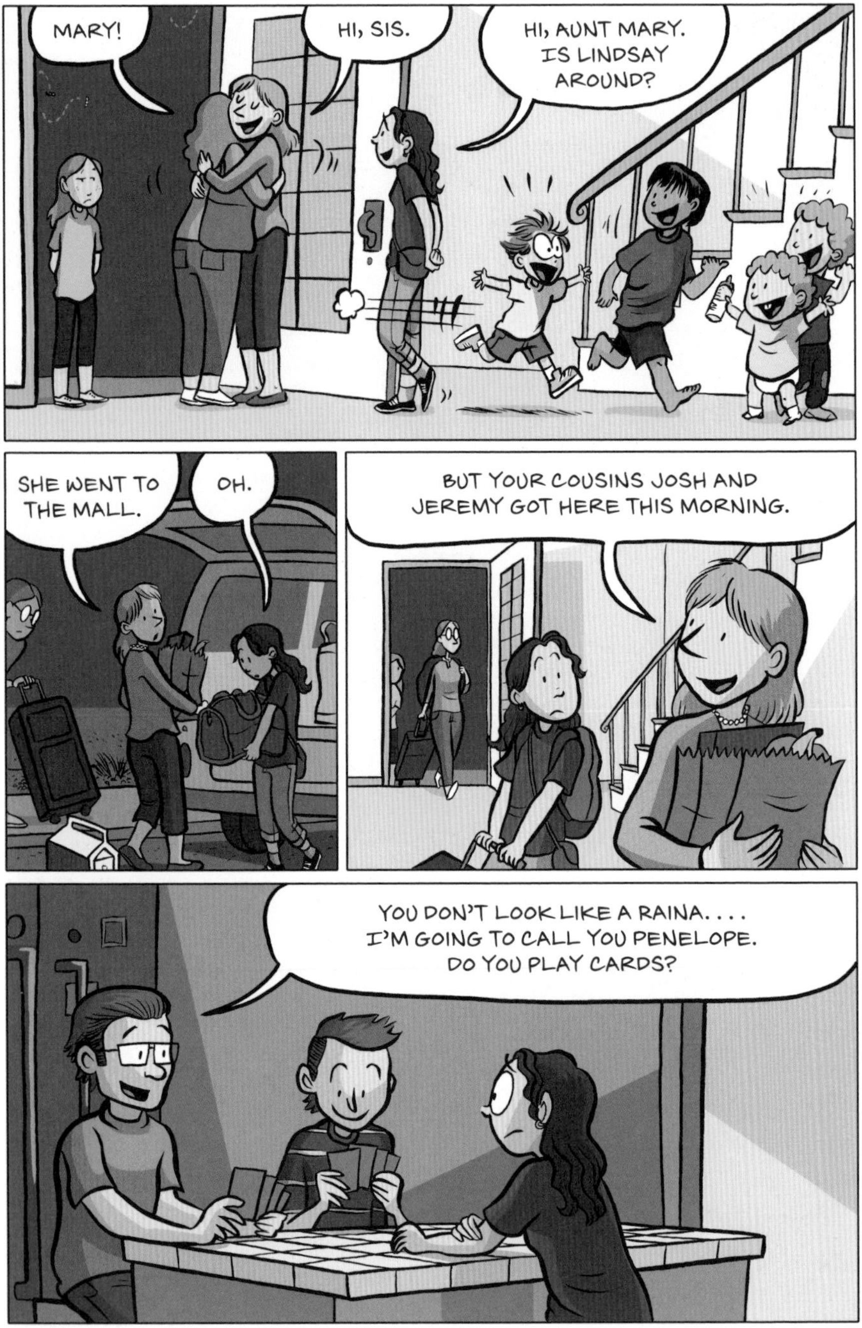
MARY!
HI, SIS.
HI, AUNT MARY. IS LINDSAY AROUND?
SHE WENT TO THE MALL.
OH.
BUT YOUR COUSINS JOSH AND JEREMY GOT HERE THIS MORNING.
YOU DON'T LOOK LIKE A RAINA. . . .
I'M GOING TO CALL YOU PENELOPE.
DO YOU PLAY CARDS?

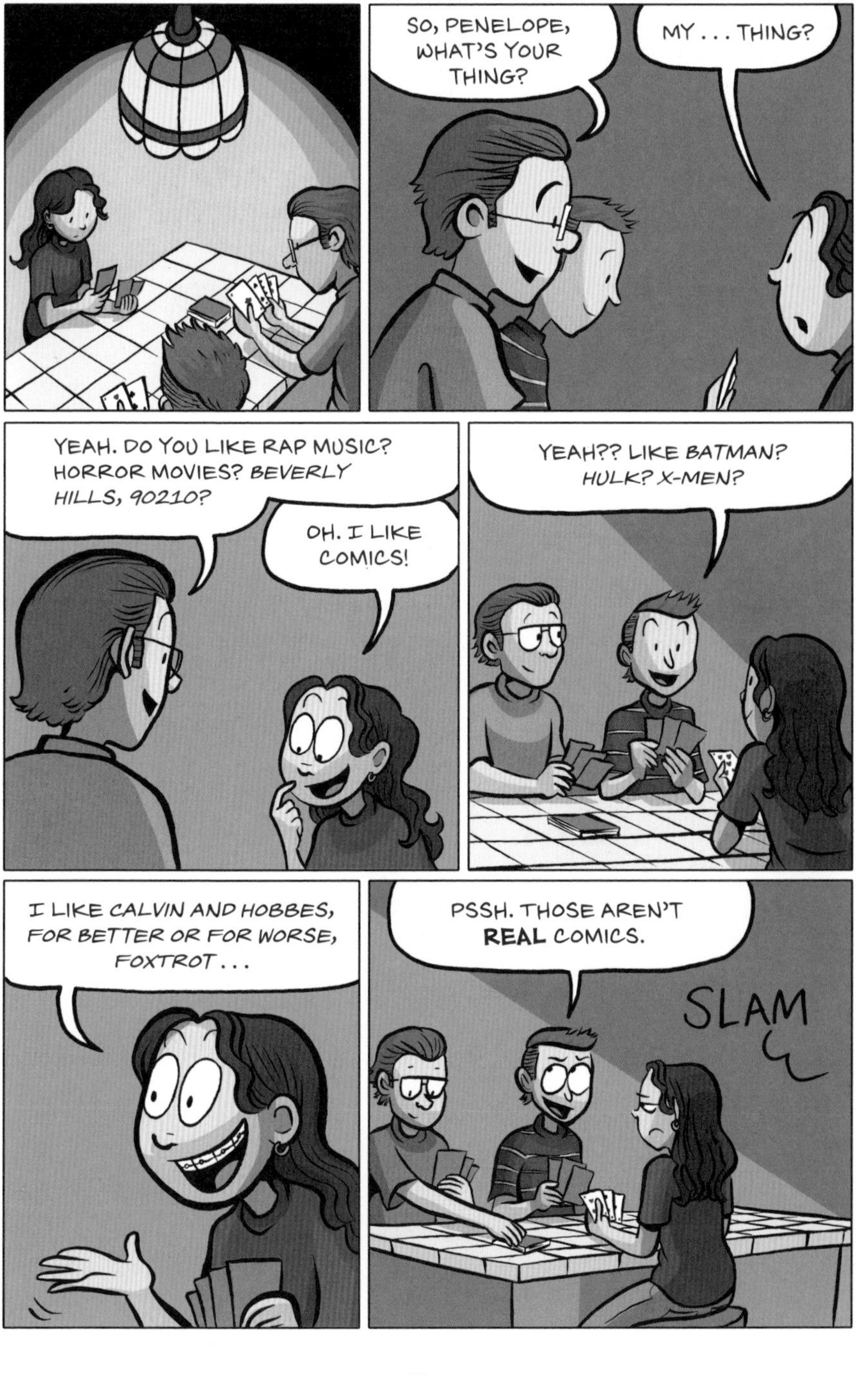
SO, PENELOPE, WHAT'S YOUR THING?
MY . . . THING?
YEAH. DO YOU LIKE RAP MUSIC? HORROR MOVIES? *BEVERLY HILLS, 90210?*
OH. I LIKE COMICS!
YEAH?? LIKE *BATMAN? HULK? X-MEN?*
I LIKE *CALVIN AND HOBBES, FOR BETTER OR FOR WORSE, FOXTROT . . .*
PSSH. THOSE AREN'T **REAL** COMICS.
SLAM

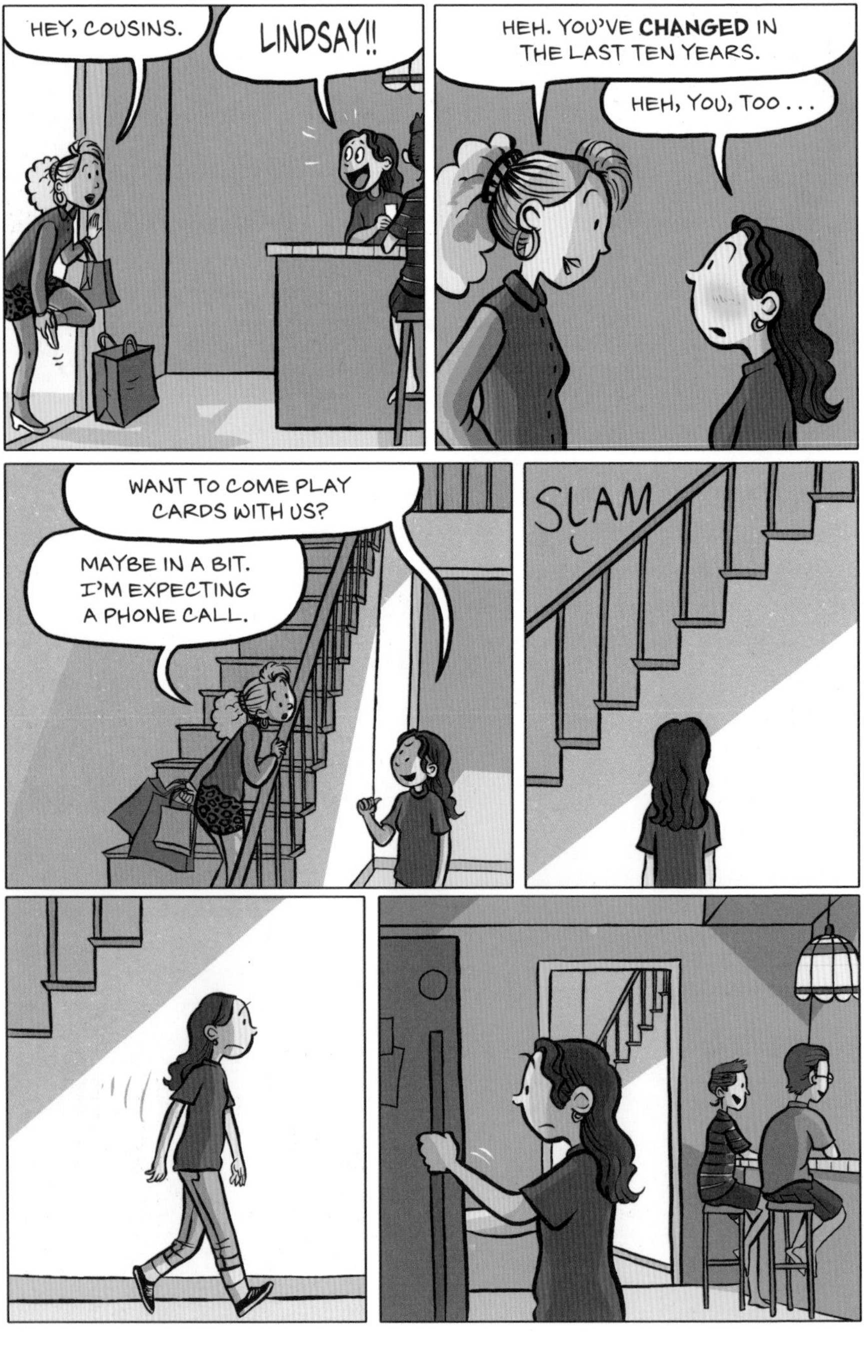
HEY, COUSINS.
LINDSAY!!
HEH. YOU'VE **CHANGED** IN THE LAST TEN YEARS.
HEH, YOU, TOO . . .
WANT TO COME PLAY CARDS WITH US?
MAYBE IN A BIT. I'M EXPECTING A PHONE CALL.
SLAM

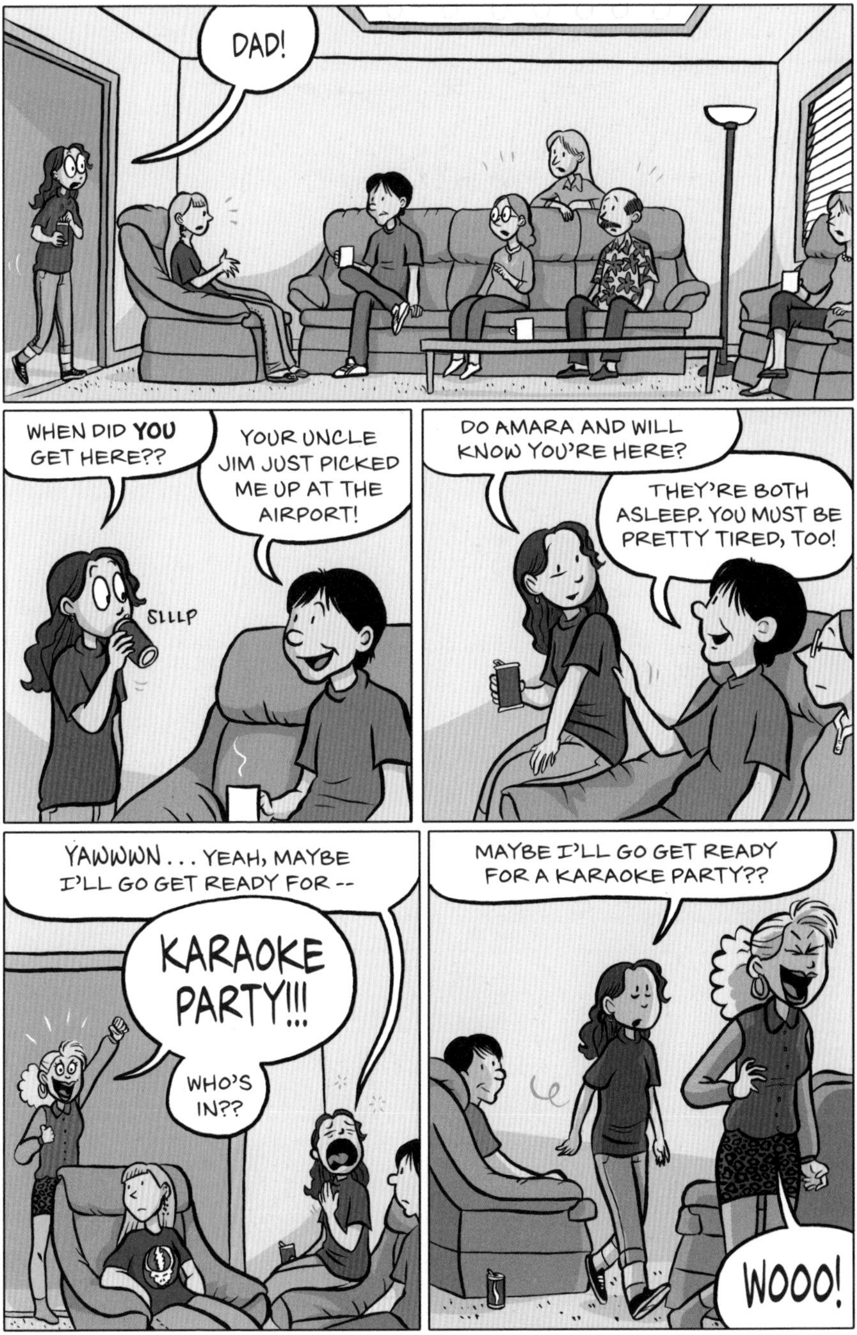
DAD!
WHEN DID **YOU** GET HERE??
YOUR UNCLE JIM JUST PICKED ME UP AT THE AIRPORT!
SLLLP
DO AMARA AND WILL KNOW YOU'RE HERE?
THEY'RE BOTH ASLEEP. YOU MUST BE PRETTY TIRED, TOO!
YAWWWN . . . YEAH, MAYBE I'LL GO GET READY FOR --
KARAOKE PARTY!!!
WHO'S IN??
MAYBE I'LL GO GET READY FOR A KARAOKE PARTY??
WOOO!

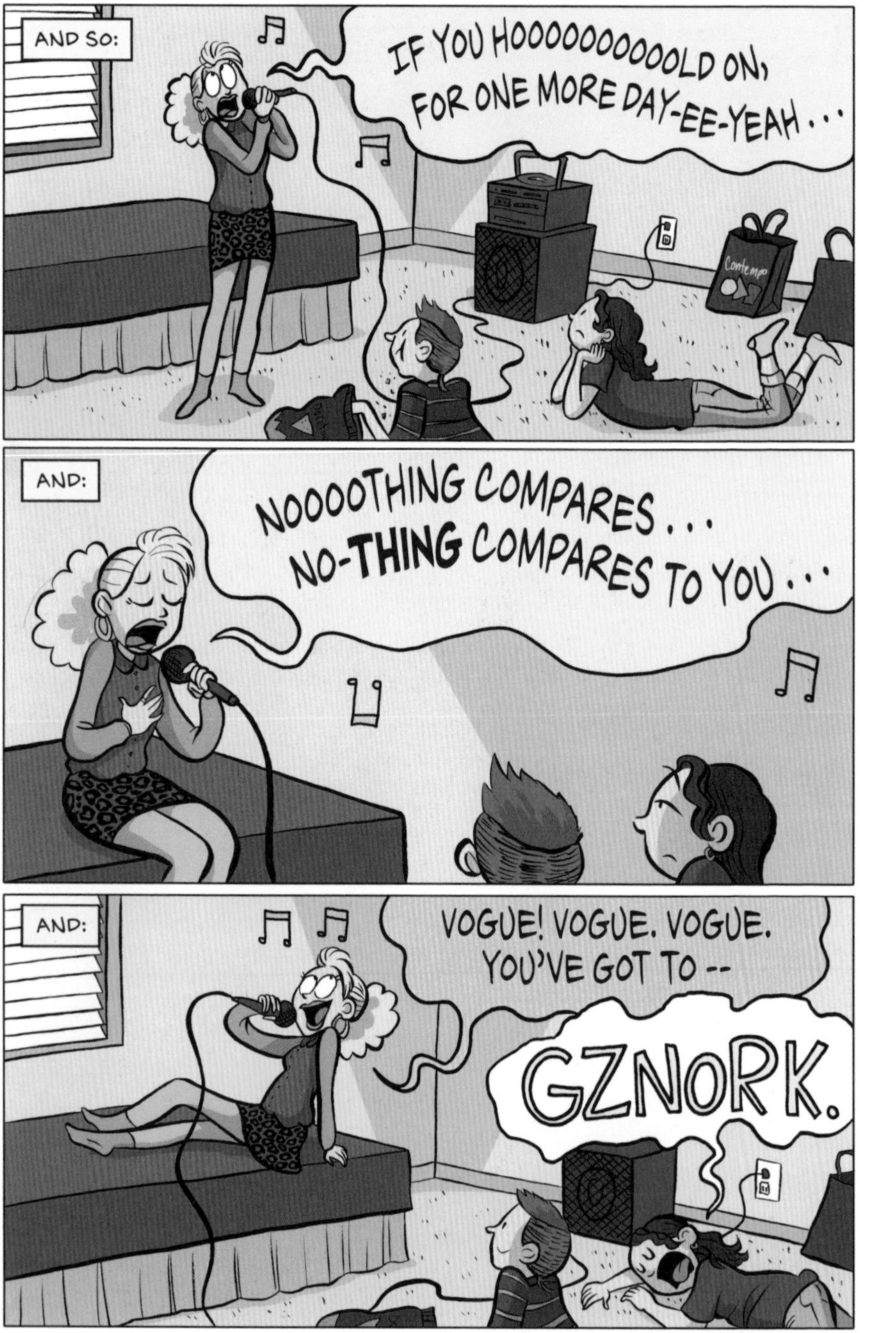
AND SO:
IF YOU HOOOOOOOOOOLD ON, FOR ONE MORE DAY-EE-YEAH . . .
Contempo
AND:
NOOOOTHING COMPARES . . . NO-**THING** COMPARES TO YOU . . .
AND:
VOGUE! VOGUE. VOGUE. YOU'VE GOT TO --
GZNORK.

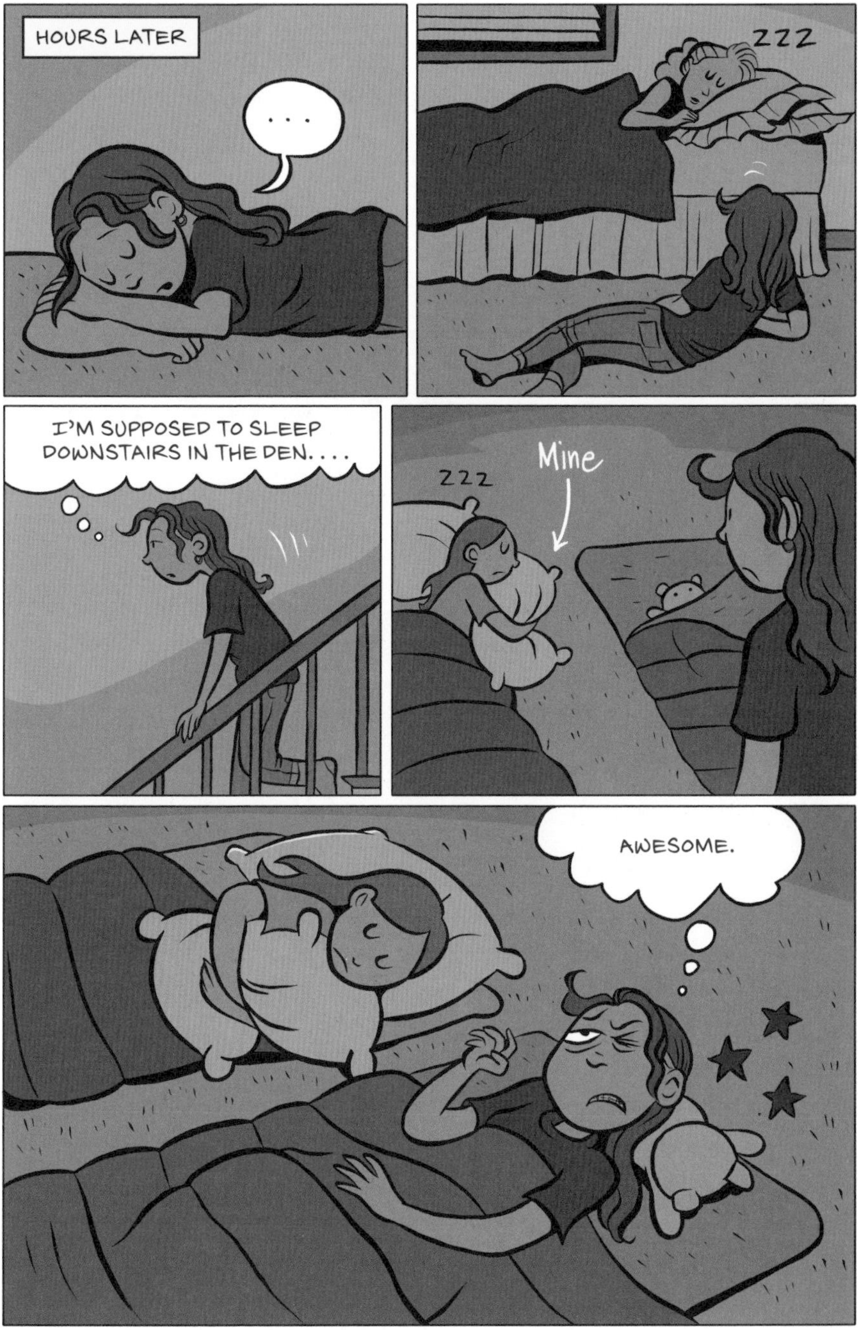
HOURS LATER
. . . .
ZZZ
I'M SUPPOSED TO SLEEP DOWNSTAIRS IN THE DEN. . . .
ZZZ
Mine
AWESOME.

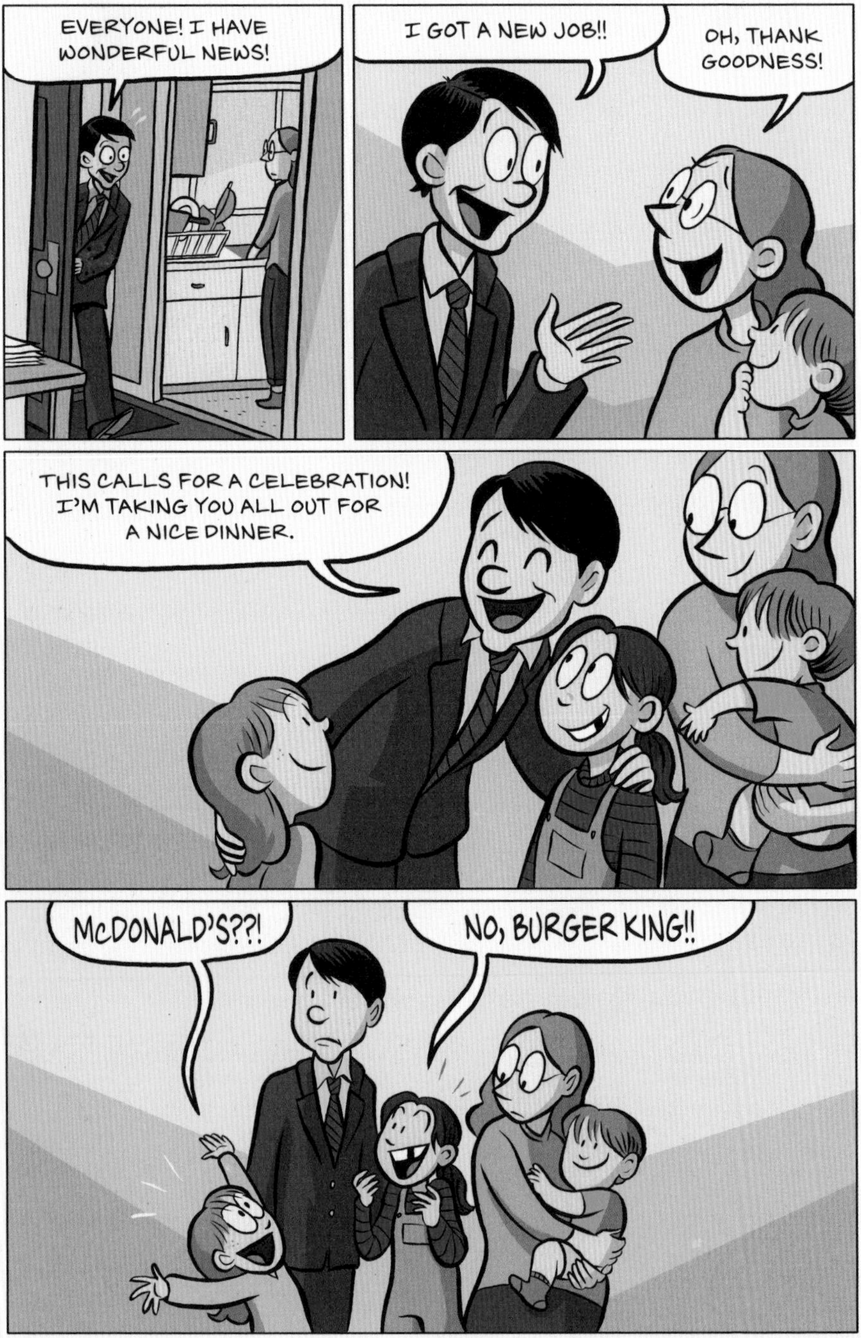
EVERYONE! I HAVE WONDERFUL NEWS!
I GOT A NEW JOB!!
OH, THANK GOODNESS!
THIS CALLS FOR A CELEBRATION! I'M TAKING YOU ALL OUT FOR A NICE DINNER.
McDONALD'S??!
NO, BURGER KING!!

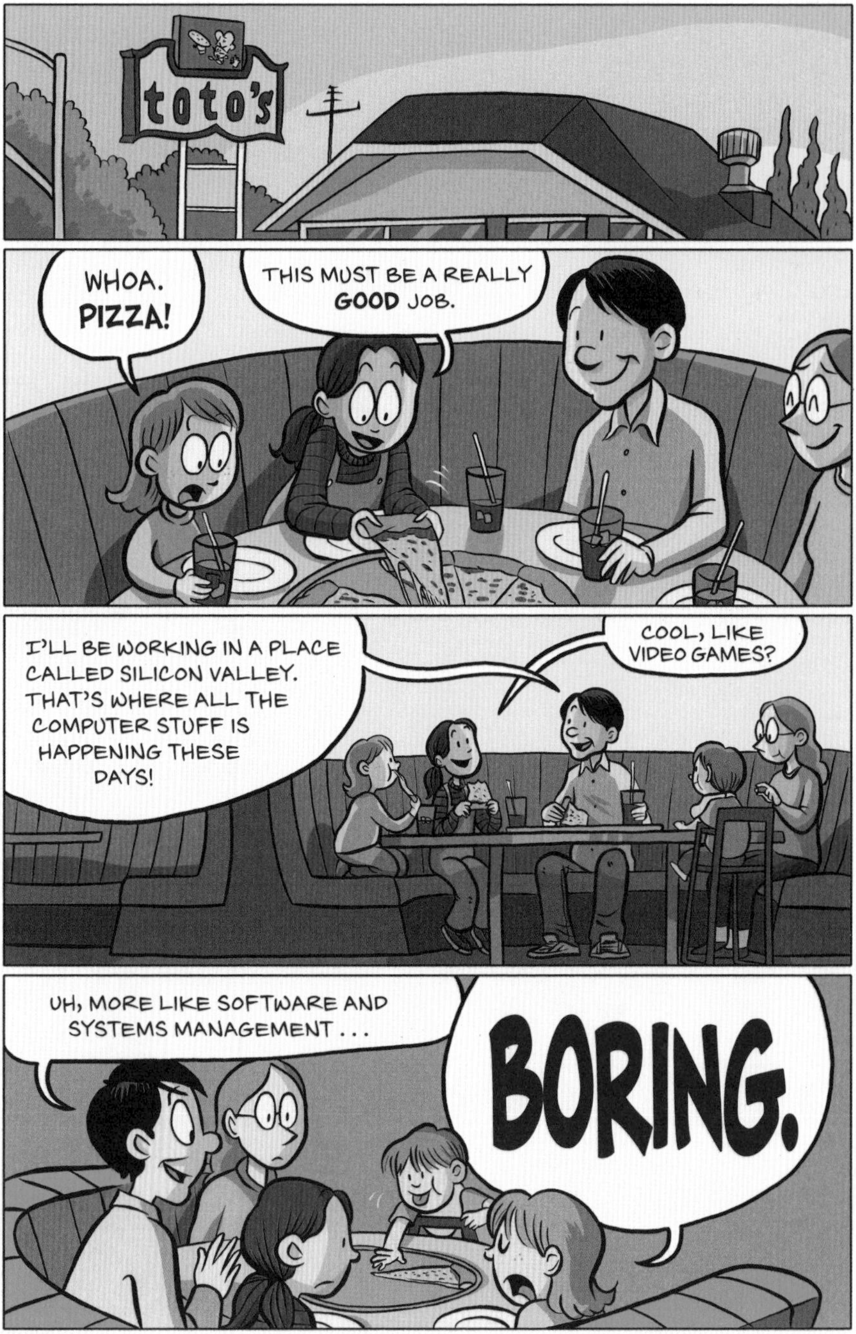
toto's
WHOA. PIZZA!
THIS MUST BE A REALLY GOOD JOB.
I'LL BE WORKING IN A PLACE CALLED SILICON VALLEY. THAT'S WHERE ALL THE COMPUTER STUFF IS HAPPENING THESE DAYS!
COOL, LIKE VIDEO GAMES?
UH, MORE LIKE SOFTWARE AND SYSTEMS MANAGEMENT . . .
BORING.

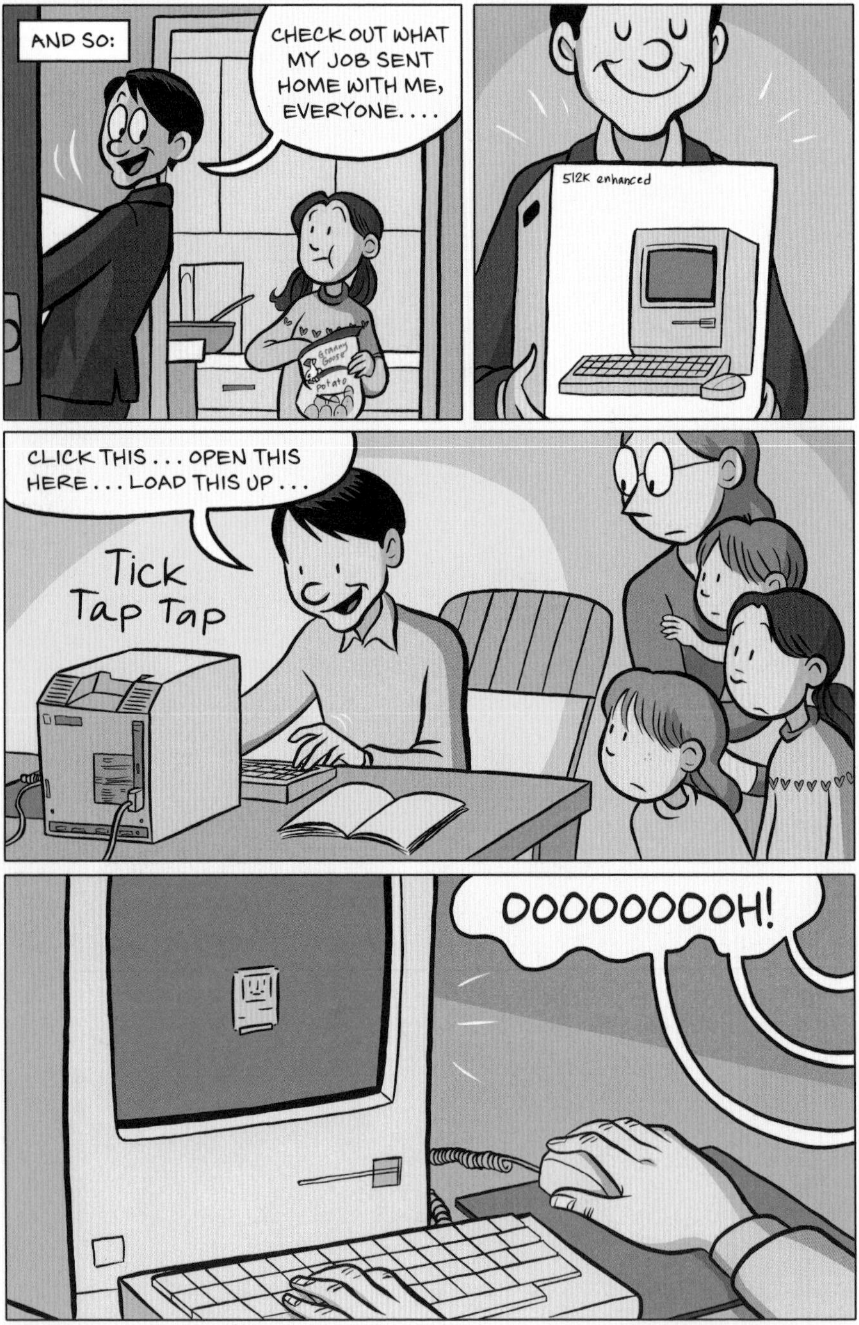
AND SO:
CHECK OUT WHAT MY JOB SENT HOME WITH ME, EVERYONE. . . .
Granny Goose
Potato
512K enhanced
CLICK THIS . . . OPEN THIS HERE . . . LOAD THIS UP . . .
Tick Tap Tap
OOOOOOOOH!

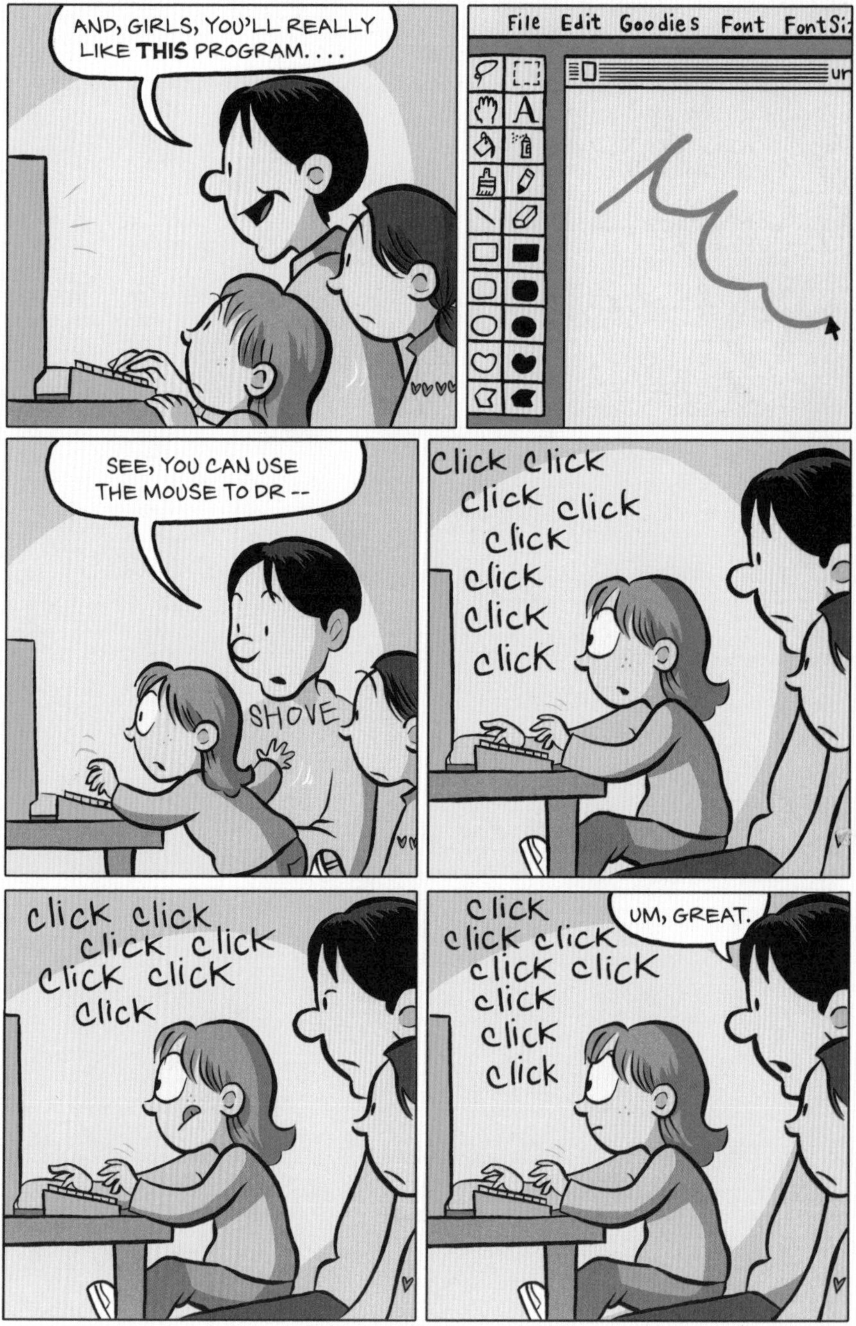
AND, GIRLS, YOU'LL REALLY LIKE THIS PROGRAM. . . .
File Edit Goodies Font FontSi
SEE, YOU CAN USE THE MOUSE TO DR --
SHOVE
Click Click click click click click click click
click click click click click click click
click click click click click click click click
UM, GREAT.

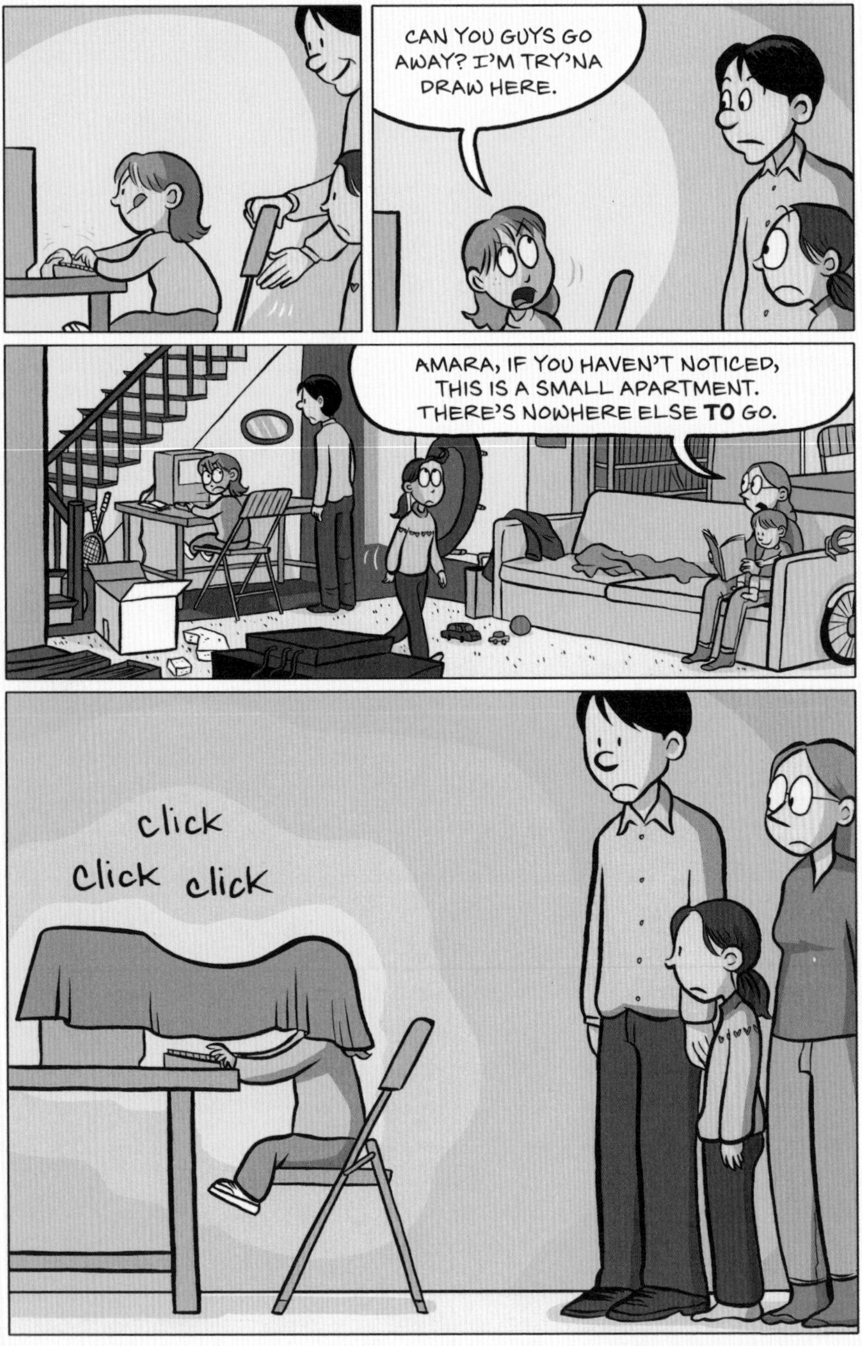
CAN YOU GUYS GO AWAY? I'M TRY'NA DRAW HERE.
AMARA, IF YOU HAVEN'T NOTICED, THIS IS A SMALL APARTMENT. THERE'S NOWHERE ELSE **TO** GO.
click
click click

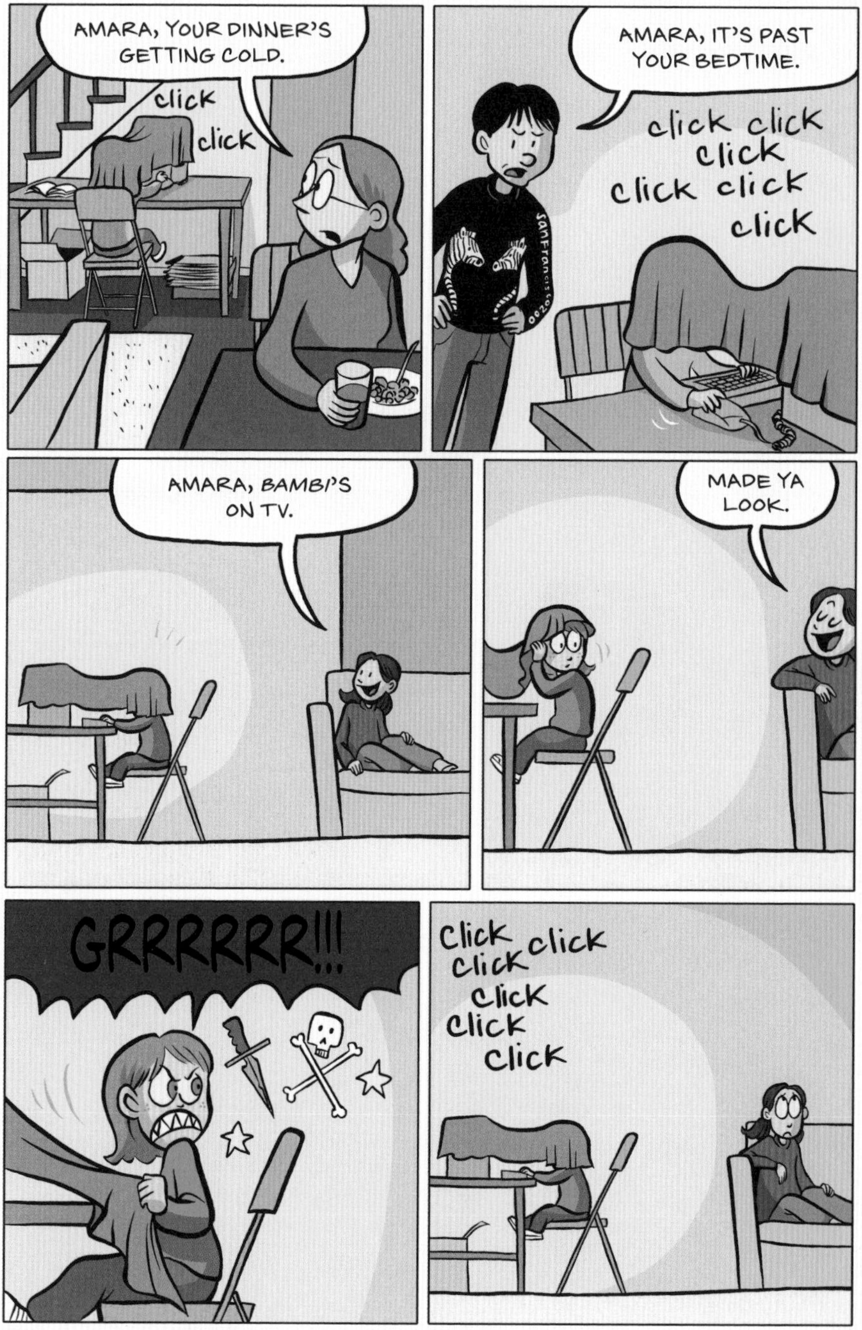
AMARA, YOUR DINNER'S GETTING COLD.
click
click
AMARA, IT'S PAST YOUR BEDTIME.
click click click click click click
AMARA, BAMBI'S ON TV.
MADE YA LOOK.
GRRRRRR!!!
click click click click click click

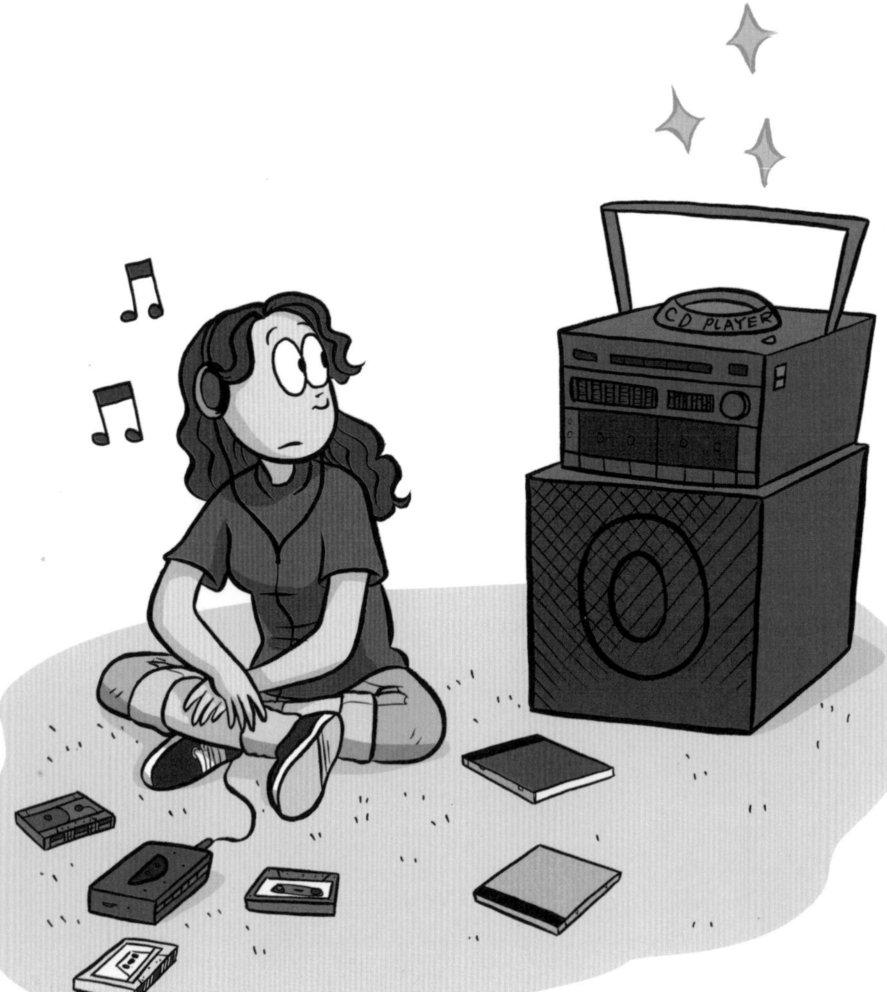
CD PLAYER

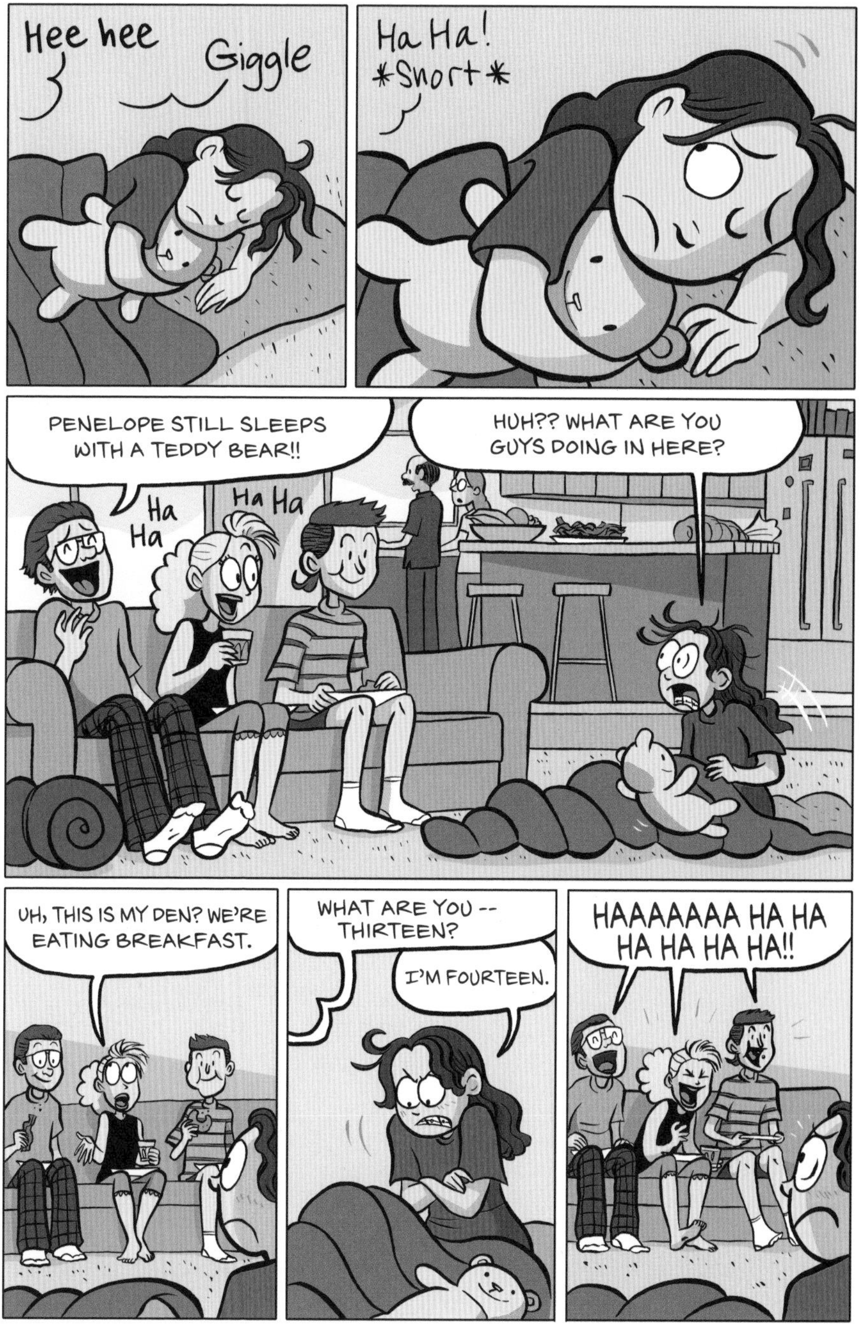
Hee hee
Giggle
Ha Ha!
Snort
PENELOPE STILL SLEEPS WITH A TEDDY BEAR!!
Ha Ha
Ha Ha
HUH?? WHAT ARE YOU GUYS DOING IN HERE?
UH, THIS IS MY DEN? WE'RE EATING BREAKFAST.
WHAT ARE YOU -- THIRTEEN?
I'M FOURTEEN.
HAAAAAAA HA HA HA HA HA HA!!

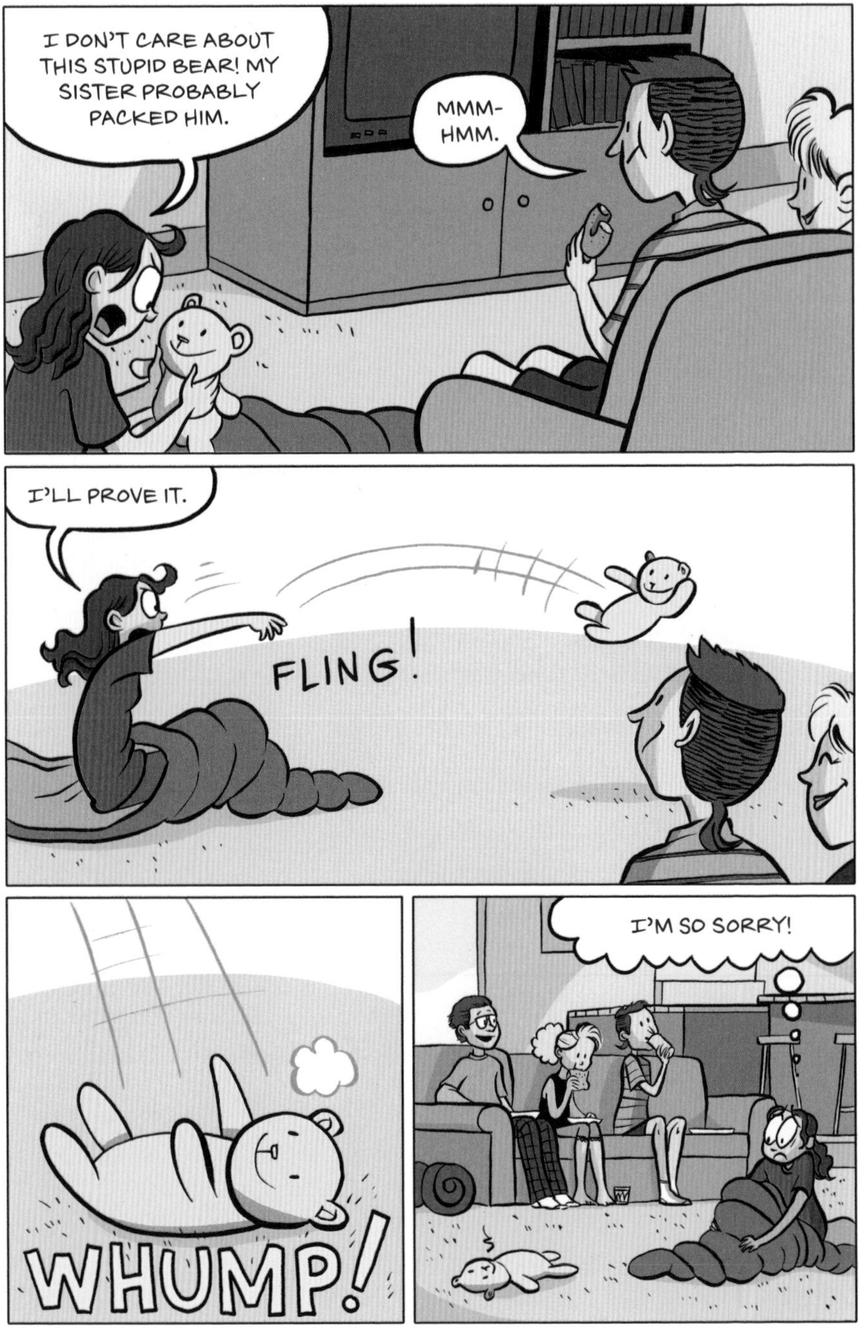
I DON'T CARE ABOUT THIS STUPID BEAR! MY SISTER PROBABLY PACKED HIM.
MMM-HMM.
I'LL PROVE IT.
FLING!
WHUMP!
I'M SO SORRY!

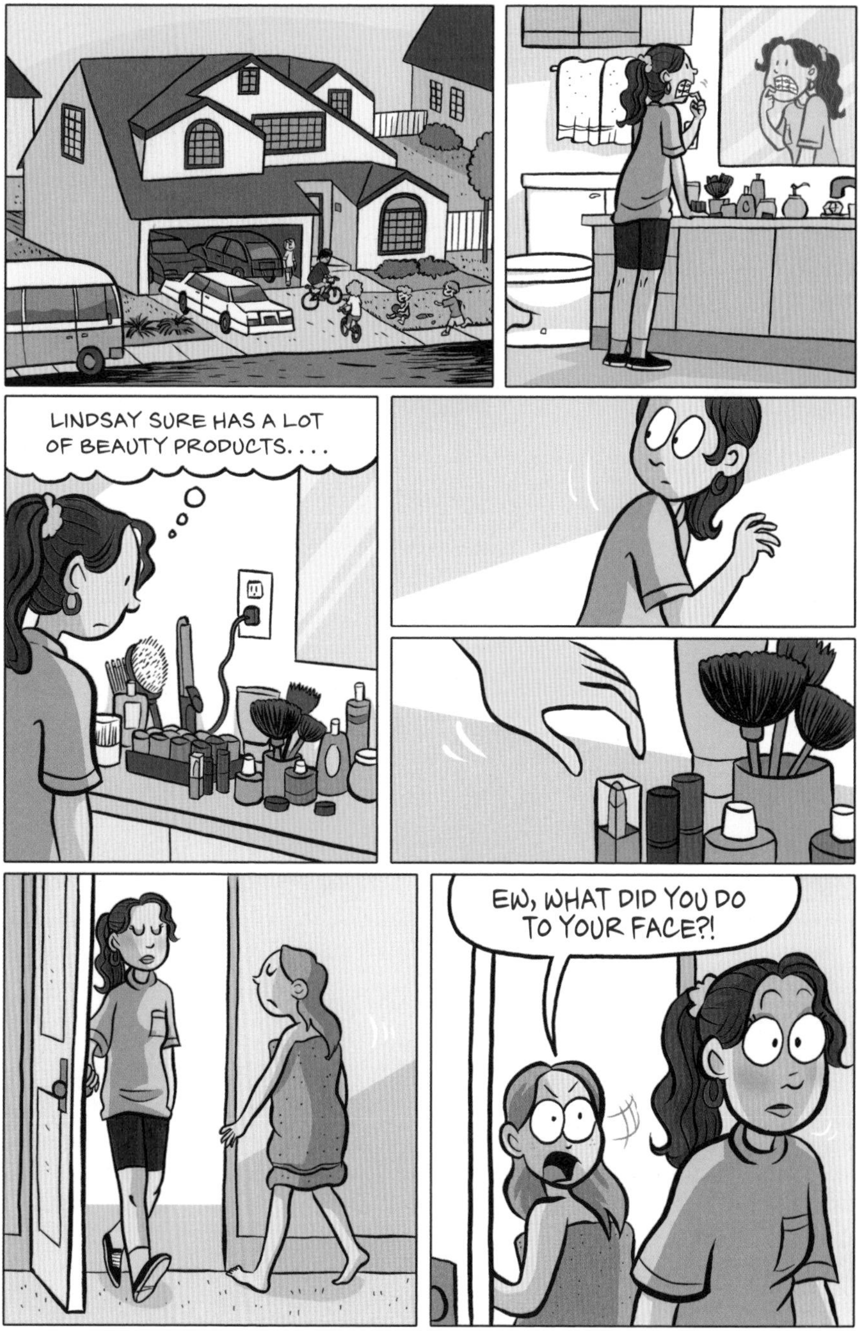
LINDSAY SURE HAS A LOT OF BEAUTY PRODUCTS....
EW, WHAT DID YOU DO TO YOUR FACE?!

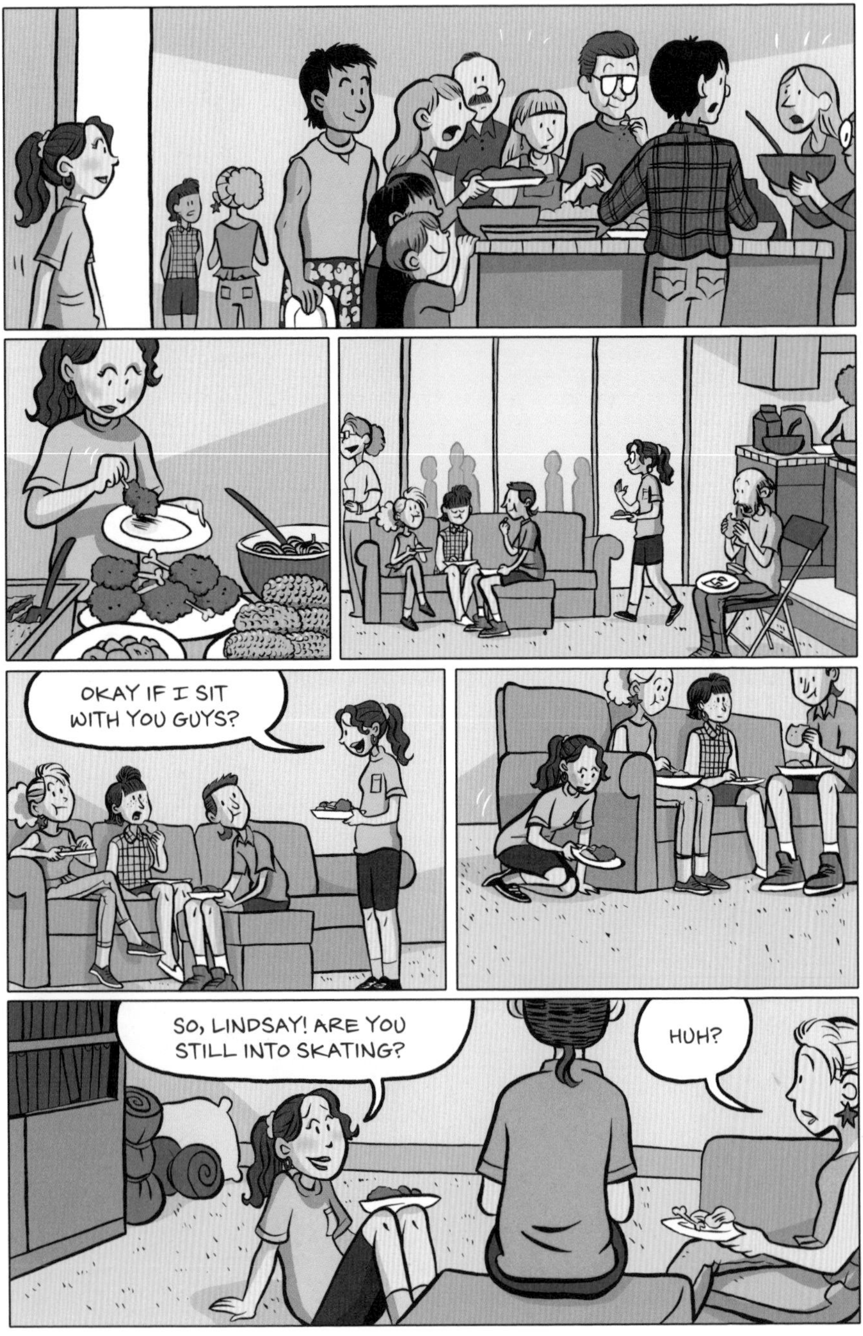
OKAY IF I SIT WITH YOU GUYS?
SO, LINDSAY! ARE YOU STILL INTO SKATING?
HUH?

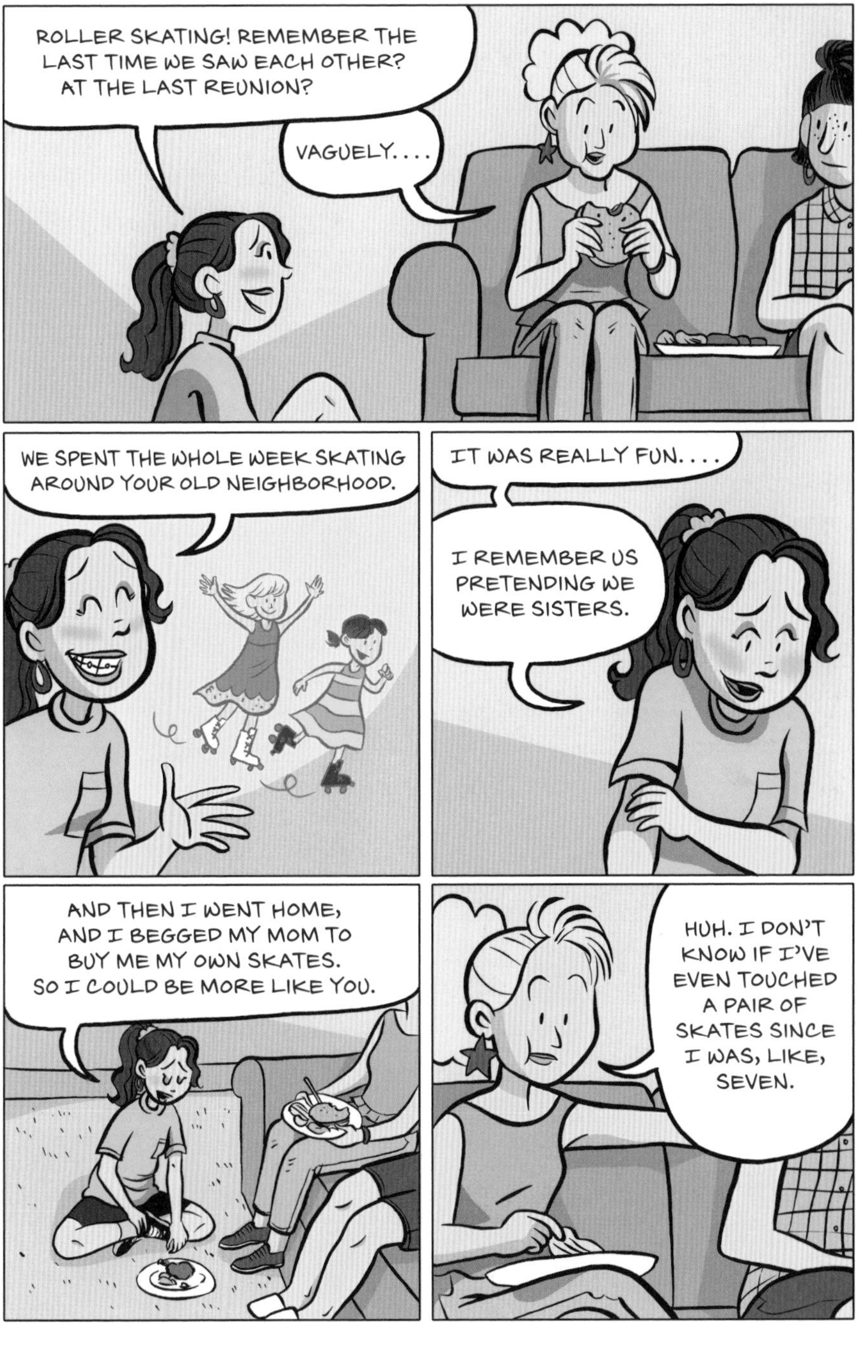
ROLLER SKATING! REMEMBER THE LAST TIME WE SAW EACH OTHER? AT THE LAST REUNION?
VAGUELY....
WE SPENT THE WHOLE WEEK SKATING AROUND YOUR OLD NEIGHBORHOOD.
IT WAS REALLY FUN....
I REMEMBER US PRETENDING WE WERE SISTERS.
AND THEN I WENT HOME, AND I BEGGED MY MOM TO BUY ME MY OWN SKATES. SO I COULD BE MORE LIKE YOU.
HUH. I DON'T KNOW IF I'VE EVEN TOUCHED A PAIR OF SKATES SINCE I WAS, LIKE, SEVEN.

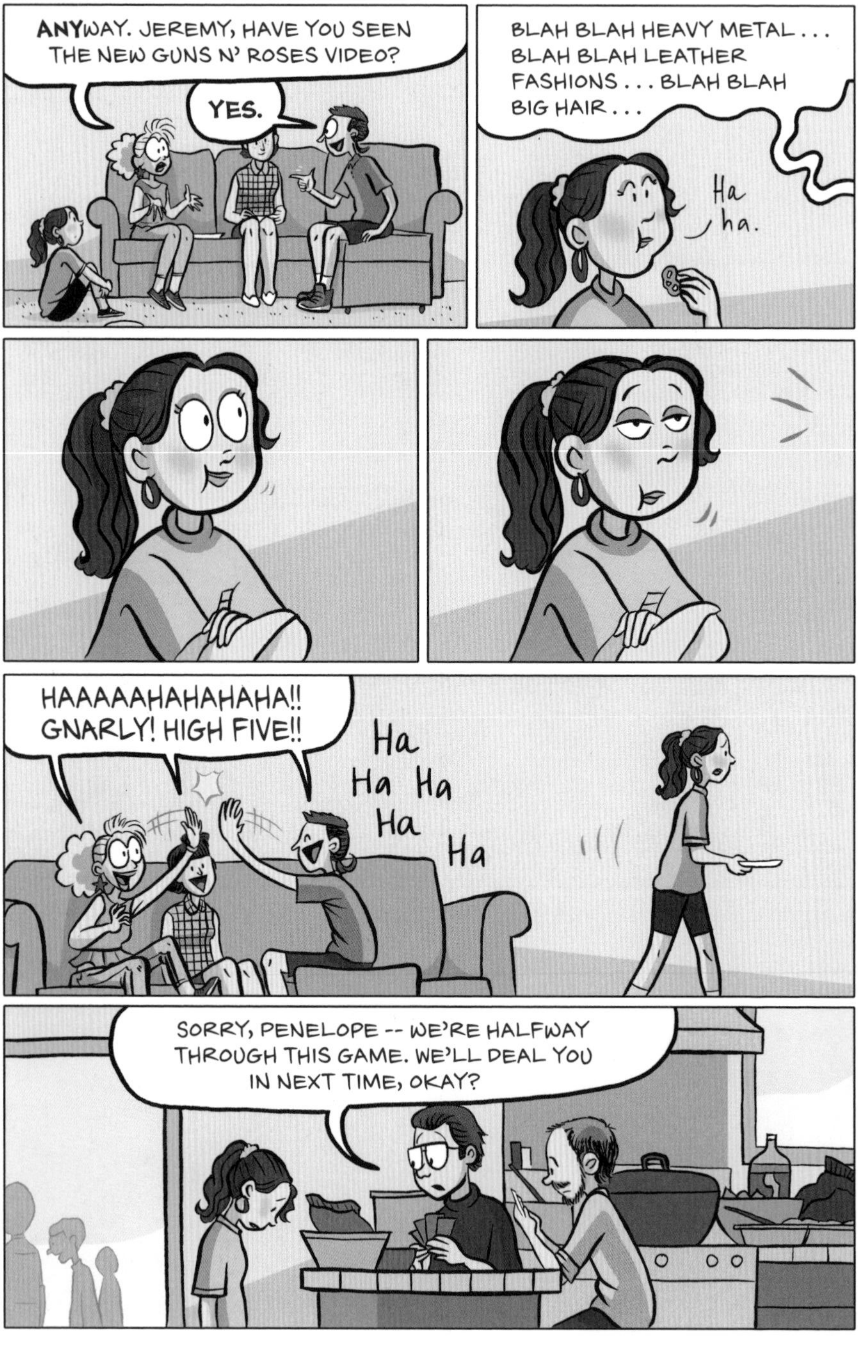
ANYWAY. JEREMY, HAVE YOU SEEN THE NEW GUNS N' ROSES VIDEO?
YES.
BLAH BLAH HEAVY METAL . . . BLAH BLAH LEATHER FASHIONS . . . BLAH BLAH BIG HAIR . . .
Ha ha.
HAAAAAHAHAHAHA!! GNARLY! HIGH FIVE!!
Ha Ha Ha Ha Ha
SORRY, PENELOPE -- WE'RE HALFWAY THROUGH THIS GAME. WE'LL DEAL YOU IN NEXT TIME, OKAY?

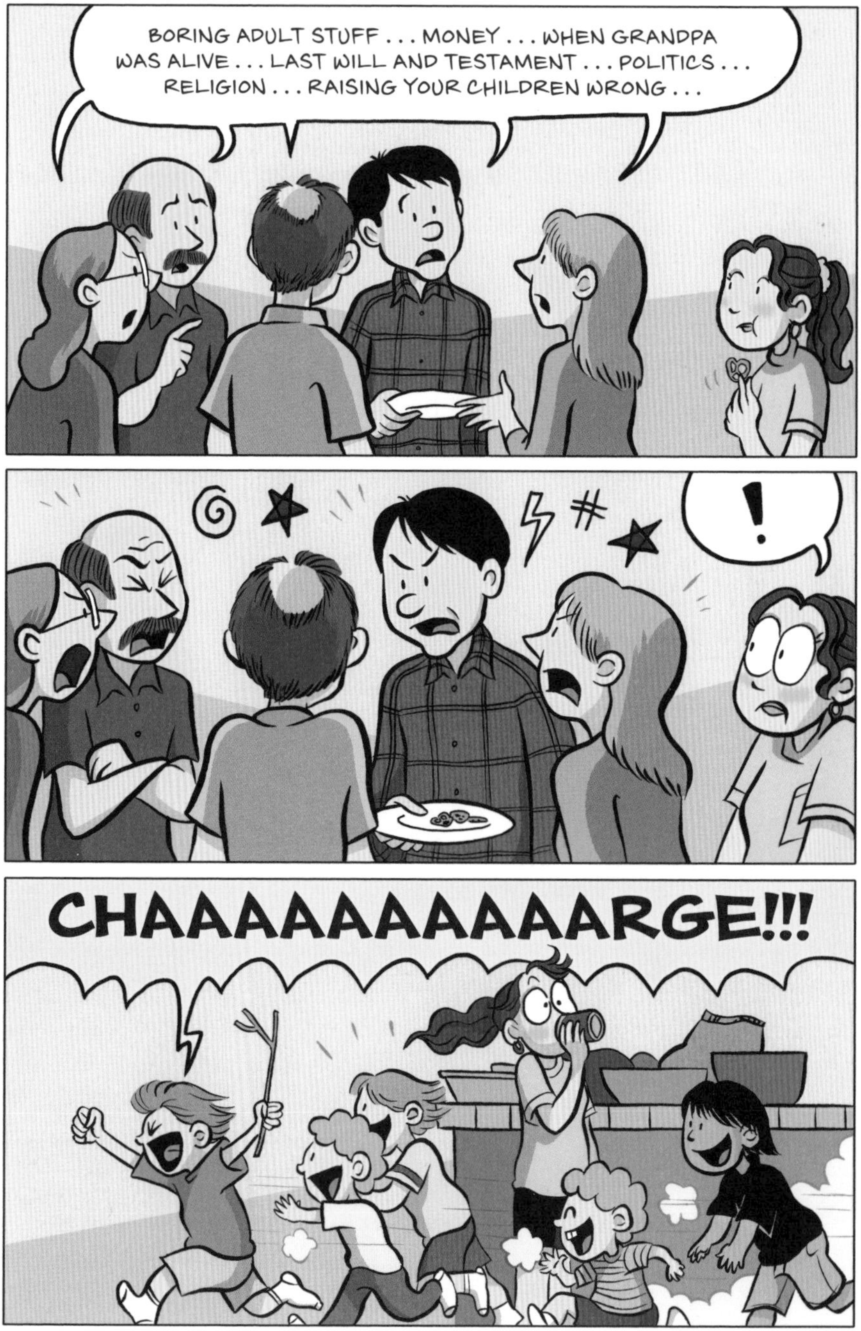
BORING ADULT STUFF . . . MONEY . . . WHEN GRANDPA WAS ALIVE . . . LAST WILL AND TESTAMENT . . . POLITICS . . . RELIGION . . . RAISING YOUR CHILDREN WRONG . . .
!
CHAAAAAAAAAARGE!!!

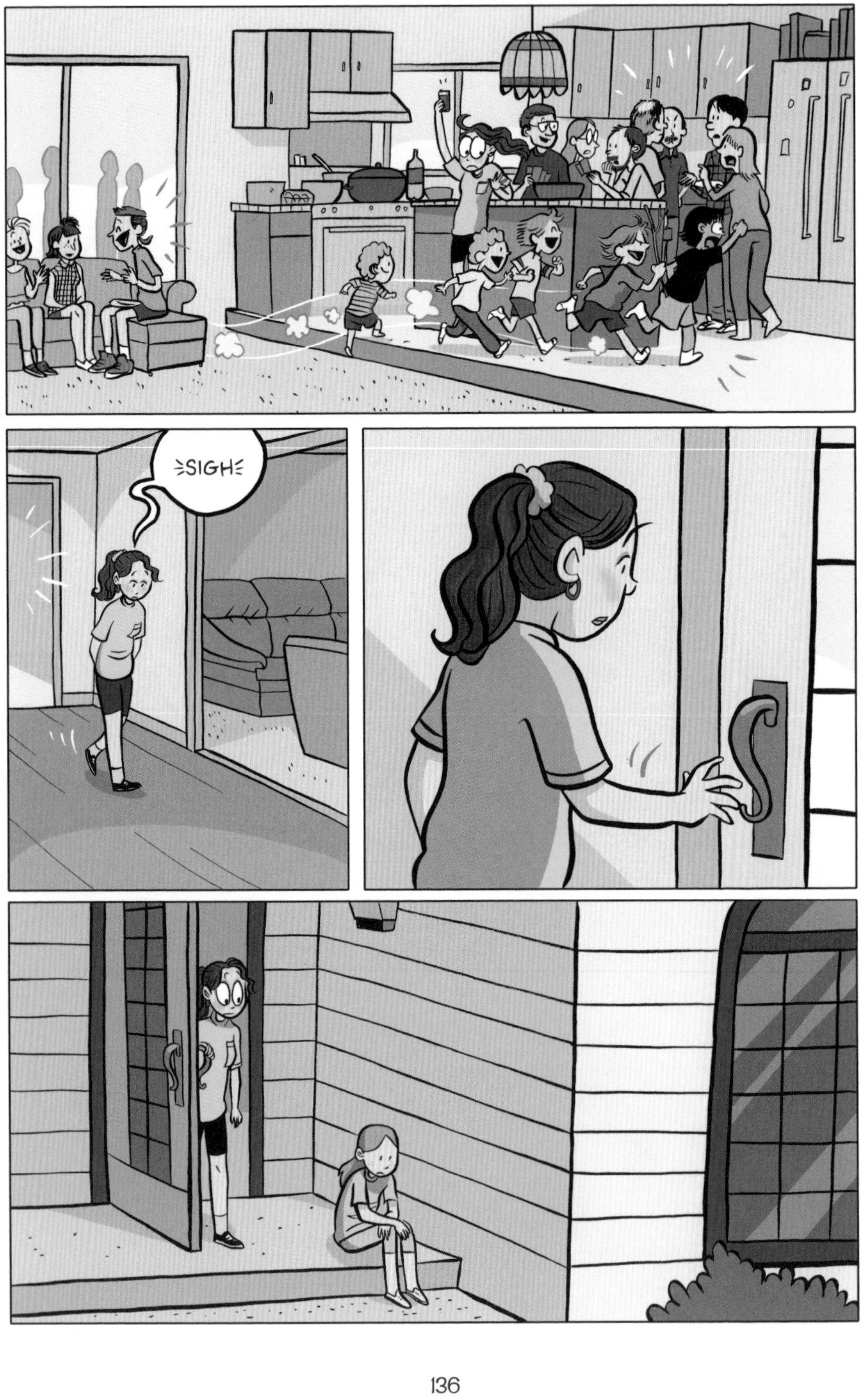
SIGH

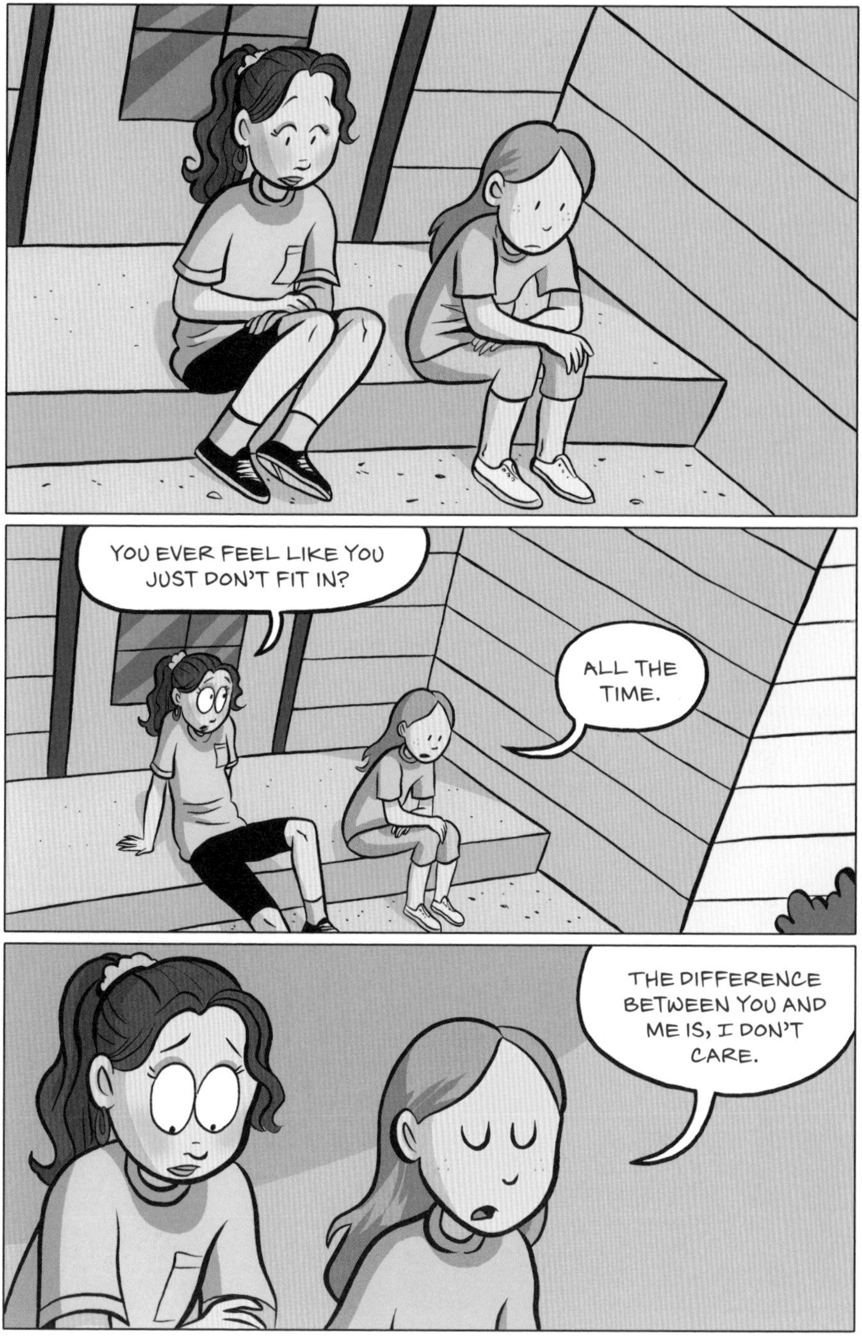
YOU EVER FEEL LIKE YOU JUST DON'T FIT IN?
ALL THE TIME.
THE DIFFERENCE BETWEEN YOU AND ME IS, I DON'T CARE.

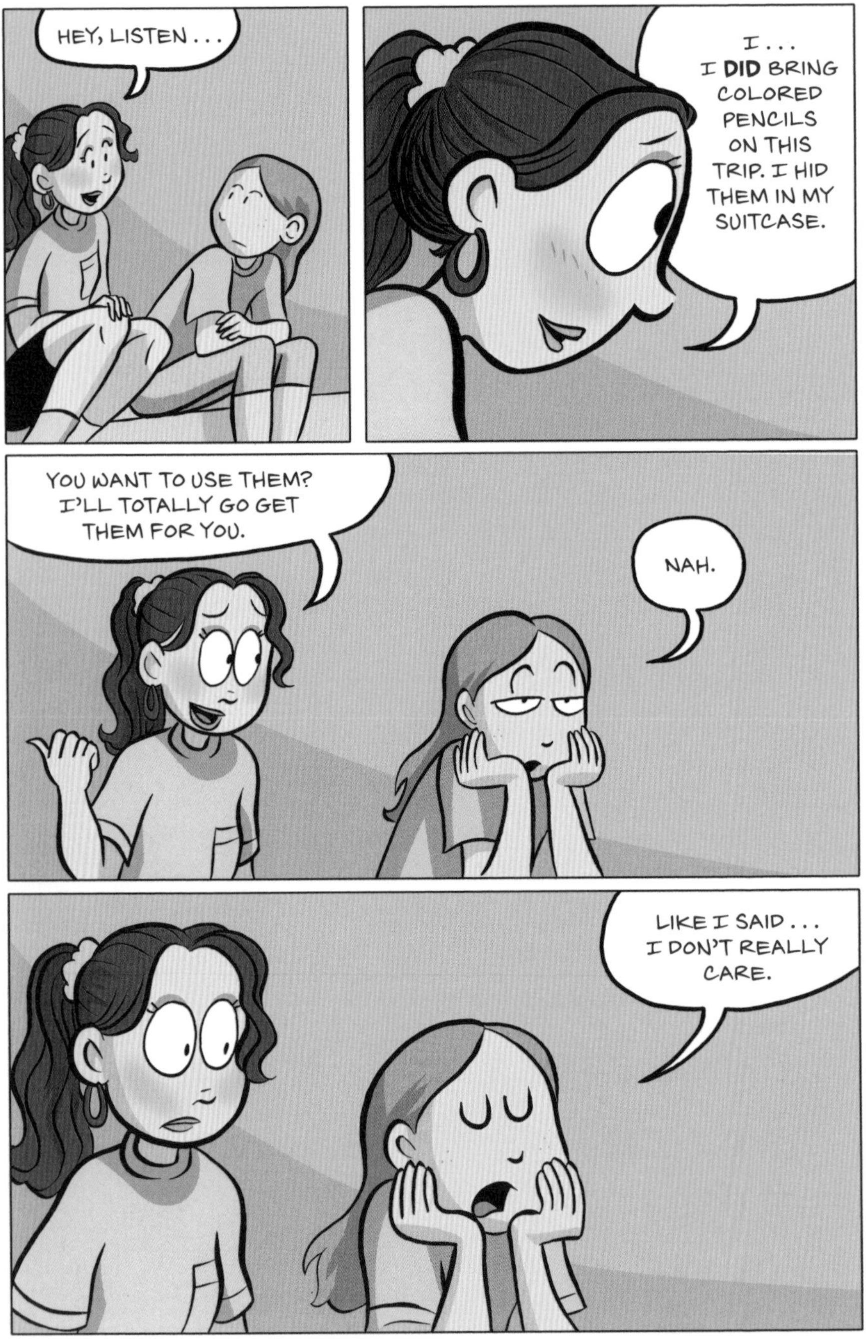
HEY, LISTEN . . .
I . . . I **DID** BRING COLORED PENCILS ON THIS TRIP. I HID THEM IN MY SUITCASE.
YOU WANT TO USE THEM? I'LL TOTALLY GO GET THEM FOR YOU.
NAH.
LIKE I SAID . . . I DON'T REALLY CARE.

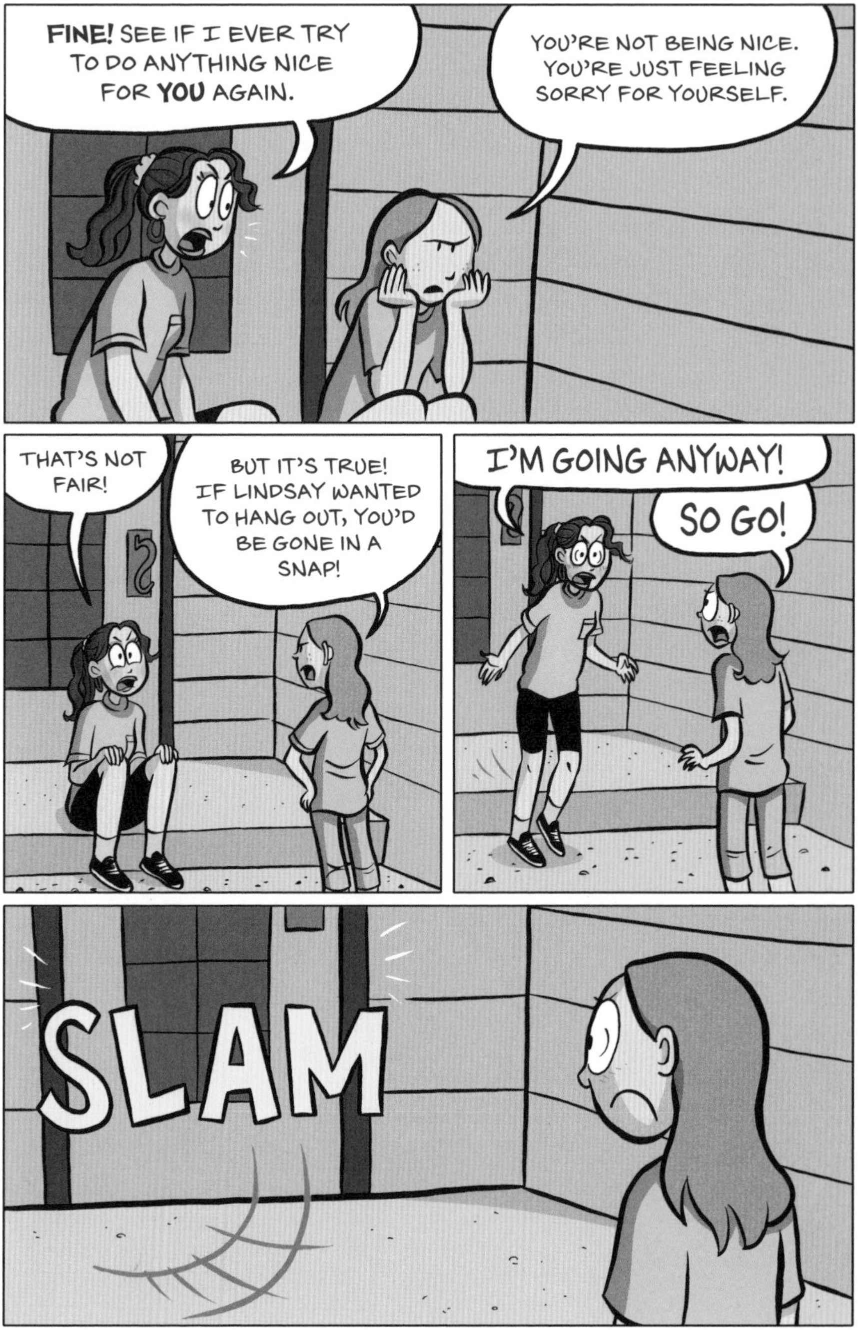
FINE! SEE IF I EVER TRY TO DO ANYTHING NICE FOR YOU AGAIN.
YOU'RE NOT BEING NICE. YOU'RE JUST FEELING SORRY FOR YOURSELF.
THAT'S NOT FAIR!
BUT IT'S TRUE! IF LINDSAY WANTED TO HANG OUT, YOU'D BE GONE IN A SNAP!
I'M GOING ANYWAY!
SO GO!
SLAM

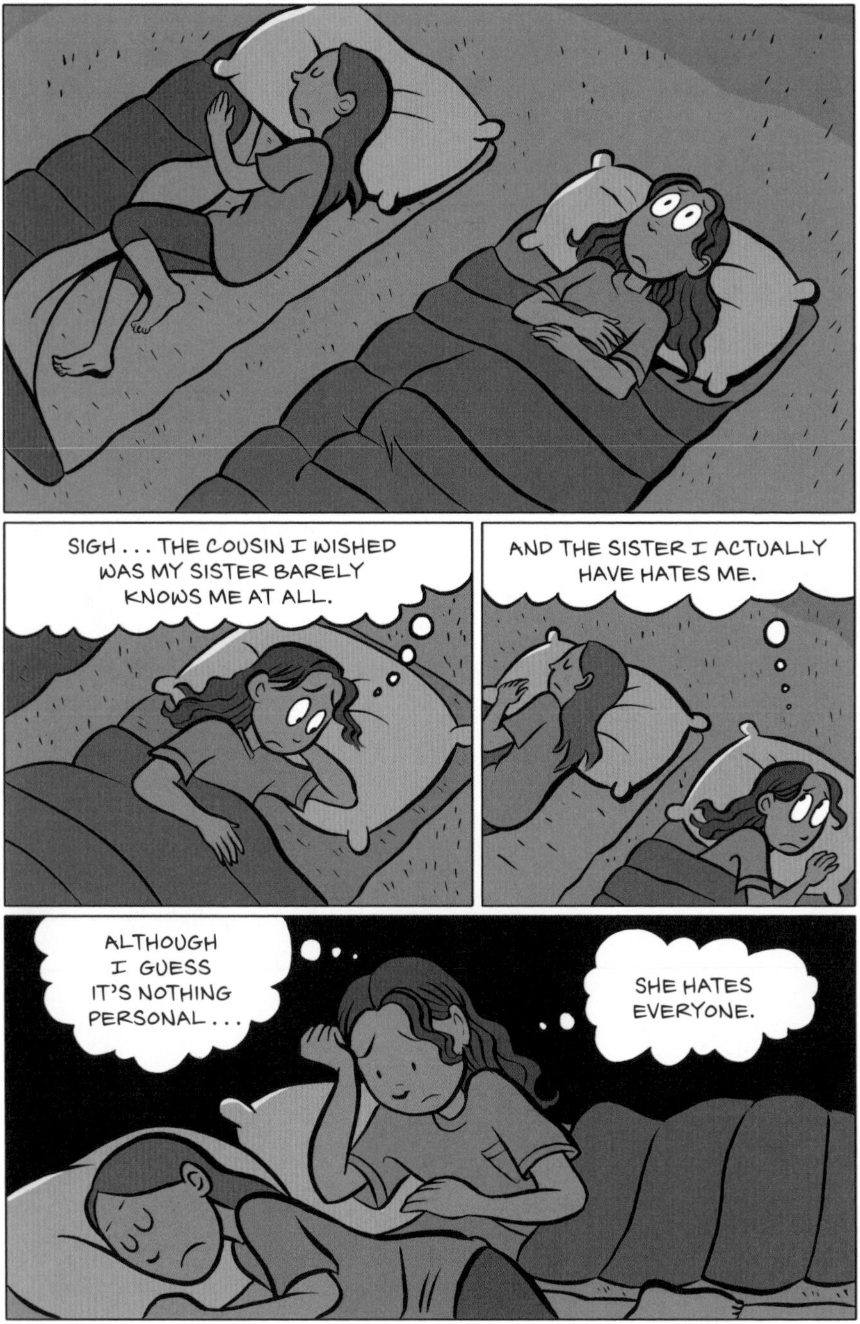
SIGH . . . THE COUSIN I WISHED WAS MY SISTER BARELY KNOWS ME AT ALL.
AND THE SISTER I ACTUALLY HAVE HATES ME.
ALTHOUGH I GUESS IT'S NOTHING PERSONAL . . .
SHE HATES EVERYONE.

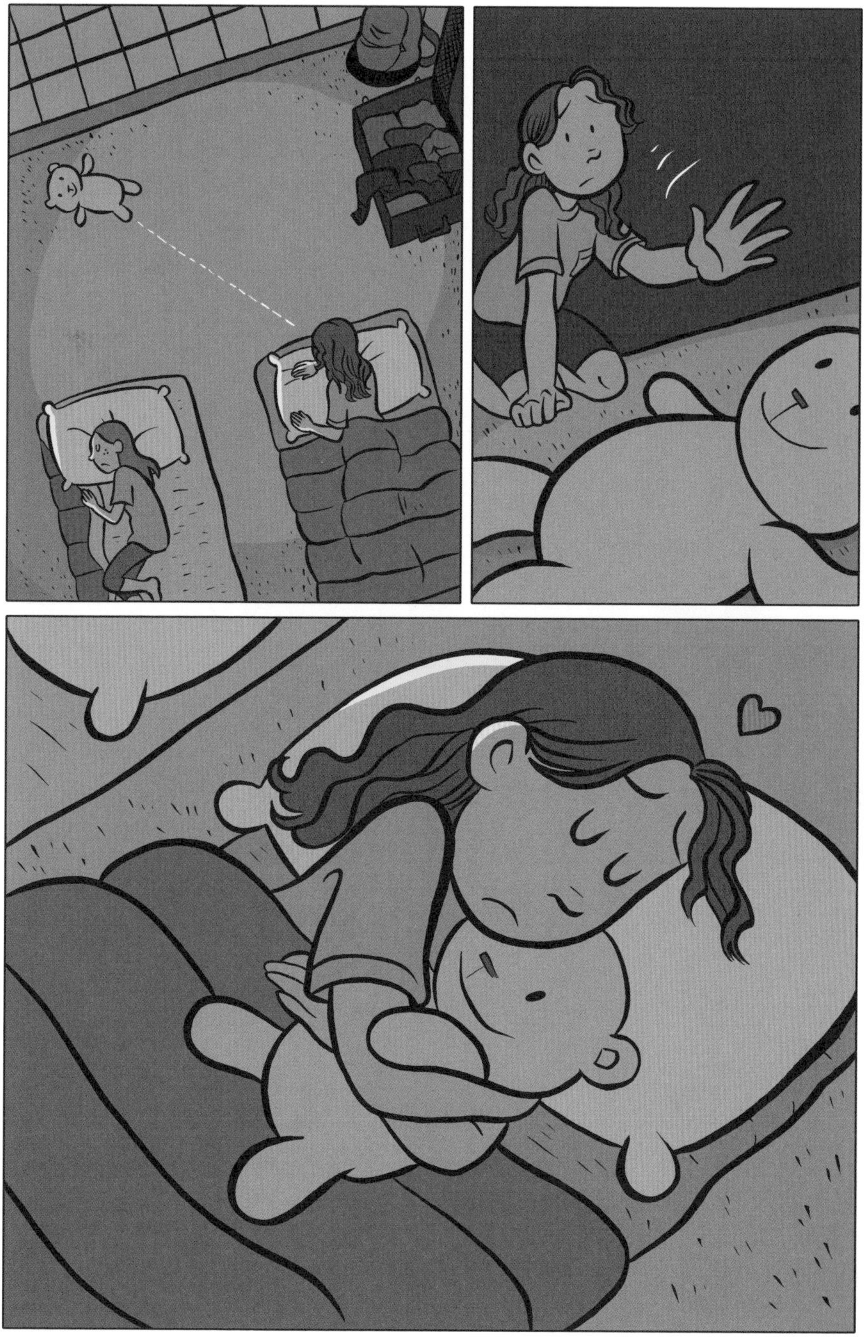

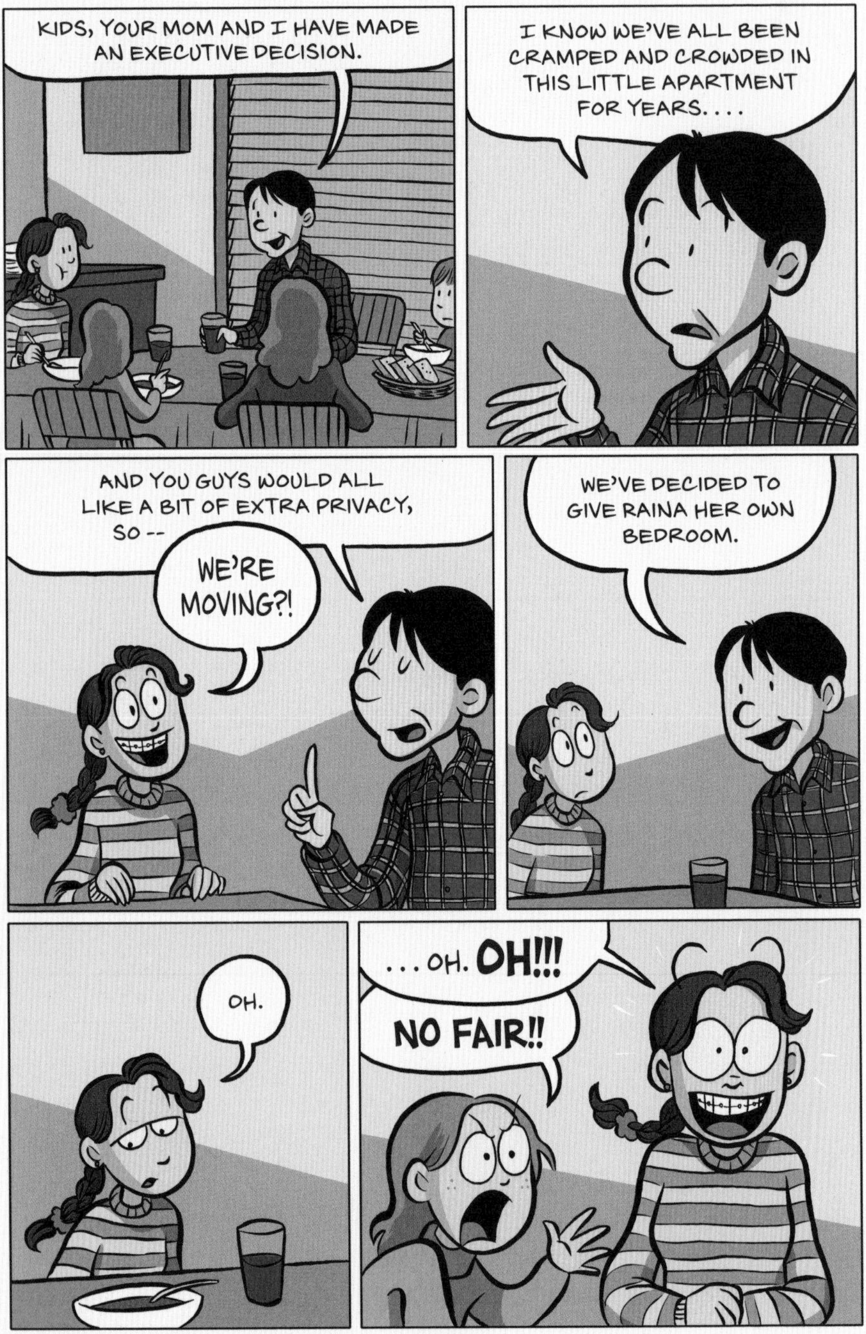
KIDS, YOUR MOM AND I HAVE MADE AN EXECUTIVE DECISION.
I KNOW WE'VE ALL BEEN CRAMPED AND CROWDED IN THIS LITTLE APARTMENT FOR YEARS. . . .
AND YOU GUYS WOULD ALL LIKE A BIT OF EXTRA PRIVACY, SO --
WE'RE MOVING?!
WE'VE DECIDED TO GIVE RAINA HER OWN BEDROOM.
OH.
. . . OH. OH!!!
NO FAIR!!

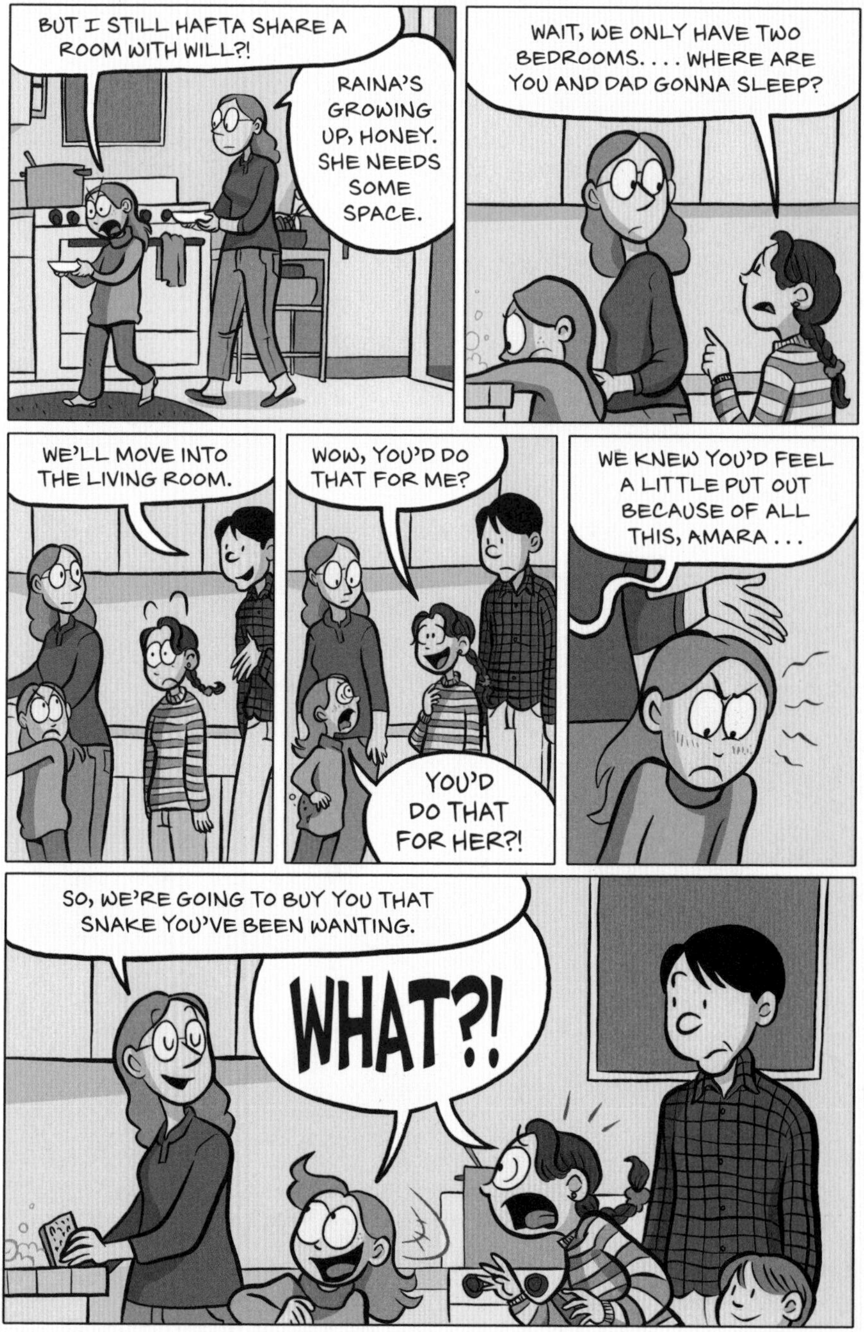
BUT I STILL HAFTA SHARE A ROOM WITH WILL?!
RAINA'S GROWING UP, HONEY. SHE NEEDS SOME SPACE.
WAIT, WE ONLY HAVE TWO BEDROOMS. . . . WHERE ARE YOU AND DAD GONNA SLEEP?
WE'LL MOVE INTO THE LIVING ROOM.
WOW, YOU'D DO THAT FOR ME?
YOU'D DO THAT FOR HER?!
WE KNEW YOU'D FEEL A LITTLE PUT OUT BECAUSE OF ALL THIS, AMARA . . .
SO, WE'RE GOING TO BUY YOU THAT SNAKE YOU'VE BEEN WANTING.
WHAT?!

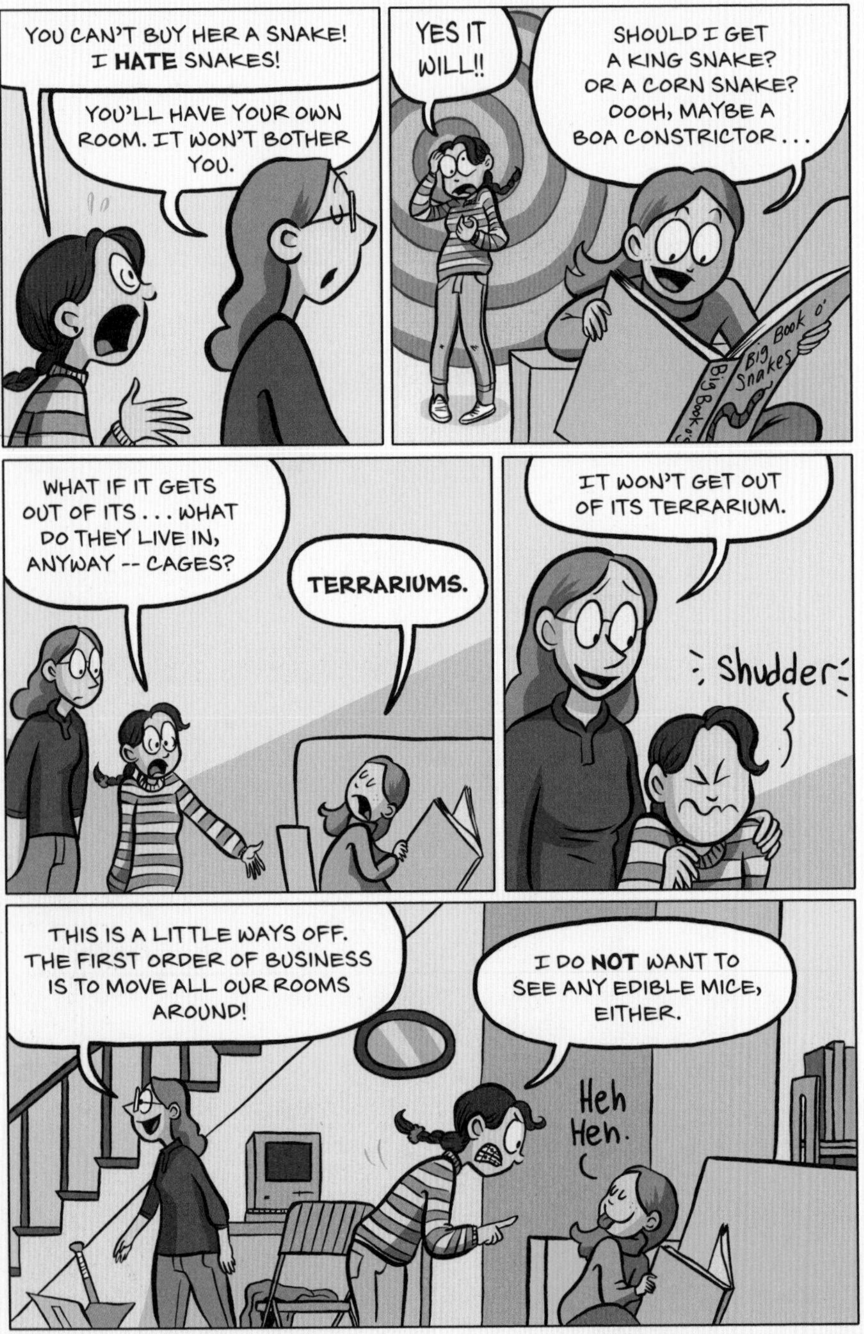

YOU CAN'T BUY HER A SNAKE! I **HATE** SNAKES!
YOU'LL HAVE YOUR OWN ROOM. IT WON'T BOTHER YOU.
YES IT WILL!!
SHOULD I GET A KING SNAKE? OR A CORN SNAKE? OOOH, MAYBE A BOA CONSTRICTOR . . .
Big Book o' Snakes
WHAT IF IT GETS OUT OF ITS . . . WHAT DO THEY LIVE IN, ANYWAY -- CAGES?
TERRARIUMS.
IT WON'T GET OUT OF ITS TERRARIUM.
Shudder
THIS IS A LITTLE WAYS OFF. THE FIRST ORDER OF BUSINESS IS TO MOVE ALL OUR ROOMS AROUND!
I DO **NOT** WANT TO SEE ANY EDIBLE MICE, EITHER.
Heh Heh.

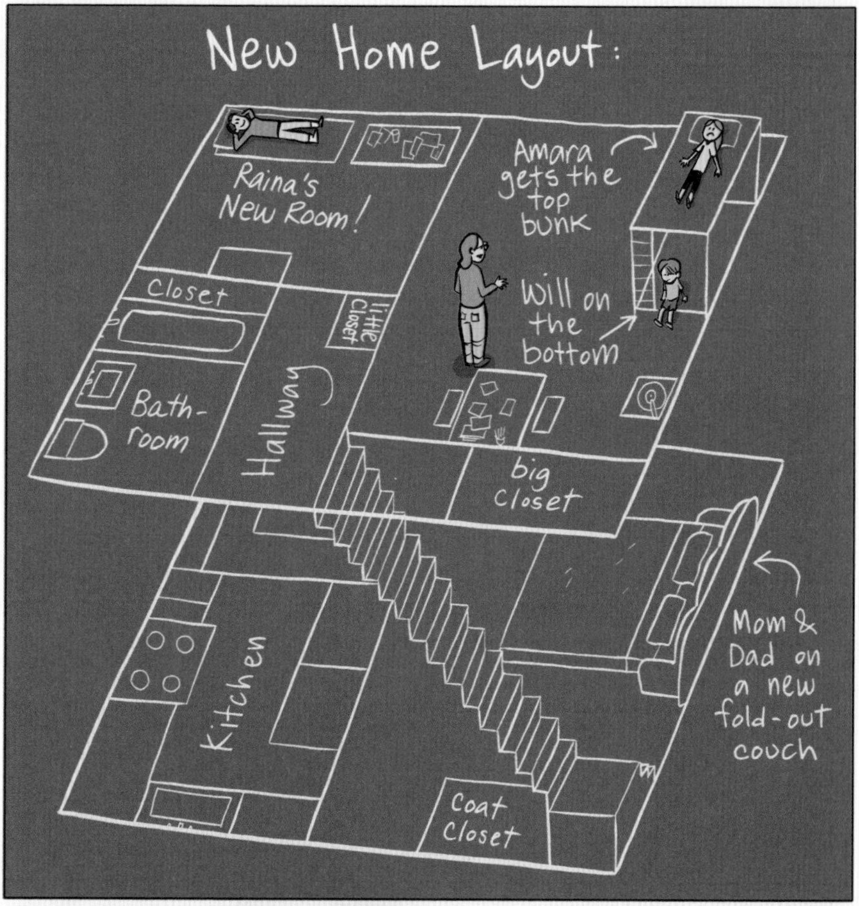
New Home Layout:
Raina's New Room!
Amara gets the top bunk
Will on the bottom
Closet
little Closet
Bath-room
Hallway
big Closet
Mom & Dad on a new fold-out couch
Kitchen
Coat Closet

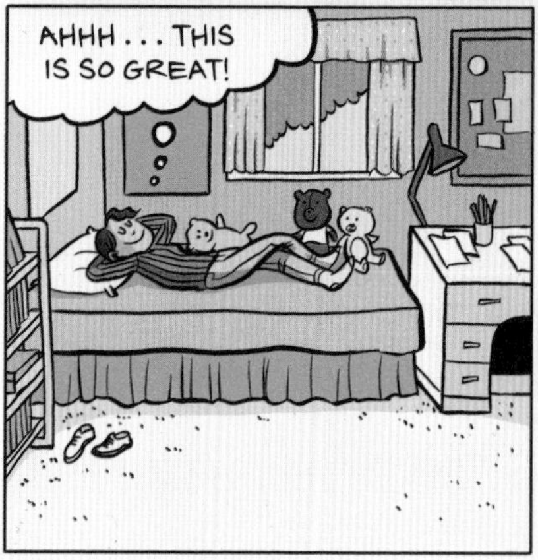
AHHH . . . THIS IS SO GREAT!

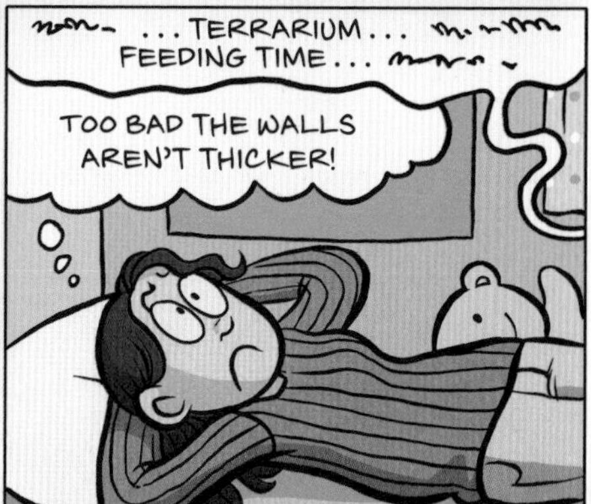
. . . TERRARIUM . . .
FEEDING TIME . . .
TOO BAD THE WALLS AREN'T THICKER!

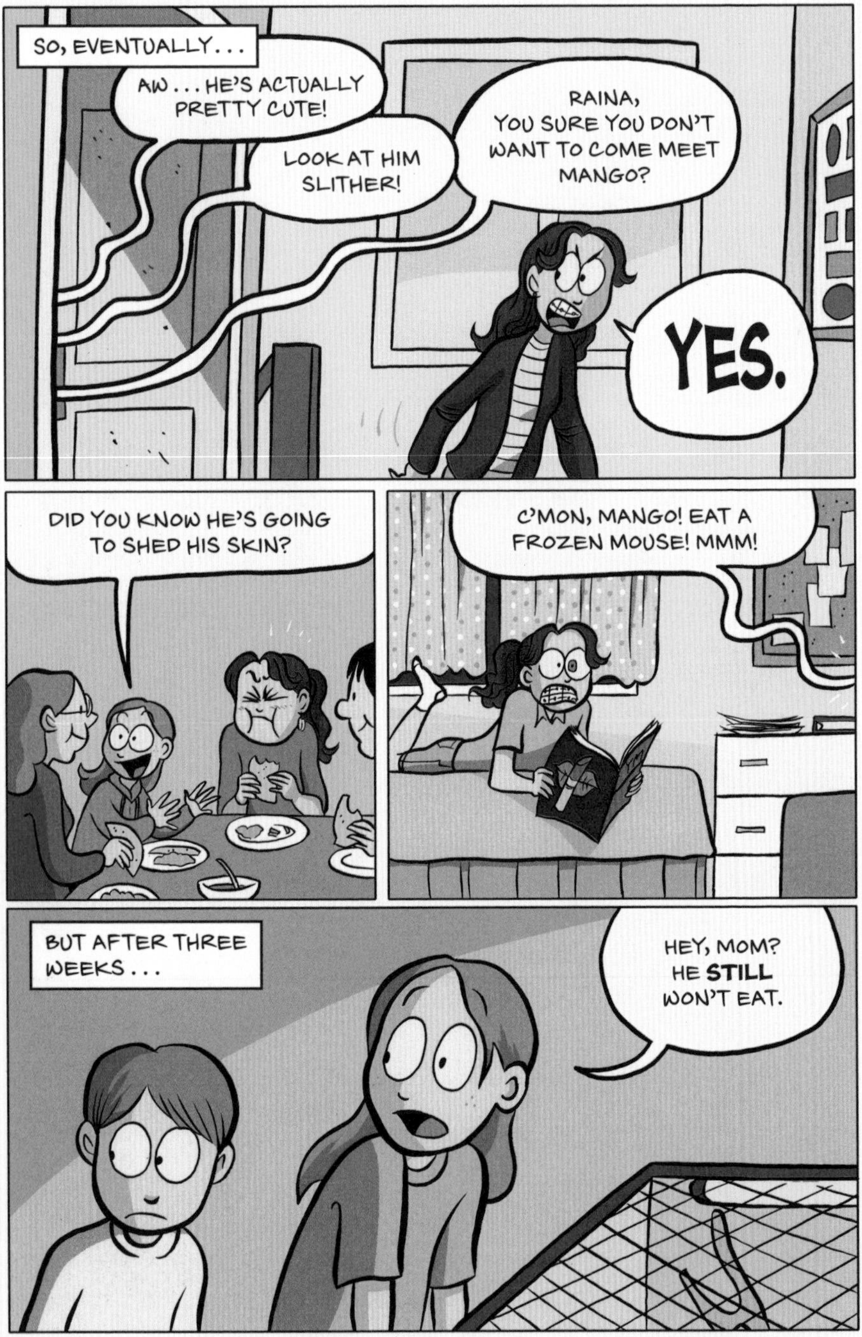
SO, EVENTUALLY . . .
AW . . . HE'S ACTUALLY PRETTY CUTE!
LOOK AT HIM SLITHER!
RAINA, YOU SURE YOU DON'T WANT TO COME MEET MANGO?
YES.
DID YOU KNOW HE'S GOING TO SHED HIS SKIN?
C'MON, MANGO! EAT A FROZEN MOUSE! MMM!
BUT AFTER THREE WEEKS . . .
HEY, MOM? HE **STILL** WON'T EAT.

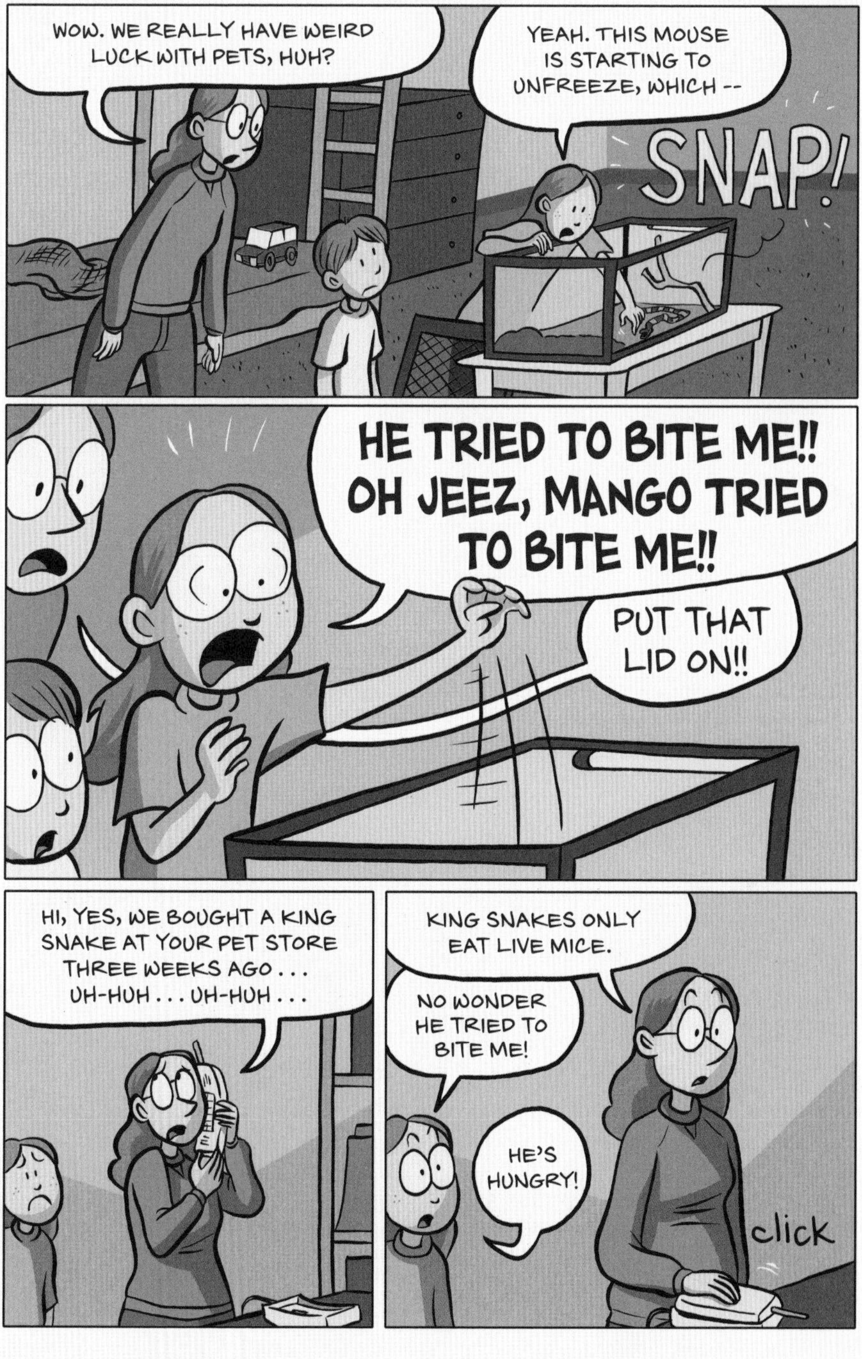

WOW. WE REALLY HAVE WEIRD LUCK WITH PETS, HUH?
YEAH. THIS MOUSE IS STARTING TO UNFREEZE, WHICH --
SNAP!
HE TRIED TO BITE ME!! OH JEEZ, MANGO TRIED TO BITE ME!!
PUT THAT LID ON!!
HI, YES, WE BOUGHT A KING SNAKE AT YOUR PET STORE THREE WEEKS AGO . . . UH-HUH . . . UH-HUH . . .
KING SNAKES ONLY EAT LIVE MICE.
NO WONDER HE TRIED TO BITE ME!
HE'S HUNGRY!
click

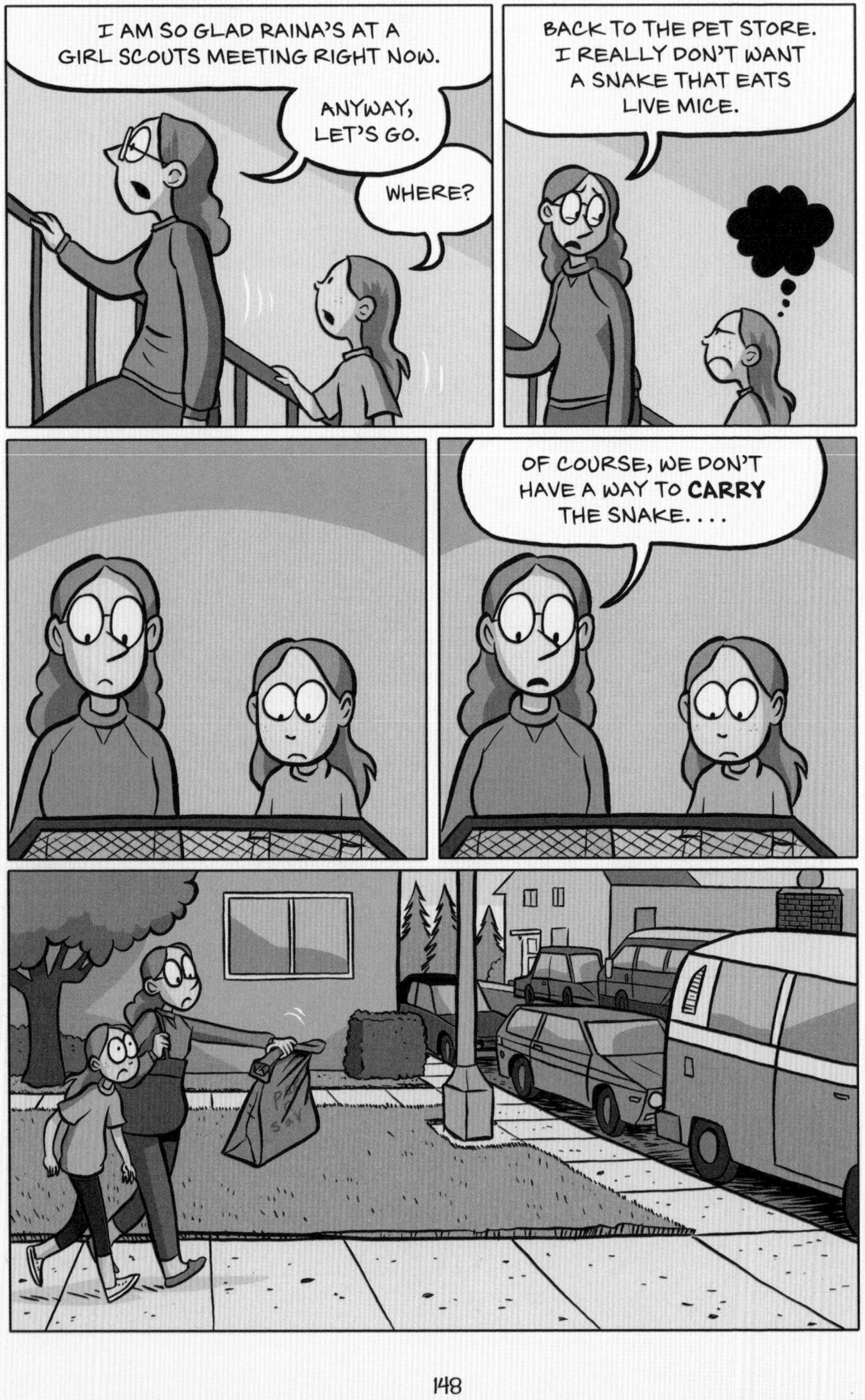
I AM SO GLAD RAINA'S AT A GIRL SCOUTS MEETING RIGHT NOW.
ANYWAY, LET'S GO.
WHERE?
BACK TO THE PET STORE. I REALLY DON'T WANT A SNAKE THAT EATS LIVE MICE.
OF COURSE, WE DON'T HAVE A WAY TO **CARRY** THE SNAKE. . . .

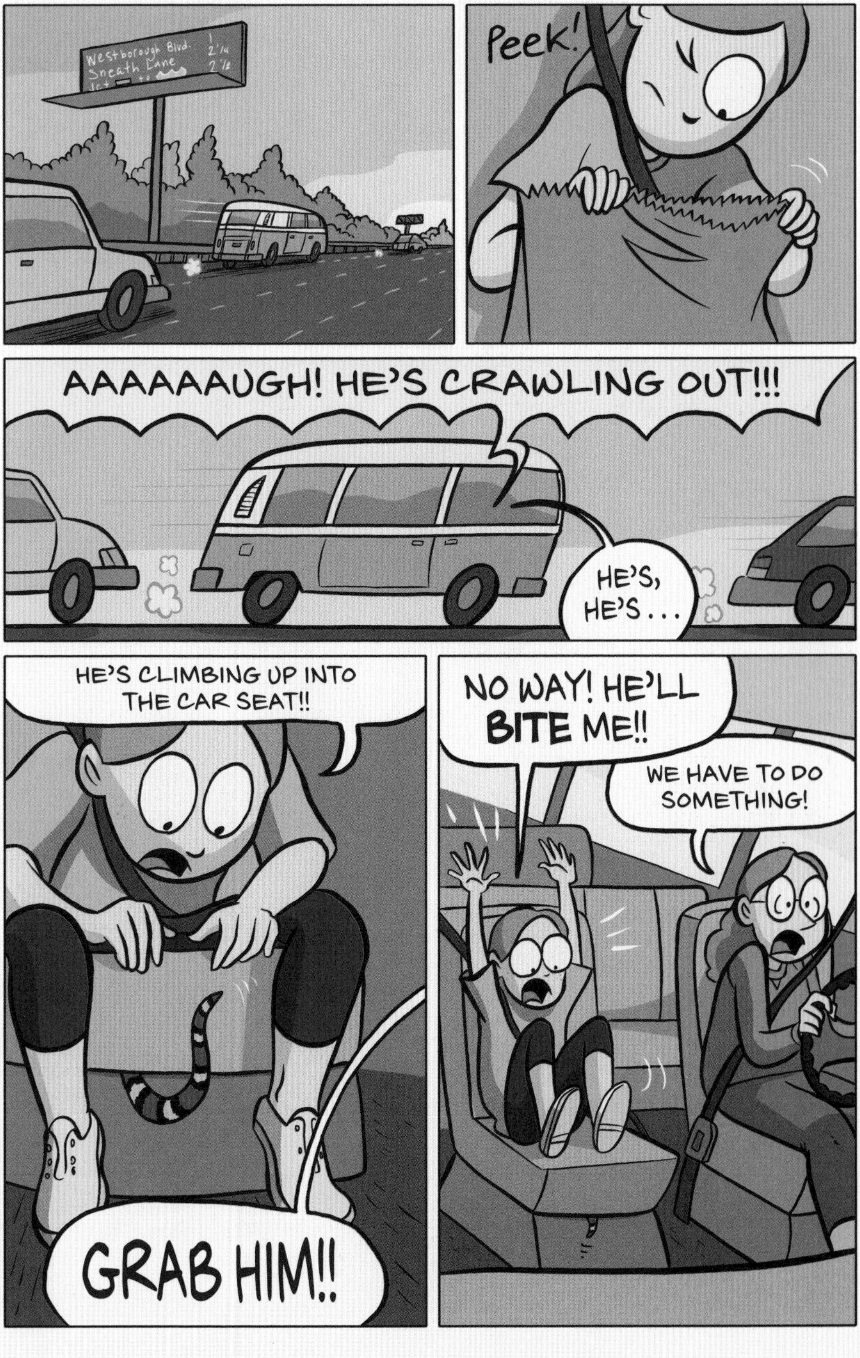
Westborough Blvd.
Sneath Lane
Peek!
AAAAAAUGH! HE'S CRAWLING OUT!!!
HE'S, HE'S . . .
HE'S CLIMBING UP INTO THE CAR SEAT!!
GRAB HIM!!
NO WAY! HE'LL **BITE** ME!!
WE HAVE TO DO SOMETHING!

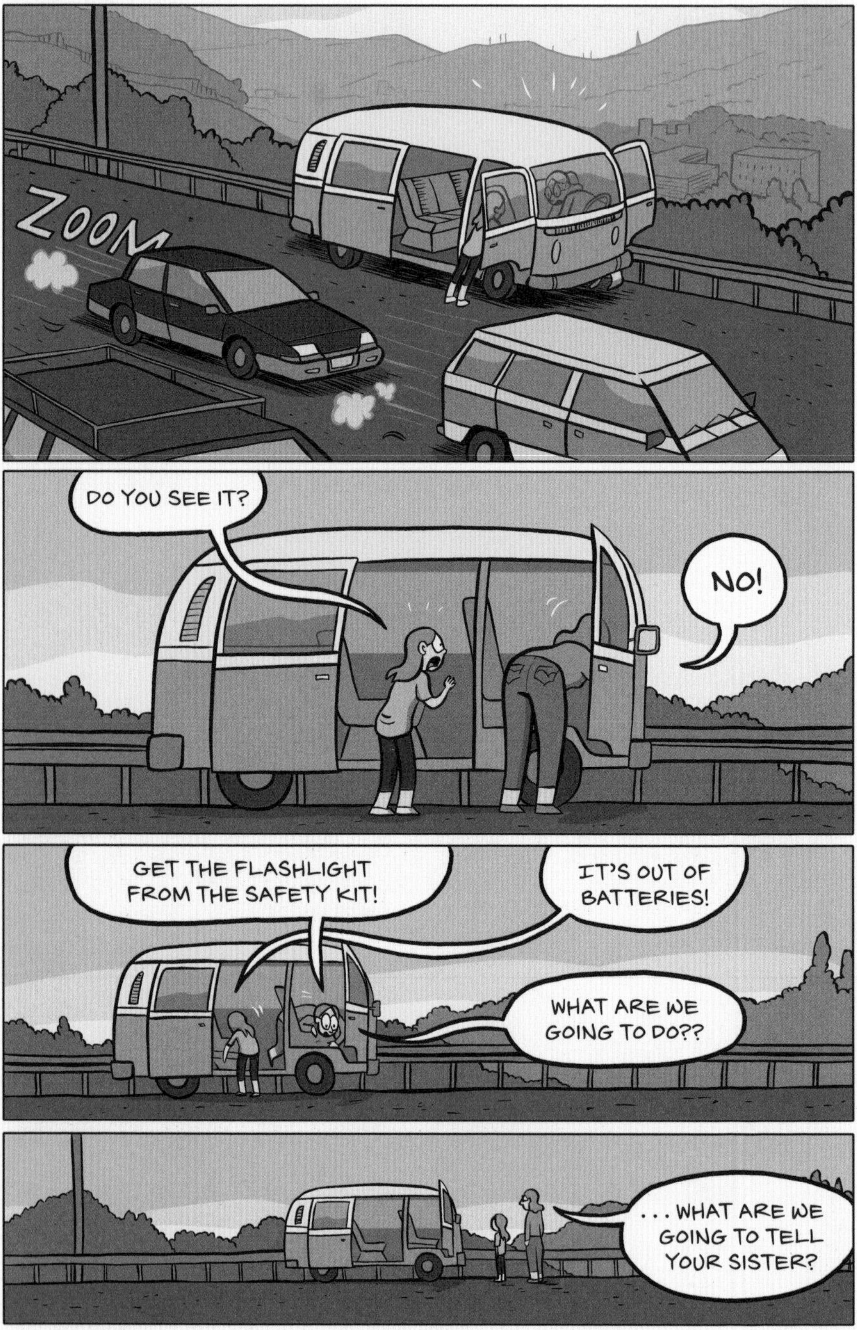
ZOOM
DO YOU SEE IT?
NO!
GET THE FLASHLIGHT FROM THE SAFETY KIT!
IT'S OUT OF BATTERIES!
WHAT ARE WE GOING TO DO??
. . . WHAT ARE WE GOING TO TELL YOUR SISTER?

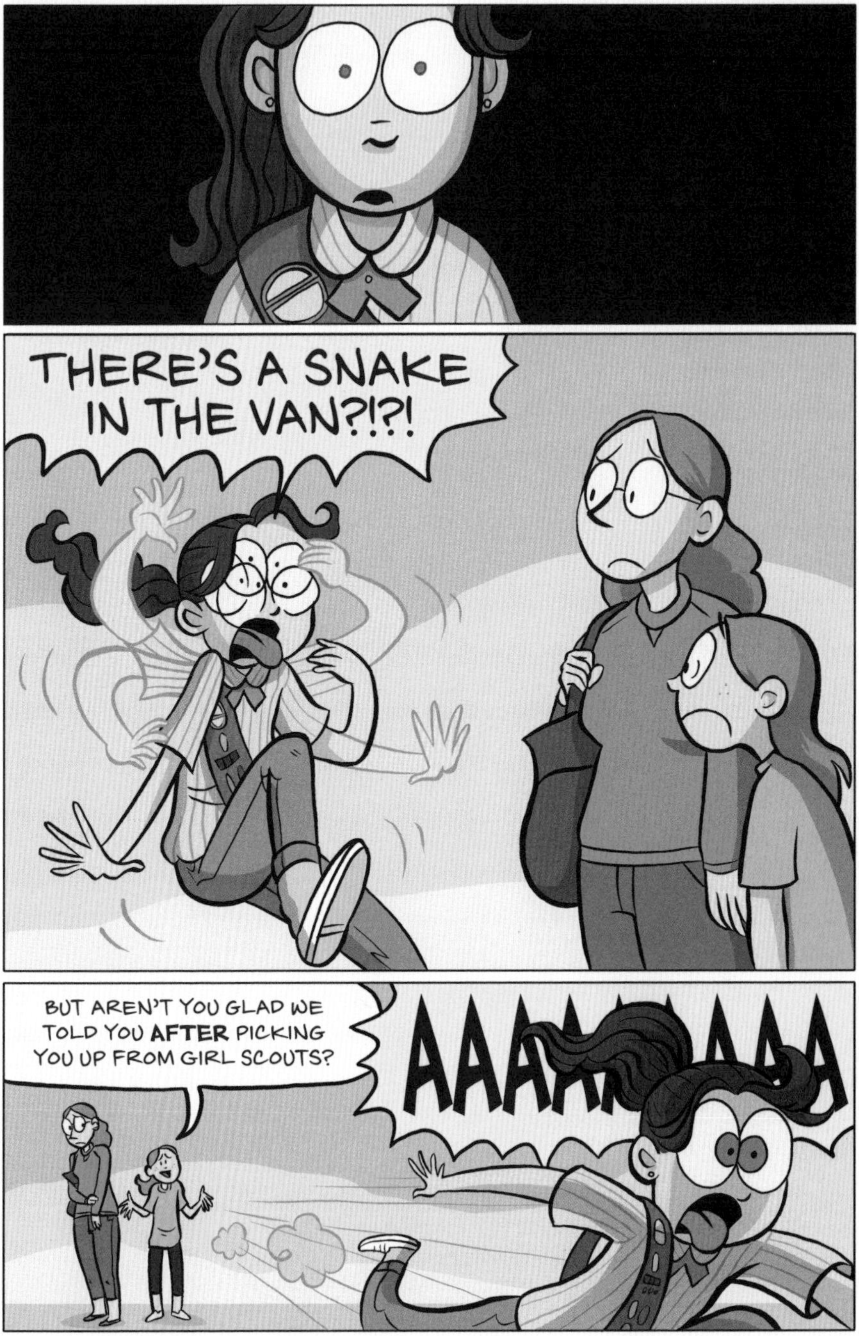
THERE'S A SNAKE IN THE VAN?!?!
BUT AREN'T YOU GLAD WE TOLD YOU **AFTER** PICKING YOU UP FROM GIRL SCOUTS?
AAAAAAAAA

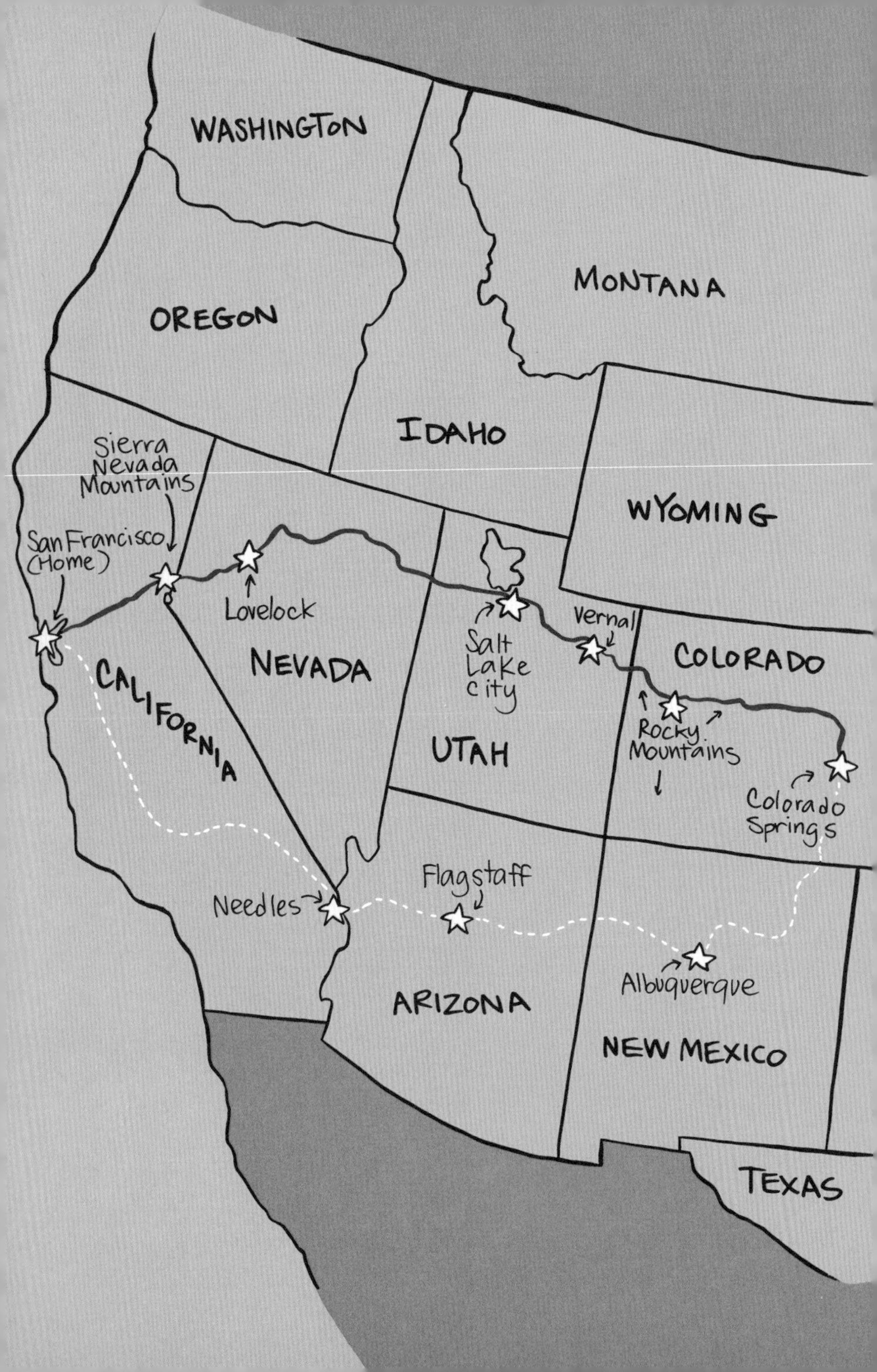

WASHINGTON
MONTANA
OREGON
IDAHO
WYOMING
Sierra Nevada Mountains
San Francisco (Home)
Lovelock
NEVADA
CALIFORNIA
Salt Lake City
Vernal
COLORADO
UTAH
Rocky Mountains
Colorado Springs
Flagstaff
Needles
Albuquerque
ARIZONA
NEW MEXICO
TEXAS

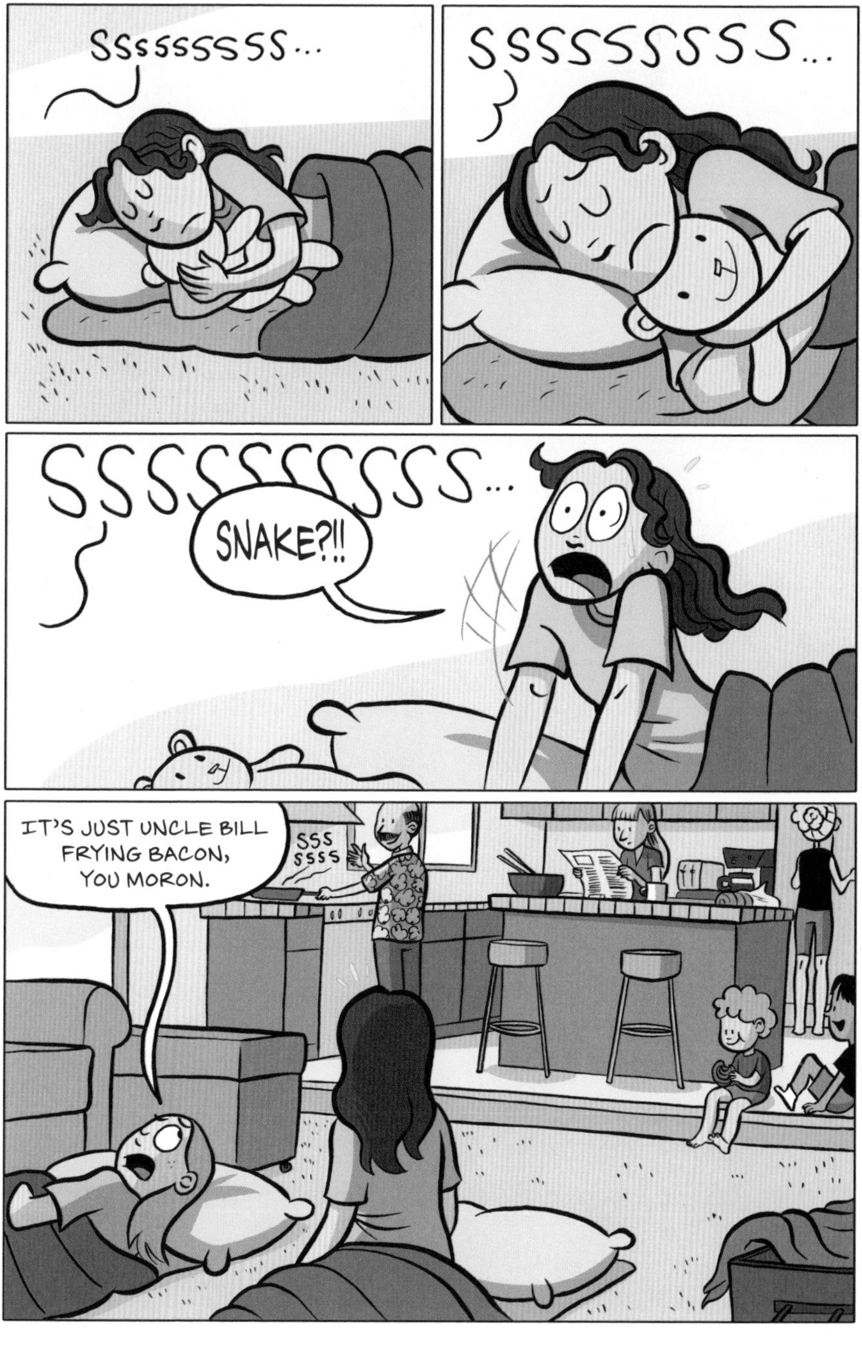
Ssssssss...
SSSSSSSSS...
SSSSSSSSSS...
SNAKE?!!
IT'S JUST UNCLE BILL FRYING BACON, YOU MORON.
SSS SSSS

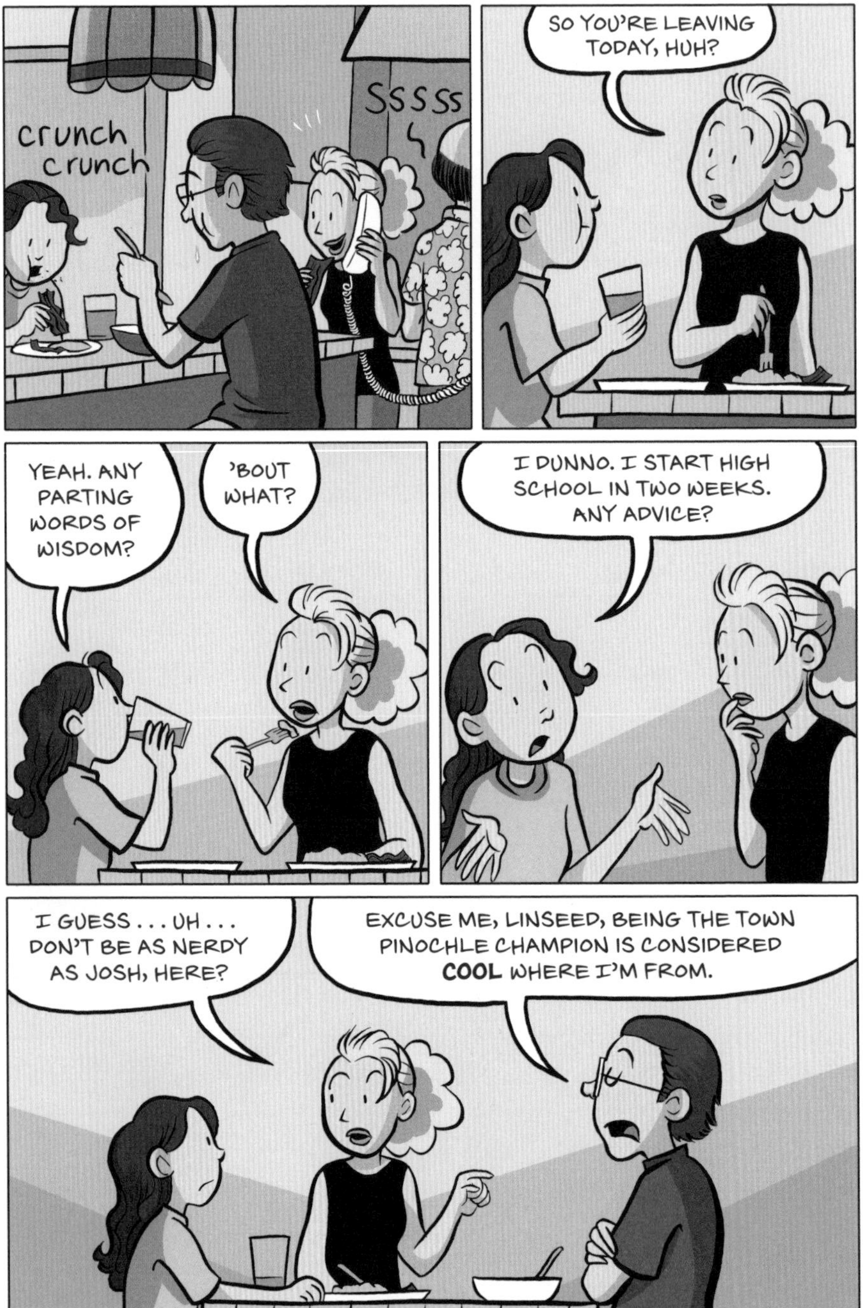
crunch crunch
SSSSS
SO YOU'RE LEAVING TODAY, HUH?
YEAH. ANY PARTING WORDS OF WISDOM?
'BOUT WHAT?
I DUNNO. I START HIGH SCHOOL IN TWO WEEKS. ANY ADVICE?
I GUESS . . . UH . . . DON'T BE AS NERDY AS JOSH, HERE?
EXCUSE ME, LINSEED, BEING THE TOWN PINOCHLE CHAMPION IS CONSIDERED **COOL** WHERE I'M FROM.

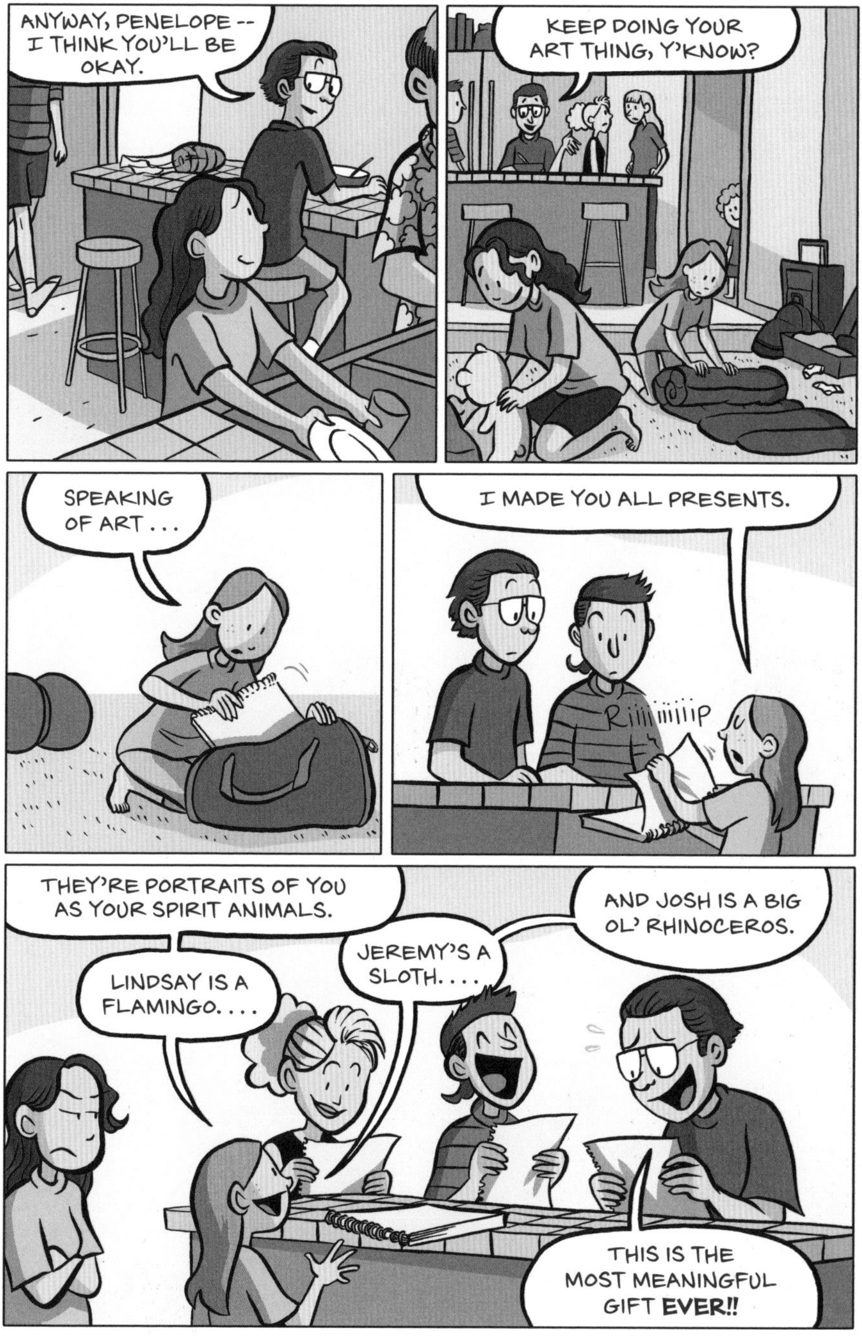
ANYWAY, PENELOPE -- I THINK YOU'LL BE OKAY.
KEEP DOING YOUR ART THING, Y'KNOW?
SPEAKING OF ART . . .
I MADE YOU ALL PRESENTS.
Riiiiiiiiip
THEY'RE PORTRAITS OF YOU AS YOUR SPIRIT ANIMALS.
LINDSAY IS A FLAMINGO. . . .
JEREMY'S A SLOTH. . . .
AND JOSH IS A BIG OL' RHINOCEROS.
THIS IS THE MOST MEANINGFUL GIFT **EVER!!**

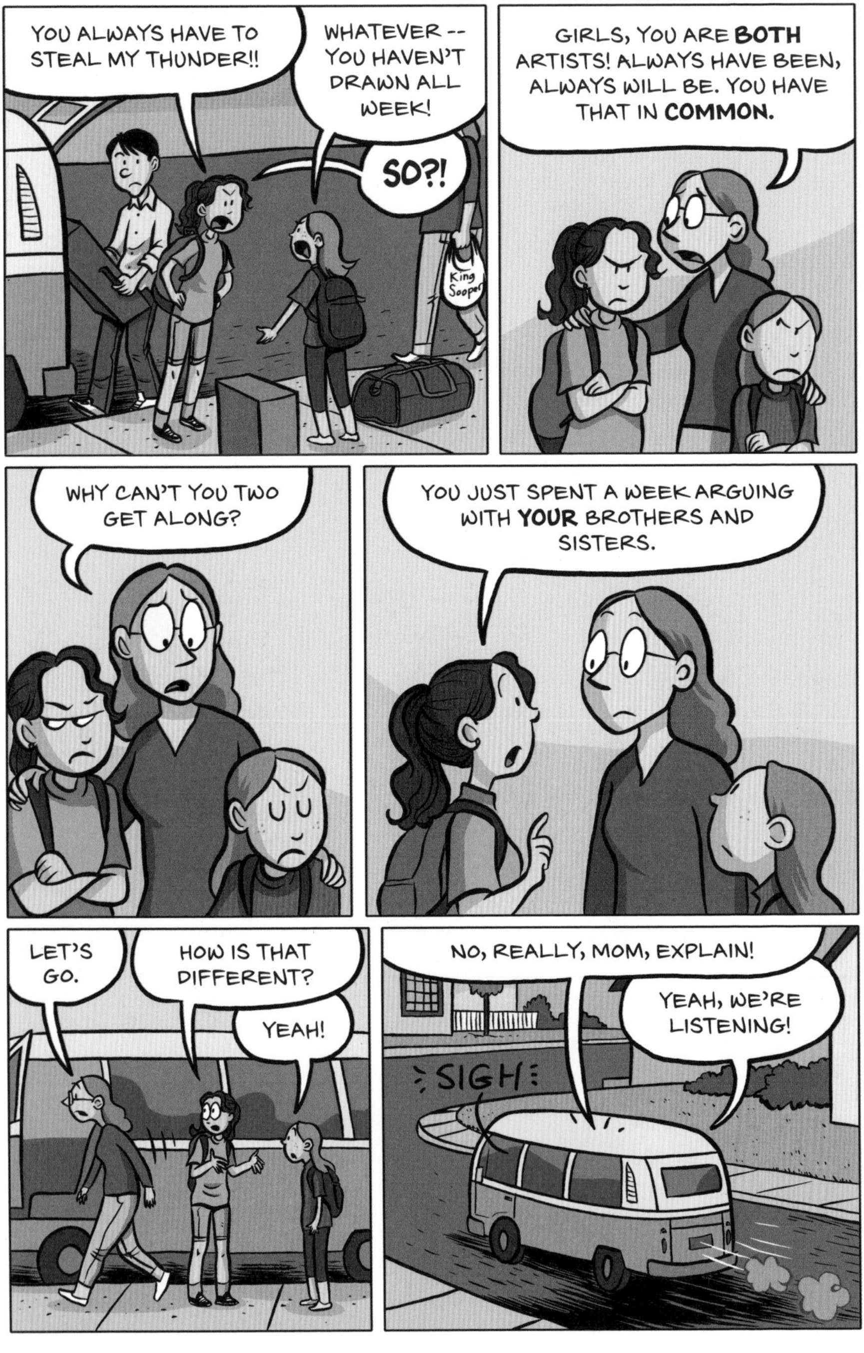
YOU ALWAYS HAVE TO STEAL MY THUNDER!!
WHATEVER -- YOU HAVEN'T DRAWN ALL WEEK!
SO?!
King Sooper
GIRLS, YOU ARE **BOTH** ARTISTS! ALWAYS HAVE BEEN, ALWAYS WILL BE. YOU HAVE THAT IN **COMMON.**
WHY CAN'T YOU TWO GET ALONG?
YOU JUST SPENT A WEEK ARGUING WITH **YOUR** BROTHERS AND SISTERS.
LET'S GO.
HOW IS THAT DIFFERENT?
YEAH!
NO, REALLY, MOM, EXPLAIN!
YEAH, WE'RE LISTENING!
SIGH

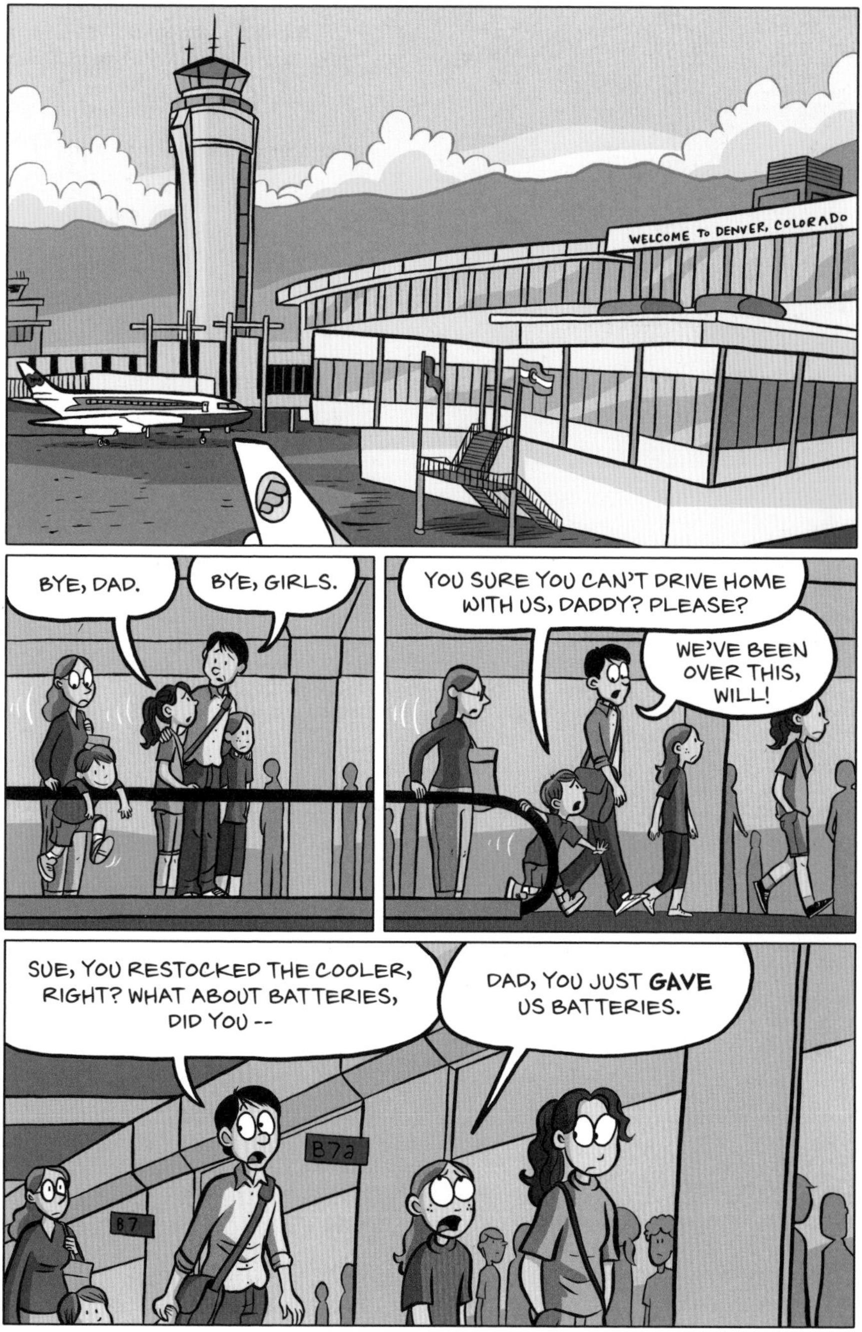
WELCOME TO DENVER, COLORADO
BYE, DAD.
BYE, GIRLS.
YOU SURE YOU CAN'T DRIVE HOME WITH US, DADDY? PLEASE?
WE'VE BEEN OVER THIS, WILL!
SUE, YOU RESTOCKED THE COOLER, RIGHT? WHAT ABOUT BATTERIES, DID YOU --
DAD, YOU JUST **GAVE** US BATTERIES.
B7a
B7

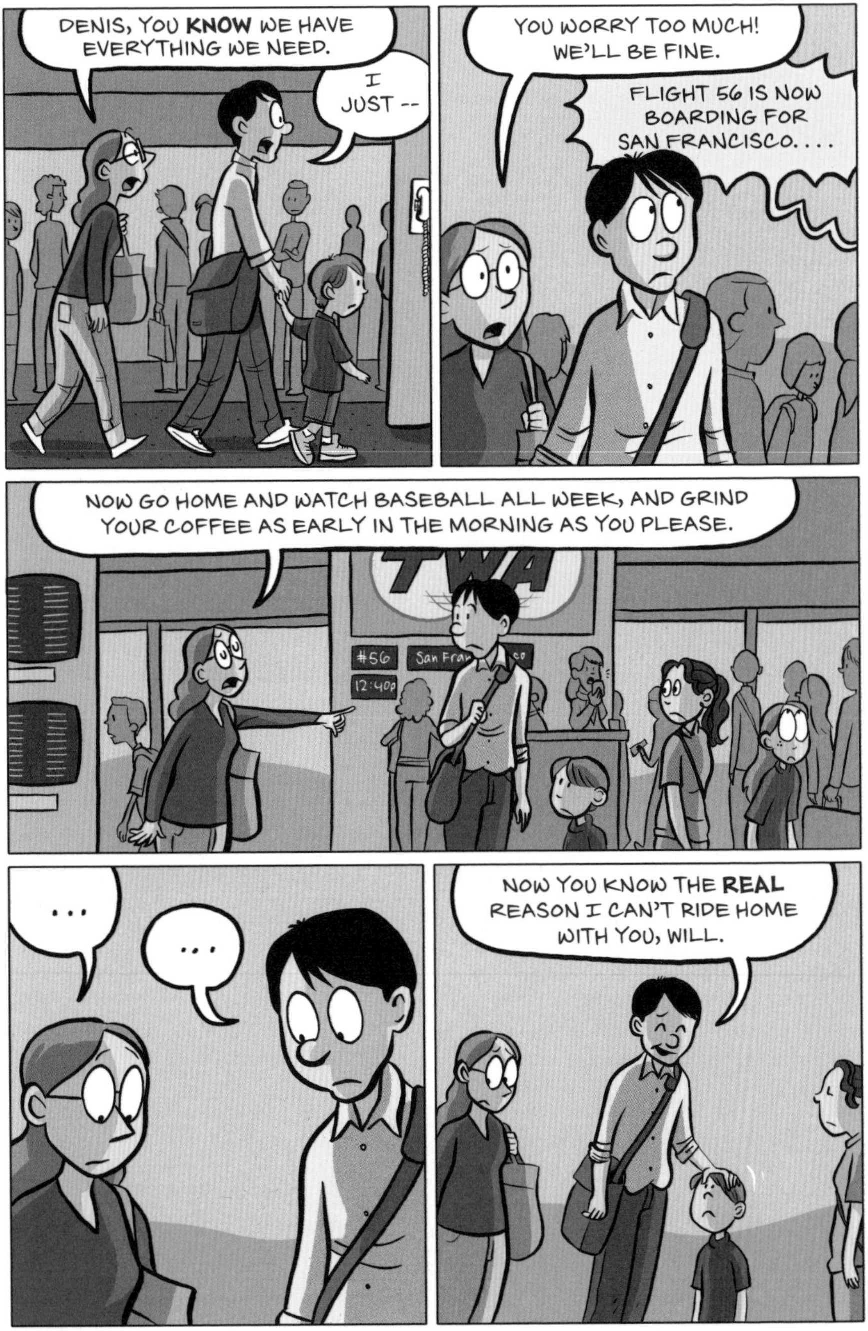
DENIS, YOU KNOW WE HAVE EVERYTHING WE NEED.
I JUST --
YOU WORRY TOO MUCH! WE'LL BE FINE.
FLIGHT 56 IS NOW BOARDING FOR SAN FRANCISCO. . . .
NOW GO HOME AND WATCH BASEBALL ALL WEEK, AND GRIND YOUR COFFEE AS EARLY IN THE MORNING AS YOU PLEASE.
TWA
#56
12:40p
. . .
. . .
NOW YOU KNOW THE REAL REASON I CAN'T RIDE HOME WITH YOU, WILL.

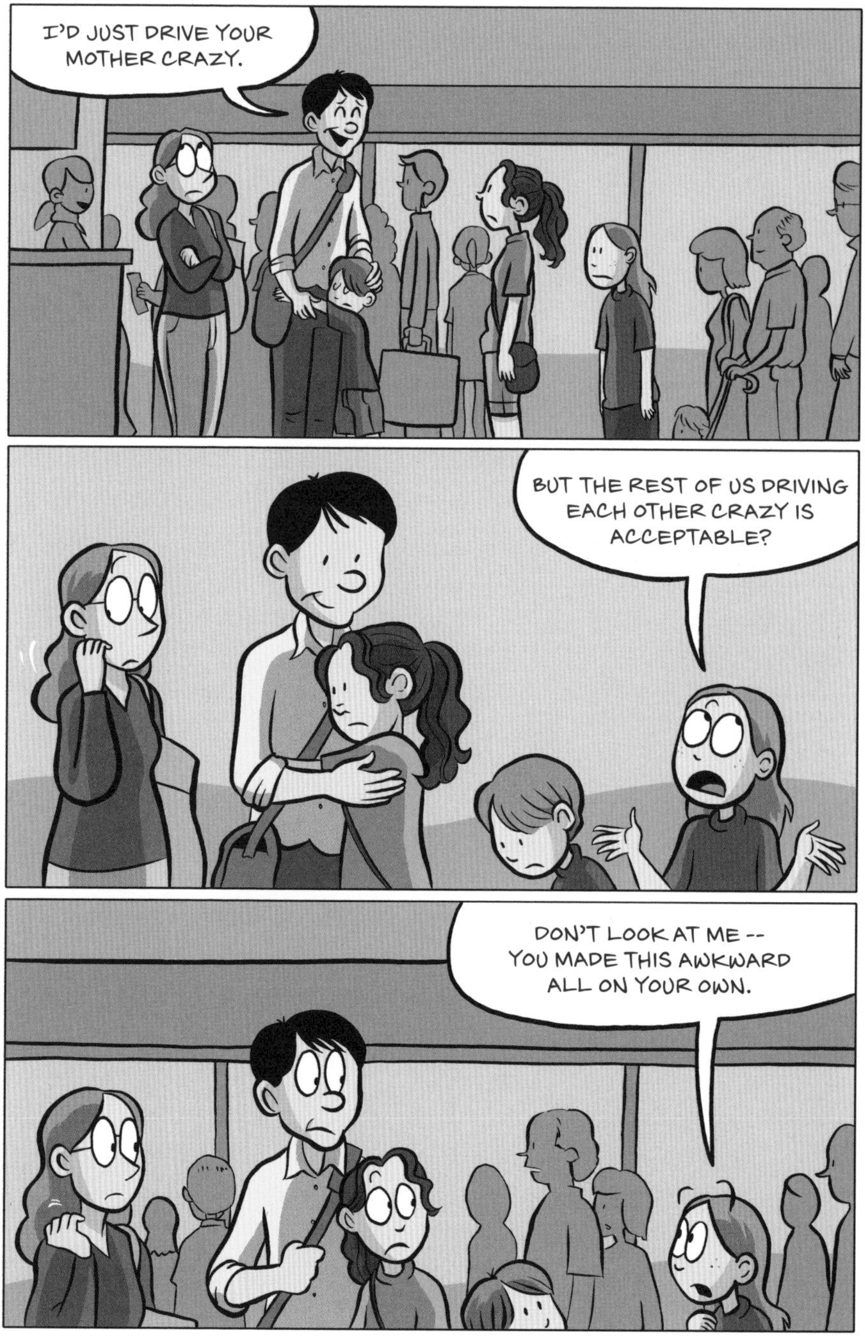
I'D JUST DRIVE YOUR MOTHER CRAZY.
BUT THE REST OF US DRIVING EACH OTHER CRAZY IS ACCEPTABLE?
DON'T LOOK AT ME -- YOU MADE THIS AWKWARD ALL ON YOUR OWN.

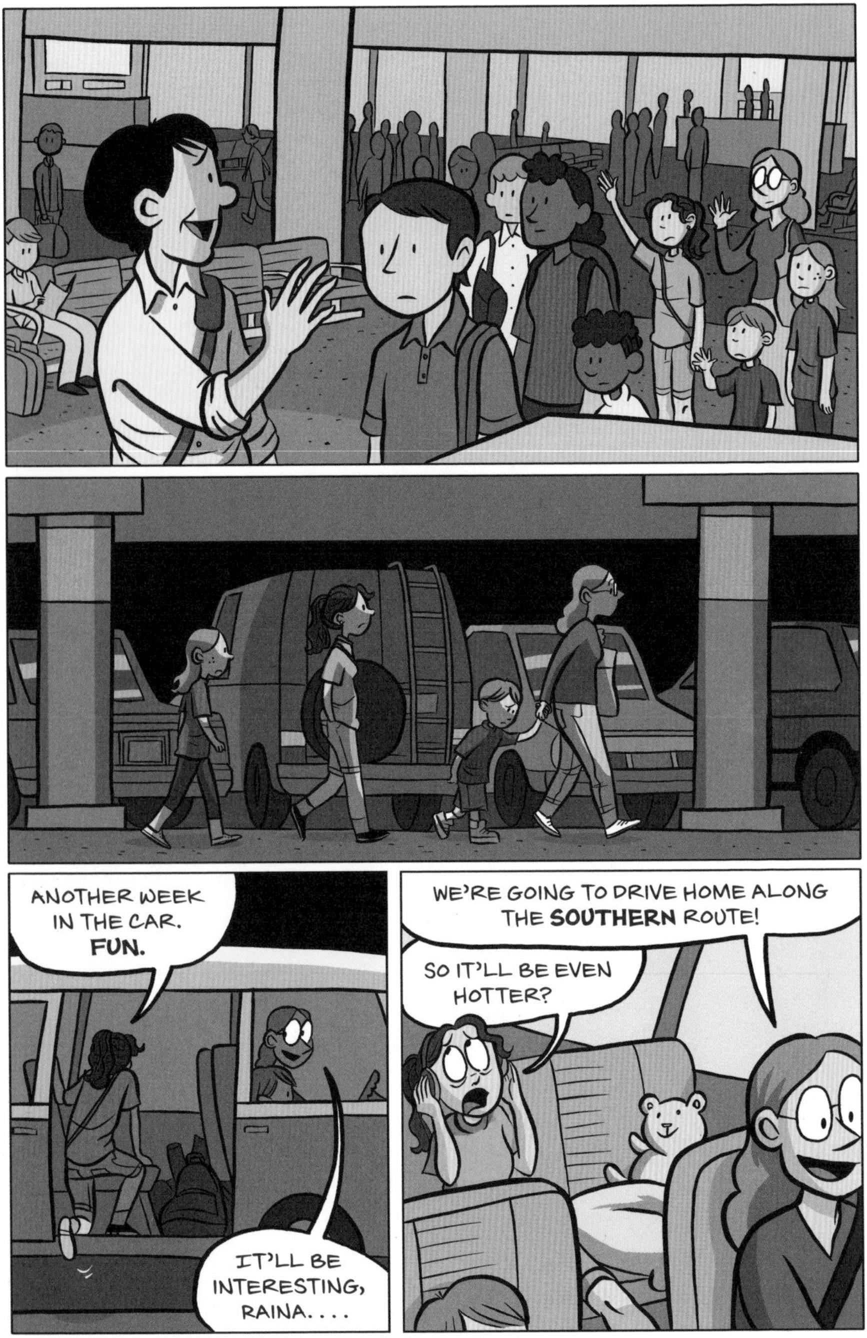
ANOTHER WEEK IN THE CAR. **FUN.**
IT'LL BE INTERESTING, RAINA. . . .
WE'RE GOING TO DRIVE HOME ALONG THE **SOUTHERN** ROUTE!
SO IT'LL BE EVEN HOTTER?

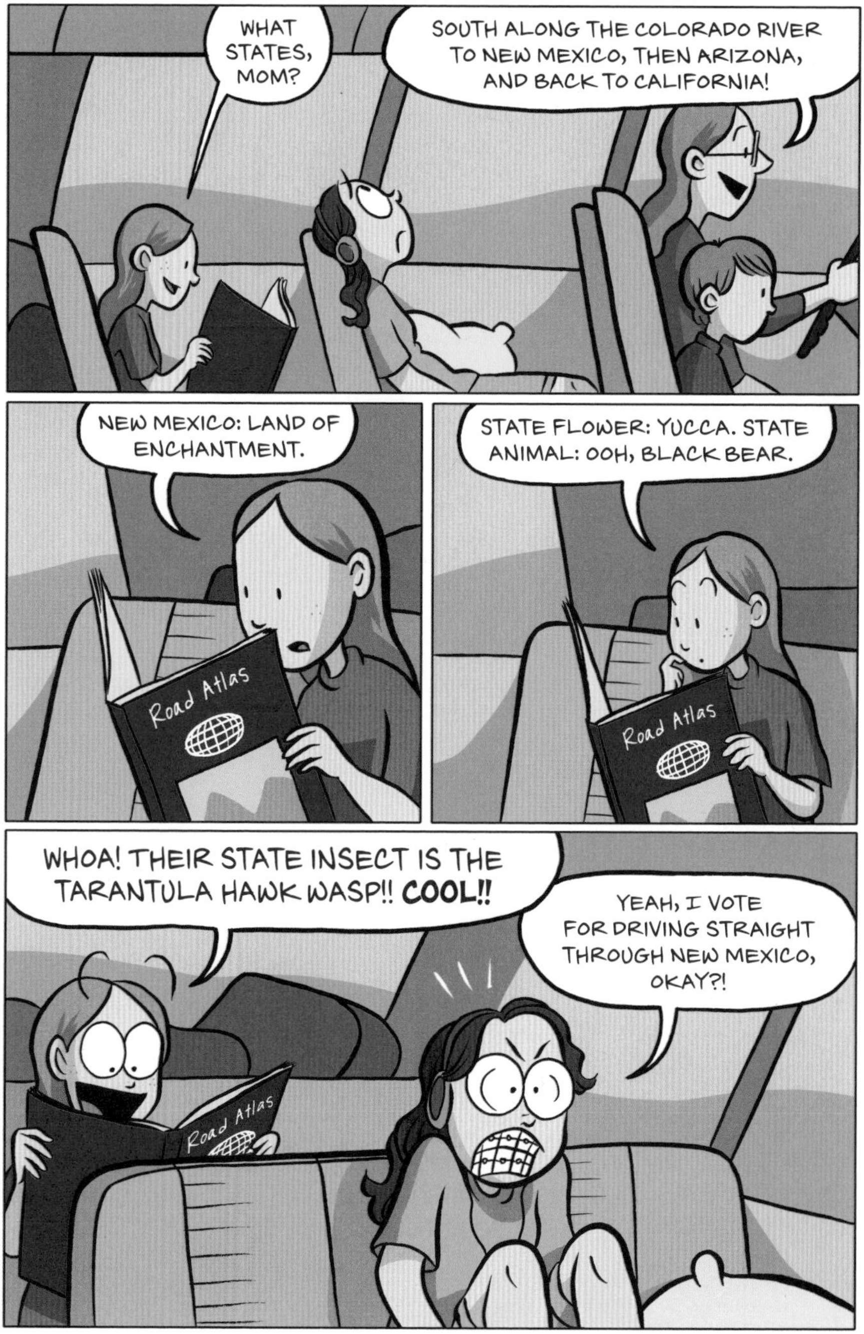
WHAT STATES, MOM?
SOUTH ALONG THE COLORADO RIVER TO NEW MEXICO, THEN ARIZONA, AND BACK TO CALIFORNIA!
NEW MEXICO: LAND OF ENCHANTMENT.
Road Atlas
STATE FLOWER: YUCCA. STATE ANIMAL: OOH, BLACK BEAR.
Road Atlas
WHOA! THEIR STATE INSECT IS THE TARANTULA HAWK WASP!! COOL!!
YEAH, I VOTE FOR DRIVING STRAIGHT THROUGH NEW MEXICO, OKAY?!
Road Atlas

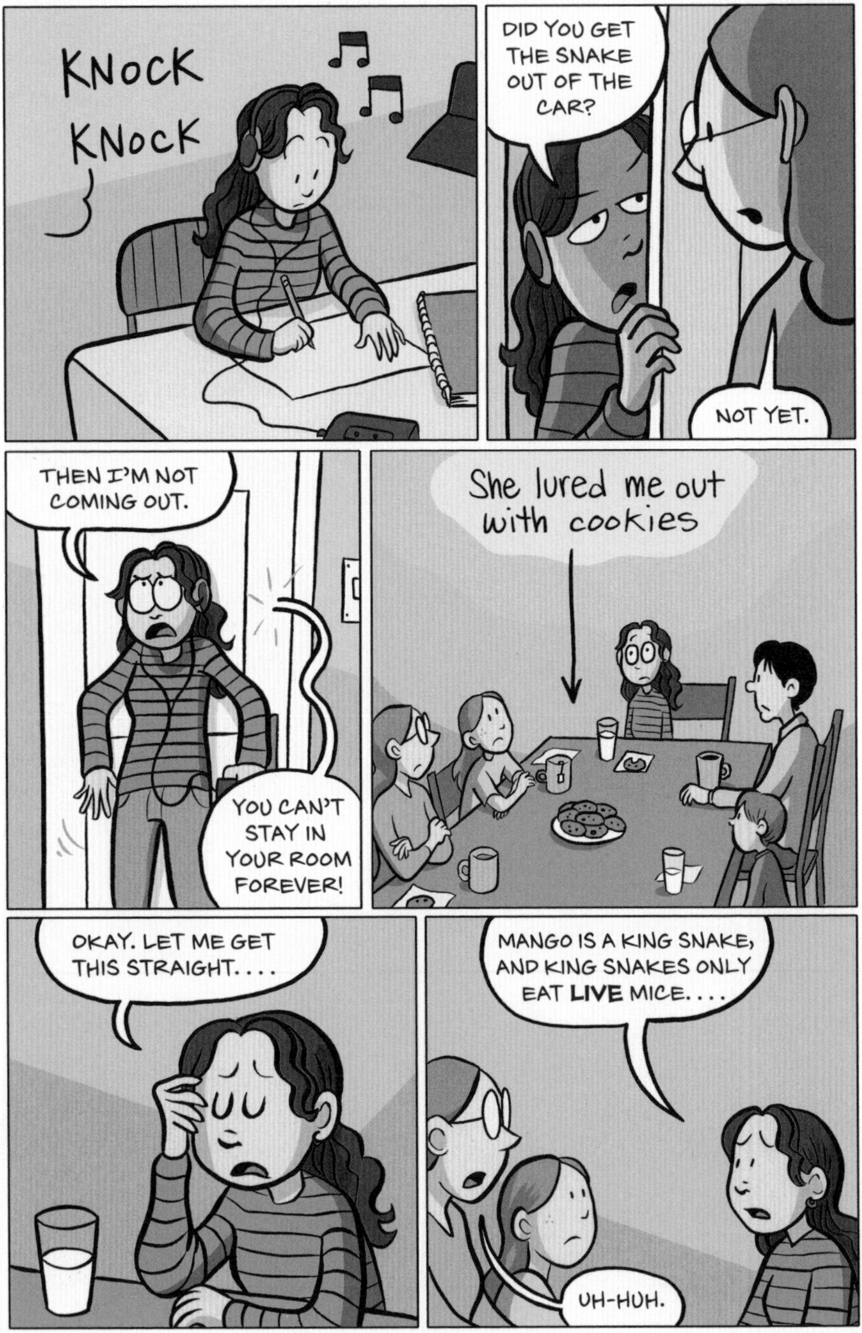
KNOCK KNOCK
DID YOU GET THE SNAKE OUT OF THE CAR?
NOT YET.
THEN I'M NOT COMING OUT.
YOU CAN'T STAY IN YOUR ROOM FOREVER!
She lured me out with cookies
OKAY. LET ME GET THIS STRAIGHT. . . .
MANGO IS A KING SNAKE, AND KING SNAKES ONLY EAT **LIVE** MICE. . . .
UH-HUH.

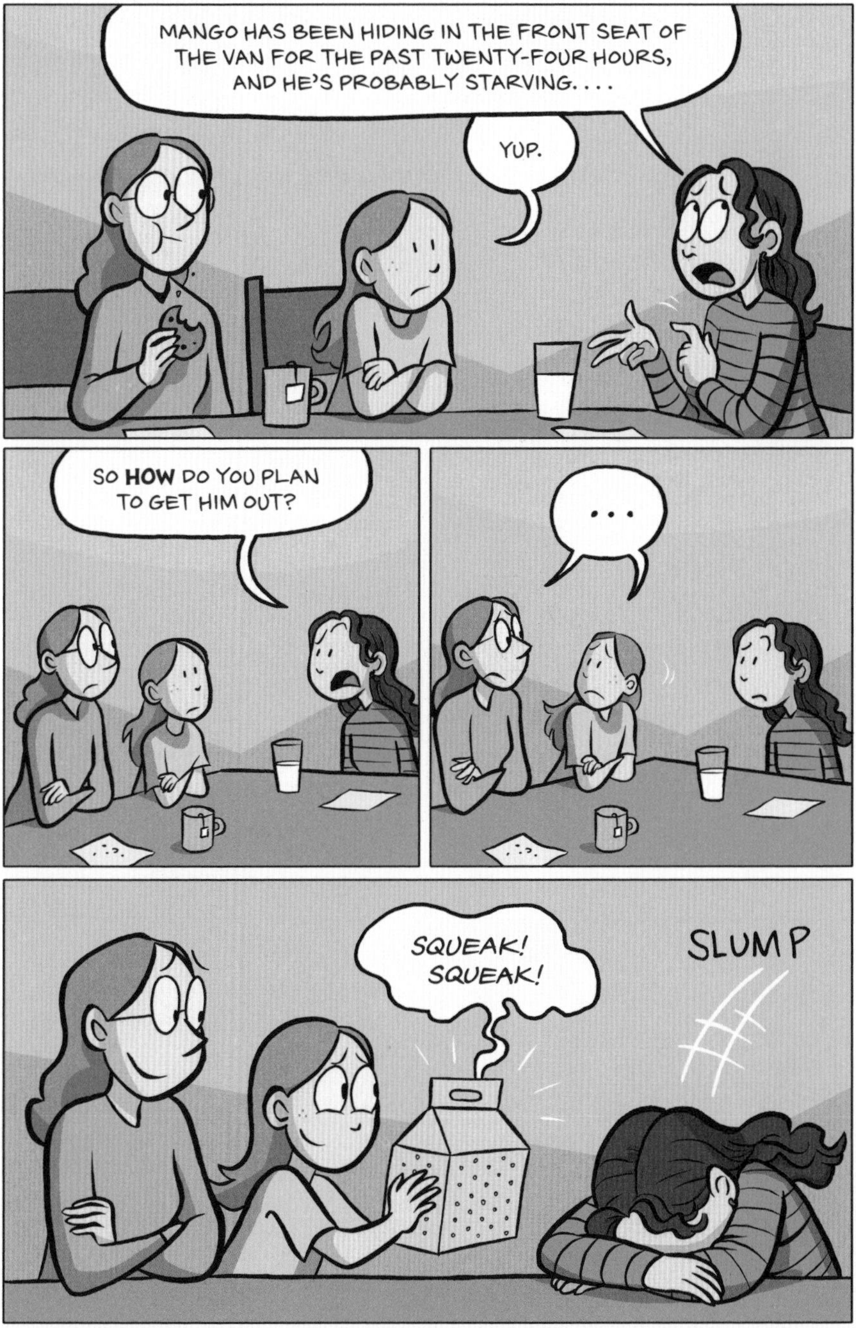
MANGO HAS BEEN HIDING IN THE FRONT SEAT OF THE VAN FOR THE PAST TWENTY-FOUR HOURS, AND HE'S PROBABLY STARVING. . . .
YUP.
SO **HOW** DO YOU PLAN TO GET HIM OUT?
. . .
SQUEAK! SQUEAK!
SLUMP

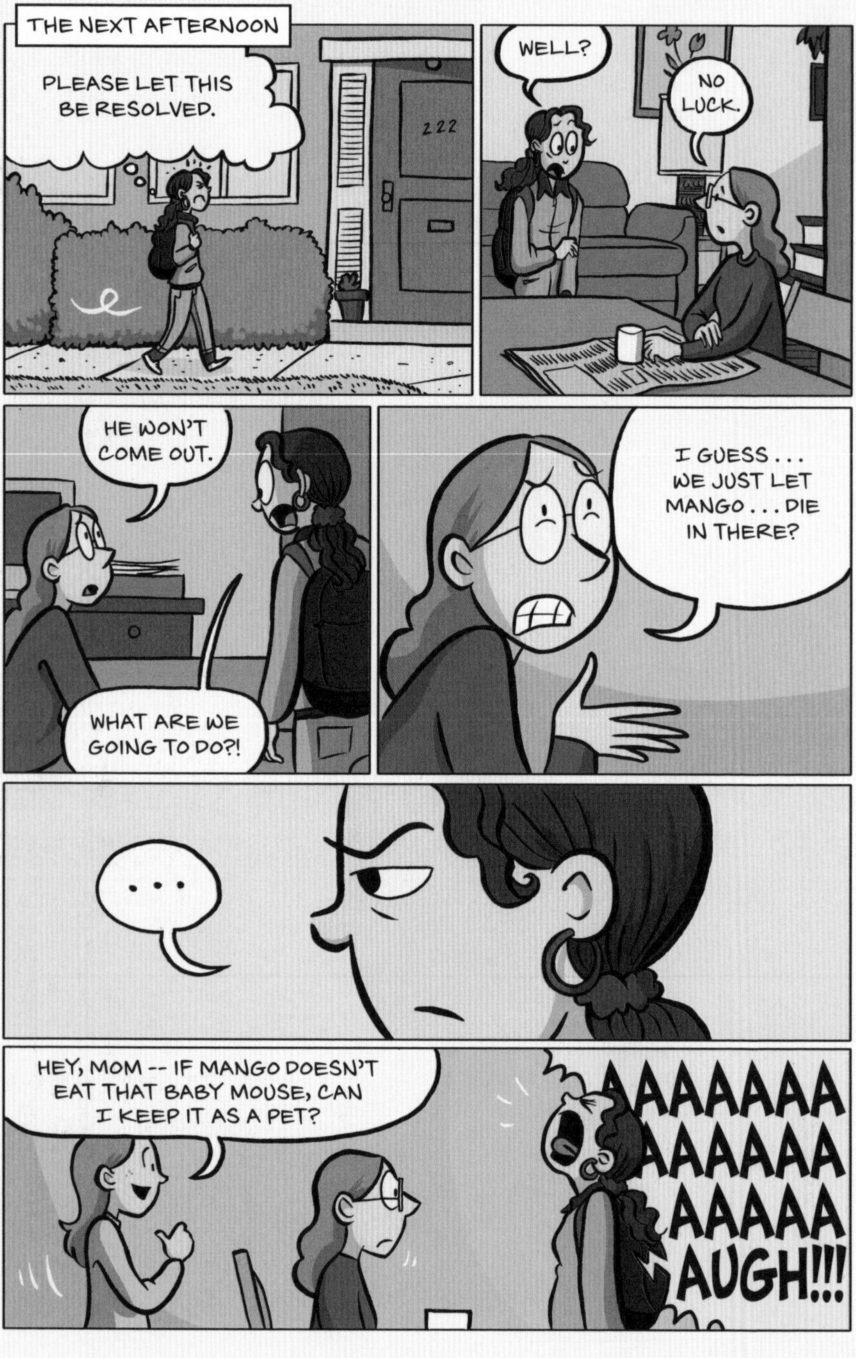
THE NEXT AFTERNOON
PLEASE LET THIS BE RESOLVED.
WELL?
NO LUCK.
HE WON'T COME OUT.
WHAT ARE WE GOING TO DO?!
I GUESS . . . WE JUST LET MANGO . . . DIE IN THERE?
. . .
HEY, MOM -- IF MANGO DOESN'T EAT THAT BABY MOUSE, CAN I KEEP IT AS A PET?
AAAAAAAAAAAAAAAAAAAUGH!!!

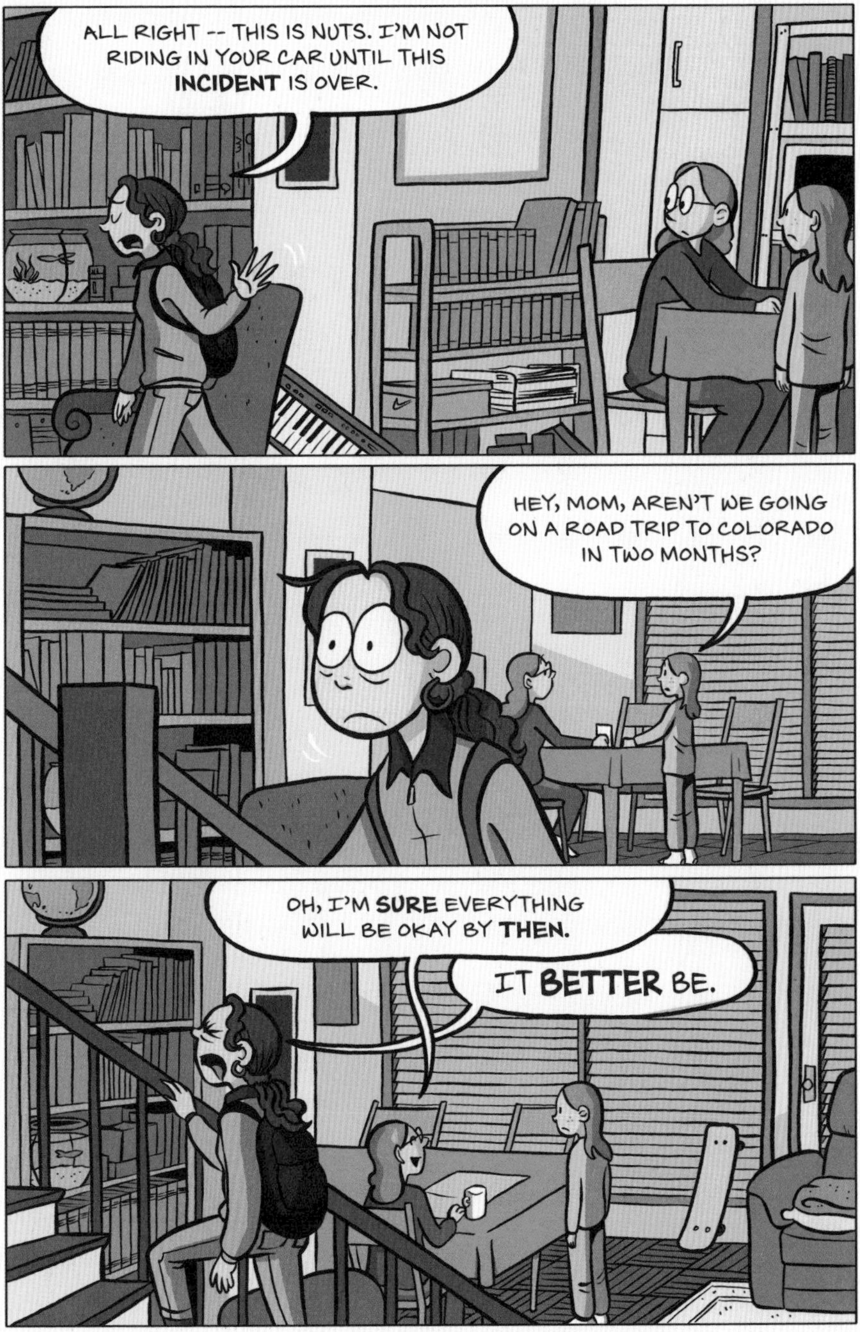
ALL RIGHT -- THIS IS NUTS. I'M NOT RIDING IN YOUR CAR UNTIL THIS **INCIDENT** IS OVER.
HEY, MOM, AREN'T WE GOING ON A ROAD TRIP TO COLORADO IN TWO MONTHS?
OH, I'M **SURE** EVERYTHING WILL BE OKAY BY **THEN.**
IT **BETTER** BE.

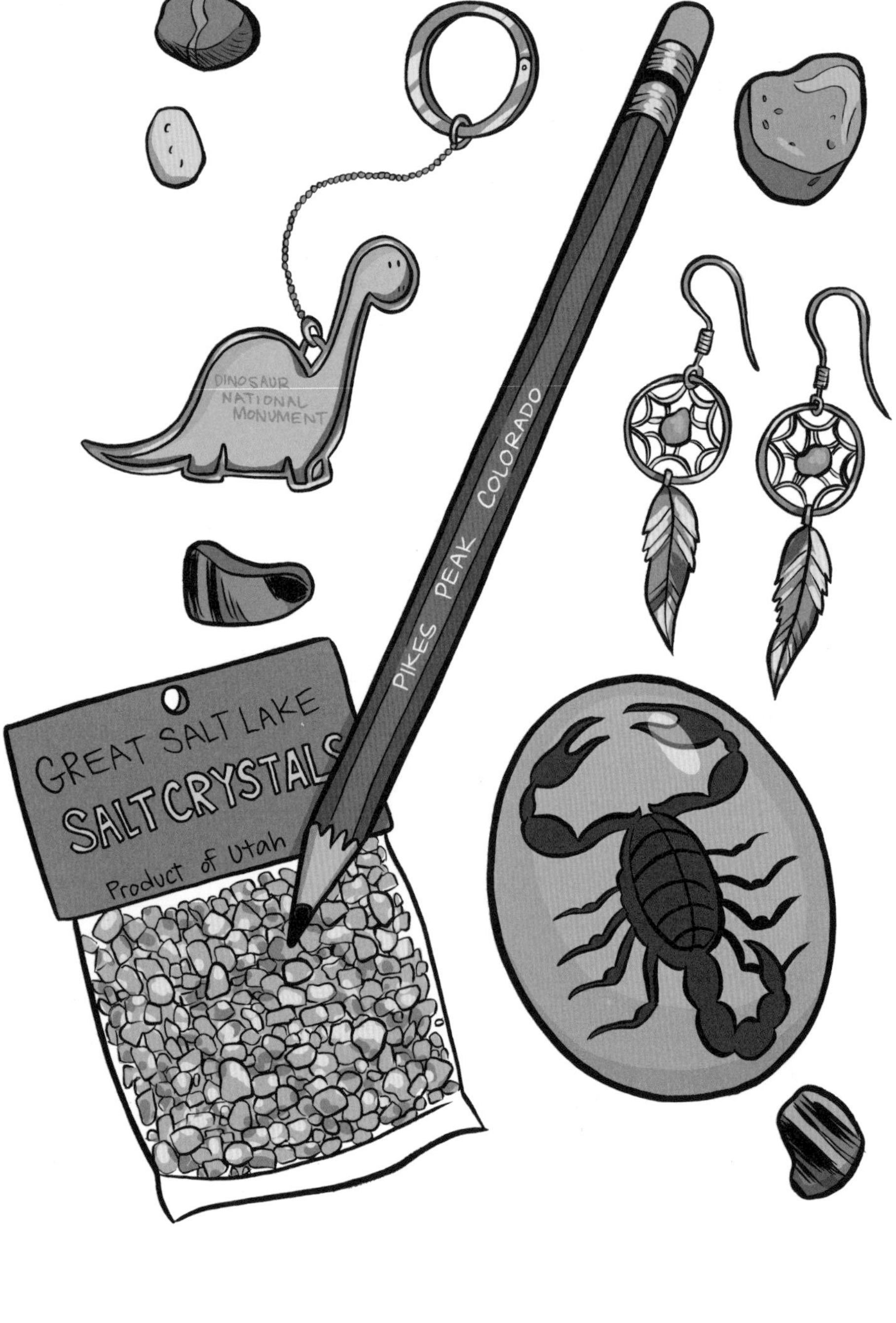
DINOSAUR NATIONAL MONUMENT
PIKES PEAK COLORADO
GREAT SALT LAKE
SALT CRYSTALS
Product of Utah

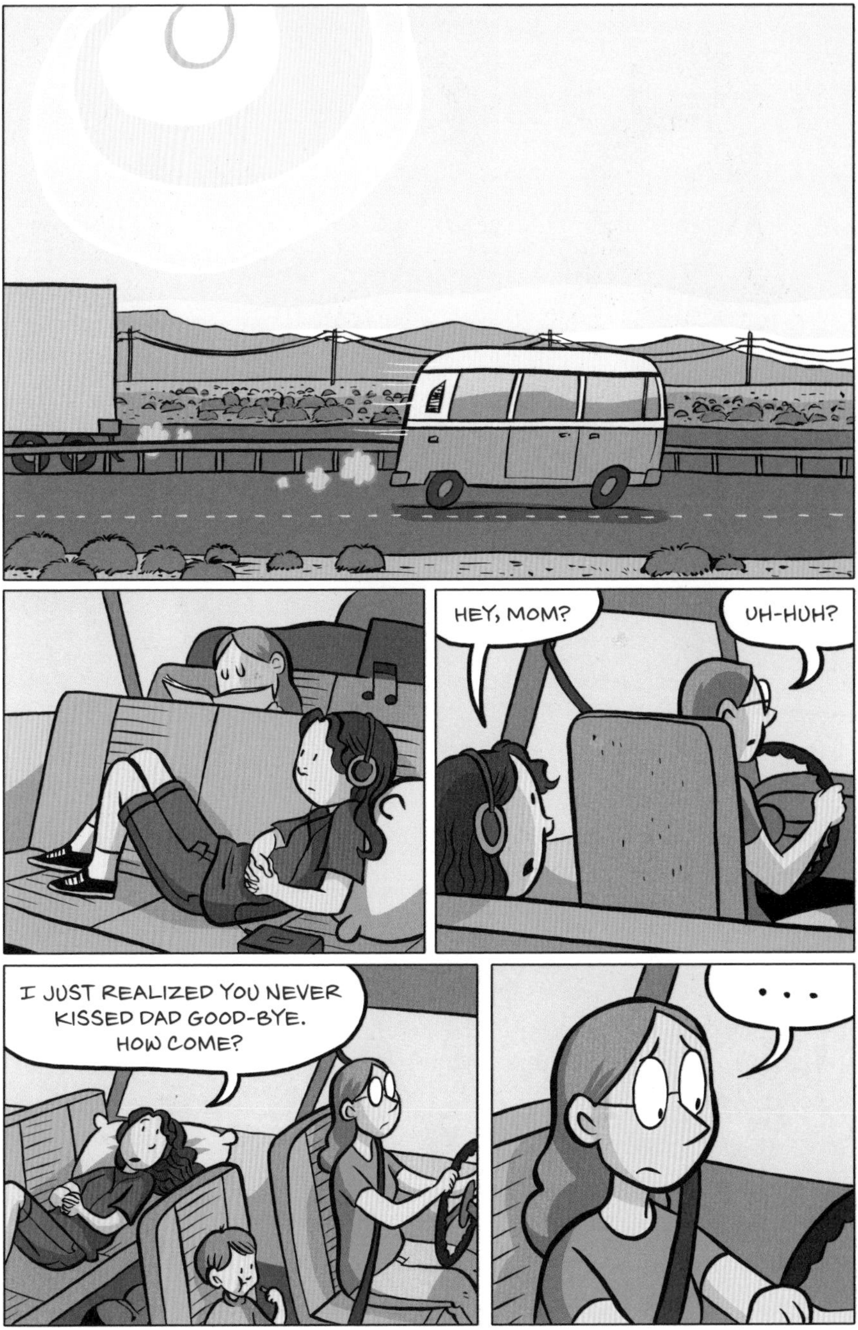
HEY, MOM?
UH-HUH?
I JUST REALIZED YOU NEVER KISSED DAD GOOD-BYE. HOW COME?
. . .

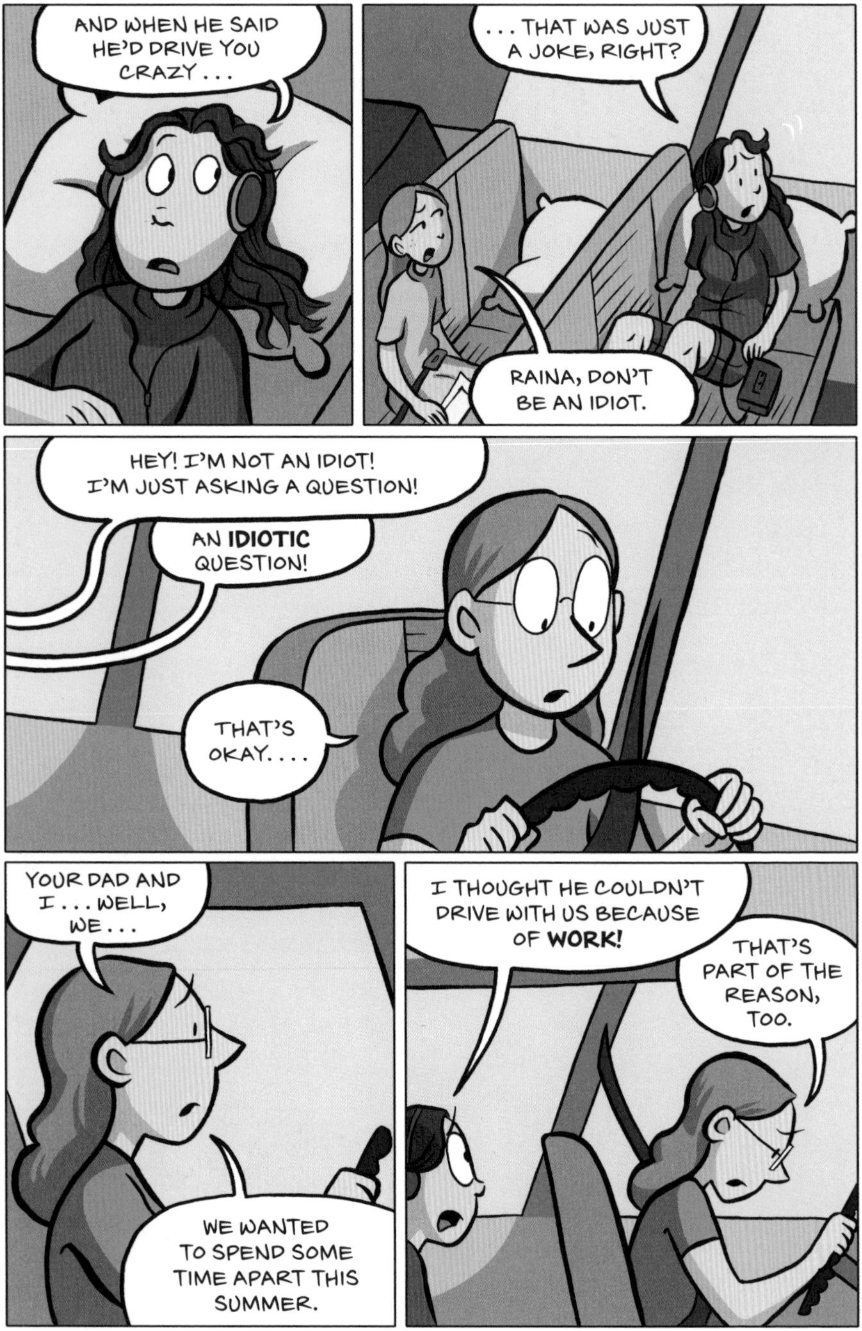
AND WHEN HE SAID HE'D DRIVE YOU CRAZY . . .
. . . THAT WAS JUST A JOKE, RIGHT?
RAINA, DON'T BE AN IDIOT.
HEY! I'M NOT AN IDIOT! I'M JUST ASKING A QUESTION!
AN **IDIOTIC** QUESTION!
THAT'S OKAY. . . .
YOUR DAD AND I . . . WELL, WE . . .
WE WANTED TO SPEND SOME TIME APART THIS SUMMER.
I THOUGHT HE COULDN'T DRIVE WITH US BECAUSE OF **WORK!**
THAT'S PART OF THE REASON, TOO.

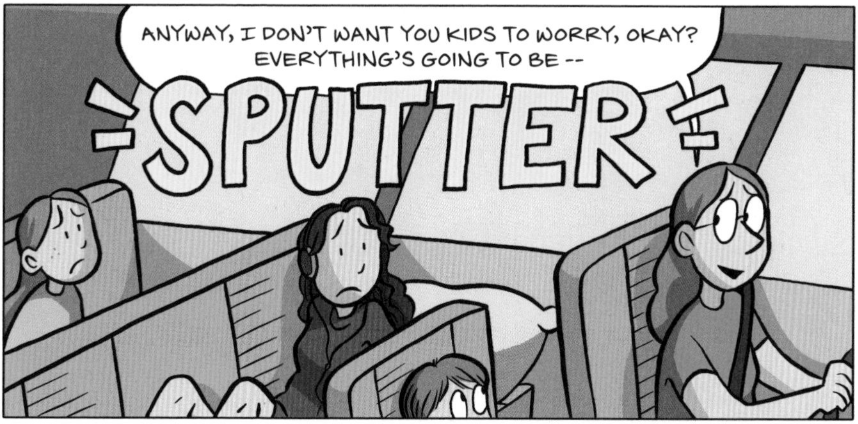
ANYWAY, I DON'T WANT YOU KIDS TO WORRY, OKAY? EVERYTHING'S GOING TO BE --
SPUTTER

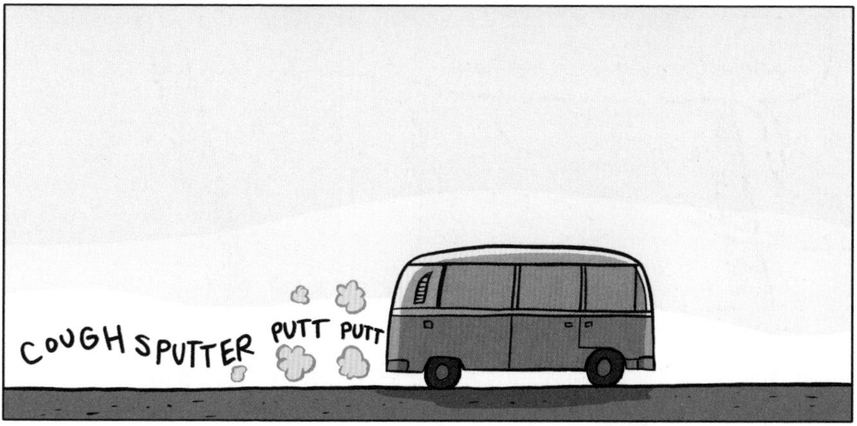
COUGH SPUTTER PUTT PUTT

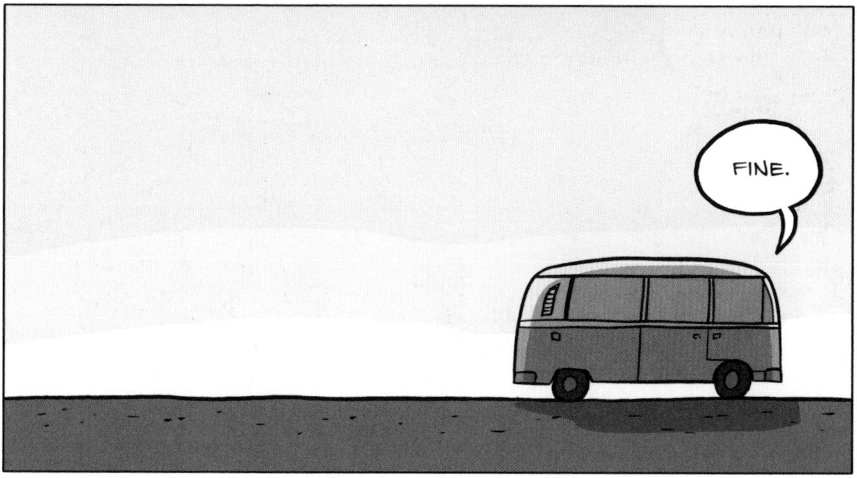
FINE.

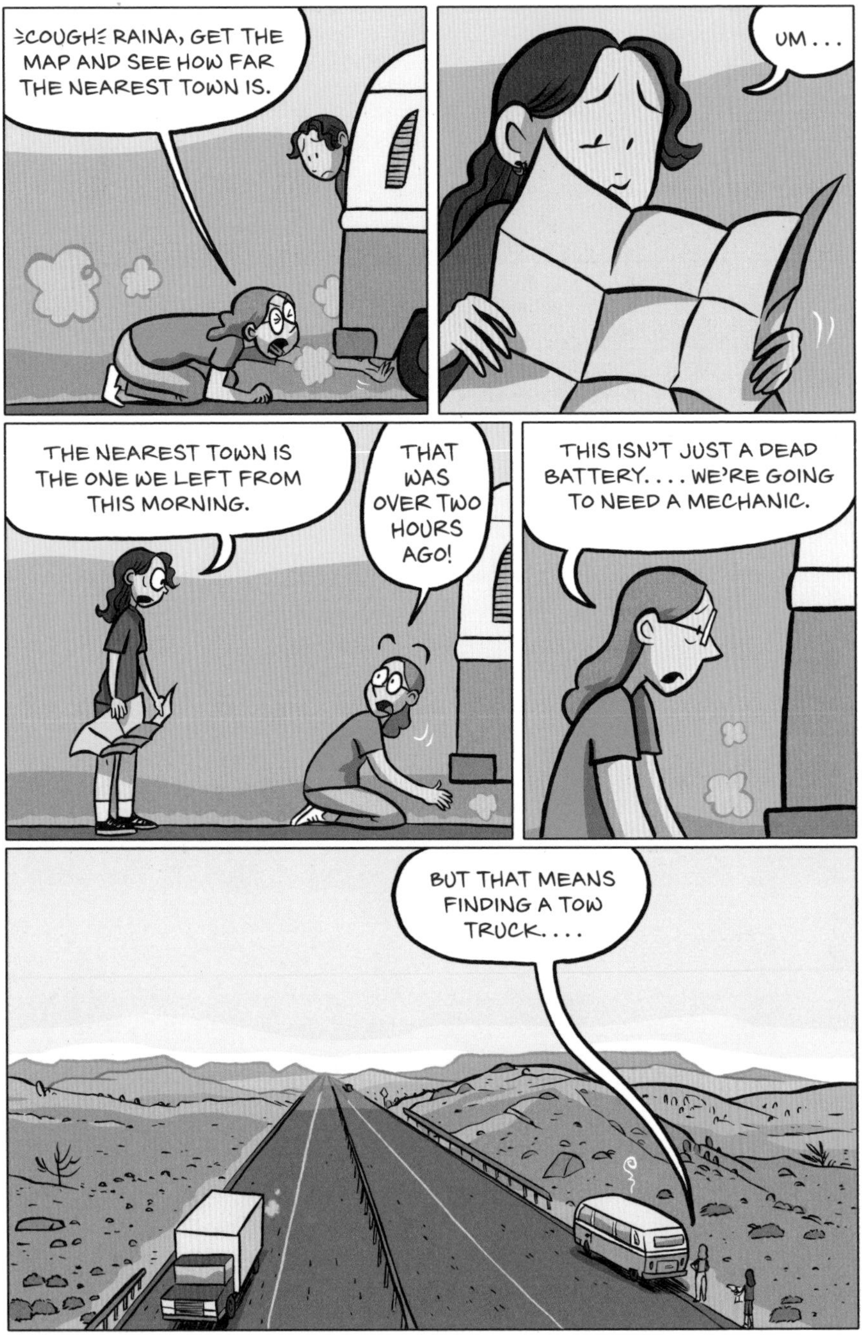

≡COUGH≡ RAINA, GET THE MAP AND SEE HOW FAR THE NEAREST TOWN IS.
UM . . .
THE NEAREST TOWN IS THE ONE WE LEFT FROM THIS MORNING.
THAT WAS OVER TWO HOURS AGO!
THIS ISN'T JUST A DEAD BATTERY. . . . WE'RE GOING TO NEED A MECHANIC.
BUT THAT MEANS FINDING A TOW TRUCK. . . .

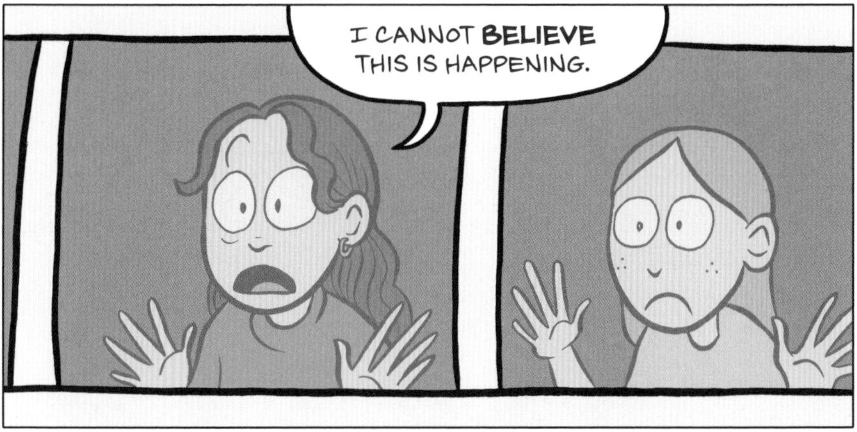
I CANNOT BELIEVE THIS IS HAPPENING.

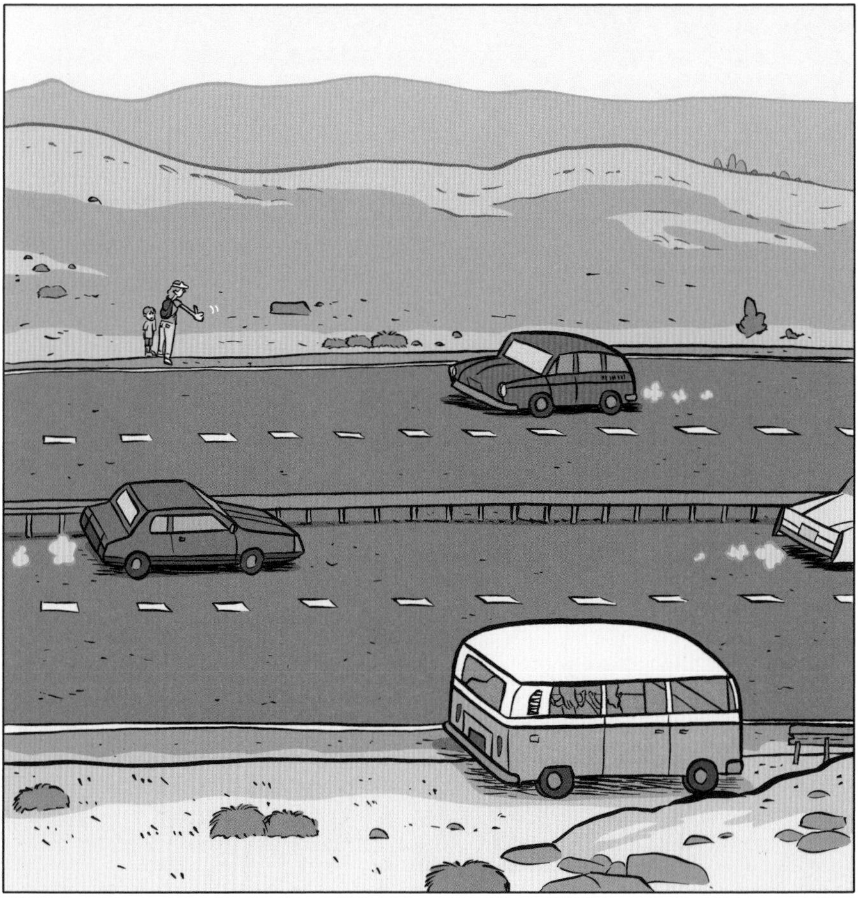

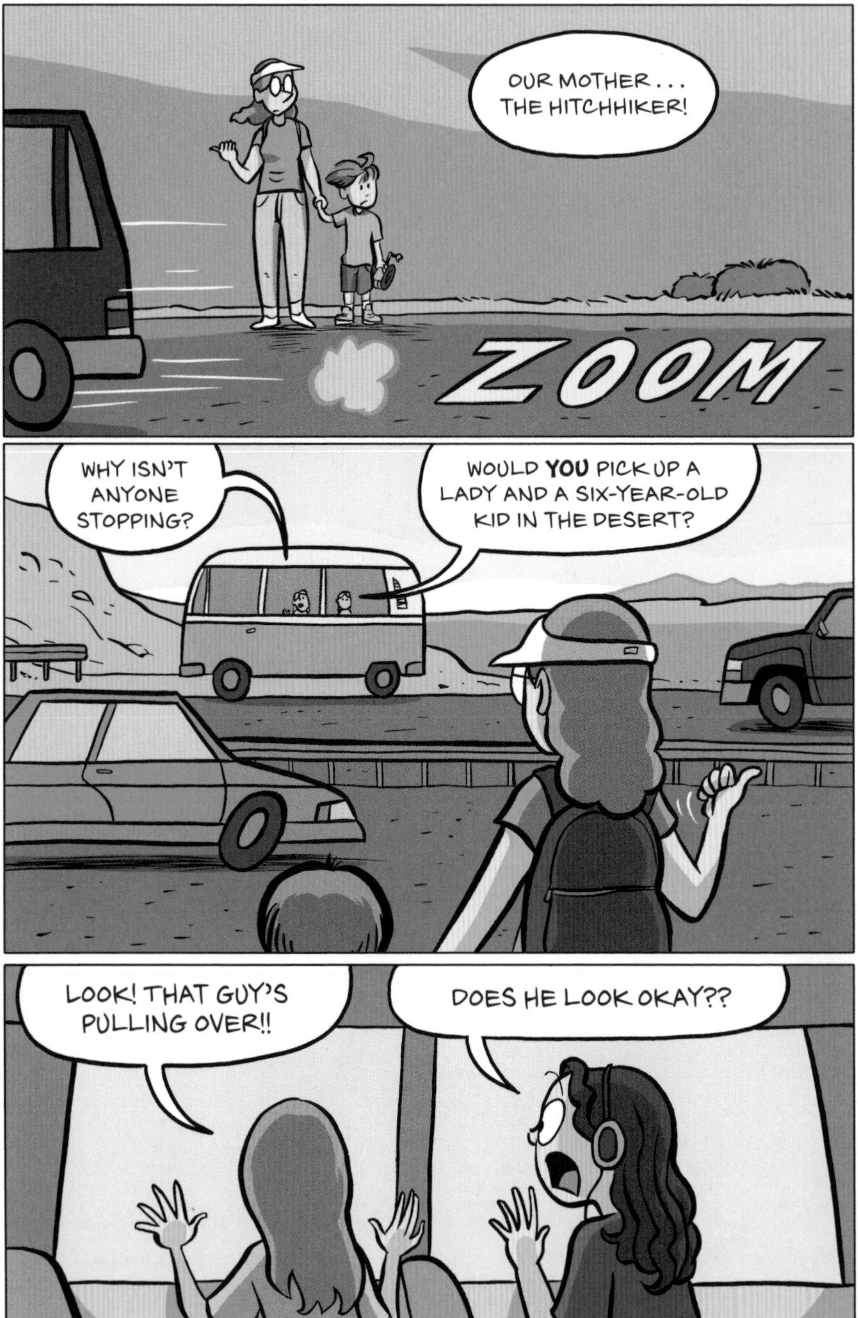
OUR MOTHER . . . THE HITCHHIKER!
ZOOM
WHY ISN'T ANYONE STOPPING?
WOULD **YOU** PICK UP A LADY AND A SIX-YEAR-OLD KID IN THE DESERT?
LOOK! THAT GUY'S PULLING OVER!!
DOES HE LOOK OKAY??

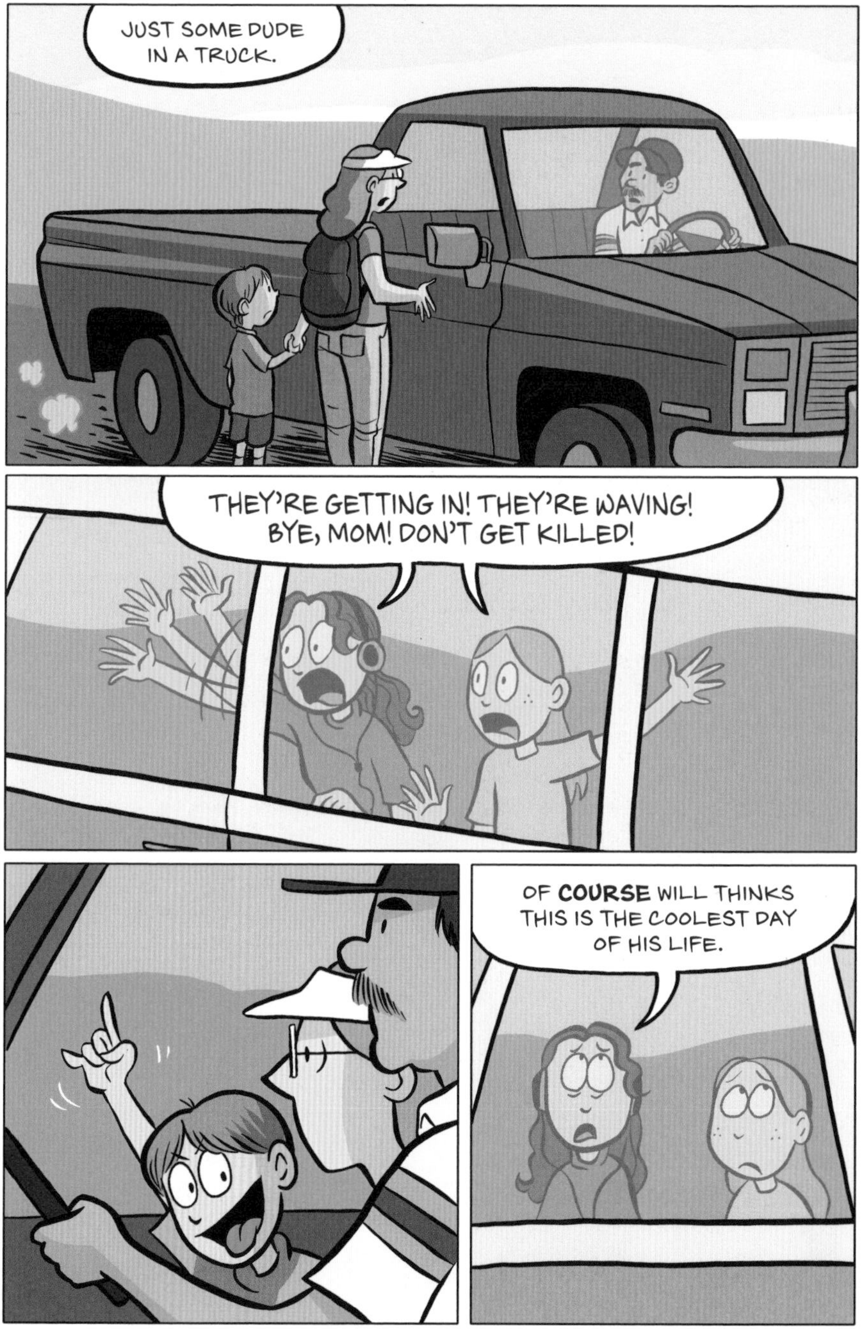
JUST SOME DUDE IN A TRUCK.
THEY'RE GETTING IN! THEY'RE WAVING! BYE, MOM! DON'T GET KILLED!
OF **COURSE** WILL THINKS THIS IS THE COOLEST DAY OF HIS LIFE.

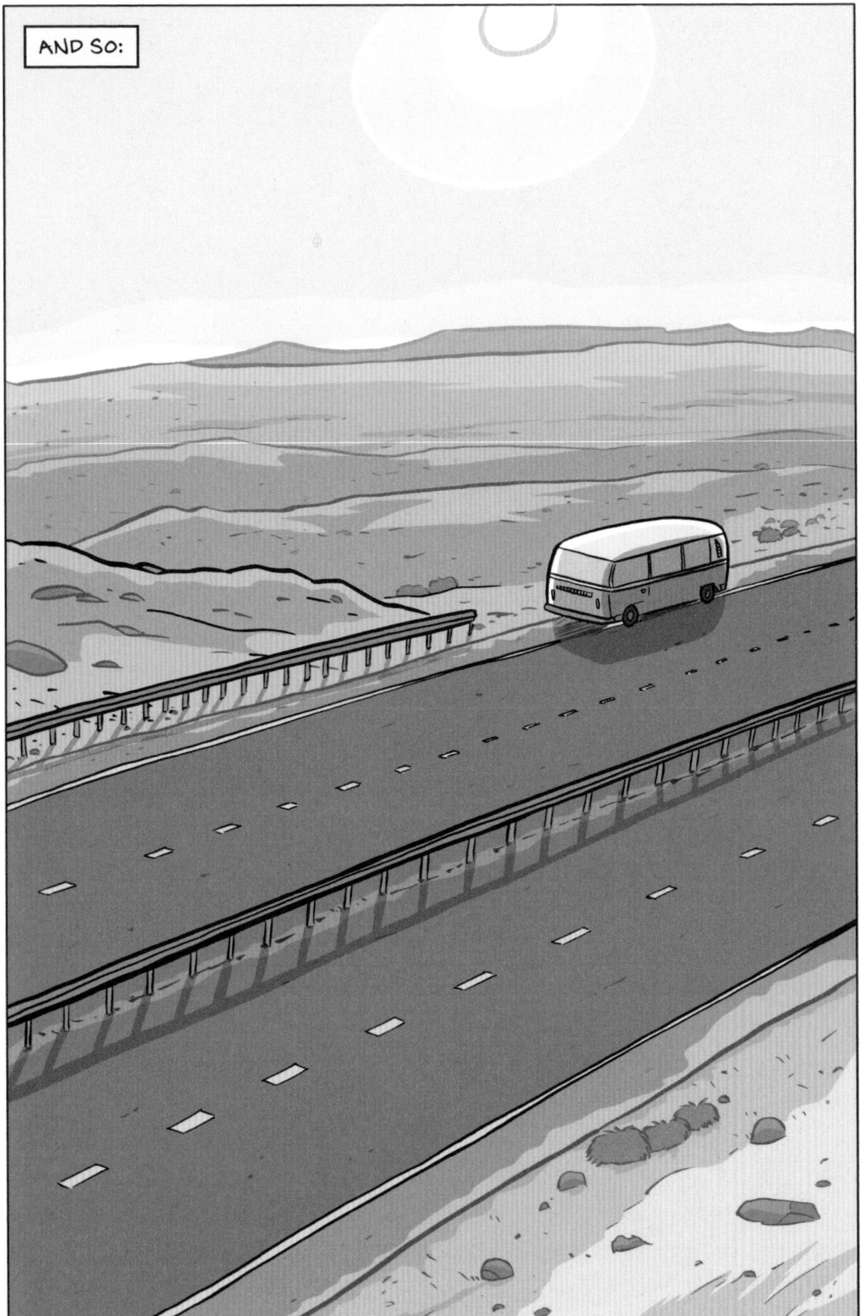
AND SO:

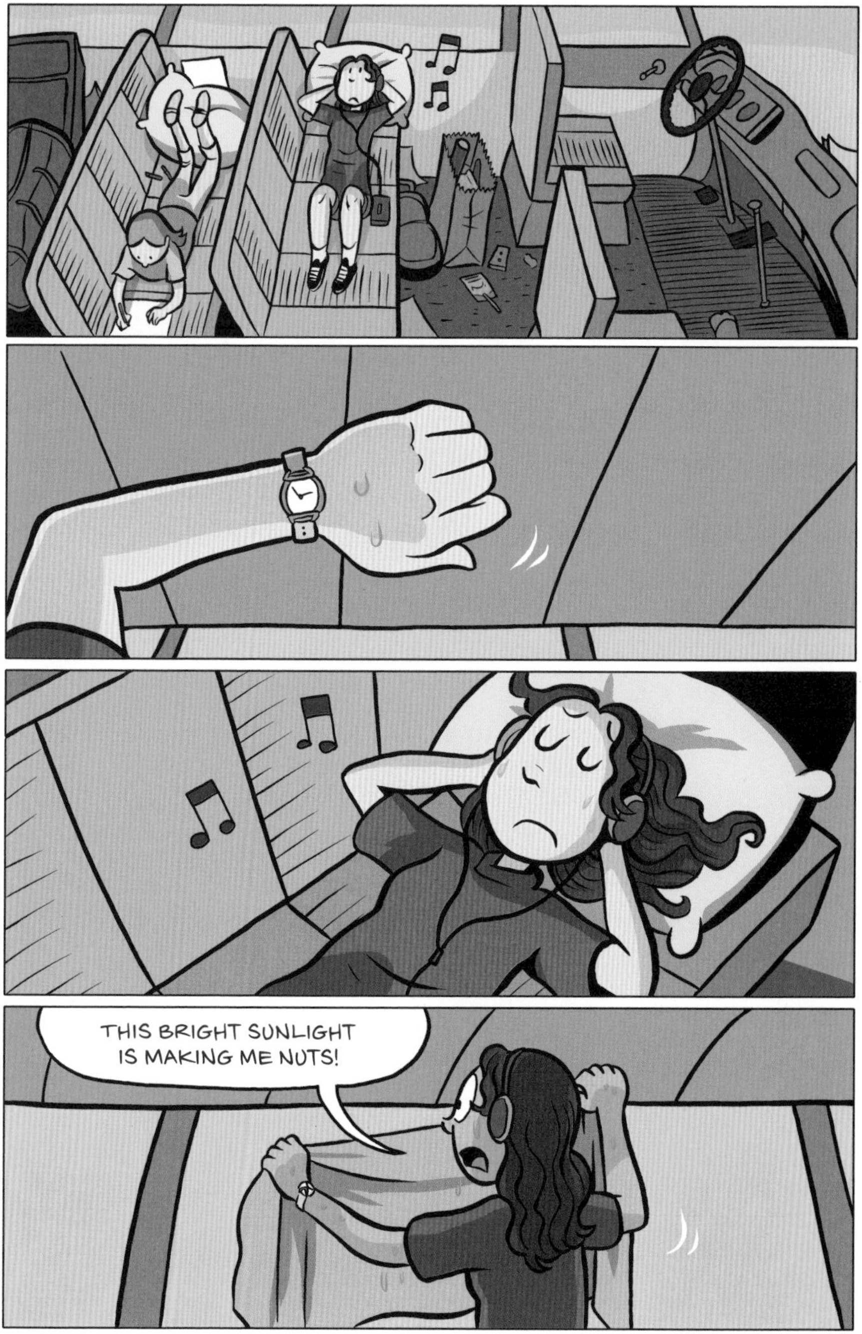
THIS BRIGHT SUNLIGHT IS MAKING ME NUTS!

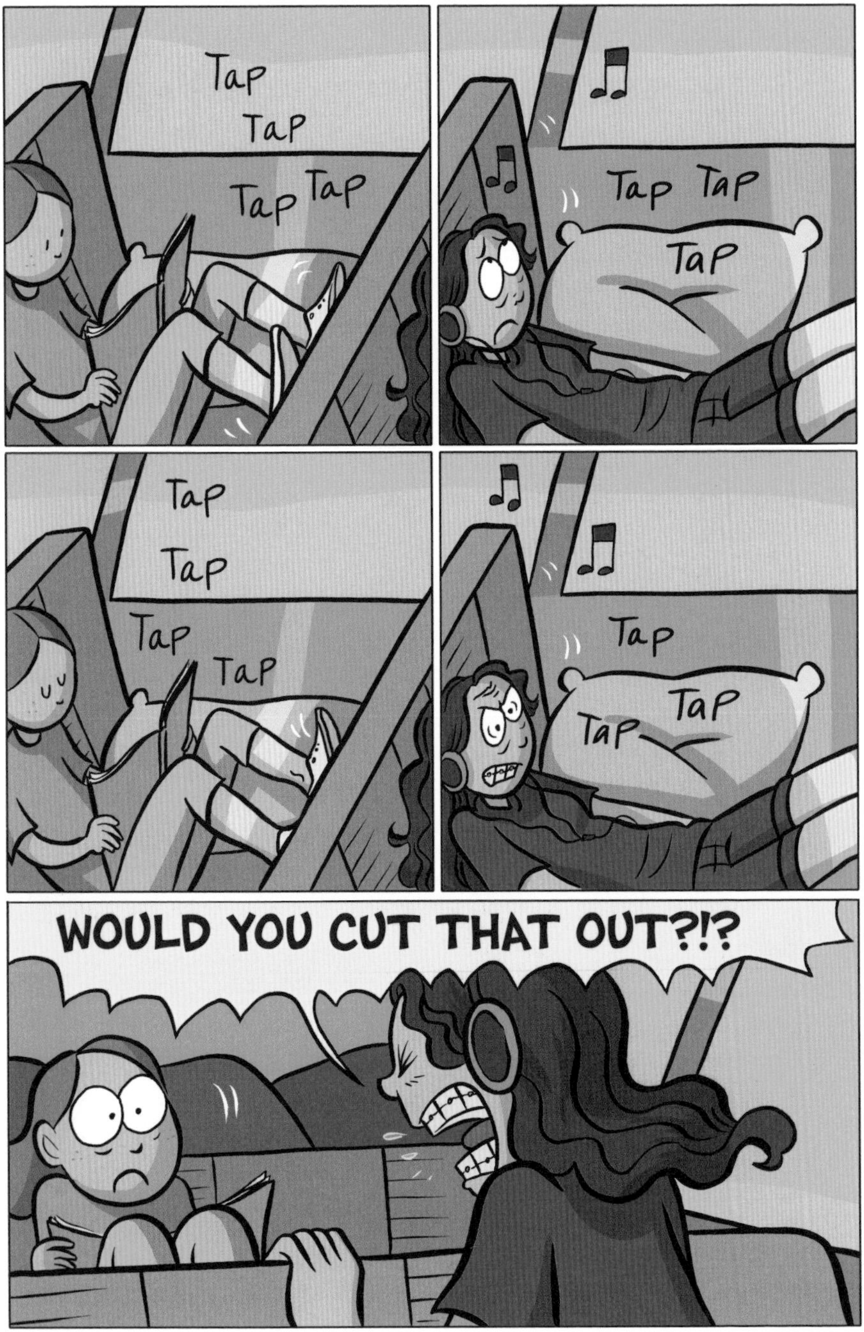
Tap
Tap
Tap Tap
Tap Tap
Tap
Tap
Tap
Tap
Tap
Tap
Tap
Tap
WOULD YOU CUT THAT OUT?!?

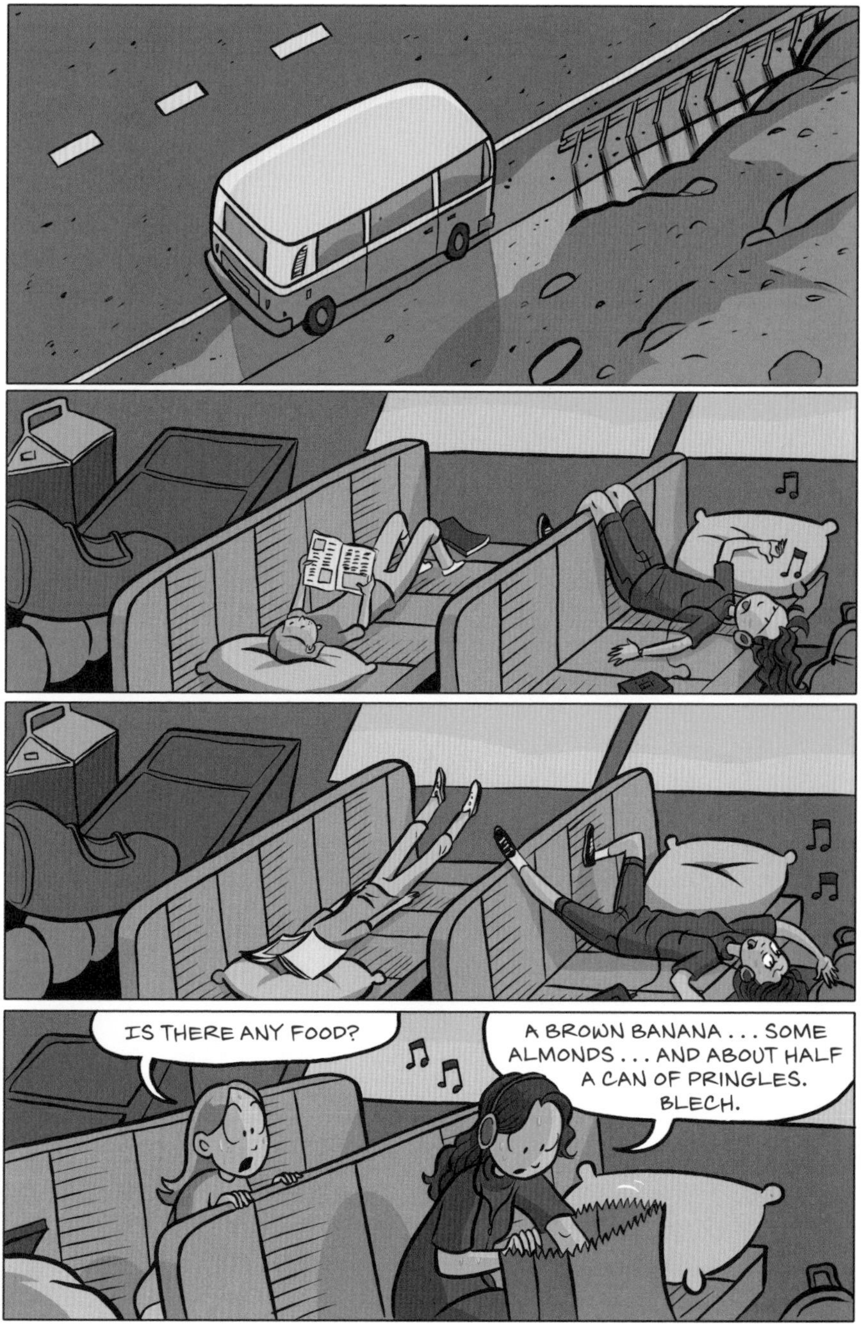
IS THERE ANY FOOD?
A BROWN BANANA . . . SOME ALMONDS . . . AND ABOUT HALF A CAN OF PRINGLES. BLECH.

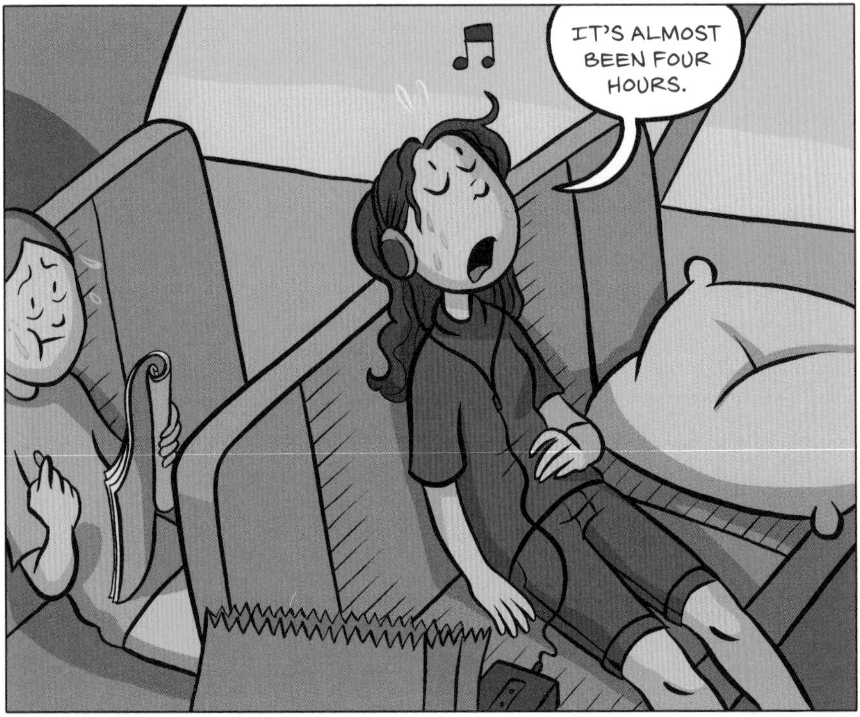
IT'S ALMOST BEEN FOUR HOURS.

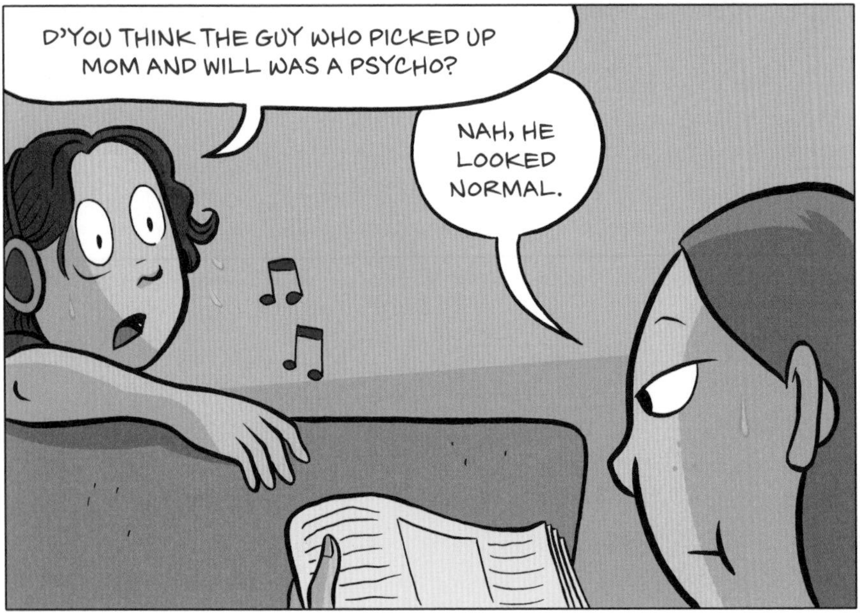
D'YOU THINK THE GUY WHO PICKED UP MOM AND WILL WAS A PSYCHO?
NAH, HE LOOKED NORMAL.

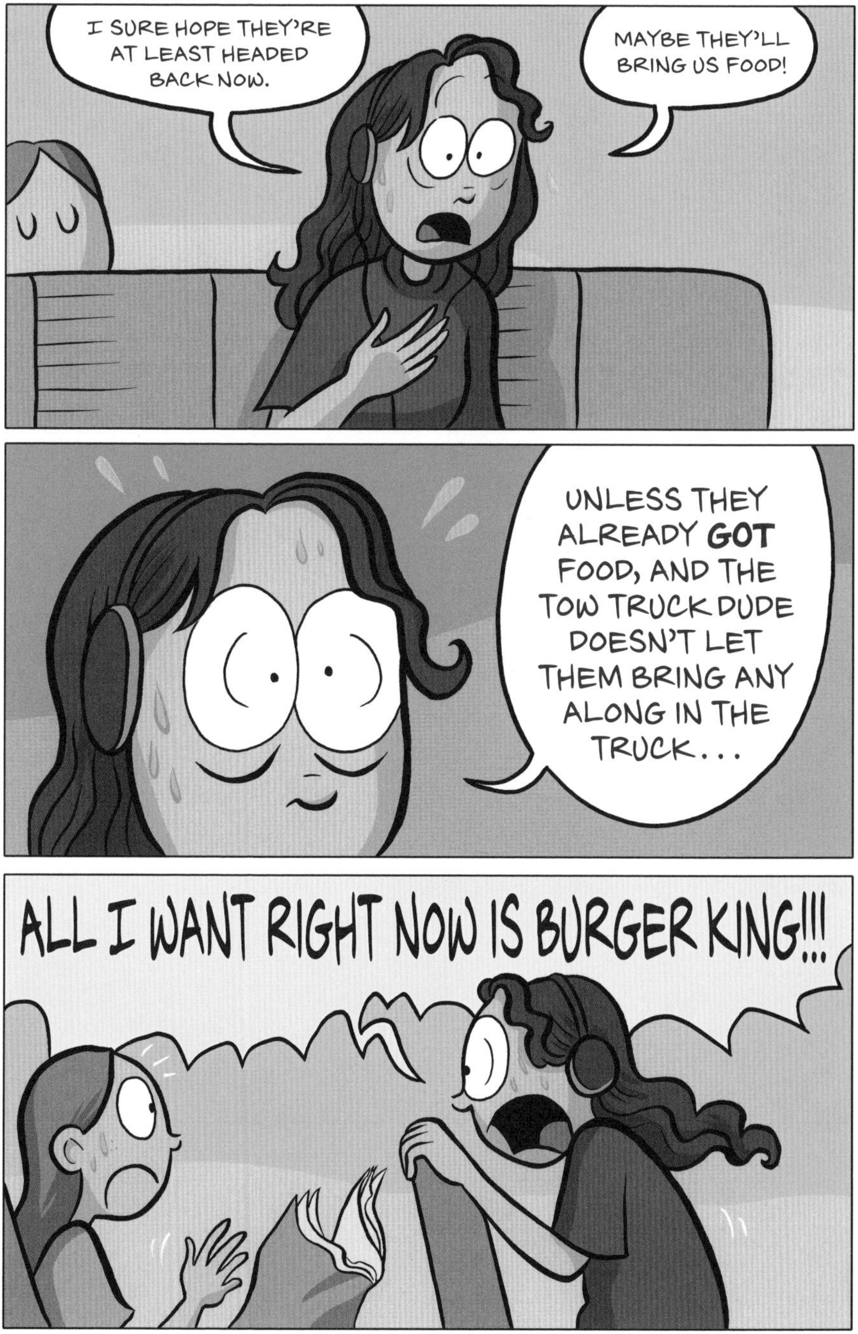
I SURE HOPE THEY'RE AT LEAST HEADED BACK NOW.
MAYBE THEY'LL BRING US FOOD!
UNLESS THEY ALREADY **GOT** FOOD, AND THE TOW TRUCK DUDE DOESN'T LET THEM BRING ANY ALONG IN THE TRUCK . . .
ALL I WANT RIGHT NOW IS BURGER KING!!!

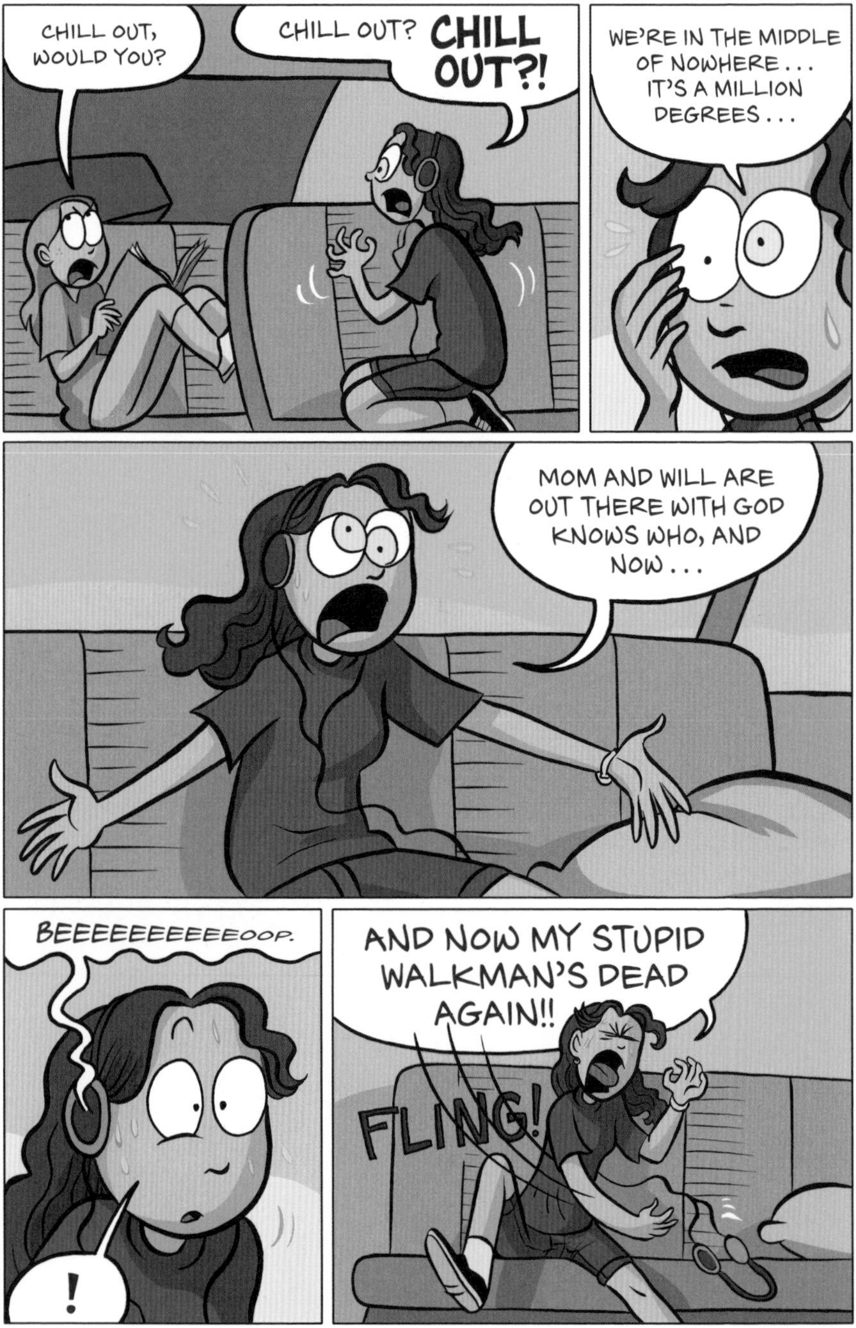
CHILL OUT, WOULD YOU?
CHILL OUT? CHILL OUT?!
WE'RE IN THE MIDDLE OF NOWHERE . . . IT'S A MILLION DEGREES . . .
MOM AND WILL ARE OUT THERE WITH GOD KNOWS WHO, AND NOW . . .
BEEEEEEEEEEEOOP.
!
AND NOW MY STUPID WALKMAN'S DEAD AGAIN!!
FLING!

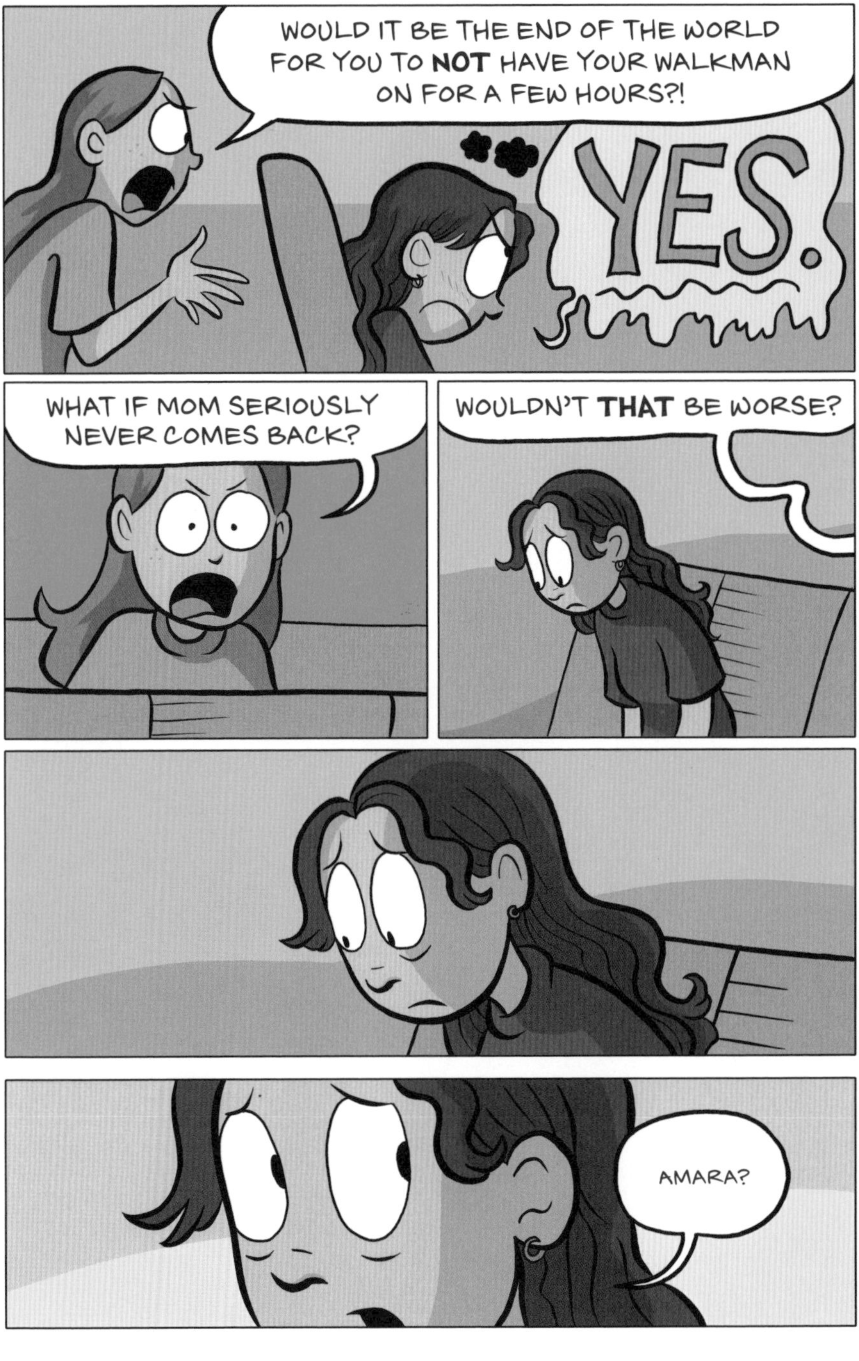
WOULD IT BE THE END OF THE WORLD FOR YOU TO **NOT** HAVE YOUR WALKMAN ON FOR A FEW HOURS?!
YES.
WHAT IF MOM SERIOUSLY NEVER COMES BACK?
WOULDN'T **THAT** BE WORSE?
AMARA?

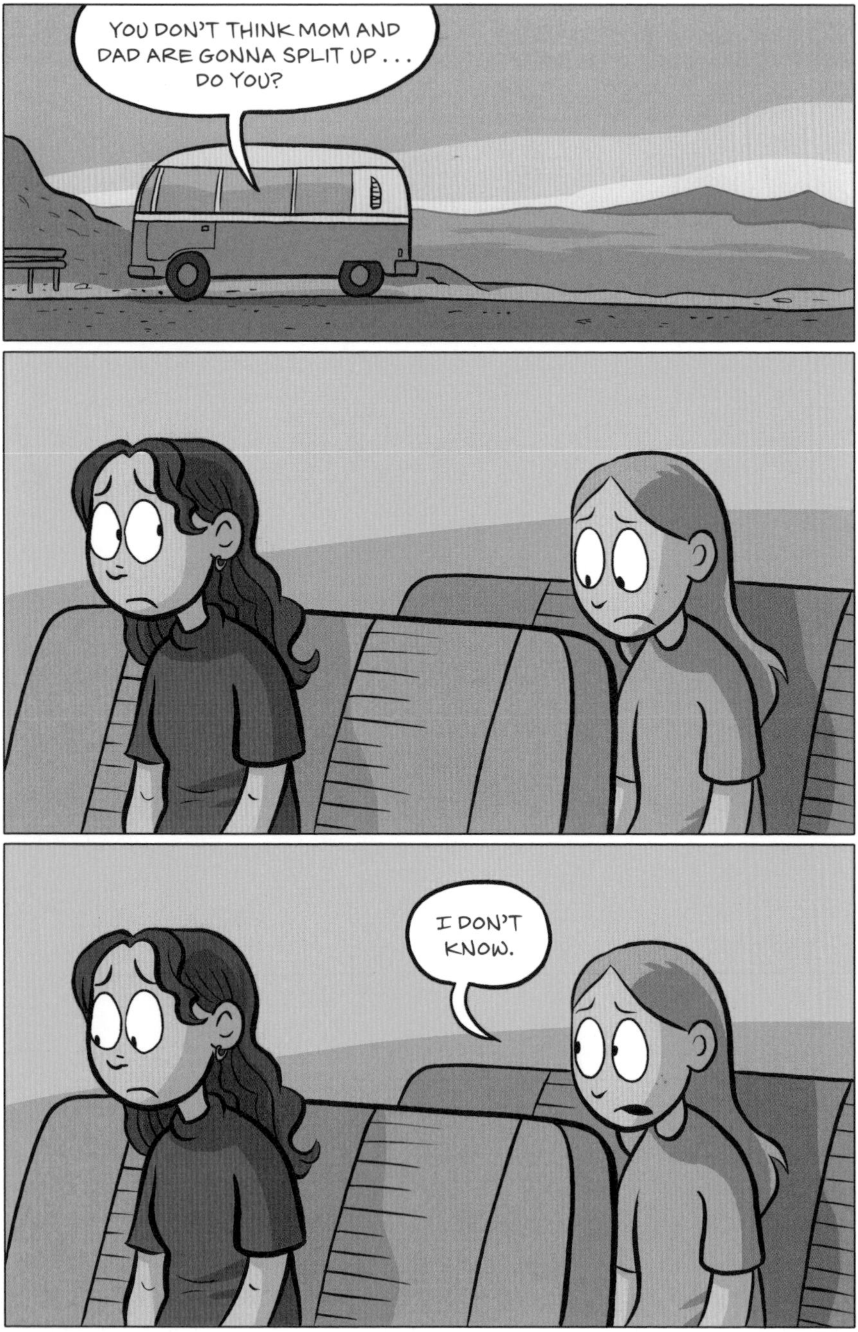
YOU DON'T THINK MOM AND DAD ARE GONNA SPLIT UP . . . DO YOU?
I DON'T KNOW.

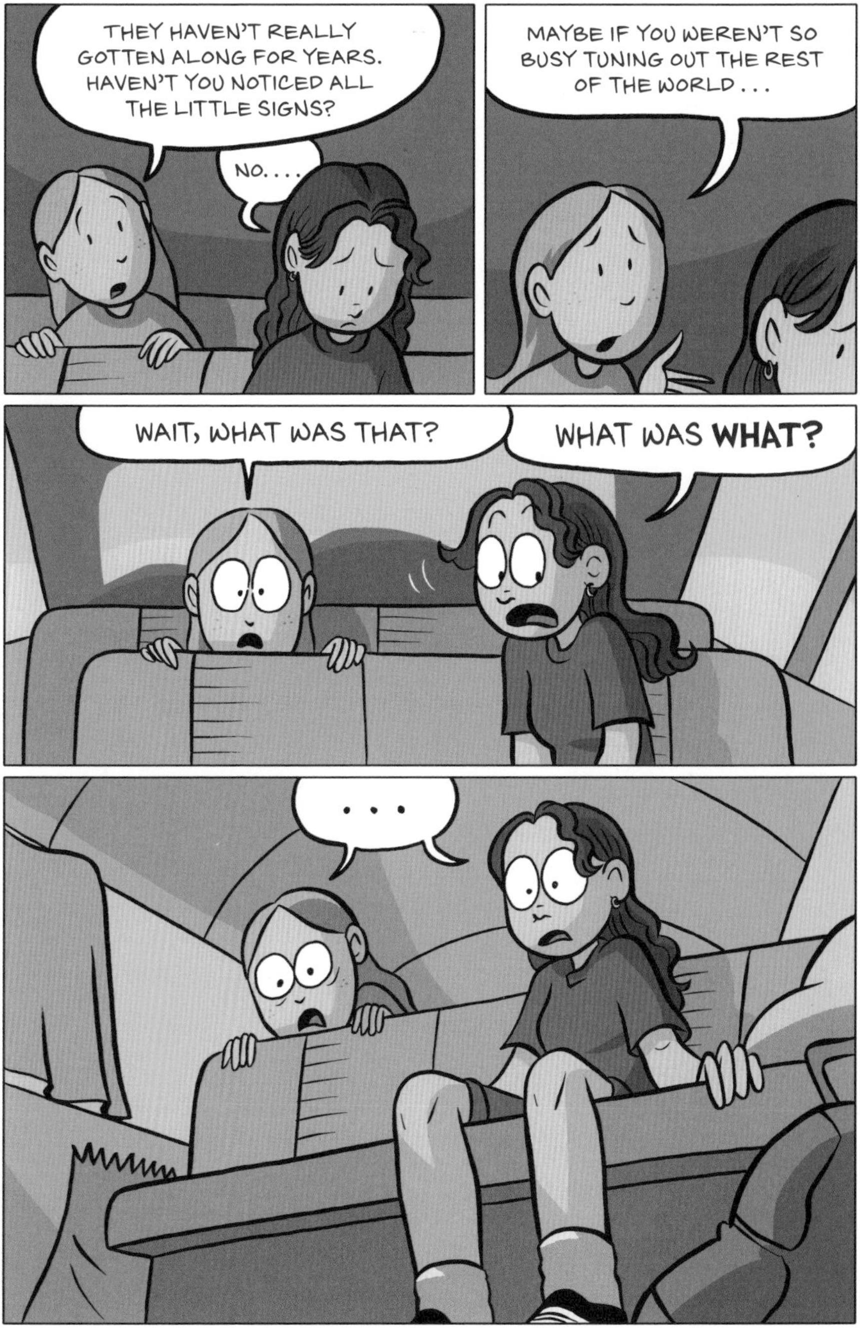
THEY HAVEN'T REALLY GOTTEN ALONG FOR YEARS. HAVEN'T YOU NOTICED ALL THE LITTLE SIGNS?
NO. . . .
MAYBE IF YOU WEREN'T SO BUSY TUNING OUT THE REST OF THE WORLD . . .
WAIT, WHAT WAS THAT?
WHAT WAS **WHAT?**
. . .

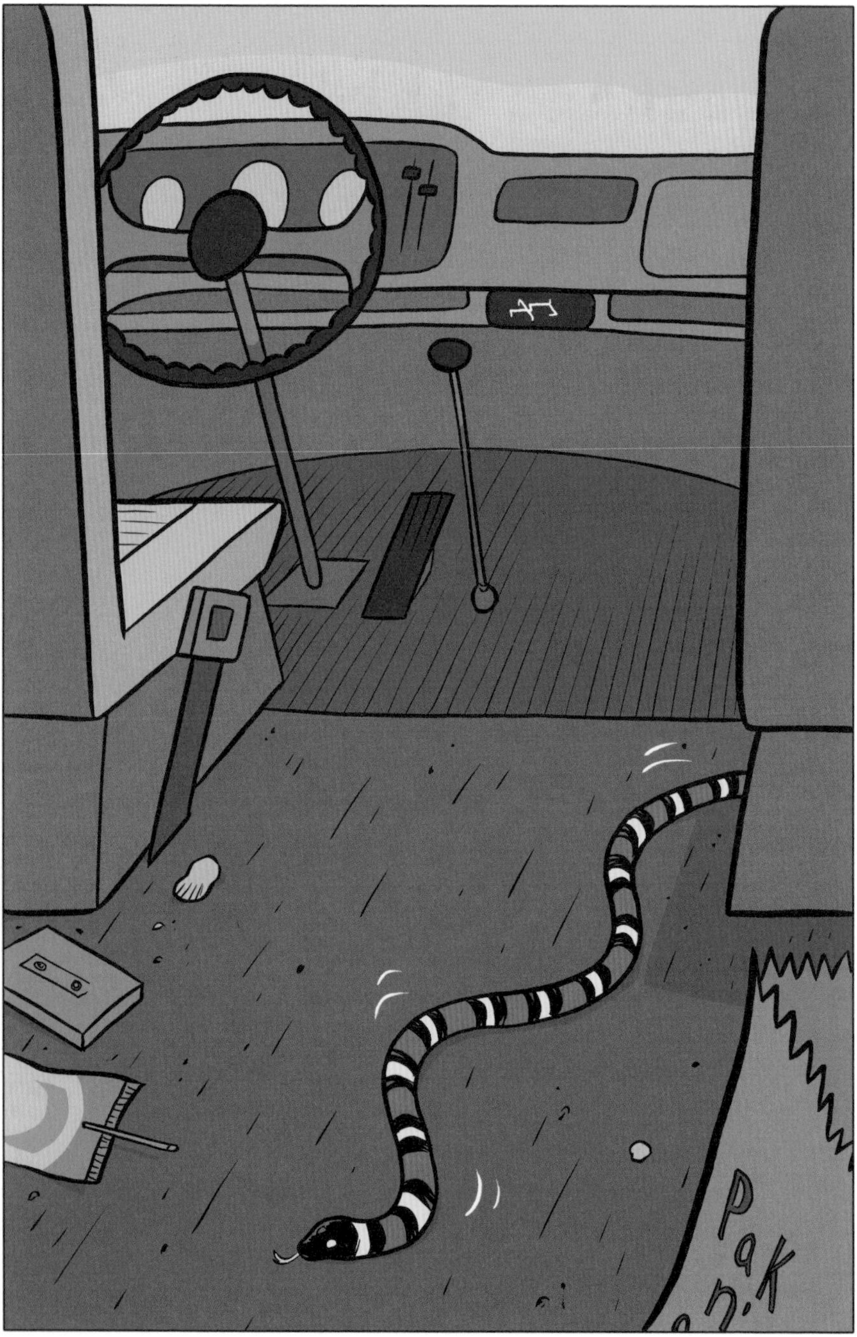
Pak

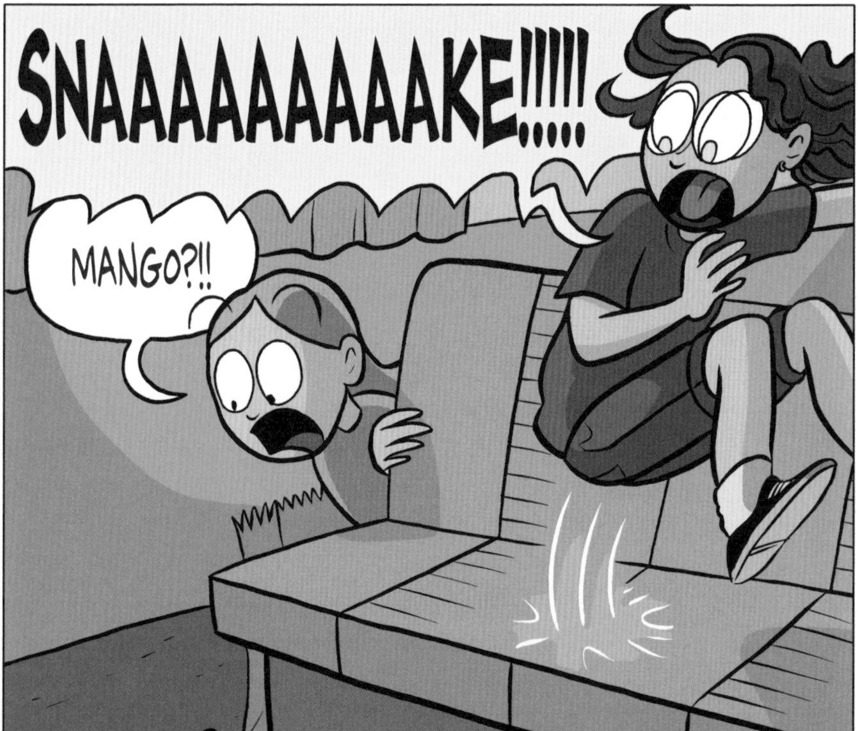
SNAAAAAAAAAKE!!!!!
MANGO?!!

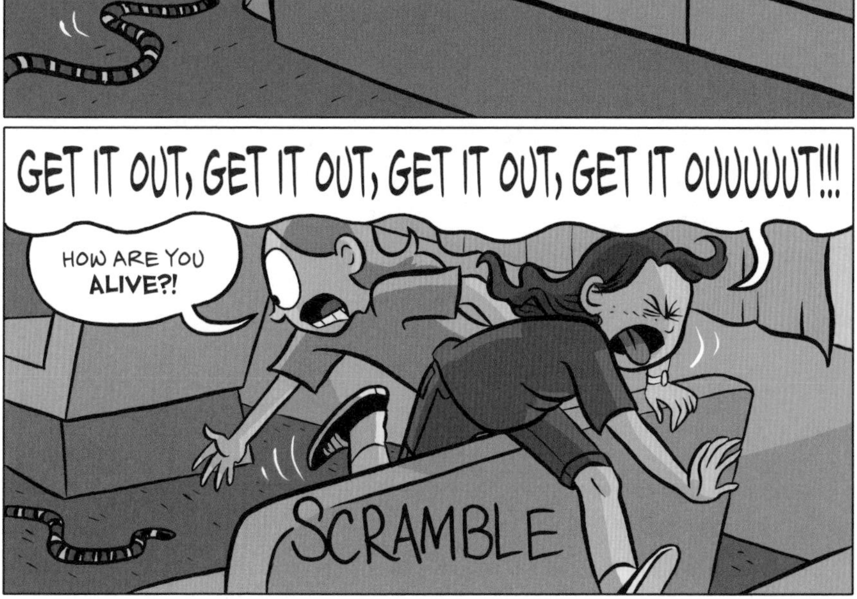
GET IT OUT, GET IT OUT, GET IT OUT, GET IT OUUUUUT!!!
HOW ARE YOU **ALIVE?!**
SCRAMBLE

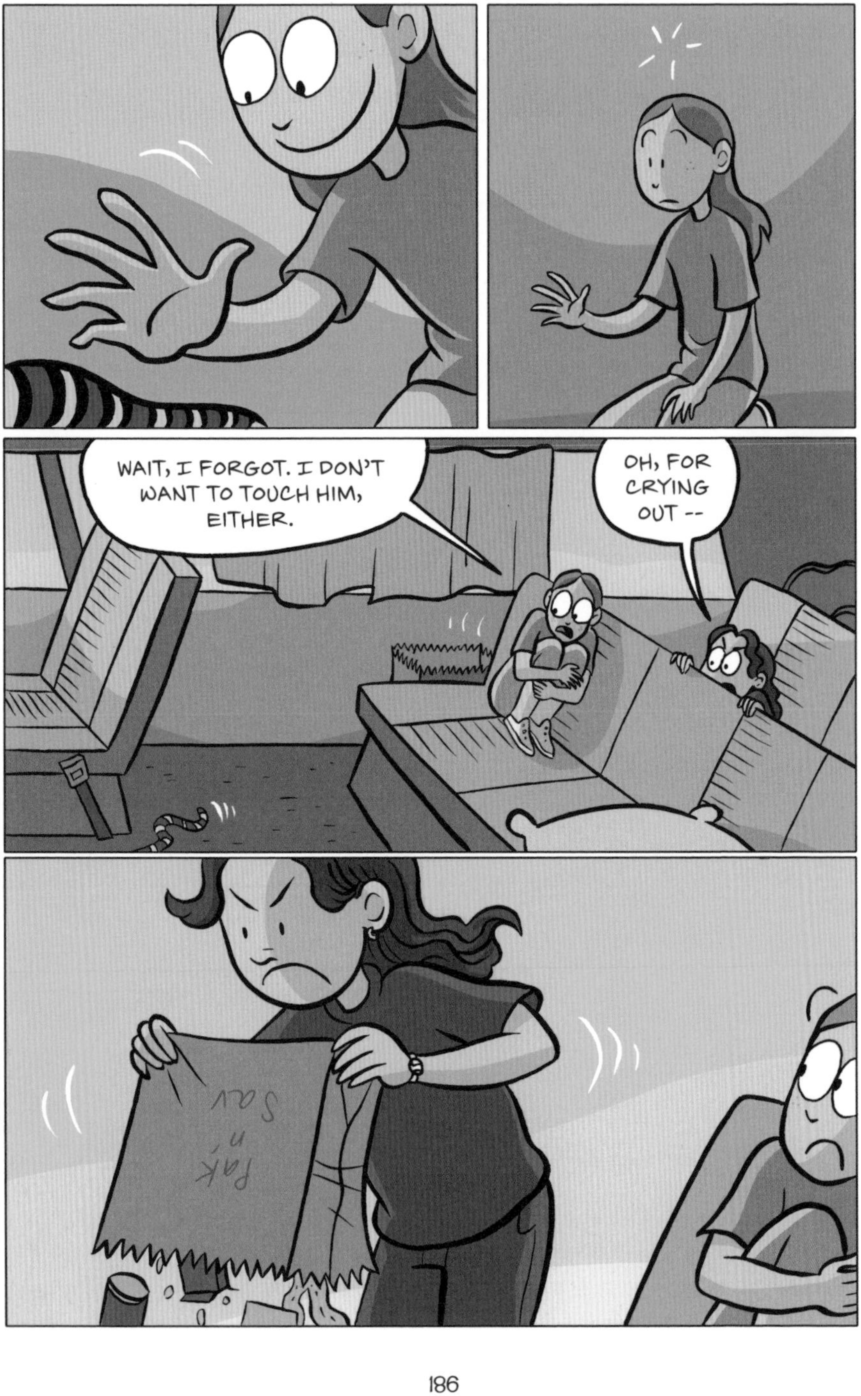
WAIT, I FORGOT. I DON'T WANT TO TOUCH HIM, EITHER.
OH, FOR CRYING OUT --

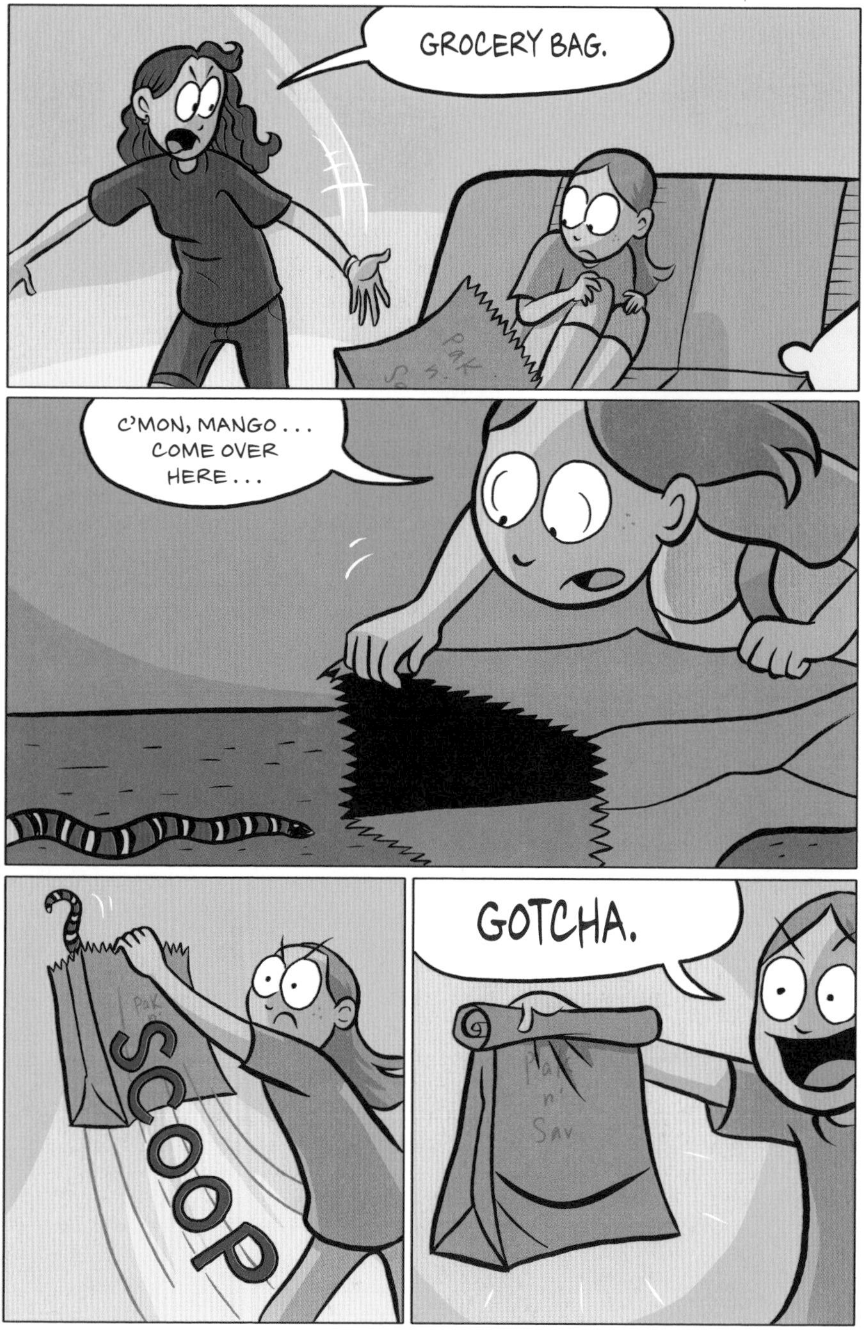
GROCERY BAG.
C'MON, MANGO . . . COME OVER HERE . . .
SCOOP
GOTCHA.

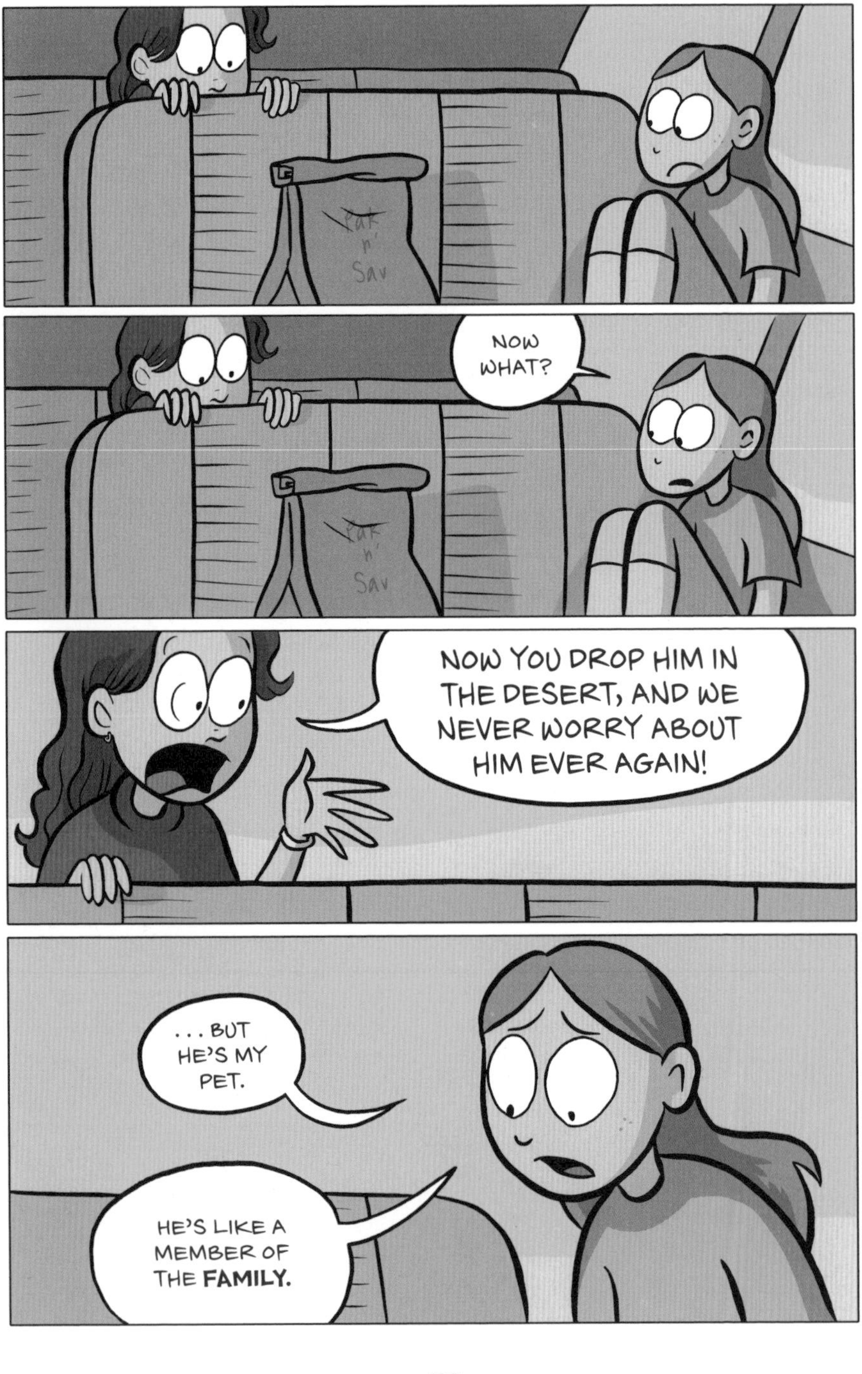
NOW WHAT?
NOW YOU DROP HIM IN THE DESERT, AND WE NEVER WORRY ABOUT HIM EVER AGAIN!
. . . BUT HE'S MY PET.
HE'S LIKE A MEMBER OF THE **FAMILY.**

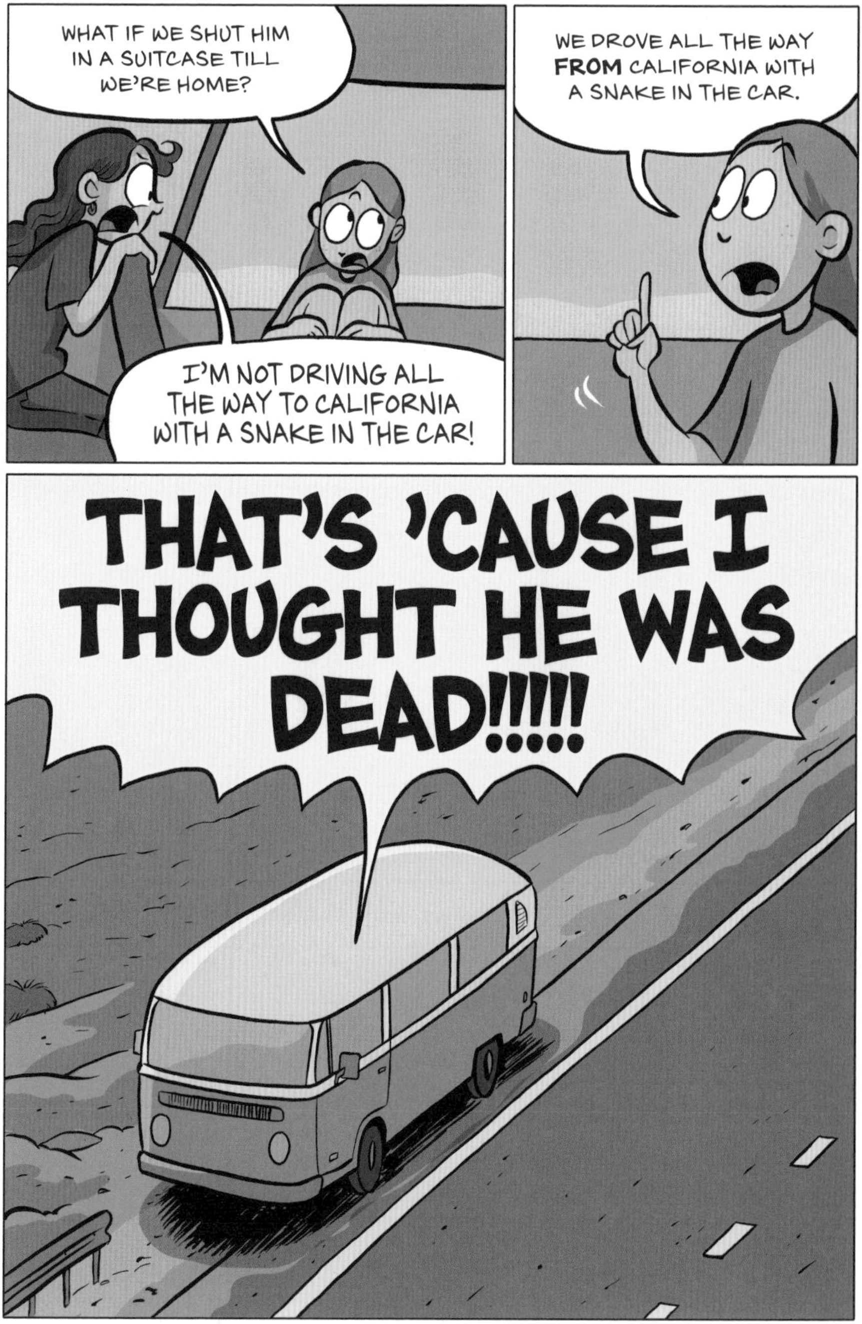
WHAT IF WE SHUT HIM IN A SUITCASE TILL WE'RE HOME?
I'M NOT DRIVING ALL THE WAY TO CALIFORNIA WITH A SNAKE IN THE CAR!
WE DROVE ALL THE WAY **FROM** CALIFORNIA WITH A SNAKE IN THE CAR.
THAT'S 'CAUSE I THOUGHT HE WAS DEAD!!!!!

LISTEN. THIS MEANS A LOT TO ME.

I KNOW.

IF YOU LET ME KEEP MANGO... I'LL GIVE YOU SOMETHING **YOU** REALLY WANT.

WHAT?

RUMMAGE

RUMMAGE

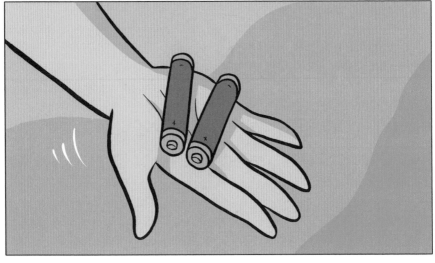

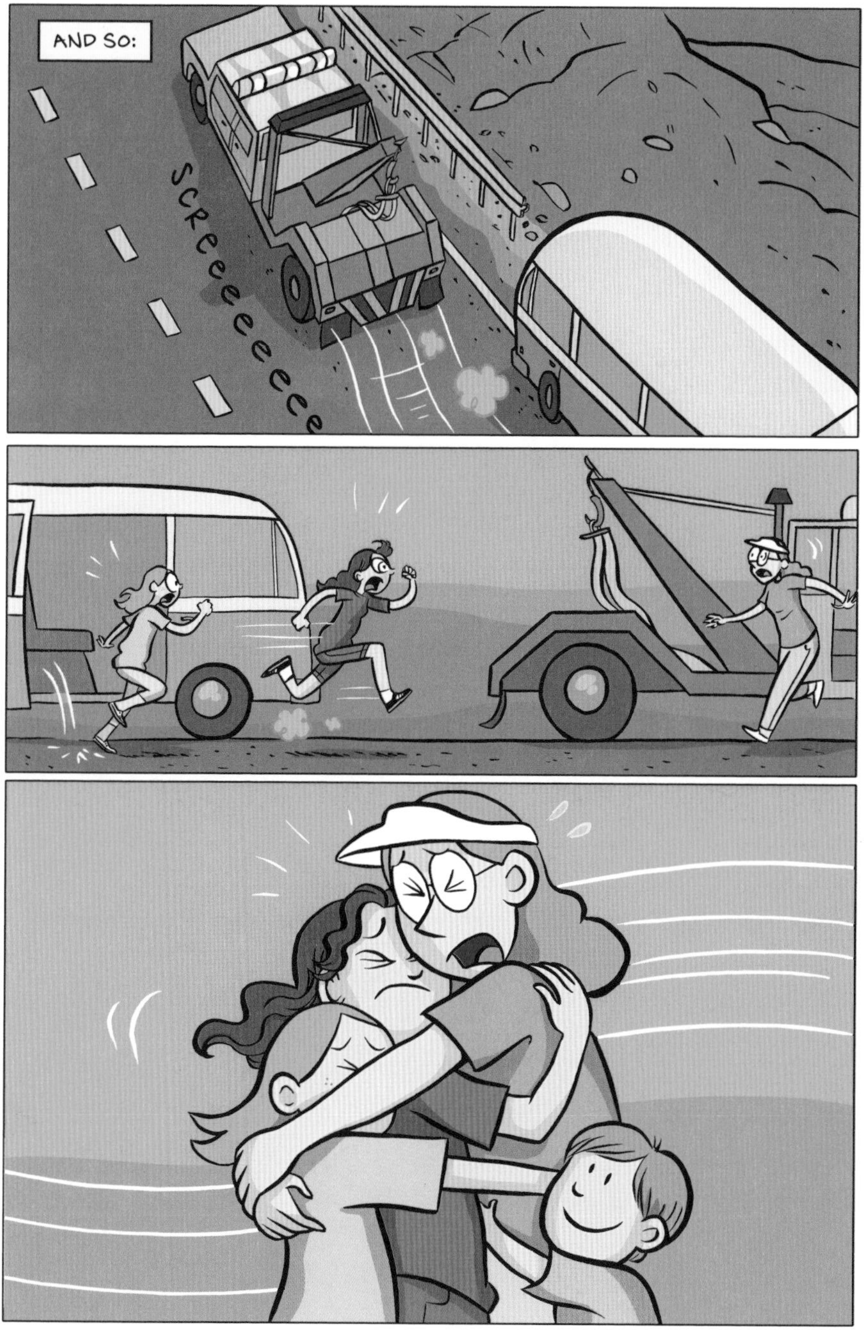
AND SO:
SCREEEEEEEEEE

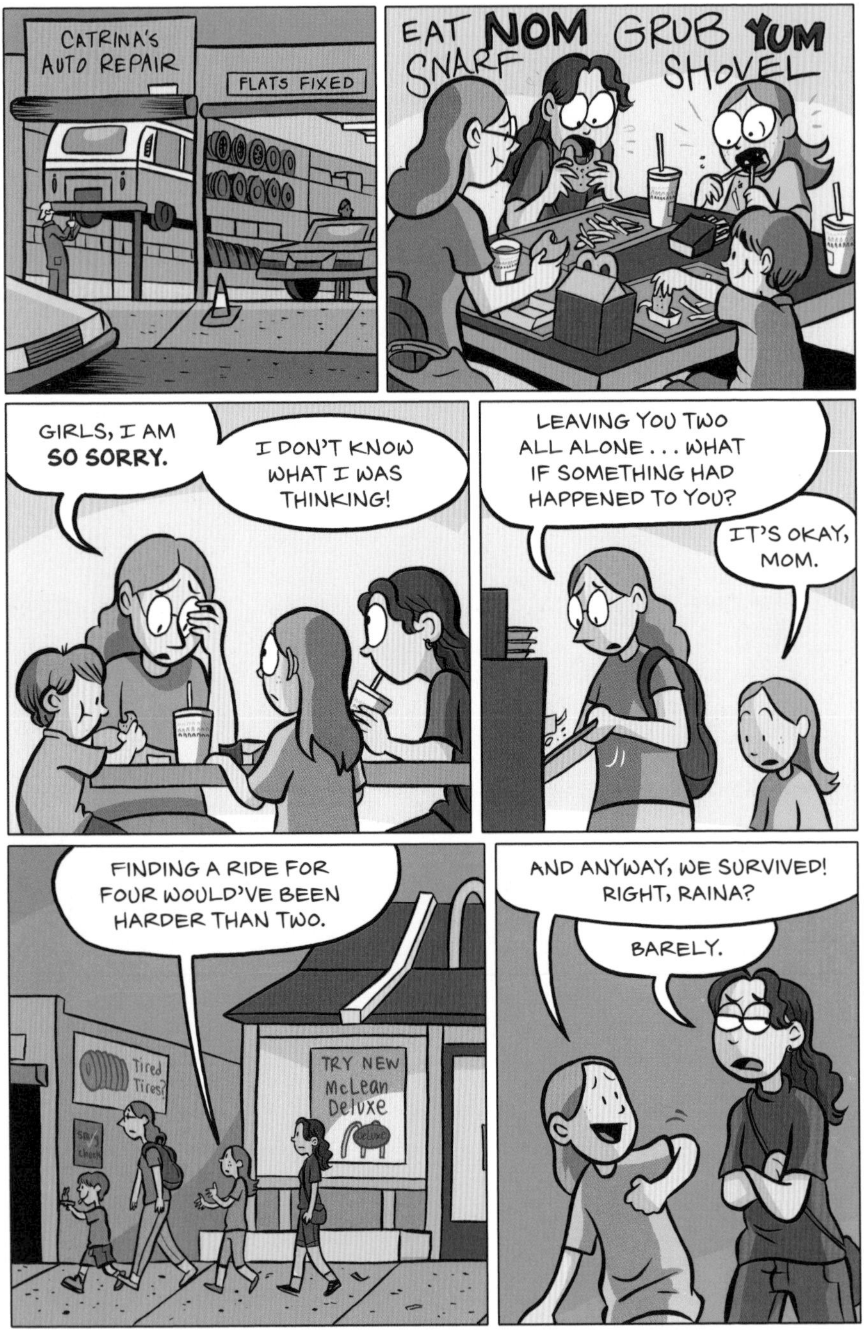
CATRINA'S AUTO REPAIR
FLATS FIXED
EAT
NOM
GRUB
YUM
SNARF
SHOVEL
GIRLS, I AM **SO SORRY.**
I DON'T KNOW WHAT I WAS THINKING!
LEAVING YOU TWO ALL ALONE . . . WHAT IF SOMETHING HAD HAPPENED TO YOU?
IT'S OKAY, MOM.
FINDING A RIDE FOR FOUR WOULD'VE BEEN HARDER THAN TWO.
Tired Tires?
TRY NEW McLean Deluxe
Deluxe
AND ANYWAY, WE SURVIVED! RIGHT, RAINA?
BARELY.

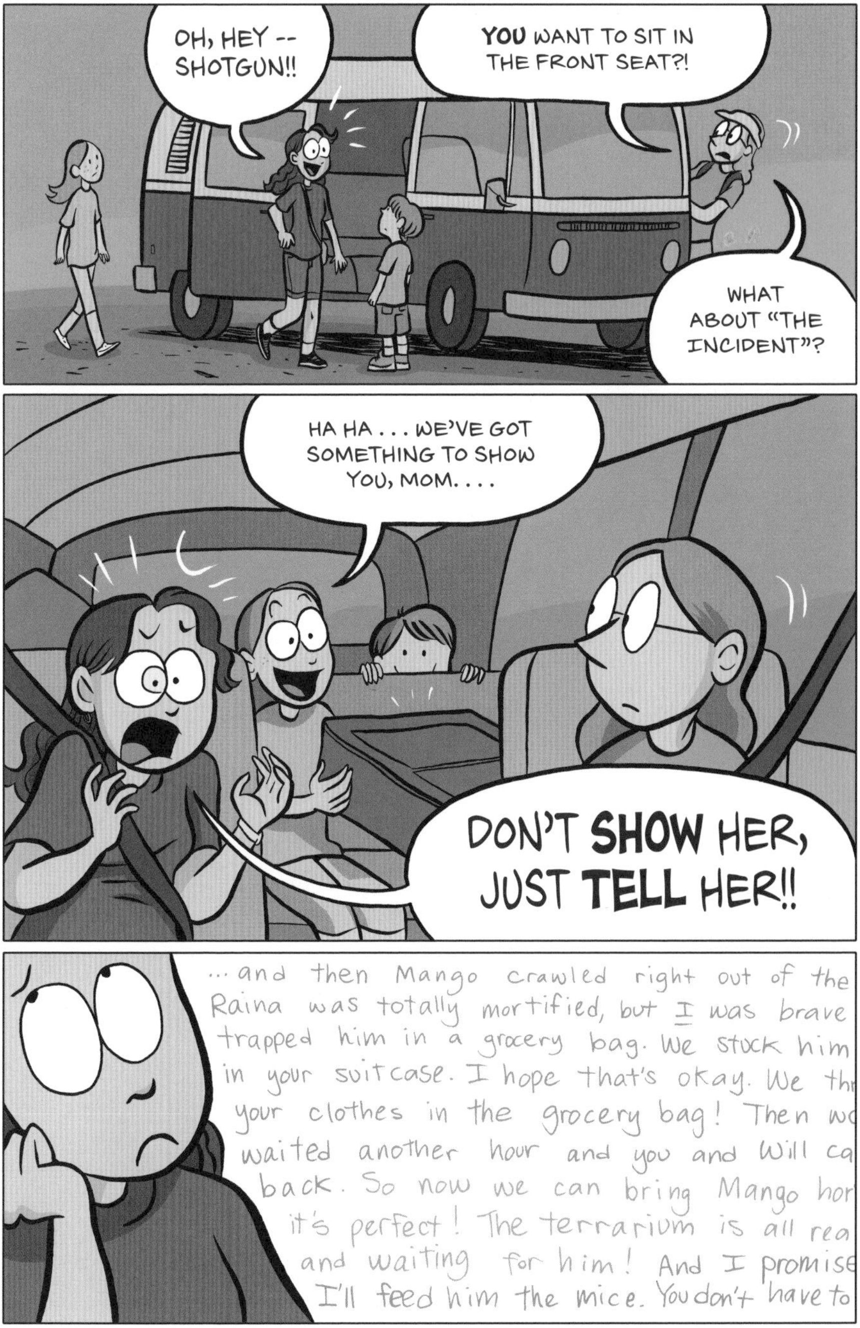
OH, HEY -- SHOTGUN!!
YOU WANT TO SIT IN THE FRONT SEAT?!
WHAT ABOUT "THE INCIDENT"?
HA HA . . . WE'VE GOT SOMETHING TO SHOW YOU, MOM. . . .
DON'T SHOW HER, JUST TELL HER!!
...and then Mango crawled right out of the
Raina was totally mortified, but I was brave
trapped him in a grocery bag. We stuck him
in your suitcase. I hope that's okay. We thr
your clothes in the grocery bag! Then we
waited another hour and you and Will ca
back. So now we can bring Mango hor
it's perfect! The terrarium is all rea
and waiting for him! And I promise
I'll feed him the mice. You don't have to

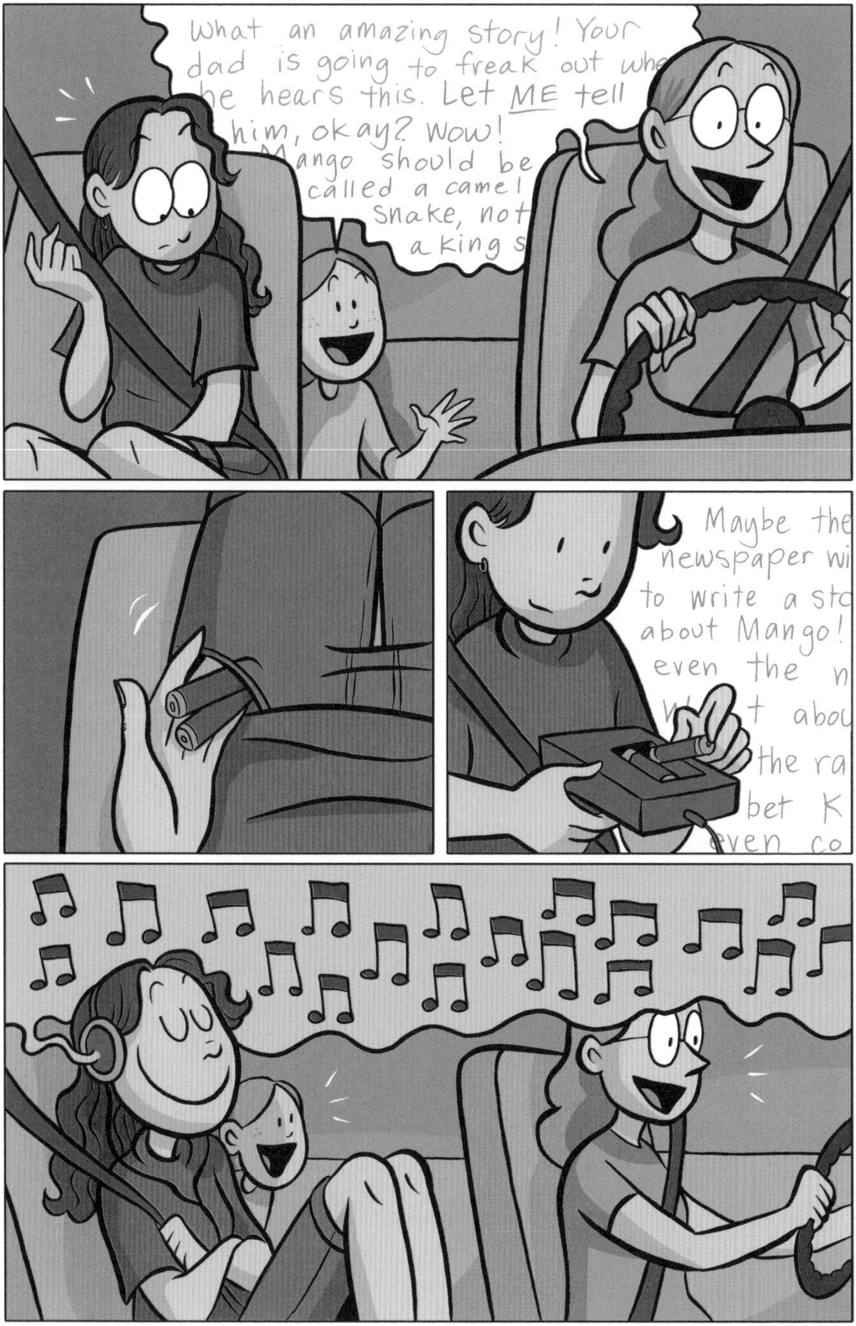
What an amazing story! Your dad is going to freak out whe he hears this. Let ME tell him, okay? Wow! Mango should be called a camel snake, not a king s
Maybe the newspaper wi to write a sto about Mango! even the n t abou the ra bet K even co

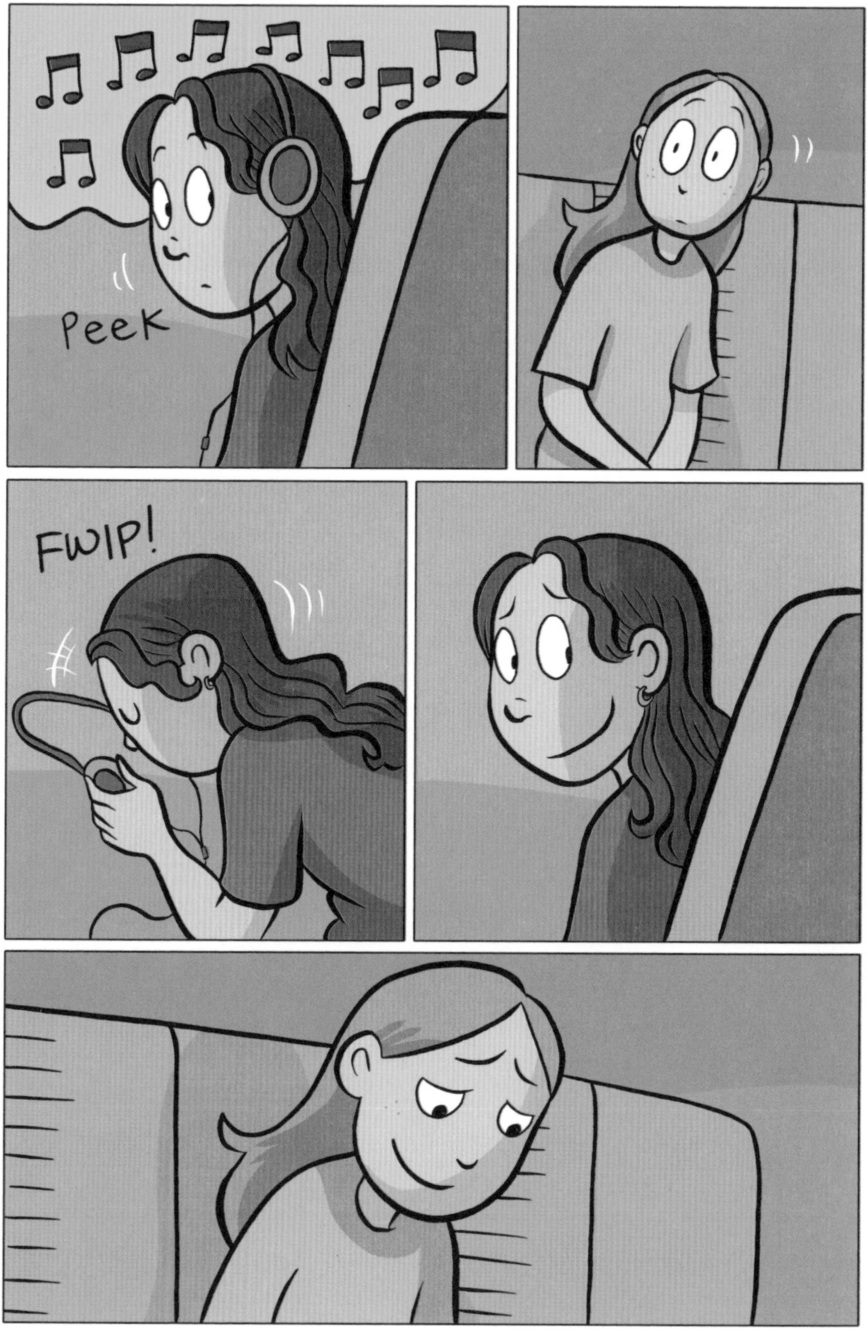
PEEK
FWIP!

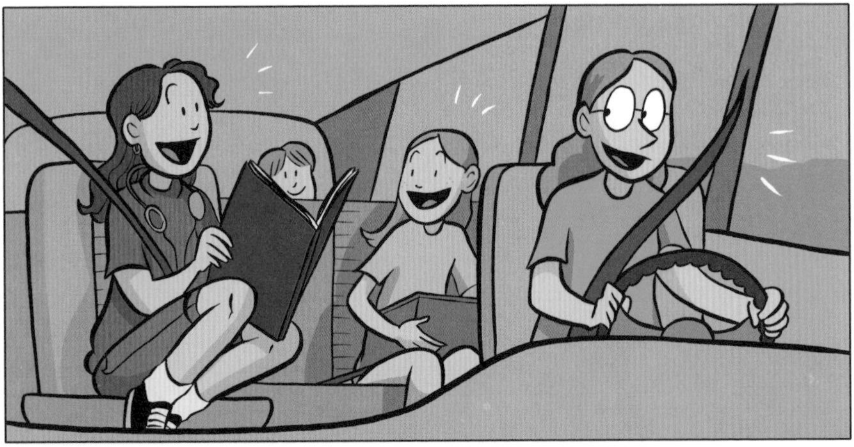

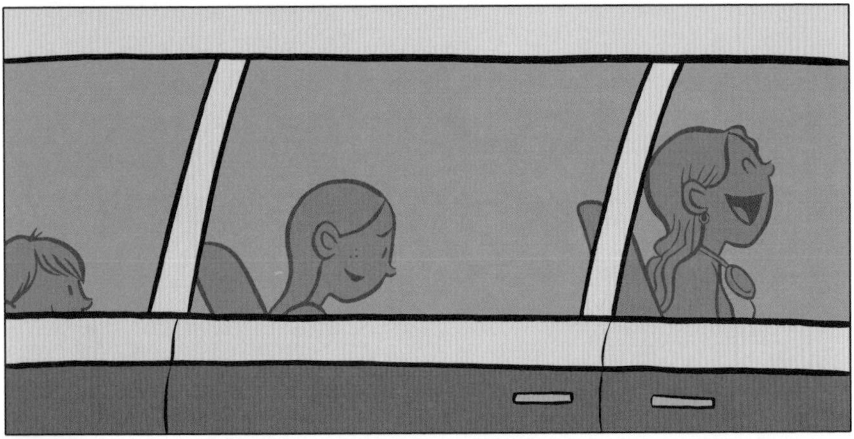

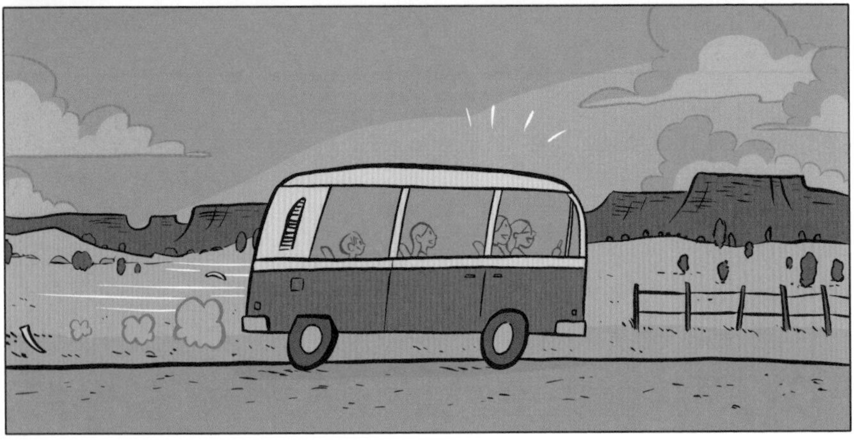

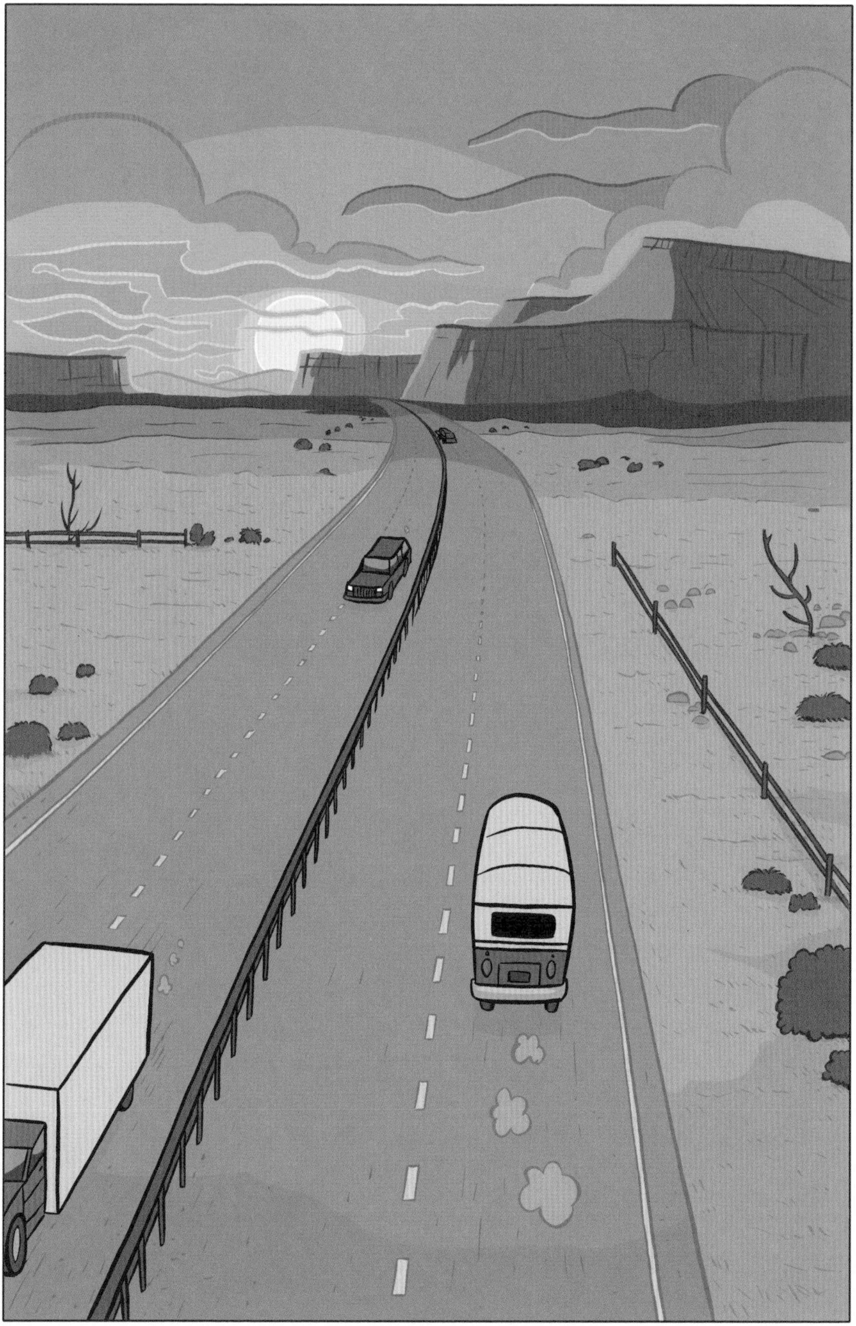

Photo Album

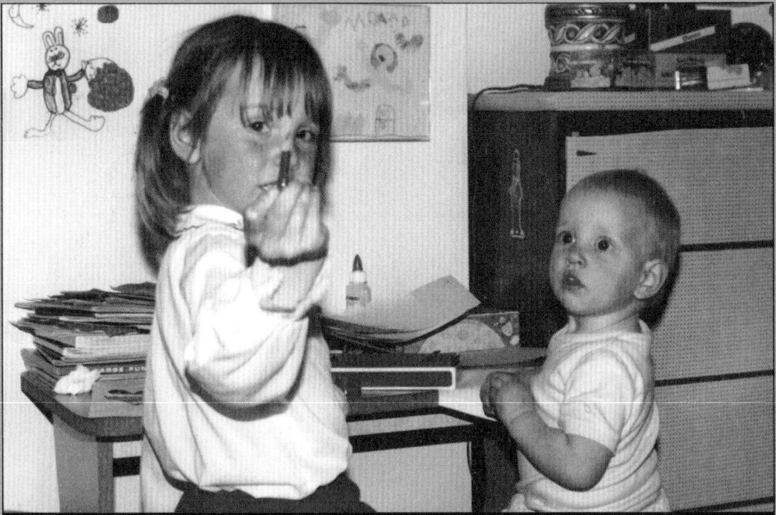

After I wrote the script for this book, my dad sent me this photo, which I had forgotten about. This picture pretty much encapsulates *Sisters* in a nutshell. We're about six and one here.

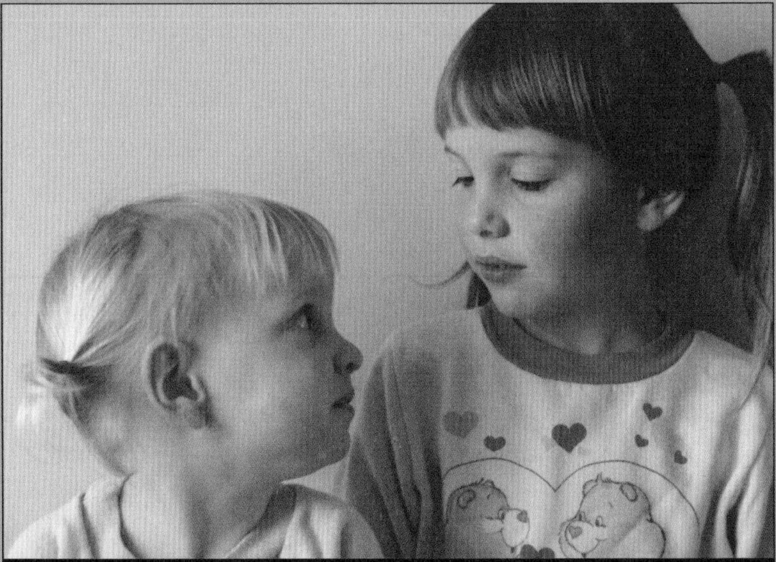

My mom took this picture of Amara and me sitting on top of a hamper in our upstairs hallway. The photo still hangs in the same spot.

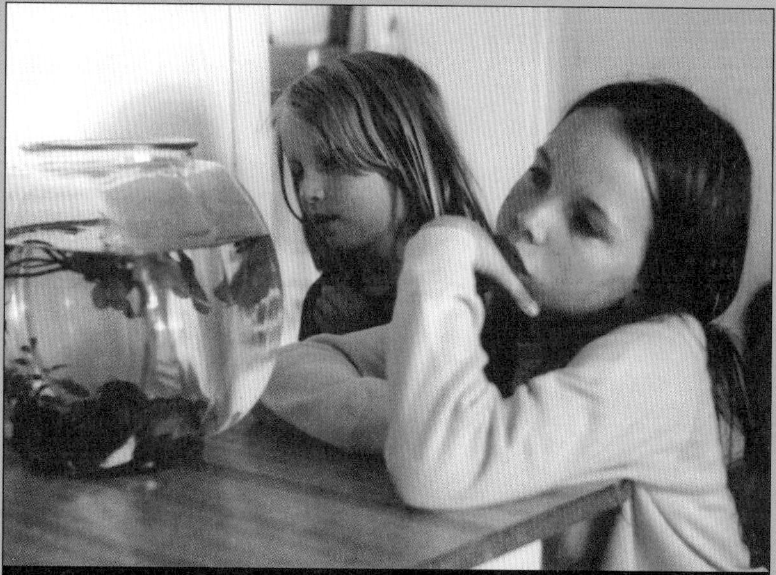

Goldfish. We look pretty excited, don't we?

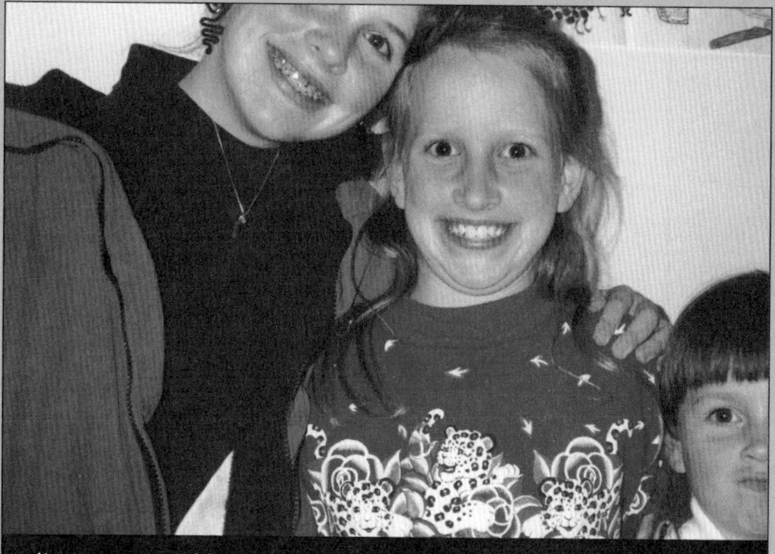

Here we are around the time this book takes place: ages fourteen, nine, and six. Amara had just won first place in an art contest I'd gotten an honorable mention for, a few years prior. I'm hiding my jealousy well!

Thanks to . . .

My family, obviously: my mom, dad, brother, sister, aunts, uncles, cousins, and grandparents. Thank you for letting me mine our collective history (and photo albums) for story ideas!

Dave Roman, who is invaluable in every way.

My editors David Saylor and Cassandra Pelham, and the tireless team at Scholastic: Sheila Marie Everett, Lizette Serrano, Candace Greene, Phil Falco, Bess Braswell, Whitney Steller, Tracy van Straaten, Ed Masessa, David Levithan, Lori Benton, Ellie Berger, John Mason, Antonio Gonzalez, Emily Heddleson, Starr Baer, Jaime Capifali, and all the wonderful folks whose time and space dovetail with mine.

My agent, Judy Hansen, for working her magic.

Braden Lamb, for his stellar coloring, as well as Shelli Paroline and Chris O'Neil, for color assistance.

John Green, for tech wizardry and his nifty lettering.

Jerzy and Anne Drozd, my beta readers.

My wonderful fans, who keep me smiling, and make it all worthwhile.

 —Raina

Raina Telgemeier is the #1 *New York Times* bestselling, multiple Eisner Award-winning creator of *Smile* and *Sisters*, which are both graphic memoirs based on her childhood. She is also the creator of *Drama*, which was named a Stonewall Honor Book and was selected for YALSA's Top Ten Great Graphic Novels for Teens. Raina lives in the San Francisco Bay Area. To learn more, visit her online at www.goRaina.com.

Also by
Raina Telgemeier

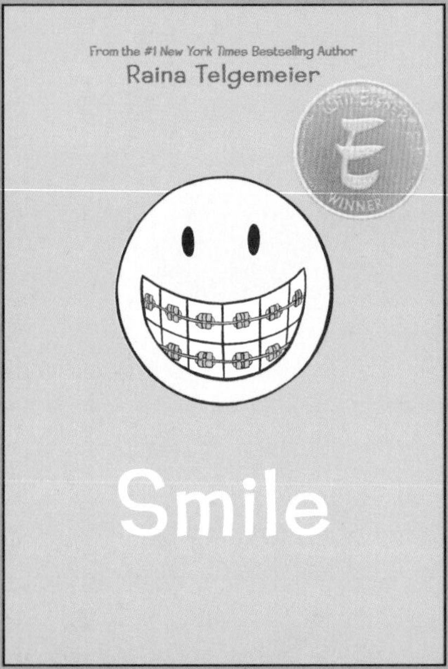
From the #1 New York Times Bestselling Author
Raina Telgemeier
Smile

This is the true story of how Raina severely injured her two front teeth when she was in the sixth grade, and the dental drama – on top of boy confusion, a major earthquake, and friends who turn out to be not so friendly – that followed!

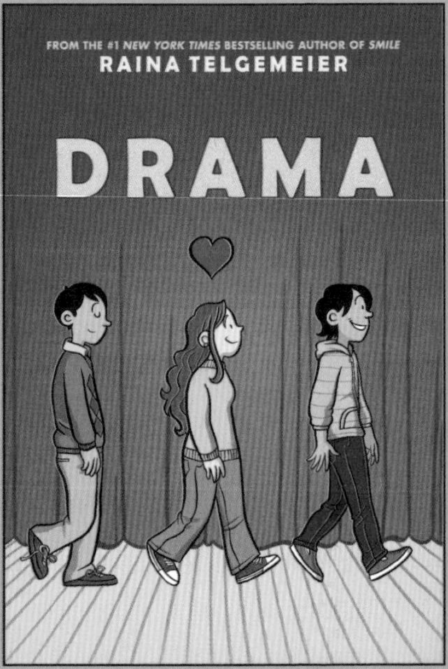
FROM THE #1 NEW YORK TIMES BESTSELLING AUTHOR OF SMILE
RAINA TELGEMEIER
DRAMA

Callie is the set designer for her middle school's spring musical, and is determined to create a set worthy of Broadway. But between the onstage AND offstage drama that occurs once the actors are chosen, it's going to be a long way until opening night!